PIMLICO

95

THE LIFE OF E. F. BENSON

Brian Masters's work is eclectic, to say the least. His prize-winning study of the multiple murderer Dennis Nilsen, *Killing for Company*, is now recognised as a classic. More recently he has published *The Shrine of Jeffrey Dahmer*. His biography of John Aspinall involved living with gorillas, and his history of all twenty-four ducal families of Britain, *The Dukes*, is a source of reference and amusement. With E. F. Benson he has returned to literary biography and the period of his definitive book on Marie Corelli, who was the source for Benson's magnificently comic 'Lucia'.

THE LIFE OF
E. F. BENSON

BRIAN MASTERS

PIMLICO

PIMLICO

An imprint of Random House
20 Vauxhall Bridge Road, London SW1V 2SA

Random House Australia (Pty) Ltd
20 Alfred Street, Milsons Point, Sydney
New South Wales 2061, Australia

Random House New Zealand Ltd
18 Poland Road, Glenfield
Auckland 10, New Zealand

Random House South Africa (Pty) Ltd
PO Box 337, Bergvlei, South Africa

Random House UK Ltd Reg. No. 954009

First published in Great Britain by Chatto & Windus 1991
Pimlico edition 1993

1 3 5 7 9 10 8 6 4 2

Printed and bound in Great Britain by
Mackays of Chatham PLC, Chatham, Kent

ISBN 0-7126-5714-2

Contents

For
ALICE
WILLIAM
and
MARY

Illustrations

(between 150 and 151)

Acknowledgements

Alice Russell, William McDowall and Mary Ferguson, three direct descendants of E.F. Benson's cousin, have given me every possible assistance in what must on many occasions have been an intrusive task, and for their tolerance, kindness and encouragement I would like to trumpet my gratitude far more boldly than these inadequate words will allow. I have also been fortunate to enjoy the very helpful co-operation of Allan Downend of the E.F. Benson Society and Cynthia Reavell of the Tilling Society, to both of whom I wish earnestly and publicly to offer thanks.

No book of this nature could be attempted without the active participation of librarians and custodians of papers, and there are many who have given generously of their time and knowledge, amongst whom I would like to thank, in no specific order, Dr Judith Priestman and Mr Colin Harris of the Department of Western Manuscripts at the Bodleian Library, Oxford; Dr Richard Luckett, Pepys Librarian at Magdalene College, Cambridge, and Mrs Mary Coleman, assistant librarian; Dr Geoffrey Bill, Librarian at Lambeth Palace, London; J. Conway and Sally Brown, of the British Library, London; Pamela Clark, Deputy Registrar of the Royal Archives, Windsor; John Kirkpatrick and Cynthia Farar of the Humanities Research Center, Austin, Texas; Michael Halls, sometime Librarian at King's College, Cambridge; Frank Walker, Fales Librarian at New York University; Vincent Giroud of the Beinecke Rare Books and Manuscripts Library at Yale University, New Haven, Conn; Dennis Bird of the National Skating Association; Anne Caiger of the University of California; Los Angeles; Mrs Nancy Steele, Archivist at Longford Castle, Salisbury.

A special debt must be acknowledged to Her Majesty Queen

Elizabeth II for gracious permission to quote from papers in the Royal Archives.

Similar gratitude must be expressed to the Master and Fellows of Magdalene College, Cambridge, for permission to quote freely from A.C. Benson's Diary; to Yale University; to New York University; to the University of California, Los Angeles; to the University of Leeds; and to the Humanities Research Center at Austin, Texas.

I owe grateful acknowledgement for the reproduction of photographs as follows: to the Bodleian Library (Plates 1, 2); His Grace the Archbishop of Canterbury and the Courtauld Institute of Art (Plate 3) – copyright reserved to the Church Commissioners; the Hulton Picture Company (Plates 7, 17); the British Library (Plate 11); Martello Bookshop, Rye (Plates 13, 14, 15); Miss Igglesden & Martello Bookshop (Plate 16).

There have been many individuals who have shared reminiscences or impressions with me, and to them all I am eager to offer real appreciation for their willingness to help. They include Sir Steven Runciman, Dr Robert Runcie (until his retirement Archbishop of Canterbury), Sir Rupert Hart-Davis, the Earl of Radnor, Ruth Pryor and Gwen Watkins, Geoffrey Palmer and Noel Lloyd, Dr David Newsome, Christopher Hawtree, and the present tenants of Lamb House, Rye – Mr W.S. Martin and his wife, Dr Ione Martin. If there are others whom I have omitted in error, I ask them to accept my thanks none the less.

Jenny Uglow, my editor at Chatto & Windus, has been marvellously encouraging and miraculous in her suggestions for improvement. Without her, this book would be impoverished, and her contribution is therefore one I wish to celebrate.

BRIAN MASTERS
1991

1 Edward and Minnie

It ought to be easy to write a Life of E.F. Benson. Some of his best books, such as *Final Edition* and *As We Were*, as well as many of the lesser-known volumes, like *Mother* and *Our Family Affairs*, are about himself. They are leisurely, meandering excursions in the autobiographical vein, memoirs which use recollection and personal observation to assemble the portrait and convey the feeling of an age. In addition, his brother A.C. Benson wrote books which cover much the same ground – biographies of their father Edward White Benson, of their sister Maggie Benson and their brother R.H. Benson, and a memoir of their childhood together entitled *The Trefoil*. R.H. Benson also wrote voluminously. No family in English letters has devoted so many pages to providing the fullest possible record of its own character and activities.

Furthermore, the Bensons were public figures whose careers might be expected to be extensively documented. Their father was the first Headmaster of Wellington College, the first Bishop of Truro, and ultimately Archbishop of Canterbury for fourteen years during Queen Victoria's implacable widowhood. A.C. Benson was Master of Magdalene College, Cambridge, and our subject, Edward Frederic Benson (known to the family, and henceforth to us, as 'Fred'), became Mayor of Rye in Sussex. One could certainly not call them obscure.

Finally, they lived in an epistolary age, when for literate men and women the writing of letters was a daily pleasure as well as a necessity, by no means confined to imparting information. The Victorians regarded a letter as a means of self-expression, an entertainment. There are thousands of letters to and from members of the Benson family which offer eloquent testimony to their concerns and their personalities.

And yet, despite all this, Fred remains enigmatic, mysterious, a fleeting ungraspable presence who leaves the merest impression of himself. A wry, ironical observer of the human comedy, witty and cynical without malice, a superb stylist and creator of wonderfully funny characters, at times mawkish and sentimental, kind and helpful, enjoying whisky, cigarettes and good company, his life seems placid and without incident. Fame and fortune he knew, and fame, especially with the *Lucia* series of novels which enjoy continuing popularity throughout the Western world, will stay with him for many years yet. A man who could write with such endearingly mocking humour must surely have had a permanent smile on his face. Moreover, his novels indicate a penetrating insight into the follies of mankind, its petty hypocrisies and absurd pretences. But what of his own follies, his own hypocrisies, his own pretences? Of these he gives no clue.

David Williams, whose *Genesis and Exodus* studies the whole Benson clan, accuses Fred of 'a marked lack of candour'. Having 'no passion for self-scrutiny', he is 'slippery . . . elusive'. Everyone who has tried to know E.F. Benson, to peer behind the curtain of circumspection, has come away disappointed and defeated. Fred refuses either to be skewered or embraced. 'If you ask: what about the whole person, what about Fred complete? Then Fred turns his back smartly on you and tells you, without for a moment ever losing his good manners, to mind your own business.'[1] Even Fred's admiring biographers, Geoffrey Palmer and Noel Lloyd, admit to detecting a cold surface and suggest there is too much detachment about the man.

Part of the reason for this apparent secretiveness lies in the revered English habit of reticence, in the precept that it is vulgar to reveal personal details about oneself and unthinkable to seek to discover them in others. A gentleman does not ask about the private lives of his fellows. Such overwhelming shyness has in the past been so refined as to lead to the risible circumstance that a man may die without his closest friends bothering to find out who he was, where he came from, or what were his antecedents.

2

Politeness to this degree is an English vice, and Fred is a perfect exemplar of the restraints it imposes upon honesty.

But obedience to social *mores* will not suffice to explain Fred's infuriating ability to disappear behind his own words. He was in fact congenitally disposed to concealment. His own family knew little about the way he lived, what he thought, or what principles guided his decisions. 'Fred is a Sphinx', wrote his mother, Mary Benson, when he was but a young man. She noted how there was always the deepest mystery about where he was going or with whom, and he even avoided indicating exactly what day he might arrive at the family home, and at what time; Fred's resentment at intrusion into his private affairs overcame his consideration for his mother's domestic arrangements. She invented a family adjective to denote this excessive attachment to privacy, and used it conspiratorially in correspondence with her other children; it was 'Freddian'.[2]

A.C. Benson (Arthur), who wrote almost as many books as Fred, also kept an exhaustive Diary which stretches to over four million words. Five years older than his brother, Arthur was, like Fred, a sedulously detached observer, one of the linesmen of history. Yet he knew Fred as well as anyone might; they met frequently and regularly throughout their lives; when Arthur was ill, Fred looked after him; they shared the tenancy of Lamb House in Rye in Arthur's latter years, and discussed all manner of subjects and problems (especially Benson family characteristics). But when they were both approaching middle-age Arthur confessed:

I know less of what Fred *really* thinks than of almost anyone of whom I see much. I expect he is rather a pagan, but a most zealous conformist. He is a very highly-strung superstitious person, and has a great terror of speaking at all frankly or giving himself away. Indeed he seems to me *never* to speak frankly.[3]

This is a somewhat aloof, damning indictment, but justified. Fred was a dissembler, innocently so, but none the less adept at wriggling away. He was marvellous company, quick with an anecdote or two (even if they had been used before, and embellished since), cheerful and amusing. But sufferings and exaltations he kept to himself. *Dodo*, published in 1893 when he was twenty-five, was immediately notorious and swept Fred to the very pinnacles of celebrity. In it, there is a character called Jack, of whom Fred wrote: 'It was his way not to blaze abroad anything that affected him deeply . . . He loved to show his brighter side to the world.'[4] That was possibly an early insight into self.

Showing his brighter side to the world, and apparently tip-toeing on the surface of life, required an adroit deflection of dangerous topics. Fred mastered the habit of never taking anything seriously, and it was this superficiality which exasperated his brother Arthur, who took himself very seriously indeed. While Arthur pondered and fretted in his study at Cambridge, Fred was having a jolly time entertaining the fatuous in Society. 'It seemed to me suddenly that Fred had never lived with life,' wrote Arthur, 'only stayed with it or lunched with it.'[5]

Over the years, Arthur grew almost obsessed with his brother's easy social success, and what he saw as its artificiality. He deplored the vision of Fred flitting from Dowager Countess to Dowager Countess and not bothering to think deeply; he went so far as to suggest, many times, that Fred knew no real emotion and held no real opinions. 'In his books he traffics with many very exotic emotions. Does he feel them *at all*? I cannot help wondering.'[6] On other occasions, Arthur descended from his lofty contempt and recognised that the coldness, the lack of visible emotion, the irrational fear of being touched, was a trait shared by all three brothers. 'There is something vulgar about me and Fred and Hugh – childish, eager, fond of success, not much feeling . . . I suppose we all have a touch of something morbid . . . of diseased self-consciousness.' Of himself, Arthur wrote, with piteous candour, 'My own real failing is that I have never been in vital touch with anyone – never either fought anyone, or kissed anyone! . . . not out of principle, but out of a timid and rather fastidious solitariness.'[7] One looks in vain for any such honesty from Fred, but there is little doubt that he shared the Benson distaste for emotional display. He simply worried about it less than Arthur, and would not let it depress him unduly.

As for his philosophy, whether religious, moral or political, that too seems to be adaptable, malleable, as soft and evanescent as an after-dinner anecdote. It is odd to discover such blatant relativity in a son of the Archbishop of Canterbury, Primate of All England, and brother of Monsignor Hugh Benson. On the other hand it is perhaps, as we shall see, precisely because he had been smothered by a stern religiosity that Fred determined not to get excited by dogma or opinion. It risked bringing unhealthy results. After a religious discussion in the family one evening, Arthur professed himself astonished that Fred should accept the cardinal precepts of the Church as a child of eight might, without question or enthusiasm. 'It is just incredible to me. I *don't think* that religion plays any part in his life. I don't think he is even interested in it. But who knows?'[8]

Who indeed? Fred delighted in keeping his family guessing, about virtually everything which concerned him, and he has kept admirers and researchers guessing ever since. In 1903 he was approached to see if he would stand for election in the Liberal interest. He declined. His mother was a strict Tory and he, though distinctly old-fashioned in outlook, leaned towards the Liberal view when he leaned at all; in essence, however, he was without political conviction. He did not bother to read newspapers. Nor did he read many books, apart from old favourites. This is not to say he was ignorant, far from it. He was, after all, a Greek and Latin scholar, a Hellenist, an archaeologist of some achievement, a knowledgeable and careful biographer, as well as the writer of amusing fables. But Fred was lazy. He did not see the need to keep up with the latest craze in literature or politics, or to clutter his mind with problems. In consequence, he gives the impression of an awesome placidity, of comfort and grace which no man can rile. Arthur put it neatly when he wrote, 'His mind is like a very definite garden, with rose-beds and grass-walks and seats – but it has nothing of the wild-wood or the waste.'[9]

Fred's moral relativism was apparent to the discerning reader from the very beginning, with the character of his heroine in *Dodo*. 'If any action doesn't seem to you wrong,' says Dodo, 'nothing in the world will prevent your doing it, if your desire is sufficiently strong.'[10] Moral absolutes were repugnant to Fred, because they were dependent upon authority and did not derive from personal choice. In *The Challoners* (1904) he was more explicit: 'Moral qualities are like corsets. If they are tight they hinder free development, and if they are loose you might as well not have them at all.'[11] This sounds like wanting to have it both ways, sacrificing choice to the beguiling balance of an epigram, but Fred remained loyal to this view to the end of his days. He certainly did not advocate moral anarchy, and was often bewildered by the dramatic changes in social behaviour which took place in his lifetime; he thought moral values should evolve naturally, through example and experience, not be imposed by precept. His sister Maggie said that he absolutely demanded 'elasticity'; tolerance and a charitable, easy acceptance of human frailties were for him a virtue, a characteristic he shared with, alone of the family, his mother. Maggie lacked this elasticity; like her father, she was harsh and unyielding.[12]

In his attitude towards morality, then, as to religion, politics, or the emotional life, Fred offers little substance for the biographer to clutch on to, no fierce prejudices, no alarming faults, no glowing, shattering sacrifice. An equable temperament with sensible views does not make for gripping narrative.

On the other hand, there is much that is positive to say about E.F. Benson. He was patient and good-natured, generous in spirit as well as materially, a fine friend and peerless companion. He worked hard at his books. He was the most independent of the Bensons, and though he would not confess it overtly, he saved himself by escaping from their repressive influence. He loved the beauty and calm of great Nature, and was just as happy to be alone with the mountains as he was to be at a dinner for ten. He welcomed that kind of solitude for the way in which it subtly invaded the soul and induced humility. But above all, as any reader of the *Lucia* books will know, Fred gloried in the rich pomposities of human life, in the ludicrous attempts of men and women to disguise what they really feel and want. His sense of humour was sharp but beneficent, not malicious or harmful; deflation was a matter of fun. Just as Fred would not allow Lucia, or Miss Mapp, or Mrs Mantrip, or Miss Howard, or any of the creations of his penetrating wit, to get away with pretending to be something other than what they were, so we shall not allow Fred to hide behind a mask of bland bonhomie.

His conversation was a joy, as the tetchy Arthur admits even as he deplores its frivolity, and that, of all his qualities, is the most ephemeral. It has evaporated with the last people who knew him and gossiped across a table with him. There are isolated snippets of wit which have come down to us, but their timing and delivery, as well as their context, are lost. We know he liked to embroider and improve a story, but we cannot know how it sounded. As Fred himself said of Oscar Wilde, whom he knew well in his youth, his talk was 'like the play of a sunlit fountain . . . Like all talk, it is completely unreproducible, for gesture and voice had no small part in it, and, essentially so, his own glee in what he said.'[13]

For the most part, then, we are obliged to seek E.F. Benson between his own lines, to find him lurking in some of his own characters, and to spot the traits of his personality as they emerge in childhood letters, are matured and refined, and find their echo in the adulthood of a successful, reserved, gentlemanly novelist. He must not complain that we make the attempt. He wrote himself, in the preface to his biography of Charlotte Brontë, that it was perfectly legitimate to examine an author's private ego in order to discover the genesis of his work. Facts may illuminate and instruct.

'Fred is a *simple* man,' wrote Arthur Benson, 'not having gone far into the labyrinths of the mind. He must be *absolutely* happy!'[14] All that this means is that Fred was not a manic depressive like Arthur. Or like his sister Maggie. Or like his father the Archbishop. How he managed to avoid the family scourge is the real story of his life.

When Edward Frederic Benson was born on 24 July 1867, his parents were in the grip of marital crisis. His father, Edward White Benson, had been Headmaster of Wellington College for seven years, and the strain of presiding over the fortunes of a new public school, founded shortly before his death by the Prince Consort, and therefore dear to the heart of the grieving Queen Victoria, was taking a fearsome toll. Edward was a perfectionist. He drove himself and others far too hard, working fourteen hours a day and overseeing every detail of the school's administration as well as dealing personally with the instruction and moral welfare of the boys. He was never satisfied. Toil was God's gift, and it followed that more toil was correspondingly more enriching. Edward adhered to this doctrine to a dangerous degree, for he suffered from a temperament easily given to depression, and the punishing worry to which he constantly subjected himself was bound to lead to illness. When in the depths of one of his moods, Edward was capable of sinking morosely into gloom and silence, locking himself in his study for days, refusing food or attention, until he emerged, cleansed and renewed, to continue the struggle. To make matters worse, he carried in his breast more than a fair portion of Christian guilt, and was always chastising himself for faults imagined or exaggerated.

His wife, Mary Benson, whom he called Minnie, and the Wellington schoolboys – some of them only a couple of years younger than she – referred to affectionately as 'Mother Benjy', was not happy or well when she was carrying Fred. Utterly different in personality from her husband, Minnie was effervescent, cheerful, liable to burst out laughing at something all too solemn, very fond of the ludicrous in life. She was completely at odds with Edward, although, in the manner of the time and their class, she strove mightily to be worthy of him and make herself more serious in line with his earnest requirements. She nearly always failed. The cause of her distress just before and for a year or so after Fred's birth was her attachment to a young lady called Emily Edwardes. For Minnie realised that the love she ought to feel for Edward did not come, however hard she tried, and that the joy she experienced in the company of female friends far outshone the dull, unwilling respect she harboured for him. So Fred was born to parents who, for different reasons, were each laid low by miserable guilt.

Minnie kept a tortured retrospective Diary of this period, which she wrote in 1875 at a time of cathartic self-examination. After Fred's arrival, she was wilful and unkind (she said), a burden to all around her, neglectful of home and children as she sought ever more often to be with Emily. She fell ill with the strain, and went with Emily to Hastings for a convalescent holiday.

Oh that sweet time with Emily! How we drew together. Lord, it was Thou, teaching me how to love. Friend of my married life, how I loved her! I remember how Thou stirred me to know what love was . . . and so it came to an end, and we went home, and my husband took me on his knee, and blessed God and prayed, and I remember my heart sank within me and became as a stone – for duties stared me in the face.[15]

Fred was their fifth child, preceded by Martin in 1860, Arthur in 1862, Nellie in 1863, and Maggie in 1865. They grew up in the nursery at Wellington under the benign care of their nurse Beth, the one emotional constant in all their lives, reliable, uncomplicated, and deeply loyal. Elizabeth Cooper had been nurse to Mrs Benson and her three brothers, and was to continue in service with the same family for nearly eighty years. All the Benson brothers and sisters adored her as a matter of course, without the need to explain why. Their love for her was instinctive, whereas they spent much of the rest of their lives trying to account for the complex of feelings they had for their parents.

Not unnaturally, 'Beth' was virtually the first word little Fred uttered. Minnie tells in a letter to Martin how she and Edward tried to coax Fred into speaking more distinctly, because they could not understand what he was trying to say. 'Bef can', was his snappy reply. 'Ah,' said his father, 'but *we* can't, and you are *our* child too, aren't you?' Fred retorted, 'Not particler.' He was just about to go into knickerbockers, so might have been around two years old.[16]

In later years, Fred was to cherish Beth's 'utterly beautiful life of love and service', and Arthur to admit that 'the love I had and have for her is almost the deepest emotion of my life.' She looked after them all with selfless devotion, protecting them from the tiniest fragments of cork from a bottle of ginger-beer, lest they swell up inside their bellies, taking them on regular walks during which the children were forbidden to pick things up for fear of catching some nameless disease. The boys never ceased to be 'Master Arthur' and 'Master Fred' to her long after they had achieved literary glory. When Queen Victoria visited Wellington College in 1864, and Beth was presented, she called her 'My Majesty'.[17]

The walls of the nursery were entirely covered with pictures cut out of illustrated newspapers and pasted on by the Headmaster himself. Outside the nursery was a staircase stretching round three sides of the entrance hall, making a large gallery, through the banisters of which Fred would peer to spy on illustrious guests as they arrived for lunch.[18]

Sometimes guests would visit the children for a few minutes, and throw Beth into a flurry of preparation. One such was the redoubtable Eton master Oscar Browning, who was closely questioned by Martin, already showing signs of intellectual precocity at the age of eight (Fred was barely a year old). Martin asked the obese and forbidding pedagogue to explain the bubbles on a pudding. 'They are imps, trying to get out', said Browning. Martin hesitated long enough to reflect, before reason won through; 'I don't believe you,' he said.[19] Fred was similarly dismissive of whimsy in his infancy, reproving his mother for calling her pencil and ruler 'Uncle Jacob and Aunt Eliza', which he said was 'silly'. When the day came for his first lesson in reading, Mama asked him what book he had been learning from. Freddy said he was not sure whether it was *Tears Without Reading* or *Reading Without Tears*.[20]

At about the same time that Freddy was grappling with his first printed word, Arthur, five years older, was proudly showing off his first written one. He told his mother 'My literary talent as an author has begun to shew itself. For I composed a story yesterday called The History and Adventures of a Needle!!! Only THINK *what* an honour to have a SON that is an author??'[21] Prophetic words indeed. Mary Benson would have more of that particular honour in years to come than she could ever have expected.

Though Mrs Benson was not herself a writer, it is certain that the literary gene passed down through her side of the family, the Sidgwicks, for they had more intellectual pedigree than the Bensons who, until Edward's generation, had been commercial. Since the brutal disparity between Edward's exigent personality and his wife's pliable one caused the problems of their early marriage, and since these problems hovered over Fred's infancy despite Beth's best efforts to keep them out of the nursery, it is as well we should consider whence these very large personalities derive. From their conflict (and ultimate adjustment at some cost to Minnie) issues Fred's perception of the world and, perhaps, his resolve to remain safely on the edge of it.

The Bensons had been established in the West Riding of Yorkshire for five hundred years, without doing much or attracting any attention. They had initially been leaseholders of Fountains Abbey, but had gradually purchased farmland of their own. The university librarian at Cambridge later assured Arthur Benson that the family was undoubtedly Scandinavian in origin, with the probable name of Bjørnsen (son of the bear); the presence of a bear in the family crest might give circumstantial support to the theory, but it is of no significance.[22] The line takes shape with Christopher Benson of Pateley Bridge, who was the ancestor of both Edward Benson and Minnie Sidgwick. It is recorded that his seventh son, John, used to walk out of York every day to smell a beanfield.[23] But it is another son, Edward, who is the progenitor of our line, and the beneficiary of a great piece of luck which improved the family fortunes. One of his cronies was a solitary bachelor called Francis White, with whom he played whist once a week in company with two others. When Francis White died he left all his property to be divided equally between these three friends, and for his part Edward demonstrated his gratitude by naming his son White; the name White was to remain in the family for four generations, until there were no more Bensons to bear it.

Captain White Benson was, alas, a hedonist and spendthrift. In his relatively short life, the savings inherited by the generosity of his namesake largely dribbled away, and his son, Edward White Benson the first, had to salvage what he could and turn to trade in order to rescue his family from penury. His talents lay in experiments with chemistry, so he worked on a new process for making cobalt and for the manufacture of white lead. Selling what was left of the property in York, he moved to the Midlands, and established his white lead factory in Birmingham. This perfectly sensible and proper displacement was to have profound and unpredictable repercussions upon the fate of his progeny, for he was able to send his eldest son, Edward White Benson the second, father of Fred, to the local school. King Edward's School in Birmingham was one of the best in the land, offering the kind of solid classical education without which no gentleman could claim real erudition. More important, its headmaster was an extraordinary, visionary, crusading teacher called James Prince Lee, who had in turn been influenced by Dr Arnold of Rugby. So it came to pass that Arnold's notions of severe Christian duty, of punishment as a purifying gift, of education as a responsibility towards God, all the paraphernalia of mid-Victorian discipline, passed through Lee to Benson, the future Archbishop of Canterbury. Other pupils, contemporaries and lifelong friends of Benson, were Westcott and Lightfoot, famous ecclesiastics of the day who were each to become Bishop of Durham.

There survives a Commonplace Book kept by Benson *père*, which opens with a Pindaric Ode on a Gooseberry Pie. It is safe to conclude that this indicates a sense of humour.[24] That apart, this industrious chemist was also a genuinely religious man. He wrote a book of meditations on the works of God which is rampant with sincerity. Yet his eldest son, our Edward, outshone him in piety. He made up his mind to be a clergyman when he was ten. By the time he reached fourteen he had converted a little room in his father's factory into his own private Oratory, which he decorated and furnished himself, draping a table for an altar, and where he went every day to say the Canonical Hours. Somewhat priggishly, he determined to keep his treasured Oratory absolutely private, and forbade his sisters to set foot therein. Once he even set a booby trap above the door to ensure his strictures were properly obeyed. They were not, and a sister was forthwith battered by falling books.

The young boy was passionately interested in liturgical history, and gave the impression that there was little else in life worthy of enthusiastic discussion than topics with a religious flavour. He was fond of the forms of worship as well as the faith, growing excited at the mere mention of churches, ceremonies, heresies, and the Council of Trent. Moreover, Edward devoured classical literature with the hunger of one who knew his future depended upon the ingestion of knowledge, spending all his spare time at the Birmingham Free Library. By the age of eighteen he had read, for his private delectation, Livy, Herodotus and Thucydides in their entirety. It was said he could recite the whole of the Psalter by heart.

Edward White Benson the first died in 1843, leaving a widow and seven young children with very meagre resources. By some accounts they were almost destitute, although still clinging to middle-class respectability with help from some of the late chemist's friends, who paid for Edward to continue at King Edward's School. Not yet fifteen, he was now the head of the family, and he seems to have embraced the opportunity to lecture his mother and siblings with rather unattractive promptness. He knew best what was good for their souls, and it was his solemn duty to advise them accordingly, if necessary to replace advice with coercion. An astounding example of this occurred in Edward's first year at Trinity College, Cambridge.

The expenses of a Cambridge education stretched the family income to breaking-point. It never entered Edward's head that he should forgo the privilege of higher education for his mother's sake: it was his destiny and his due, and, as we shall see, Edward never escaped the habit of thinking of himself before all else. (In fairness, it must be made clear that Edward did not live in luxury at Trinity, but in conditions of extreme hardship.) His mother possessed her late husband's patent for the manufacture of cobalt, and she considered it might be a splendid idea to turn this to profit by starting a business of her own. Her clever and ambitious son was horrified. It was out of the question that any mother of his should enter into 'trade'. He wrote from Cambridge more or less instructing her to keep out of it and abandon the scheme forthwith. Why? Because 'it will do me so much harm here, and my sisters so much harm forever!'[25] Mother obeyed.

Edward then had to take part-time pupils to help make ends meet, and send half his earnings to his mother. Upon this poor woman there now descended what her grandson would accurately describe as 'a tempest of woes'. She invested what was left of her capital in a newly-floated railway company, and lost it all. Two of her daughters then caught typhus. Edward was on his way from Cambridge when he received the news that one of them, Harriet, had died. Mrs Benson went to Harriet's room to take one last look at the corpse of her daughter, then lay down on the bed beside another daughter and went to sleep. She never woke more, but died without movement in the night, and was found, cold, by the terrified girl lying next to her.

So Edward had a double funeral to arrange, and the full responsibility of a surviving family of orphans to shoulder. He knew he was equal to the task. His first discovery was that all his mother's capital had disappeared, and that they were, for practical purposes, penniless. There was no hope of keeping the family together; the children had all to be adopted by various relations. Two went to a grandmother, the others were dispersed into distant and sometimes strange homes. Edward's sister Ada, who was later to cause him such anguish because he failed to offer her a home with his family, was brought up by their cousins the Sidgwicks, who will soon come to the forefront of the story. There was also an uncle on the mother's side, Sir Thomas Baker, a successful and wealthy businessman. This generous man offered to adopt the youngest orphan, a boy of eight, and bring him up with all the advantages which would accrue to his own son. Edward, who at twenty-one had to bear the burden of every decision, would not countenance such an offensive idea. The one terrible problem with Uncle Thomas was that he was a Unitarian.

Correspondence between uncle and nephew on this matter has survived and is painful to read. To a modern mind it appears incredible that Edward should sacrifice the future and well-being of his little brother to arid principle. Thomas Baker insists that he has no intention of indoctrinating the boy, that he will educate him according to the strict ideas that Edward upholds, that no hint of Unitarian propaganda will ever be allowed to approach his ears. Edward would not be moved; there remained always the appalling hazard that the child might be contaminated and thereby forfeit God's grace.

Edward undertook full responsibility for his little brother's education. His final letter on the subject heralds many of the characteristics which will make him at once a stunning achiever in life, and a difficult husband and father. They are obtuseness, stubbornness, self-satisfaction, an inability to understand any point of view which differs from his own, and a rigid belief in salvation through hardship. 'My religious principle is not a thing of tender feelings,' he writes, 'warm comforting notions, unproved prejudices, but it consists of full and perfect conviction, absolute belief, rules to regulate my life, and tests by which I believe myself bound to try every question the greatest and the least . . . This is a very serious matter, and I hope you will not think bitterly either of the young man's presumption, or the young churchman's bigotry. Bigot, thus far, a conscientious Christian must be.' When his son Fred read this letter many years later, he said that 'it burns with the uncompromising faith out of which, in days of persecution, martyrs were made.'[26]

The words Edward uses to describe the kind of religion which excites his contempt, a religion of 'warm comforting notions', might with equal justice be applied to the much gentler spiritual feelings of his wife. That they should be so much at odds at this level does not augur well for harmony in marriage.

Meanwhile, back at Cambridge, Edward was rescued from penury and the ruin of his chances by yet another *deus ex machina* with a warm heart and a deep pocket. Francis Martin, the middle-aged bachelor bursar of Trinity College, offered to pay not only all Edward's expenses at Cambridge, but all future maintenance until such time as he was able to earn enough to support himself and his siblings. He beseeched Edward to accept, and he won. According to Fred, Francis Martin had a romantic affection for Edward, and would have written sonnets to him had he known how. And with reason, for Edward at twenty-one was extremely handsome and, apart from the bigotry already referred to, wonderfully sensitive. He loved long walks in the country, swimming, talking. He was splendid company for a lonely, white-haired, gruff old man. Martin furnished Edward's rooms at Trinity entirely anew, gave him a supply of cheques to cover every need, put aside £500 for each of his sisters as a potential dowry, took him on holiday and looked after him with parental tenderness. Martin entirely changed Edward's world, enabling the poverty-stricken and orphaned undergraduate suddenly to savour university life to the full. Edward never forgot his patron's kindness, and was to name his first son after him.

After two more years, Edward graduated in a blaze of glory, with a first-class degree in the Classical Tripos and the Chancellor's Gold Medal, given by the Prince Consort. He was staying at the house of his widowed cousin, Mrs William Sidgwick (descended from Christopher Benson of Pateley Bridge), when Francis Martin came panting across country from Cambridge to convey the astonishing and delightful news of his success. The Sidgwicks made a huge fuss of Edward, as well they might, for they were a family to value academic achievement above most of the blessings of life. William Sidgwick had been the Headmaster of Skipton Grammar School. His widow brought up four children, three boys and a girl, and each of the boys would rise to the very peaks of academic life. William junior won a scholarship to Christ Church, Oxford, and became tutor at Merton College. Henry would be Professor of Moral Philosophy at Cambridge for nearly twenty years and have a remarkable influence on two generations of scholars. Significantly, in view of E.F. Benson's subsequent dabbling with the occult, he also founded the Society for Psychical Research. Arthur Sidgwick was eventually a master at Rugby and tutor at Corpus Christi. They were all but boys when cousin Edward White Benson received the news of his glittering gradu-ation, and they were suitably proud of him. But it was their sister whom Edward most wanted to impress, little Mary, known within the family as Minnie. She was eleven years old. This is what Edward wrote about her:

> As I have always been very fond of her and she of me with the love of a little sister, and as I have heard of her fondness for me commented on by many persons, and have been told that I was the only person at whose departure she ever cried, as a child, and how diligent she has always been in reading books which I have mentioned to her, and in learning pieces of poetry which I have admired, it is not strange that I . . . should have thought first of the possibility that some day dear little Minnie might become my wife.

Everyone who has read this passage has professed to be shocked by it. Fred wrote that his father 'rather chills us by the painstaking quality of his emotions', which is a just observation as far as it goes. Others have found something distinctly prurient in the idea of a grown man paying court to a pre-pubescent girl. The diary entry goes on to record a conversation they had on the sofa one evening. Minnie asked her cousin how long it would take for her to be as tall as she would be now, if standing on a stool. He replied that he thought it would take about five years. Minnie asked if she would be taller still at the age of twenty. Yes, said Edward. And how old would Edward be when she was twenty? Thirty-two, he told her. 'Thirty-two,' she exclaimed. 'Edward, I shan't look so little compared to you, shall I, when I'm twenty and you're thirty-two, as I do now that I'm eleven and you're twenty-three.' Edward confesses that he blushed at this point, and the palms of his hands 'grew very hot'. He then confides the embarrassing reflection, 'Whatever she grows up to be, she is a fine and beautiful bud now.'

Edward told Mrs Sidgwick that Minnie was a sweet and clever girl and would one day make him a fine wife. The mother demurred at this startling suggestion and more or less told the young man not to be in such a hurry (she may have wanted to marry him herself). But the following year he asked her permission to raise the subject with Minnie herself. Amazingly, Mrs Sidgwick relented, and so Edward took the little girl, sat her on his knee in an arm-chair, and proceeded to propose to her.

> I asked her if she thought it would ever come to pass that we should be married. Instantly, without a word, a rush of tears fell down her cheeks, and I really for the moment was afraid. I told her that it was often in my thoughts, and that I believed that I should never love anyone so much as I should love her if she grew up as it seemed likely.

He then told her that he would not dream of asking her to promise anything at this stage, but she took his handkerchief, tied it in a knot, and placed it in his hand. He was 'much affected'.[27]

Within days his ardour had conquered his reserve. 'I love you *very very* dearly and wish much for you,' he told the little girl after a long chat with her mother. It was settled between them that Minnie should sit next to Edward at table, and that her portrait should hang over his dining-room chimney-piece – 'I gave it a kiss before I came away tonight.'

And now – what do you think? William *knows*. Your Mama told him, and he was very glad, and very pleased that you wished him so much to know. He thought, *of course*, that I should be a very lucky man – whether he thought you a very lucky Minnie is not for me to say.

Nevertheless, he would say it often enough in the years to come. Another note in the same summer ends with the valediction, 'With many kisses to your sleeping eyes.'[28] She said she now knew what love and happiness meant.

She knew nothing of the sort. She *expected* love (whatever that was) to come in due course, as it did in the poems she and Edward read together. From that moment, she considered herself beholden to him, and her mother must bear some of the responsibility for this, by reason of her complicity in Edward's selfish deed. In later years, Minnie remembered that earnest chat on the sofa with horror. She was too much of a child to understand the implicit commitment she was making, and in the years to follow she regularly answered Edward's letters (which her mother read) in the hope she would grow worthy of his love and fulfil the role marked out for her. As Edward's letters were those of a pedagogue, always trying to *teach* her something, telling her what to read, what architecture to look at, how to evaluate it, and almost offering marks out of ten for her replies, it would have been surprising had love grown from such dry and dusty soil. What offends the modern reader in Edward's approach is not so much the disparity in age (for he intended nothing improper), but the idea that she had to be built up into a woman who would deserve him. He had selected her because he intuited she would be a useful spouse, and what was most important in his scheme was that his every need should be met. It was paramount that his career in the service of God should not be thwarted. He would have a hard task. He would need a helpmate. Minnie would do very nicely. Worse still, she was gradually made to feel, that if she did not learn to love Edward, then in some obscure way she did not love God.

In March of that year Edward wrote his infant fiancée what is to modern ears a truly horrible letter. He told her that he had a 'grave matter' to discuss with her, and that this would be his most serious letter. Everyone, he pointed out, has a besetting sin or fault: 'I believe that you are anxious to control yourself, and grow up a good and useful woman, a *true woman*.' He proceeds to tell her that her besetting sin is thoughtlessness and itemises its dangers and manifestations:

> You must remember that if you do *not* cure yourself you will go on *always* perpetually giving pain, and perpetually causing trouble to those whom you most love and wish to please; and you will expose your love for them to perpetual suspicions, for they will say, '*could* she do so, if she really and constantly loved me, and thought how she might please me?'

The nastiness, priggishness, self-righteousness of this attitude were surpassed in postscript by an exhortation that Minnie should read the letter several times![29] The calamity of their marriage was presaged in that instruction.

Mrs Sidgwick moved house to Rugby at about the same time as Edward was offered a part-time post teaching at Rugby School. It was therefore a matter of course that he should take lodging with the Sidgwicks, as his sister Ada had already done. As he taught only in the mornings, he was afforded ample opportunity to educate his future wife in the delights of architectural style, poetic metre and liturgical doctrine. 'Lessons with Ed,' she wrote later, 'so dreaded – architecture and physical geography.' As a present, he inscribed for her a copy of the Book of Psalms and Hymns used in Rugby School Chapel.[30]

Later that year Edward was elected a Fellow of Trinity and ordained by his old Headmaster, James Prince Lee, in 1854. This was followed by a trip to France and Italy with his friend Lightfoot, during which he sent frequent letters to Minnie explaining the history of cathedrals in suffocating, leaden prose. She was still only thirteen. As one of the Bensons' biographers has put it, 'the Victorian child was very much thought of as the Victorian grown-up only not yet quite so large.'[31]

When Rev. Frederick Temple took over as Headmaster of Rugby, Benson decided to stay on rather than accept a tutorship at Trinity. It was a wise decision, for from this modest beginning was to develop a career of uninterrupted, startling progress. Not long afterwards, the Prince Consort announced his plan to found a new public school in memory of the Duke of Wellington, which would rank with Eton and Marlborough, and be set among the Berkshire hills. It would offer first-class education at low rates to the sons of officers, though others would be admitted, and it would be firmly based on the classical curriculum. The new school was well under way in 1858, when Prince Albert asked for a list to be drawn up for the post of Headmaster. Over thirty names were presented to him, but not one of them was thought worthy or energetic enough for a pioneering job such as this. Whoever was appointed would have to combine academic brilliance with a flair for organisation and a talent for disciplined innovation. Temple thought he knew the man for the job, and wrote to Prince Albert a letter of fulsome recommendation in favour of Edward White Benson. He praised Benson's 'very high attainments', averred he was 'intellectually a very superior man, a first-rate scholar', and concluded that 'he is one of the best teachers I have ever met with.'[32]

Benson was duly offered the post, which he accepted. Suddenly transformed from an impecunious schoolmaster to a man of position and prestige, with a house and a handsome salary, Edward decided the time had arrived for Minnie to embark upon the role in life for which she had been groomed. He was now thirty, she eighteen; there was no need to wait any longer. He composed a poem for her:

> I have loved her so long and so well
> These seven bright years of gladsome life.
> I have loved her so well that I scarce can tell
> If she be Ladylove more than Wife.
> . . . . . .
> Will the thrilling embrace and the rapture new
> Change thee from Ladylove swift to Wife?[33]

Alas, no! After a brief trip to Germany to observe methods of education in Prince Albert's homeland (which did not impress

Edward, who from the beginning was to demonstrate that he was his own man, with his own ideas), the couple were married at Rugby by the Reverend Temple himself in 1859. They went to Rouen, Rheims, Paris and Switzerland for their honeymoon, and returned to their new home at Wellington, due to open in January 1860. By this time, Minnie had discovered the implications of marriage, for which she was lamentably unprepared. She was a wretchedly unhappy young woman, not least because she felt she *ought* to make Edward happy, and with equal conviction knew she could not.

There are two journals of this period in Minnie's hand. The one, clearly undertaken on the instructions of a husband still bent on improving her, is a careful travelogue, describing perpendicular arches as if they were part of a boring school exercise. It is an exceedingly dull document, with not a word of spontaneous personal thought in its nicely-bound pages. The other was a private outpouring of anguish, rapidly scribbled with no regard for syntax and balance (how Edward would have deplored such slapdash prose!), and painfully, pathetically honest.

Wedding night – Folkestone – crossing. Oh how my heart sank – I daren't let it – no wonder – an utter child, with *no* stay on God . . . danced and sang into matrimony. [Edward was] twelve years older, much stronger, much more passionate, and whom I didn't really love – I wonder I didn't go more wrong . . . no one had told me about God *this way* . . . But let me try and think how hard it was for Ed. He restrained his passionate nature for 7 years, and then got *me*! this unloving, childish, weak, unstable child! Ah God, pity him! . . . misery – knowing that I felt nothing of what I knew people ought to feel – knowing how disappointing this must be to Ed, how evidently disappointed he was – trying to be rapturous, not succeeding, feeling so inexpressibly lonely and young – but *how* hard for him! I have learnt what love is through friendship – how I cried at Paris! poor lonely child. The nights! I can't think how I lived.

It is not difficult to picture the scene, the man virile, handsome, passionate, responsible; his wife frightened and bewildered. Throughout the long courtship, she had pretended to love him because she knew such was expected of her. 'I had to strain the truth in order to satisfy Ed by expressions of love,' she wrote. Additionally, she had been called upon to demonstrate to her own mother that she loved him, and shrank (her word) from encounters with her. One year before the marriage, Minnie had felt affection for an unnamed girl, which she refers to as 'first friendship'. Now she wonders if she had done wrong. 'I fell in love with her and spent a great deal of time with her . . . No, I trust there was not much amiss here. Now and then I neglected something for her and vexed Mama.'

This is what she meant by having learnt love through friendship. To her immense credit, this vivacious, frisky, warm young woman does not blame her husband for subjecting her to boredom by day and terror by night; she is constantly thinking how terrible it must have been for *him*, and castigating herself for having failed to grow into the proper wife she should have been. She could not know, then, how profoundly marriage hones the emotions, nor that Edward would eventually come to rely upon her as the perfect spouse.

Back in England, she was determined no one should be aware of her distress, but she was constantly on edge lest he appear and demand something, lest he want her company:

> I would have died rather than that anyone should have thought for a moment I wasn't happy . . . Did I love E? I cannot quite tell. I used to be anxious for his appearance – used to watch his looks – he must have had a good deal to bear.[34]

So must she. Edward was in the habit of correcting her in public, of pointing out her mistakes in front of others, possibly even in front of schoolboys. He would not consider this an humiliation, but a duty before God. Minnie had to learn to put up with it, as she said, to get into the *habits* of life. 'But where was the Stay, the Rock, the Helper?' From the earliest years of her marriage, and directly consequent upon her husband's deplorable lack of understanding, Mary Benson began to lose her faith.

Fortunately, there were children to rear. They came in quick succession, the first five born within seven years. Martin gave cause for anxiety because he stammered, an affliction he never entirely conquered. Arthur was very ill at the age of only five months, and his mother scarcely thought he could live. In the meantime, Minnie was expected to fulfil the role of Headmaster's wife and run a household with thrift and care. Gradually, she found herself rebelling against this endless round of chores and duties and imprisonments. 'A great difficulty is, I cannot *obey* as I should. I am not yet large-hearted enough. Please God to help me.'[35] The largeness of her heart was never, would never be, in question. The trouble was, she was intelligent, thoughtful, reflective, with a mind set quite differently from Edward's, but no less admirable. In 1860 and for long afterwards, wives were meant to be subservient to their husbands, to suppress whatever personality they might inconveniently possess and devote themselves entirely to the satisfaction of their husbands' whims, desires, or orders. Minnie Benson obviously tried to fit the mould, but her character was too bright, too full to accept the need to be smashed and obliterated in such a way. Despite herself, she was assertive, and when quarrels reminded her that she was not behaving as meekly as she should, she fell ill with remorse. Edward, too, was straining under the load of his responsibilities. The worry of Wellington, which *had* to be a success, for nothing less than brilliance would satisfy the Queen, frequently sank his spirits, and back in his private married quarters he would make a drama out of the smallest trifle.

One such erupted in January 1864, not long after the birth of Minnie's third child, Mary Eleanor (always known as Nelly). Edward lectured his wife on one of his favourite topics – DUTY; she *must* learn to organise the household bills so that they are correctly dealt with, and on time. Furthermore, she must keep the servants on their toes, a task she avoided, for she did not like to make a fuss or upset anyone. One of her duties, he told her, was to correct anything that was wrong in the household, and that included correcting those under one's care when they were found wanting. It was sinful to turn a blind eye or be lenient. 'It is a law of God that cleanliness and order should lead to Godliness,' he said. She sulked, and told him she knew he would say something like that. 'Now, Minnie,' he said, 'I think you need not be pettish with me.' Far from being angry at this treatment, Minnie wrote, 'He is kinder and kinder, and I always feel, even when he speaks severely, that he really does it *for my sake*.'[36] At this distance, we may be forgiven for interpreting his behaviour with less charity.

Later the same year there occurred another marital squabble over an unspecified problem which Minnie identifies with a capital letter; it is interesting for Edward's response to it:

> After dinner we had a conversation about S, which was renewed upstairs. E very vexed and spoke very strongly, and seemed to think that I knew he must disapprove, and denounced it as 'either a sin or a folly'. I said I was very sorry that he forbad it for the future. He was still more vexed at that. I *can't* feel that it is so wrong – when undertaken in a reverent spirit, anyhow I suppose it is over for me now, and I must be content.

The following day Minnie returned to the subject. 'I still take the same view,' she wrote. 'One thing E said was that he would not for worlds have it known, it would hurt his reputation so. I don't know why it is, but I always rebel against this argument.'

Whatever 'it' was, the image of Edward standing before his distraught wife and ordering her to keep quiet for *his* sake is peculiarly unattractive. It appears to be appallingly selfish ambition, although Edward would maintain it was God's purpose that needed protecting, not one man's *personal* reputation. Nevertheless, Edward cannot escape the charge of arrogance, and blatant disregard for Minnie's own idea of her happiness. Her happiness must be subordinate to keeping him in a good mood. 'E complained of my want of power (or *will*) to "pick him up" when he was downhearted.' No wonder she rebelled against egocentricity of this order; Minnie was not made for self-effacement.

None of this was allowed to be seen outside the private parlour. Perhaps Beth knew something of Mrs Benson's distress, for she had nursed her from a baby and enjoyed that confidence which needs no articulation, but what Beth heard Beth swallowed. Minnie undertook her public duties at the side of her husband with grace and charm. The boys at Wellington adored her, while they stood in fear of the Headmaster. Even as she endured these private humiliations, she played hostess to Queen Victoria herself in the full glare of public attention. It was in 1864, three years after the death of Prince Albert, that the Queen paid a visit to Wellington College and was received by Mr and Mrs Benson, who conducted her through the court past the busts of generals 'which dear Albert took so much trouble about'. Her Majesty was shown the classrooms, dormitories, kitchens, and finally the chapel, 'of which my beloved one laid the first stone in July 61'. She told her journal that she had to struggle hard not to break down, but Edward remembered seeing tears stream down her face. The Queen already knew the Bensons from previous encounters. She does not mention Minnie this early in their acquaintance, but she has nothing but praise for Edward, 'such a pleasing, nice, clever man . . . an intellectual man, whom Albert liked so much.'[37]

Victoria presented Edward with a copy of the Speeches and Addresses of the Prince Consort, with her own personal inscription: 'In recollection of the great and good Prince, Who took so deep an interest in the success of the Wellington College, from the beloved Prince's broken-hearted Widow, Victoria.'[38]

The Queen's confidence in Benson was amply justified by events, as he showed himself to be an educator of the first rank, an honest champion of the principles established by Arnold and Lee. Benson believed that the ultimate aim of education was not so much the ingestion of information as the attainment of moral perfection, and that this precious goal was reached through earnest, unending effort to make oneself worthy of it. Happiness lay in making the attempt to strive towards good, and if one discovered faults in oneself along the way, so much the better, for there was joy in self-chastisement. It followed that much of the teacher's job was to control behaviour, to show boys how to lead a righteous life and how to combat sin, and Benson rose to this task with messianic fervour. He was an absolute autocrat, impatient of opposition, who could tolerate no dilution of his authority. Having made clear from the beginning that he would rule according to his own lights, and not by committee, he strode forth majestically convinced of the rightness of his mind. His son Arthur, who would himself be a master at Eton in due course, and one moreover with much gentler notions of his calling, said that Edward White Benson 'did not desire that his pupils should develop on their lines but on his own.'[39]

The precepts Benson laid down were simple but severe. Honesty and accuracy were the prime virtues (and how many times would we hear poor Fred chastised for his want of the latter). To tell a lie was practically beyond God's capacity to forgive, and any boy detected in falsehood was made to suffer such perturbation of spirit as he was unlikely ever to forget. It was partly for this reason that fiction was regarded by educators like Benson as injurious to health, for it celebrated pretence at the expense of accuracy. More important, fiction was frivolous, it did not elevate the mind or induce moral improvement. It was nothing but a worthless amusement, to be condemned at every level. The Headmaster abhorred waste of time. Even leisure must be used for instruction, not idleness. There was much to be learnt from a walk on the lawn. To set an example, he was wont to read the Greek Testament while shaving. For his part, Freddy had to learn a psalm each morning and deliver it before breakfast.[40]

Benson was naturally aware that boys were weak, and so he laid great store on vigilance, establishing a prefectorial system which resembled a secret service. Every morning he had two senior boys to breakfast with him. His own family thought that was incredibly decent of him, but they could not have known that he might in this way hear of misdemeanours which merited his attention. The purification of morals was his ideal, and his prefects, always on the watch for sinful conduct, would assist his discovery of the devil's work. They prowled and they reported. To make quite certain, Benson had barbed wire placed on the tops of dormitory partitions.[41]

Every evening after prayers, Edward shook hands with each boy in the school and bade him goodnight, thereby establishing a rapport which would render the breaking of any rules a personal affront to him. He almost made discipline a private compact with each boy. 'Misconduct, a slackening of effort, childish flippancy all pained him deeply. It was as if the offender were consciously letting him down, deliberately flouting the most sacred principles of life.'[42] His wife and his own children were also to feel the bitter wounding of this oddly sensitive man. Minnie was forever trying to live up to him.

When, however, the code laid down by Benson was breached, he was utterly relentless in punishing the offender. A great believer in flogging, he used the cane to drive out sin, and a pupil who grew up to be General Sir Ian Hamilton was flogged every day for weeks on end, simply because he had arrived late for school. Benson did not question the efficacy of such treatment. As David Williams has put it, he was a man 'corseted in frozen attitudes . . . girt about with certainties'[43], for whom compromise would be tantamount to weakness. One thing is sure – Benson did not have a cruel or vindictive nature; punishment afforded him no satisfaction beyond the utilitarian. He could not bear the thought of pain being visited upon man or beast. He was excessively kind to animals, and wept at the image of cruelty inflicted on a defenceless creature. The family had a collie called Watch, adored by all the children. It was Edward who fluffed up his rug every night to make sure the dog was comfortable.

The significance of all this in any enquiry into the life of E.F. Benson is that his father did not leave his schoolmasterly principles in the classroom or the Headmaster's study, but carried them with him into domestic life. The family, after all, lived at the school, and Benson expected his own children to set an example to the boys in his care. They were to be perfect, he must be proud of them, they must never let him down. This was a harsh and almost impossible demand. Almost, because perhaps his eldest son, Martin, did very nearly attain the perfection Edward yearned for, but he was not to live long enough for adulthood to confirm the assessment. The highest praise for Martin was that he never once in his life was detected in a falsehood. The other children, however, were flawed as children are, and were constantly reminding themselves what a disappointment they must be to their revered, faultless, fierce and dominating father. Fred spent much of his life as a writer trying to escape Edward's influence, embracing frivolity, cherishing forgiveness, glorying in the weaknesses more than the hallowed virtues of humankind. In this he took after his mother who, unbeknown to Edward, learnt more about human nature from her despised novels than he could possibly encompass in his principles. Where the father made no allowance for lack of initiative or imagination, and was ruthless towards the second-rate, the son celebrated their humanity with an affectionate chuckle. Occasionally, as in his novel *The Challoners*, he would revert to his father's lack of sympathy and the chuckle evaporated, for Fred did not approve of sanctity on earth. His problem would be that the man he loved and admired as a miracle of achievement was not a man he liked.

His mother, on the other hand, excited his undisguised commitment for the rest of his life. He valued her temperance, her whimsy, her fondness for larks and games; he admired her intelligence and her intuition; he cherished the largeness of her heart and her constant willingness to help anyone laid low by unhappiness. Fred liked his mother without reserve, but it was not until after her death that he discovered how miserable she had been immediately following his own entry into the world. Then he saw the oppression of matrimony, the squabbles over household bills, the humiliation of Minnie having to borrow £100 from her mother to avoid the dreaded ticking-off from her husband, and the waywardness of her affections. Emily, Annie, Susan Wordsworth, all were the recipients of Minnie's innocent, yearning affection, at the same time as she was imploring God to teach her how to love Edward with that overpowering desire which he felt for her.

Minnie once had her horoscope read anonymously. The sage declared that the subject under scrutiny had 'a strong loving nature [with] great capacities for love . . . yet great trouble in love matters . . . I am not told whether this lady is married or not . . . I may say I hope not, for this latter would be a very disturbing element in married life.'[44]

The troubles continued sporadically until Fred was four years old. Then his brother Hugh was born, in 1871, the last of the Benson children. And Minnie finally had the breakdown which had been long in preparation.

2   Progress of an Infant Snob

When he arrives at the year 1873 in his heavy two-volume history of his father's career, and the family's translation from Wellington College to Lincoln, Arthur Benson states that 'My mother was ill at the time we moved, and was much away.'[1] It is typical of the Benson style that a crisis can be concealed in a sentence which is bland, truthful, but completely locked against the inquisitive.

Mary Benson's illness was in fact a profound searching of the soul, a protracted and devastating experience from which she was to emerge a totally formed woman in her own right, no longer the laborious creation of her husband. It began immediately after the birth of her last child, Hugh, in 1871, and was the product of various adverse influences colluding at once to undermine her. She was worn out by incessant childbirth, and needed to protest. She was fatigued by the effort of trying to become the woman Edward wanted, and needed to assert her individuality. And she was so hurt by Edward's vision of a punitive, unrelenting God that she was in danger of losing her faith altogether.

Thus it happened that, just as Fred was born at a time of difficulty between his parents, so by the age of five he was made painfully aware yet again of the perils of bonding. He cannot have failed to notice that his mother was unhappy, and though at such an age he was obviously unable to assess the causes, he would remember and reflect in maturity.

Fred must also have observed his father's wounded, uncomprehending distress. For there is no doubt, despite Edward's hard, didactic manner, that he loved his wife deeply and genuinely. He simply did not know what was going on in her heart, and his world of certainties permitted no room for the subtle analysis of personality. When she was away from him, he wrote letters which cry out with bewildered affection, addressing Minnie as 'my dearest, dearest, dearest Wife', or 'My sweet', and signing off 'Your lover'.

Minnie first took refuge in Scotland, and then for a period of months in Wiesbaden, Germany. It was probably there that she met Miss Elizabeth Hall, though the sequence of events is confused. We have only her staccato jottings in the diary to guide us, but it is clear that she felt a closeness to Miss Hall that seriously threatened her marriage. There is talk of an ill-advised letter she wrote, now missing, of arguments, of Miss Hall being turned out of the house, then returning. It looks as if Miss Hall accompanied Minnie from Germany after the dangerous letter had been written, and that Minnie went back to Wiesbaden as a result. Anyway, we must let her relate the anguish of this time in her own way:

Then I began to love Miss Hall. No wrong surely there – it was complete fascination . . . the continuous seeing of her . . . I have learnt the consecration of friendship. The other fault thou knowest – I will not even write it – but O God forgive me – *how* near we were to that! my sudden illness – I know the misery of this time – tossings, doubts, indecisions, jealousies. [after coming home with Miss Hall] how I grieved E[dward] to the heart. So she left our home, that March morning.

The letter – ah! my husband's pain – what he bore, and how lovingly, how quickly. *Our talk* – my wilful misery – my letter to her – Ah Lord, how blind thou allowdst me to get. [. . .] So E.H. came again at the end of July, and I *saw*. Friendship has its duties like marriage – enable me to do mine, and make my love ever grow and grow. So we left Wellington, I with this great stain, which till now I have never asked entire forgiveness of.[2]

The children all wrote to Mama in Wiesbaden, and she to them, but to none more than Fred. She felt an affinity with Fred which was to endure, and she could be humorous with him. His letters are naturally sparse. Nelly, aged nine, wrote, 'Fred has written a letter which neither himself nor anybody else could read', and Maggie, seven, saw fit to comment that 'Freddy sometimes forgets that he is the eldest son at home'.[3] The older boys, Martin and Arthur, were away at school.

Mary Benson admitted to Fred that she was bored. 'Here I am sitting upstairs in my own room, and the rain is coming steadily down, and if it goes on all the day as it did yesterday I really think I shall have to put all the drawing-room chairs in a row and jump over them.' Nor was she afraid of showing that she missed the family. 'I do like to hear all about Baby [Hugh] – mind when you next write you tell me all about him. I like to hear about his teeth and his crawling and his talking. And did *you* ever hear him say "mama"? Goodbye, my dear old Fred, mind you get on nicely with your reading, for when I come back I shall hope you will be quite able to read me a little story.'[4] Fred replied with some sweet reminiscence about a character his mother invented called 'Lady Abracadabra'; she used to dress up in fantastic garb covered with cheap jewels and surprise the children with little gifts – Fred missed Lady Abracadabra.

Minnie deserted her husband (for that is what it amounted to) at a time of great travail for him. Shortly before, he had been offered the headmastership of Rugby, which he had declined for reasons of loyalty to his school. Yet he was by now tired of teaching little boys things they did not particularly want to know, and felt disprized, unappreciated. His calling was to the church, and he longed for the panoply of ecclesiastical ritual as well as the sheer joy of preaching to people willing to listen. The deciding factor was a row with the school governors, who were rash enough to question Edward's judgement on a matter of morals. Three boys had been detected in 'grave moral delinquency' involving a kitchen maid, as a result of which one of them had contracted a venereal disease. Edward had requested the parents of each to remove them from the school. The parents of two of the boys had made the sensible observation that the offences had taken place in school holidays and were therefore a private family matter. They petitioned the Governors, who asked Benson to re-admit the boys. He was furious and made it absolutely clear that he would resign on the spot. He won the day, but the affair wounded his immense pride. It is an interesting story in its own right, for it sheds

31

appalling light upon this man's right and duty to interfere with schoolboys' behaviour at any time and in any place.[5]

Benson's opportunity to discard such irritating challenges to his authority came obliquely through a man who joined the staff for two terms as Sixth Form assistant to the Master, John Wordsworth. Wordsworth formed an immediate attachment to the Benson family, which was quickly endorsed and enlarged by the whole Wordsworth clan. The father, Christopher Wordsworth, was a nephew of the poet, and it was he in particular who became a fast friend of Edward White Benson; they shared ideals and ideas, and were soon visiting one another at frequent intervals. As Arthur was to say, 'it was an intellectual partnership, tinged with ecclesiastical romance, and illuminated by deep and genuine affection.'[6] Wordsworth would come to stay at Wellington College, and great important debates would take place after dinner by the fire, in company with Lightfoot, Temple, and others. In return, the Benson family spent holidays staying with the Wordsworths, Mary Benson being especially fond of the daughter Susan, and Edward coincidentally taking a shine to another daughter, Elizabeth, later to be Head of Lady Margaret Hall at Oxford. The two families dwelt together in perfect amity and unity; little Fred was impressed by Christopher Wordsworth's enviable ability to skate on one foot, lifting the other completely off the ice!

Wordsworth possessed weightier talents than this. In 1869 he was appointed Bishop of Lincoln, and three years later he invited his friend Edward to accept the post of Chancellor and Canon of Lincoln, with a home in the Chancery, facing the fourteenth-century cathedral, and the challenge presented by a plan that he should start a theological college. Edward loved hard pioneering work, and had already proved himself a brilliant administrator with the huge success of Wellington. Besides, the attraction of working in close proximity with congenial and like-minded friends was very strong. The only sadness was that Edward had to make the decision alone, as his beloved wife was absent at the crucial moment.

So much did he miss her, so anxious was he becoming for her good opinion, that he posted the letter from Lincoln, offering the Chancellorship, to her in Wiesbaden, appending a note of his own asking her what he should do. He admitted the new post would demand a severe cut in salary, but it offered 'the cloistered existence I have always wished for'. He also sent her careful drawings of the Chancery, and a plan of the house. Edward wanted assurance that Minnie would accept the change for his sake, yet he is constantly enquiring after her health and insisting she look after herself properly. At no time does he beg her to come home, except by painting a picture designed to foster homesickness. 'Fred contrasted my administration of the dinner-table very unfavourably with yours,' he said, 'and was very serious on the severity of my rule.'[7] Mama sent him a sweet note for his birthday. 'I said to myself, there is such a beautiful toyshop and booksellers at Rugby I will send him a *Post Office Order*.'[8]

She did however come home for the emotional leave-taking, when the Headmaster made his last speech to the assembled throng, and walked through the cloisters for the last time. The boys of Wellington were determined to give their chief a rousing send-off, and forgave (or at least forgot) his severity and his self-righteousness, remembering only his long labour on their behalf. It was the kind of occasion the emotional Victorians, ever given to blubbing, might relish. Arthur Benson described it twice, in *The Trefoil*, and in the *Life* of his father. Following the speech, the Head was joined by his family and said goodbye to his colleagues. Then he walked into the cloistered courtyard, which was packed with boys who surged forward thrusting out their hands to shake his. Benson appeared to be taken by surprise. His lip trembled and tears brimmed in his eyes. The gusty wind swayed his surplice and hood. He walked through the crowd, his wife and children behind, shaking all hands and wishing everyone goodbye. Then a voice cried out, 'God bless you, sir!' This was too much for Benson, who gave way to the tears which ran down his face, as he smiled and called back, 'Goodbye, God bless you, my dear, dear boys.' Arthur wrote, 'It was the most affecting and beautiful thing I had ever seen or shall ever see.'[9]

While Edward supervised the preparation of the house at Lincoln, Minnie, Beth and the younger children, including Fred, stayed with the Sidgwicks at Rugby. There is no specific complaint from

Edward about Minnie's detaching herself from domestic concerns, but we do know from Arthur that Edward suffered one of his worse attacks of depression in those first lonely weeks. The unfamiliar surroundings and the contemplation of the task ahead conspired to weaken his resolve; they would not have been so potent had he not also been worried about his wife's spiritual health. In time, that would improve, and his achievements at Lincoln would be correspondingly dramatic.

For the children, who moved into the Chancery in the latter part of 1873, Lincoln was to prove a period of unalloyed magic and discovery. The fourteenth-century house might have been designed to provide for childish delights, as there were sufficient corridors, unexpected staircases, dark corners, and hidden cupboards to entertain a small platoon of children for weeks on end. Nelly was inordinately fond of frightening Maggie and Fred out of their wits, by leaping on them from nowhere or screaming in the dark. She was the unchallenged prankster in the family, fond of practical jokes and much given to giggling. Fred once found her prone and lifeless on the floor of an empty attic room draped in cobwebs, and stood paralysed above her, pleading 'Oh don't, Nelly, don't', all the while trembling lest it was not Nelly at all but a horrid corpse. None of the uproar which they together created in the rambling old house reached the ears of their stern Papa (though Nelly was the only one of his children not to tread in fear of him); Mama, on the other hand, when she was better, might well join in the fun. So, too, did her brother, Uncle Arthur Sidgwick, to whose visits the children looked forward, as he could be relied upon to invent some devilish new game.

Their most repeated game was 'sieges', which took place on a winding stone staircase and was elemental in its simplicity. One child stood at the top while the others attacked from below and tried to topple him. Fred remembered having a bloody nose as a result of this particular romp; Nelly denied she had kicked him – she had put her foot on his face and pushed! They also loved to climb into the bell-tower just before Great Tom clanged out its thunderous noise and then run like blazes before the reverberations deafened them.[10]

The children had whole portions of the house they could call their own and which they protected with profound territorial instincts. There was a day-nursery and a night-nursery, and a very small room which Fred called 'My Room'; though it served little purpose, Fred was concerned to keep others out of it. At the top of the stone stairs was another room, which Edward one day offered to the children for them to use as they wished. Excitement could not be contained! The notions of privacy and secretiveness were intoxicating. This room immediately became 'The Museum', and it was the centre of Maggie and Fred's life. Martin and Arthur were at school, Nelly was slightly older, Hugh was still a baby. From the Lincoln days and the establishment of The Museum dates the close companionship of Fred and Maggie which was to survive the calamity and darkness which eventually poisoned Maggie's adult life. To the end, it was always Fred she felt safest with. Together they created a kingdom in The Museum and stuffed it full with an ever-increasing array of exhibits. They collected butterflies, birds' eggs, fossils, minerals, coins, almost anything collectable, labelled them and arranged them in professional order. Sometimes Mama was invited to the Museum, on which occasions she would put on a special hat for visiting and behaved like a guest. This Fred found very impressive.[11]

It was at Lincoln that several strands of Fred's personality were woven. He was six when he arrived there and nine when he left. This was the age when he first distinguished the differences between grown-ups and observed their rituals and hierarchies. He was taught to raise his hat to certain church dignitaries, and behave with greater deference to others. It was at Lincoln that his love of literature was first kindled, not the 'improving' literature which his father recommended, but the literature of exciting words and images, of gripping stories and outlandish characters. His mother would read Dickens to him (surreptitiously, one is bound to suppose) for half an hour before bedtime. It is also there that Fred developed his love of Nature. As with Proust's *madeleine*, Fred reacted all his life with involuntary happiness to the smell of lilac, which reminded him of the gorgeous odours which filled the garden of the Chancery. He had his own little corner of the garden, where Nelly one day made for him a 'little kind of lake at the bottom of my garden path, it is a jar in a hole.'[12]

There were also regular visits to Riseholme, where Bishop Wordsworth and his family lived. Here one could walk among mysterious dark woods and hope never to be found, one could catch frogs and snakes, one could dart and run and taste freedom as nowhere else. Fred and Maggie, accompanied by Watch, would have long outings together at Riseholme, delighting in Nature and her varied population. 'At Riseholme we went on a cow's back and took a rabbit up in our arms,' Freddy wrote. 'I saw the funniest thing, it was a goose turning somersaults in the water . . . it could not quite get over when its head was right down in the water, its legs flapping about . . . when it was pruning itself the wind blew it round and round.'[13] Most of his letters from this period are to his big brother Martin, who was then fourteen and to Fred a scholar of renown. There was some hero-worship in Fred's admiration for Martin, with good reason, and the letters are full of endearments and attempts to be as hearty as Fred imagined Martin would be; his favourite words are 'heaps' and 'jolly'.[14]

Something akin to hero-worship was likewise awakened by a chorister at Lincoln Cathedral. Fred did not share his father's insatiable appetite for church services, and used to dread Sundays precisely because worship and prayers would continue virtually all day long. By the evening Fred was heartily sick of it. But everything changed when the face and voice of the chorister, probably only three years older than Fred but immeasurably grander, transformed the cathedral into a place of strange, enthralling emotion. Instead of the usual reluctant murmur, Fred gave forth an exultant treble which so impressed his father that he predicted Fred might one day sing in the choir himself. That was indeed a prospect of bliss. 'Oh God, let me enter into Lincoln Cathedral choir,' Fred prayed, 'and abide there in happiness evermore with Thee.' 'Who "Thee" was I cannot determine,' he wrote. 'I believe it to have been a mixture of God and the chorister, and, I think, chiefly the chorister.'[15]

Lincoln broadened Fred's understanding of the world considerably, and always in a delicious, rosy way. Everything was felt with new, incredible intensity. As he wrote in a novel forty years later, it was 'that completeness of emotion that only children know, who are unable to look beyond the present and immediate future, the happiness or misery of which possess them entirely.'[16] Fortunately, it was mostly happiness at Lincoln. The only blight came, sadly, from Edward Benson himself, whom Fred could now begin to perceive as a person, and not just as an overpowering presence. Edward's failings as a father mirrored his virtues as a teacher (in the widest sense), and it was his tragedy that he could not cease teaching even when he most wanted to be fanciful and at ease with his children. For they all say he longed to be with them, and they all confess they could scarcely wait for him to go away.

In her autobiography, Dame Ethel Smyth openly admits that she stood in deadlier awe of Edward Benson than of anyone she ever met in the whole course of her life. 'The sight of his majestic form approaching the tea-table scattered my wits as an advancing elephant might scatter a flock of sheep.'[17] If a hard-boiled adult, confident in her own attested achievements, could be rendered speechless and limbless by the man, it is impossible to imagine how grim and forbidding he must have appeared to small children. His sons were so obsessed by him they felt bound to grapple with his influence long after they should have outgrown it. Fred tells us that they were inhibited by him and consequently always on their best behaviour: 'all spontaneity withered'. They feared his displeasure more than anything in the world, and would avoid him rather than run the risk of incurring it. Edward's disapproval might descend on such unpredictable, unimportant follies, that they never felt safe. Pathetically, Fred says his father 'brought too heavy guns to bear on positions so lightly fortified as children's hearts'. So they sat on the edge of their seats, wooden, attentive and obedient, ever ready to be ticked off for something or other. They made themselves tidy and clean, they kept their voices low, and they never said what they wanted to say, but rather what they thought he might want to hear. Sometimes they got it wrong, and a formidable, terrifying rebuke would be their reward.[18]

In later life, Fred recalled several instances of his father's unyielding habit of finding fault with trifles, be it an umbrella improperly folded or some potato on his plate unpleasantly mashed with gravy. In these years before he went to school, the infant Fred grew to recognise that Edward had something mysteriously wrong with him, that when he descended into the gloom of one of his moods his defences were absolute. If Fred spoke, he was reprimanded for the silliness of his chatter; if he was careful to hold silence, Edward would wonder why there was nothing that interested him enough to tell his father. So Fred, with a hole in his belly, yearned for the interview to be at an end. Arthur had very similar memories. 'I can recollect being paralysed as a child', he wrote, 'by having my meagre conversational stock criticised, and by being required to produce from my lessons or my reading something of more permanent interest . . . It was always a certain strain to be long alone with him.'[19]

Even Hugh, who as the youngest was indulged rather more readily than the others, wrote: 'My father's influence upon me was always so great that I despair of describing it. I do not think that he understood me very well; but his personality was so dominant and insistent that the lack of this understanding made very little difference.'[20] He was afraid of showing ignorance, afraid of shocking him, afraid of doing anything at all which he might *notice*. Edward's disapproval cast such a wide net that, paradoxically, the effect of his moral teaching was diffused and rendered less potent. If walking too fast was as sinful as telling lies, then they are both less, not more, important in the long run. 'His imagination, instead of removing mountains, created them.'[21]

In like manner, Edward's wish to enrich his children's lives with useful leisure activities made these activities suspect if they actually produced enjoyment. He had a puritanical notion that simple irresponsible fun was dangerous to moral fibre. Hence Fred could not throw a ball without the principles of the parabola being explained to him, and when Arthur was rash enough to tinker with the piano, his father reproached him with the cold words, 'Hadn't you better be reading a useful book?' Arthur never dared experiment with music again. In Edward's mind, music was merely an adjunct to worship and must not be encouraged for its own sake. Botany, on the other hand, was *very* useful, for it taught about the Creation. Edward offered a prize for the best botanical collection, and the children competed gladly, pasting their speci-mens in with utmost care and writing the *genus* in Latin. What they were in reality competing for was his affection.

Had they but known, they each possessed it in abundant measure. Edward's strictures arose from a deep fountain of love. He would have been overjoyed had he found a way to be at ease with his children, for though he repelled intimacy, he longed for it. He wanted them to improve themselves because along that road true happiness lay. With Martin he managed a closeness denied to the others, but it was largely intellectual in expression; and with Nelly, who inherited her mother's sense of fun and mischief, he failed to inspire the requisite awe. After receiving one of Papa's lectures, Nelly irreverently asked, 'Why does respecting people make you love them more?' She then determined she would save up and buy him a pair of slippers for his birthday, and have them made up all by herself.[22] She would love him whether he deserved it or not.

Fred did not know that his father loved him until, after his death, he found that Edward had kept every one of his children's absurd letters written in infancy, scraps that could only be of value to a sentimental man. And he remembered an occasion when Edward had displayed uncharacteristic sympathy. Fred had a precious talisman, a little brown model of a dog from the Noah's Ark collection he played with on Sundays. The legs had been broken, but Beth had repaired them with skill, and Fred carried the thing in his hand wherever he went. One day, walking in the wood with Beth, he dropped it. They went back to search, but to no avail. Martin offered to stay behind in the wood and have a further look, which Freddy thought incredibly brave, but he too returned empty-handed. Fred was downcast.

The next morning Edward gave Freddy a cup of milk to drink, which was an odd thing for him to do. As he neared the end, he was told to drink more slowly. Then he heard a chink, and there in the bottom of the cup was a shilling, all for himself! One can but picture the gleam in the proud parent's eye, and wonder why he did not melt more often. Arthur tells how he could make the family roar with laughter, but the occasions were few.

The brooding, scowling presence of Edward Benson crops up again and again in his son Fred's books. The hero of *David Blaize* says, 'He knew quite well that his father was fond of him, and was anxious about his well-being, but somehow the serious talks froze him up, and he could not feel all the things he knew he was expected to feel.'[23] The father in *The Challoners* says of his son, 'I want to be kind to the lad, to make him happy, to make a friend of him. But when that which I consider my duty leads me to correct him, and again and again to correct him, I am so afraid that his estimate of the love I bear him will be lowered, eclipsed. And nothing in the world could be sadder to me than that my children should not think of me as their friend.'[24] Even when writing an historical biography, Fred finds occasion to use his father's huge personality in order to illuminate his subject. It is of Edward Benson that he is thinking when he writes of the father of *Alcibiades* that a man without weaknesses himself or indulgence for weakness in others risks being led to faulty conclusions about human nature.[25]

It was never far from Fred's mind that his father's sad thwarted love was a terrible lesson pointing to the perils of moral absolutism. It coloured his life and his work, it stunted his affections and made them subject to rigid control. He took after his mother, who realised that one could not forever be learning, scrabbling about to grab knowledge and instruction from every tiny experience of life. 'If one wants to understand life, one must be content sometimes to sit and watch it.'[26] That is emphatically what E.F. Benson would grow up to do.

Mrs Benson had been trying to understand life, all those weeks in Wiesbaden, and her long introspective anguish finally bore fruit at Lincoln. The two strands of her torment – the direction of her emotional and of her spiritual life – came together and were resolved in tandem. Indeed, the one informed and supported the other; they would thereafter be fused into a single perception of the source of feeling.

Her marriage had stifled her, made her subservient, and she knew in her heart that this was not right. 'What, and how far, is the union of two souls in matrimony, and what is the individuality?' While she prayed earnestly for God to teach her that passion which Edward felt, and which would surely then promote the 'union' which eluded her, at the same time she had been buffeted by the intensity of her friendships, the desire she had for the proximity of female companions. There had been Susan Wordsworth. 'Oh my vanity! how I fancied attracting her – how I thought she was thinking of and looking at me when far other and nobler things occupied her.' Her letters to Miss Wordsworth betrayed the rawness of her heart. 'Oh Susie, do write me a long letter full of scoldings and good advice and 'arf pints – I am dreadfully thirsty. Goodbye my Susie. How nice it is to write your name over and over again – Susie Susie Susie Susie Susie.'[27] Then Miss Hall and the discovery, renewed exile and the loneliness of Lincoln. That first Christmas had been dreadful. 'Unsympathetic to my boys. How they felt it. Arthur crying. Oh Father, forgive and cleanse, Amen.'

Salvation came in the guise of a woman unlike all the others, the wife of a theological student at the college Edward was establishing in Lincoln, Mrs Mylne. Minnie called her 'Tan', for reasons unexplained. Annie, Miss Hall, Susan Wordsworth, had all been young and mystified, like Minnie herself, whereas Tan was middle-aged, mature and wise. She was also evangelical, with a firm belief in the goodness of God rather than His power; hers was a God one could trust, not only revere, a God who cared for the unhappy, not one who merely demanded obedience to dry laws and ceremonial rituals. There is no doubt that salvation is the correct word – Minnie certainly saw it as such, and without Tan, she might well have broken loose and upset the marriage, thus ruining Edward's chance of advancement for ever. Without Tan, this could well have been a different story.

And dimly, in the midst, came Thy messenger, my beloved Tan – and I did not know her at first – played even with my human love for her and hers for me – felt it coming, felt how different places were when she was there – but played, played – and all the while Thou hadst sent her and she has led me to Thee – my darling Tan.

Mrs Mylne's evangelical faith was revolutionary to Minnie; it explained everything, made everything acceptable and lovely where it had been resisted and ugly. Her inward rebellions ceased. The Diary itself was undertaken as a direct result of Mrs Mylne's

41

influence, as Minnie went back over her marriage and repented her weaknesses and sins. She yearned for a personal God, one who would listen and help, and when she found Him, she was released from bondage. She now expected that Christianity 'would do away with the necessity of my *accommodating myself* to him [Edward].' Religion through blind Faith was not for her, and she should never more attempt to emulate Edward in this sphere. Her God would be Love – the Redeemer, the Comforter, the Father – a God approached through the heart, not the head, a God whom one *feels*. The realisation made Minnie better able to cope with Edward, for she now saw him as a human being, flawed like the rest of us, and loved him the better for it. She no longer had to obey, but to share and sympathise, perhaps to understand him better than he did himself. This would eventually give her the superior edge, and he would come to depend upon her alone in the world. At Lincoln, one can spot the signs of change, the shift in emphasis:

> He thinks more of little remarks, is more sensitive, more easily wounded, than I am. Therefore I must not think of *being at my ease*, but of suiting my ways of saying things to his feelings – and this without a shadow of thinking my ways better than his. *I* like them better.

Minnie's rebirth came as the consequence of much soul-searching, a long struggle with ideas and concepts and feelings with Mrs Mylne as her guide. Edward's kind of religion did not produce the love she had been meekly expecting all this time, perhaps Tan's gentler religion would succeed. She went to Tan with every problem, sought her succour at every turn. There was an occasion when she went to the circus (presumably with the children, though Fred never mentions it), and was uncomfortably aroused by what she saw. 'The suppleness, litheness, movements of the limbs stirred me to an uneasy restlessness, a fierceness, a tingling.'[28] Again she went to Tan, and Tan comforted her and explained. How much of this did Fred realise? It is impossible to tell, but the parallel with Maddox and David in *David Blaize* is arresting. It is quite clear that Tan was the saviour, not the tempter, that she rescued

Minnie from herself by giving her the one love which is not shallow and sensual, the love which is truly unselfish. It is a pity that, after fifteen years of marriage, it took a woman to reveal to Minnie where her inner strength lay. Edward naturally did not approve of Mrs Mylne; he did not understand her influence and justifiably felt excluded from their intimacy. Yet he should have been eternally grateful, for Mrs Mylne enabled Minnie at once to love her husband and stand up to him without fear or self-reproach, and it must be due to her that Mrs Benson grew into the sustaining rock which Edward wanted.

'I need *discipline, discipline, discipline,*' Minnie told her diary. '*I must guard myself against unnecessarily opposing,* and if I oppose, I must be patient and give good reasons, and *not* give in rather than make a disturbance – here comes my childishness and want of *maturity,* that which Tan has woke me up to at last.'[29]

Arthur Benson says that Tan was loved by all the children, and he certainly was aware that her influence was crucial. We may safely assume that Fred did as well, and that Maddox's salvation by David in *David Blaize* was some sort of echo. Arthur wrote that Mrs Mylne exercised a tranquillising effect upon his mother and kept her from tumbling into scepticism and unbelief. 'They had long and earnest colloquies; and I am sure that my mother always felt that Mrs Mylne's quiet and mystical apprehension of the essence of religion had been like an anchor to her own troubled spirit in a time of urgent doubt and mental turmoil.'[30]

Edward's success at Lincoln was whole-hearted. From hesitant beginnings, when his depression and anxiety over Minnie had made him wonder if he had taken the right step, he developed the theological school into an institution known and respected throughout ecclesiastical circles. (Again, Mrs Mylne must be allowed some of the credit, for Edward worked better when Minnie was happy). He taught himself how to preach, with signal success, so that people flocked to hear him. He realised that a church, not a school, was home to him, and he blossomed in the cathedral atmosphere. He opened night schools for men as well as boys, and poured out his convictions in passionate swaying language. The men revered him, because he gave all his energy to them, without stint, and because he made clear his belief that education was their due and their right, however poor they might be. In this, E.W. Benson was a genuine democrat; he had accepted half his Wellington salary to meet the challenge of Lincoln.

So famous did he become that grand places were offered him. He turned down the chance to be Professor of Divinity at Cambridge, because he would rather remain with the illiterate of Lincoln whose joy in learning touched him so, then another opportunity to become Bishop of Calcutta. This he did consider seriously, drawing up a painstaking balance sheet of 'pros and cons'; the final (not the first) disadvantage he lists is 'wife suffers under hot temperature'.[31] Calcutta would have been torment to a young family, anyway, so the refusal was timely. Then there came a letter from Disraeli offering the new bishopric of Truro. That was another matter entirely. There had been no bishop in Cornwall for nearly a thousand years; there was as yet no cathedral – it would have to be built; the job would call upon all Edward's gifts for organisation as well as his pioneering spirit. Everything was in favour.

When Edward announced that he was leaving Lincoln after only three and a half years, his students felt bereft. So, in a way, did he; he had been happy there and was proud of his work. Some members of his Bible-class presented him with a set of bronze dessert dishes. They were not especially fine, and had probably been made by the donors themselves, paid for out of their own small change. But Edward was deeply touched. For the rest of his life he insisted they be placed on his table at the end of dinner, and he prized them above all other gifts. Similarly, he kept a bust of his old teacher, James Prince Lee, on his desk. Benson may have appeared a bully; in his heart he was a sentimentalist.

With the move to Truro we catch our first glimpse of Fred as we would know him, or at least a manifestation of one of his most salient characteristics. There being no house as yet assigned to the bishopric, a lease was arranged for the vicarage of Kenwyn, just outside Truro, as the vicar no longer wished to stay there. It was a perfectly lovely house (when they established permanent residence they named it 'Lis Escop', Cornish for Bishop's House), set in a beautiful garden and high on a hill overlooking Truro.

The air, the smell of fresh flowers, the views of patchwork fields dotted with sheep and indolent cows, all made it a paradise to the senses. Beth loved the scenery, Maggie said she was 'fearfully glad', little Hugh said 'How jolly!'; but what mattered most to ten-year-old Fred was his father's new title. He asked his mother, 'Will Papa *really* be addressed as the Right Reverend the Lord Bishop of Truro?'[32] His interest in status began to blossom.

To be fair, Fred was as much enamoured of the countryside as the rest of the family. His response to stable-smells, haystacks, butterflies, every living plant or insect or animal was positively sensual. He wrote of returning home after long walks 'with heart and shoes alike drenched with the spring-dew'.[33] Every afternoon the entire troop of Bensons would set out for an adventurous ramble, led by Edward who was stern in his admonitions not to pick a plant specimen from some spot where its absence might be noticed and lamented, but only from an obscure clump. He also forbad slashing at plants with a stick, lest they be unnecessarily hurt. The collie Watch came along for the walk as well, and Maggie's nanny-goat, whom Watch had to keep in check. The children were obsessive collectors, still competing with one another for the best show of leaves, or butterflies, or whatever. Fred bought a special cabinet in which to keep his various speci-mens. 'It is made of deal and is oak-stained and varnished', he proudly wrote to brother Arthur. 'I keep my eggs and as many of my shells as I can get into it . . . it does look so nice. I have got exactly 100 kinds of eggs.'[34]

Father laid down regulations about eggs, too, and they were very much to the advantage of the birds. No more than one egg was ever to be taken from a single nest, and that only when there were at least four eggs in the nest at the time. Thus did Benson impart his feel for the dignity of Nature to all his children. On one occasion a tiny bird fluttered into the church and flew blindly into a window-pane. Edward picked it up with the most tender care and released it into the open.[35]

Twice Fred told the story of the stickleback which he and Maggie brought home for their aquarium.[36] It was their most exciting acquisition. Every day they would change the water in the aquarium by emptying it through gauze into a drain and then replacing it. Maggie held the gauze, but her hand slipped, and the stickleback slithered down the drain to eternal oblivion. Fred retains the sense of childish anxiety, telling that he and Maggie were left 'looking at each other in incredulous dismay'.

Games continued at Truro as they had at Lincoln, but were gradually becoming more sophisticated. The children together founded a Society of Friendship and Goodwill, the charter of which they drew up very carefully to look like sixteenth-century parchment, in ancient script and with a proper seal. Arthur was named as the Warden, Maggie as Subwarden, Nelly was Chancellor and Hugh a Fellow and Senator. Fred, perhaps already recognised by the others as a wizard with money, was appointed Treasurer.[37]

The family made two new friends at Truro, each to have some effect on the growing boys. Benson's chaplain was Arthur Mason, an eager youth with flamboyant emotions and a conquering spirit, who shared Edward's desire to make a mark for Truro. Equally emotional was the curate-in-charge at Kenwyn, John Reeve, who Arthur said 'flung his heart about in handfulls'.[38] In a neat echo, Fred admitted that he lost what he called 'my sloppy heart' to Mr Reeve, who evidently adored him and thought he was destined for the priesthood. Every Sunday evening after tea Mr Reeve took little Fred to a spare bedroom where he read him the sermon he was about to preach that evening, all the time with his arm round Fred's neck. Neither the sermon nor the arm appears to have impressed Fred much, but he certainly enjoyed being flattered.[39] That first winter at Truro, Mr Reeve took Fred on holiday with him to Dartmouth for a week.

There was also Mrs Carter, who played the organ and made noises therewith which thrilled Fred's embryonic musical sense, to the extent he imagined himself in love with Mrs Carter, when he was really in love with the organ. He was able to disentangle this confusion before making any embarrassing declarations.

The See of Truro was created by Order in Council on 15 December 1876, and the next few years witnessed the inspiring erection of a new cathedral. Inspiring, that is, to Edward, who threw himself into the work with a zeal which would have exhausted anybody else. Fred was lamentably indifferent. All the children laid a foundation stone, but when Papa said, 'There! You have helped to build Truro Cathedral', Fred could not understand why such a fuss should be made. When Benson applied to the College of Heralds to design the arms for the new See, Fred became much more interested. They had a pony-carriage to drive around in, and looked horribly smart and correct. Mary Benson wrote to Martin, 'Fred becomes rather extra pompous at all this, which afflicts Nellie's heart very much. I drove them down into Truro the other day, so says Fred, as we drove along, "are the arms painted on the panel yet?" '[40]

The truth was, young Fred was already something of a snob, and this trait was all the more marked because he was alone in the family to possess it. As we have seen above, Nelly was positively embarrassed by his posturings. In a letter to Arthur, who was away at school, Fred is blithely unaware that his interest in such matters might seem odd to the others. 'One of the judges was staying here last Sunday,' he wrote. 'He was very stately, but he and the sheriff had the same number of horses and the judge generally has 4 and the sheriff one, but the judge had two and so did the sheriff, and he had *such* a dirty wig.'[41] At about the same time as he develops these observations on the relative importance of people, Fred also begins to demonstrate his own. He stops signing his letters to Arthur and Martin as 'Freddy', choosing instead the more impressive 'E.F. Benson', written with a flourish to cover the whole page. He is still only eleven years old. Arthur remembered that as a child Fred always behaved like an old grandfather to them all.[42] He disagreed with his siblings, finding fault with their arrangements of moss, criticising their taste, being generally captious and superior. His father used the word 'sententious' to describe his young son, and Martin wrote to Nelly, 'I suppose Freddy is as grave as he can be'.[43]

The Bishop of Truro took his responsibilities very seriously indeed. They included visiting every parish in the county, including some which were beyond the reach of railways and had not received a visitor of any kind for many years. Edward undertook these punishing journeys with joyful vigour, setting off from Lis Escop with flowing black cloak and shovel hat (looking much like David's clergyman father in *David Blaize*) in a carriage laden with papers, books and luggage. In vain Minnie begged him to be more generous to himself, to allow more time for rest. 'But he won't listen to the voice of Wisdom (ME)', she complained to Freddy.[44]

Fred occasionally accompanied his father on these trips, and encountered pastors so isolated they were encrusted in rich eccentricity. There was the vicar who chose vintage wine for his services, a choice claret one day, a burgundy the next; another who never went inside his church, for he had no parishioners and felt no need. Fred tells how his father enchanted these lonely souls. 'They found him personally irresistible, so intensely jolly, so full of enjoyment and keenness and humour.'[45] Fred was receiving early lessons in the manifold layers of human personality, for this was unlike the stern Papa he knew. There were occasions when Edward was moved to pity by the poverty which hung about these remote vicarages like the devil's revenge for piety. He came upon one which was bare of furniture save a kitchen table and chairs, and the only food in evidence was a bowl of porridge. The vicar had a congregation of five or six – it had once been eleven – and from Sunday to Sunday he saw no one; villagers did not wish to speak to him. A man of education and charm had been reduced to wretchedness by the demands of his calling. Edward implored him to be brave and faithful, though his work might appear unblest, and there were tears in his eyes as he left.[46]

Edward did not like to enquire into divine motive, it made him uncomfortable, made him feel disloyal. He was not intellectual in that sense, preferring to rest in the certain knowledge that God's will was always good. He shed tears for the lonely, beaten pastor because God's will was occasionally hard to understand in simple human terms. His greatest trial came at Truro, when Edward's true and solid faith was shaken by the worst tragedy ever to befall the Benson family.

Benson's ideal of a good Christian scholar was so exacting that none of the boys at Wellington, however bright or willing, had quite managed to realise it. Disappointment had been a contributing factor in Benson's decision to abandon the schoolmaster's life. As the years progressed, however, he grew to recognise with boundless joy that the ideal was attainable, and was being attained by his eldest son Martin. The academic brilliance of the boy was astonishing. At his prep school, Temple Grove, he had effortlessly risen to the top and was able to read Carlyle's *French Revolution* at the age of twelve. He was reading and writing in Latin well before that, and learnt Italian by himself for the pleasure of reading Renaissance literature in the original. He seemed able to master any subject with ease, to cope with abstruse philosophical matters, to study genealogy and heraldry, to write poetry, with a precocity which would have been alarming had he not, at the same time, been a normal boy of high spirit endowed with a sense of mischief. Moreover, he was fascinated by liturgy and ecclesiastical history, and held to a genuine religious belief without the need for coercion. Edward glowed with pride at Martin's advance towards Christian maturity; it seemed the boy was God's reward for years of piety and industry.

Martin won the first open scholarship at Winchester at the age of fourteen, and immediately set about building up a personal library of such distinction that he was the wonder of teachers as well as of his contemporaries. At the beginning of 1877 he won the Sixth Form Prize, in October that year he became a prefect, and at the end of the year he was runner-up for the Goddard Scholarship. From the Sidgwicks he had inherited an enquiring mind which delighted in picking over complexities. It was the opinion of his elders that Martin Benson was destined for a career in moral philosophy, that he would examine the basic tenets of the Christian religion with profound and original insight.

His younger brothers viewed him with awe. They could not hope to emulate the power of his intellect, and they respected him almost as the third adult in the family when he was but seventeen. Fred later wrote, a trifle ruefully, that he had 'a gay passion for sheer learning which made its acquisition more of a pastime than a task', which would certainly never be the case with Fred.[47] Martin's moral character was likewise above reproach. Though by no means a passive or priggish individual, he did not commit that worst of all schoolboy misdemeanours – the telling of lies. 'I never, his mother never, no master ever found any falsehood in his life,' wrote Edward.[48] Father and son gradually became companions, able to converse freely and frankly with each other in a way denied to the younger children. They had interests in common, and shared a vision of the future. There can be no doubt that Edward saw Martin as his spiritual heir, his partner, the one marked out by God to carry the torch of the Church after Edward himself.

Perhaps he expected too much. It has been said that Edward drove Martin relentlessly, but there are signs that he was aware of the danger of too intense an application. At the end of 1876 he had been to visit Martin at Winchester and afterwards wrote to his wife, 'Martin seems fairly strong and works too hard I think. He loses time and effort through inaccuracy . . . but he is a dear good most loving hardworking boy.' Edward thought he would do better 'slightly to reduce rather than increase his devotion to work', and one must suppose he said as much to his son.[49]

During the course of 1877 Martin appeared listless and languorous. The congenital moods which afflicted his father may have begun to weigh upon him too, the vision of perfection to oppress him. That Christmas, the first the family spent at Truro, found him especially quiet, and when the time came for him to bid goodbye to his brothers and sisters at the front door, to return to Winchester, he uncharacteristically burst into tears. Arthur walked with him to the station, and they hardly spoke.

In February there came a telegram from Winchester which made the Bishop cancel every appointment and hasten to his son's side. Martin had suddenly, at tea, found himself unable to speak. When asked what was the matter, he could hardly write either, but laboriously drew, in capital letters, the word 'paralysis'. He had no control over digestion or bowel movement. By the time his father arrived, the doctor had diagnosed 'brain fever'; we should now call it tubercular meningitis.

Martin recovered his speech over the next few days and much enjoyed his father's company, in particular his reading of the psalms. But he stayed in bed, and grew weaker and more feverish. Three days later there was a relapse. Benson was told there was cause for the very gravest anxiety. Minnie was summoned. When both parents were by his bed, Martin spent much of his time taking their hands in his, or placing his father's hands together so that he might pray. Mostly, he slept in profound slumber, but when he awoke it was with a look of happiness and affection on his face. At one point he gazed into thin air and said, 'How lovely!' They were to be the last words he uttered, as paralysis again gripped his young body.

Benson scarcely knew what was happening, or was too frightened to admit the knowledge. It was incredible, it was wrong, it was impossible. He prayed and prayed but would not see. Minnie, on the other hand, immediately recognised the truth and grasped it fearlessly. To Martin she said, 'Do not be afraid, darling; you are in the Valley of the Shadow of Death; but do not be afraid; don't fear, darling. God is with you.'[50]

Arthur was at Eton, but all the other children were gathered together at Truro, and each day Minnie wrote them a collective letter assuring them Martin was in no pain, and asking them to place their trust in Jesus Christ. Above all, they must not be down-hearted. 'Resolutely eat and go out, and sleep, and *do things*, and think of everybody else, and comfort them, and don't leave any duty undone because your heart is faint.'[51]

On the last day Martin suddenly assumed that look of awe and pleasure, as he gazed at something in the room, and urged, with his finger, that his parents should look as well. They saw nothing. Benson said to the nurse, 'Does he want something? He is pointing to something he wants, is he not?' She replied, 'No, no, he sees more than we see.' He took his father's cross and kissed it, then did the same with his mother's. His breathing was heavy, his eyes did not react to light. Then the breathing relaxed, and the nurse placed his hand across his eyes. He was sobbing gently. His parents watched him die at ten o'clock on a cold February evening.

'My dearest wife understood it all more quickly – better – more sweetly than I,' said Edward. Minnie wrote to the children a letter of consummate peace. Martin, she told them, went to God 'without a stain on his gentle spirit, kept from all evil . . . Martin is ours, now, forever, if we will only follow him – for there is nothing that separates but sin, and from that he is free forever.' To Beth, who was utterly inconsolable, she wrote a poignant letter addressed 'Dearest Friend and Mother Beth' from which all thought of self was banished. 'My heart aches for the dear ones at home', she said, 'but I know you are a mother to them, and will support and comfort their hearts, and keep before them that God is love, and that He is loving us in this thing also. And I want them to think of Martin, our darling, in perfect peace forever, free from fear, free from pain, from anxiety for evermore, and to think how he will rejoice to see us walking more and more in Love for his dear sake. We cannot grudge him his happiness.' She signed off, 'Your own child, your fellow-mother.' The resilience and confidence of Mary Benson at this time of cruel loss was quite extraordinary.[52] Here was stark proof of Mrs Mylne's beneficent influence upon her previously troubled spirit. Long afterwards she told Fred she had experienced great happiness on that awful day, realising that though God had taken, she could give.

The contrast with her husband the Bishop could hardly be more vivid. He was devastated. Quite simply, all his hopes and plans perished with Martin, and he was struck dumb with incomprehension. That God should allow such a monstrous deprivation to occur threatened even to undermine his faith. Martin was buried in the cloisters at Winchester and the whole family assembled there for the funeral. Both Arthur, coming from Eton, and Fred, from Truro, were haunted ever after by the sight of their father on the platform of Winchester station, the pain on his pale and agonised face against the night air emphasised by the flaring gas-jets of the lamps. In his Diary Edward wrote:

> It has changed all my views of God's work as it is to be done both in this world and the next, to be compelled to believe that God's plan for him really *has* run on sweetly, and rightly for him and for all – and yet – he is dead. 'One's views of life change very quickly', he said to me that last hour in which he spoke to me. My sweet boy, thou hast changed mine.[53]

'My mother never faltered,' wrote Arthur in an unpublished memoir. 'She spoke and encouraged us to speak freely of Martin, "even as he were by". But as we thus talked, I have seen my father rise and leave the room suddenly.'[54]

Every year Edward would visit Martin's grave on the anniversary of his death. When Archbishop of Canterbury he still confessed the event was an inexplicable grief to him, and, as he sought the consolation which came so naturally to Minnie, he further admitted that he could not reach to that degree of acceptance, and felt himself wanting. Benson's altered personality had a profound effect upon the family, for it tempered his strictures towards the children, terrified as he was that undue pressure might provoke another disaster, and it confirmed his emotional dependence, from that moment on, upon his wife. Little Hugh, only six years old, drew the greatest benefit, as he would be treated with such indulgence as his siblings had never known, and grew, in consequence, into a pampered and spoilt adult.

And what of the older boys? Significantly, Arthur recalled the occasion with a degree of wonder at his own equanimity. 'In 1878 Penny[55] told me so tearfully of Martin's death. I remember it came like a blow, and I went and sate down and leant my head on my hands, and then was surprised that I did not *feel* more *acutely*.'[56] Fred also says that he was so much younger than Martin, as if that is sufficient to account for his apparent coldness. If he grieved, it was with the intellect. As Martin lay dying, he sent some flowers – violets – which his mother had told him were Martin's favourites. 'Dear Fred,' she wrote from the bedside, 'thank you for your dear little note. The violets are in his hand.'[57] Minnie gathered her dead son's poignant belongings from Winchester and bundled them up in a parcel labelled 'Martin's Things' – they are still so labelled at the Bodleian Library.[58] They contain a collection of old coins, a school exercise book, a book of pen and ink drawings of bishops and saints, and an 'Ecclesiastical History of Thomas of Malmesbury', carefully written in Latin. Minnie never parted with these objects as long as she lived.

Fred does not disclose whether or not he shed tears. The vision of his father's appalling pain certainly frightened him, and the death of a brother not yet eighteen made him think. But he will not allow us to know what he felt. In one of his earliest books, he was to write, 'Life and death often walk hand in hand, and when we clasp the hand of life, we cannot but feel that we accept death as part of our union.'[59] That is hardly a reflection born of deep feeling. It is more than likely that Fred observed the agonies of emotion, differently manifested by each parent, and experienced the effect, while he merely noticed the cause.

3 Marlborough

After the Easter holidays of 1878, Fred was sent to boarding school and his first experience of living away from home. He was approaching his eleventh birthday and had thus far been taught mostly by his mother. The preparatory school selected for him was among the best in England, with a fine record of scholars going on to Eton, Winchester and Marlborough. Both Martin and Arthur had passed through the school, as had M.R. James, later to become the Eton schoolmaster and champion writer of ghost stories. This was Temple Grove at East Sheen near Richmond, a prep school destined to be recalled in dozens of memoirs, due entirely to the huge personality of its Head, O.C. Waterfield.

Temple Grove was a lovely eighteenth-century villa set in gardens of some twenty acres. There were smooth lawns, tall impressive cedars and elms, rows of brilliant shrubs. Over a hundred boys lived there in cubicled dormitories, with a dozen schoolmasters, which made Temple Grove somewhat larger than the usual prep school. The man who presided over this mini-paradise, where terror and laughter habitually overlapped, was a genial eccentric, very tall (to little boys the very incarnation of a giant), with fierce eye above a lush dominant beard. Ottiwell Charles Waterfield was an old friend of Edward's, an Old Etonian and a Fellow of King's College, Cambridge. Arthur wrote of him, 'I have never in my life been so afraid of a human being as I was of him.'[1]

For a son of E.W. Benson to say as much Waterfield must have had a terrifying manner indeed. He was an autocrat, but not a brute. Misdemeanours were punished with several strokes on the hand with a ruler, after an elaborate teasing ritual with keys to the drawer wherein every boy knew the ferocious instrument was kept. Another boy had to open the door for the criminal to exit, as his hands were for the moment rendered useless. When Waterfield once broke a boy's finger with the ruler, he burst into floods of tears, and it was usual for him to frighten the wits out of a child with a stentorian harangue, then exclaim 'Well, that's all over, my boy,' and bend down to kiss him. With one leg shorter than the other, Waterfield walked with a kind of menacing roll, allowing boys to scatter well in advance of his approach. Although everyone at Temple Grove strove at all costs to avoid the Head's displeasure, there were many who toiled with equal effort to win his approbation. Fred was to depict him very accurately in *David Blaize* nearly forty years later and show that, at bottom, the boys of Temple Grove were fond of Waterfield; 'he was probably omniscient, and of his omnipotence there was no doubt whatever.'[2]

Nevertheless, the first impression of a little boy faced with this awesome figure was not conducive to ease. Edward took his son to Temple Grove on 11 May, and Fred visibly trembled when he was introduced. 'Fred *looked* very much *appalled* at the sight of Mr Waterfield', he wrote to Minnie, 'but they were very kind to him, and he was committed to the especial charge of Dr Hort's son[3] – a very handsome and nice-looking boy.' Thus was Fred abandoned to this strange new world. 'He wished me goodbye very steadily. Let him have plenty of letters, especially at first.'[4]

Minnie needed little prompting. She deluged the homesick boy with affectionate missives, addressed to 'Dearest Laddie', 'Dearest of dear boys', 'Dear Old Fred', or just 'Old Man Fred'. She promised he would have the engine he had set his heart upon for his birthday, only a few weeks away. If anything, Mama fretted too much, for Fred settled in at Temple Grove very quickly indeed, subsequently admitting that he enjoyed himself enormously. There were two reasons for this. First, he found he was top of the class almost without trying, which naturally gave him confidence. Second, his incipient talent for the observation of human types found much to practise on, for Waterfield was not the only unusual specimen there. 'I cannot believe a stranger set of instructors were ever got together,' he recalled.[5]

One of them used to stab boys on the back of the hand with a pen dipped in purple ink. He had one arm, and would sit a favourite on his knee with this single limb wrapped around while the chosen one's gaze inexorably focused on what was missing on the other side. Another teacher slept throughout classes, a third spent his day, feet propped on the desk, reading the *Sporting Times*. And there was a Frenchman genuinely called M. Voltaire. Mrs Russell played the piano and encouraged Fred to try his hand, thus nurturing the early delight in Bach which had been born at Lincoln.

Fred warmed to this atmosphere redolent with eccentricity and charm. He learnt that Waterfield could inflict far more damage with his tongue than with the ruler or the birch, and that 'elderly persons' (i.e. those over twelve) did not cry when whacked. He accepted the wisdom among boys that school food was disgusting, and therefore shovelled his perfectly appetising pudding into an envelope to be buried in the garden, because someone had said the currants in it were squashed flies and the suet fashioned from yesterday's left-overs. In common with every other boy Fred developed a passion for stag-beetles, probably because they bred in such abundance in the grounds. 'There are such heaps of stag-beetles here,' he told his mother at the end of his second week, 'and some of them such monsters.'[6] He kept two in a match-box, releasing them into his wash-basin at night and feeding them with elm-leaves and strawberries in the morning before matron came round; she had made it clear that any stag-beetles she found would be hurled out of the window, and that was a fate to be wished upon no creature.

Further, the rules at Temple Grove were relaxed on half-days, when boys were permitted to explore in Richmond Park unsupervised. Fred loved watching the deer and looking for undiscovered insects beneath the trees. On Waterfield's birthday, the boys shared the intimate family celebrations by accompanying him and his wife on a trip to Crystal Palace, which again impressed Fred with its shimmering, delicate beauty. Papa and Arthur came to visit once, and Fred was allowed a whole day off to go with them by river-steamer to St Paul's Cathedral, the Tower of London and Greenwich. Fred noticed that Arthur was now taller than Papa (he was sixteen and glumly handsome), but confessed he dreaded further parental visits. Temple Grove was very quickly adopted by Fred as 'his' demesne, and while he was proud of his father's exalted status as Bishop of Truro, he did not relish father spoiling the effect by appearing in person and looking foolish. In the way of adults who wish to show how easy-going they are, Edward would ostentatiously banter with the boys (Fred's own friends!) and show himself odder and more shame-making than he actually was.

Fred wrote happily home to mother in his first term with letters full of gossip and adventure. 'On Saturday we went over a line and were jawed horribly by an old pointsman about something which I could not or did not care to understand. We went by today and heard that he was dead! Run over by the train on Sunday. How uncertain is life!'[7] This is authentic E.F. Benson, both in the rueful comedy of the conclusion and the slightly arrogant tone of the detached observer. Mother wrote back in a style which, too, was an embryo of the later relationship she was to enjoy with Fred, both confidential and larky. She tells him she well remembers those dreadful days at Wellington College, when one 'existed and endured', then strides into a chatty scene which she paints with the liveliness of Mme de Sévigné: 'Hugh is writing the comparison of some adjectives, and you'd think he was doing some tremendous thing. There! It is over, and he is off. I believe Papa is going to buy a new COW today, only it is a DARK MYSTERY.'[8] By contrast, Edward's letters to Fred are written with a wrist chained to duty – no lightness, no fun, but remorseless sermonising. He pays one compliment, that Fred's letters are well-written; otherwise he exhorts and forbids and chastises.

Life in a boarding school suited Fred perfectly. He enjoyed the forming of secret friendships which required skill and circumspection to conceal – tip-toeing to another dormitory before dawn to wake up a best friend and whisper confidences for an hour before furtively regaining one's own dorm before the bell sounded to dress. The risk attached to possible discovery made it all the more daring and important. Fred knew as well as anyone that to be caught in another boy's dormitory was just about the worst offence in the canon, though he confessed, also as most boys of that age would, that he could not imagine *why*. As Christian names were 'effeminate and disgraceful things',[9] the opportunity to use one surreptitiously added a savour the potency of which he yet but suspected. Then there was the glorious fun of telling stories, just as he used to with Maggie at Lincoln, and the delight in finding a rapt audience. Fred was good at spinning a yarn, and soon realised that if he embellished it, decorated it, improved it, the audience was even more attentive. A rude warning in the form of a note marked BENSON'S LIES, prepared by jealous boys who simply would not believe a word he said, made him control his imagination. But not for long. He was learning how to sacrifice veracity to credibility.

One excitement he did not need to exaggerate was the visit to White Lodge in Richmond Park on Guy Fawkes Day. Teck Major and Teck Minor invited Fred to come and take tea with their mother, the formidable Duchess of Teck. A great barrel of a woman, she was immensely popular with the crowds for her good humour, and embarrassing to the Royal Family for her extravagance. So often was she in debt that she was known as the Big Duchess of Tick, and Queen Victoria had eventually to send her to Florence (where life was cheaper) to retrench. She was probably the first flamboyant older woman Fred had met. Her daughter, sixteen-year-old Princess May, was also at the tea-party. She would grow up into Queen Mary, and be entertained by Fred to tea in Rye over fifty years later.[10]

When the time came for Fred to return to Truro for the Christmas holidays, he desired to demonstrate his new maturity by making the journey alone (and, undeclared, his hope of thereby avoiding the embarrassment of having his father present himself again at the school). He enlisted his mother's support. 'I think I could quite manage it,' he wrote. 'Temple Grove to Waterloo 1s. Waterloo to Paddington I suppose about 2s 6p. Paddington to Truro I suppose £1.0.0. I suppose I had better get something to eat at Slough . . . and about 1s for accidents.' To ensure agreement, Fred added the titbit of news that he had won a prize, by calculating the date 1878 years and 11 months to seconds, and *proving* it. He was duly rewarded with his independent journey.[11]

Soon after his return to Temple Grove there fell the first anniversary of Martin's death. 'Just a year since our dear Martin left us,'

Mama wrote to Fred, 'God help us to love each other better – for that is just all – is life itself.' The sadness was relieved by pride in Fred's manifest progress at school. 'God bless you, Dear; you have been, and are, a great joy to us, with all your work and perseverance, and good character in all your school life.'[12] Alas, the honeymoon was not to last. Throughout the next three terms, Fred plunged out of favour time and again, and always for the most trivial reasons. When a boy flipped a towel at him he said, 'Shut up', and was reported for it. 'Please don't tell anyone, except of course Papa,' he pleaded. What he meant was, especially not Papa![13]

Fred continued to do reasonably well in class, but his previously effortless supremacy began to slip. He told his mother that he wanted to get a microscope 'most awfully' and dropped hints that she might want to help, yet he felt obliged to explain that he was third in the class because there were two boys who had been there before and knew all the work. She said she would contribute to the cost, as he had an important birthday coming up. '*Twelve* sounds a portentous age, and I promise to hear you with due respect when you have reached it.'[14] The truth was, Fred was congenitally lazy; the fatal facility which had seen him coast through his first year and a half was deserting him as he found more in the beauty of language, which was difficult to measure or earn marks for, than in arid translations from the classics. When Mr Waterfield read poetry aloud Fred was entranced by its power to move and to impose balance, but the rest of the time he was frequently bored.

Escapades and japes brought disgrace upon him, and he became very unhappy at the thought that his father must needs be informed of every peccadillo. Just before Christmas Fred was reported for what looked like capitalist enterprise (as an adult he would be an addictive player of the Stock Market), bartering postage stamps for servility. Benson still smarted with shame that his own father had been involved in trade, and looked to little Fred to rest pure and unsullied by the temptations of Mammon. Little idea did he have of the heartbreak he could cause as he vented his fury upon the twelve-year-old with earnest and selfish passion. Fred wrote an abject letter:

I did not give him the stamps to buy things for me with at all, they were entirely for himself to do what he liked with. I was very wrong indeed I know and I don't want to excuse any. I only tell you the plain simple truth. Please don't write about this to Mr Waterfield or tell anyone. I am as ashamed as I can be. Besides if you wrote to Mr Waterfield it might get other boys into a row. P.S. I daresay all this will sound untrue, but it is not.[15]

There is pathos in the prediction that Papa will immediately assume a lie is being told.

With his mother Fred was not afraid of showing his fragility. 'Oh I do want to come home so,' he wrote the very next day, 'and yet it seems somehow, I don't know what to say about it, as I have been reported. Please write to me a letter saying that you have forgiven me, and all about the holidays. You see it is a full fortnight since you wrote to me about jolly things.'[16]

There was the occasion when he and three others spent a school-boy fortune on Turkish Delight, which they then smeared over the bedsheets; one of them threw up in a manner which could not be kept secret, and Fred was identified as the ringleader. That meant, of course, another letter to the formidable Bishop, although Mr Edgar, who was to succeed Waterfield, was less likely to make a meal of it. None the less, Fred was summoned to his father's presence and treated like a pariah. Freddy was not fit to be included among his children, he said. He must henceforth take his meals alone and apart, banished upstairs where his siblings were safe from his contaminating influence. As the only one who was not afraid of Papa, Nelly intervened to reduce this appalling sentence.[17] When the time came to return to school, Fred was more unhappy than ever, because he knew his father's displeasure had not really abated. 'Dear old Fred went off yesterday,' said Minnie, 'very brave at the last, but, Beth told me, having had two good cries in bed, in the evening before, and one in the morning when he woke. Dear lad! He was *very* sorry to leave home this time, and followed one about all Sunday, and asked for letters, and kissed me so warmly.'[18]

Temple Grove was no longer the entirely carefree place it had promised to be. An event of shattering solemnity occurred when two boys were expelled for an undisclosed crime. They had been at breakfast, but had disappeared before classes began. Then they were paraded before the whole school and publicly humiliated. They were told they had brought disgrace upon their families and would bear the stain of their sin forever. Fred had not the faintest idea what it was all about; he knew only that it was terrible. He was told to go to the Head's room, where he found Mr Waterfield blubbing freely. 'Do you understand why those two boys were sent away?' he asked through his sobs. 'No, sir,' said Fred. 'Thank God for that,' exclaimed Waterfield, and no further elucidation was forthcoming. Fred was to allude several times in adulthood to this incident, and use it in one of his fictions. He remembered that the elder of the two boys had said friendly things to him, and on occasion had asked questions which he did not understand. It was up to the boys to work out for themselves what viciousness could have caused such turmoil, and of course their imaginations were probably far more prurient than the reality. Fred declared when older that the silence which surrounded boyhood sexuality was 'libellous' and 'criminal'.

The combination of these threatening mysteries and Fred's inability to do well in class brought distress and failure upon him. Both Martin and Arthur had won scholarships, to Winchester and Eton respectively, and covered the family name with glory. Martin was now dead, and Arthur could do no wrong, having just won an Eton scholarship to King's College, Cambridge as well. Nelly and Maggie were doing splendidly at the school in Truro. So it was up to Fred to show himself worthy, and incidentally save his father some money, for the Bishop had only his stipend to keep the family going. Fred was not so ambitious of academic distinction, and dissipated his energies on poetry and music and friendship. He flouted the rules by speaking to a younger boy at a time when such fraternity was forbidden. He showed off his skill with conjuring tricks and sent home for some more, but was surprised when, for once, his mother failed to oblige him. 'We think you had better *not* have your conjuring tricks just now, *altogether* on account of your work – don't let anything come between you and it – it is always your snare, this trifling with a number of things.'

She could not, however, be hard for long, especially with Beth hovering beside her, and relented in a postscript – 'Judging by Beth's face, I should say the hamper will be *very* satisfactory.'[19]

Fred sat for a scholarship to Marlborough and failed dismally, not even being mentioned as a runner-up. He sat for entry as a scholar to Eton, and failed again. Many more attempts did he make, and each was attended with a bold lack of distinction of any kind. His parents were perplexed.

Mama was quick to make excuses for him. Perhaps he was poorly? She did not want to believe that he was just not taking any trouble. After the second failure, Fred wrote that it was 'hard not to despair', which was a hideous reflection for a thirteen-year-old to make. 'Poor little man!' said Mama. 'Little Fred's letter is sad, my dearest, is it not?' Edward, as ever, betrayed less concern about Fred than about the reflection upon himself. 'I own to being very much disappointed about Fred,' he told his wife. 'I did not look for such utter failure among nine scholarships. He must I suppose now stand for Eton, but the hope is very small, if he has been doing his best . . . I'm afraid he has not worked well. I must write to him but scarcely know how.'[20]

Minnie tried to reassure Edward, without giving the impression that she was taking sides. They ought not to be so downcast about Fred, she said. 'God bless him, and make him a good boy.' To Fred himself she assumed an admonitory stance, showing solidarity with her husband, but then regretted she may have been too censorious. 'Poor laddie. If *only* he will learn by this, one will *bless* his failure!' She was determined to distil some goodness from the catastrophe. Minnie knew, of course, that the real cause of Fred's 'despair' was his father's extreme reaction to any disappointment, the black moods and grim self-pity which rendered filial duty an impossible mountain to climb. As nothing short of perfection would satisfy Papa, nothing was what he would get. Fred was already self-willed to a degree.

When Edward went away to London on ecclesiastical business, Minnie determined to beard him with this problem once and for all. The memory of Martin's death, possibly as the result of over-exertion, was too recent for her to keep silent, and she felt sure Edward was clinically ill. There were serious grounds for such a suspicion. One of Edward's brothers was what we should now-adays call psychotic, and two of his sisters were subject to those erratic swings of mood sometimes diagnosed as cyclothymia; this condition, unknown in Benson's day, is on the borderline of disabling psychotic disorder, but not so severe. Edward's father and grandfather had also most likely suffered from cyclothymia. As for Minnie's own family, she cannot have failed to notice the dangerous behaviour of her brother William, and the oddness of brothers Henry and Arthur, each of whom were attacked by wild moods of gloom from time to time. She saw the symptoms in her husband and felt she ought to make him face their implications, writing him a long, dignified, frank and tactful letter:

My dearest, I have another thing still more at heart, and one about which I want to *implore* your real consideration. I have tried to talk to you about it, but you didn't really listen, and I get more and more troubled and anxious about it. You know what it is – I want you to see a good doctor in London, on Monday. My dearest, I don't think you at all realise *how* depressed you get when you are not well ... how very great the depression is, and how terribly it reacts upon everyone around ... and you must know how intense your influence is, and how widespread, and how when you are in gloom, and each little difficulty seems insurmountable, and a grasshopper a burden, and when other people's faults stand out so clear as they always do at such a time, *then* just think how difficult it is for everybody. I mean, just as your power of *brightening* is, so is your power of depressing ... you can't shut yourself up and say you won't depress us all, but will keep out of the way ... and thereupon you come, come silently, and look gloomy and go away quickly – these things make our hearts so heavy. I want you to *recognize* that this is physical. Forgive all this long beseeching – it has made me more and more unhappy now for many months. I don't often talk about this now – please God I never will again as I know I have done, and seemed so mean in the doing of it. Your most loving wife, Minnie.[21]

It is a pity we do not know whether Minnie's courage was rewarded and whether Edward did seek help, but it would be some years yet before the family came into contact with the one medical practitioner who understood their predicament.

Fred duly went up to Marlborough as a normal fee-paying schoolboy. Edward, much calmed, delivered him in person on 17 September 1881, all unaware that his odd dress of black gaiters, a hat with strings at the side, and an apron, might excite comment among boys. Fred would rather he had looked like anyone else's parent, and was very quiet. Still, he was impressed when the boys took off their caps as soon as they realised the Bishop was among them, and felt a private glow of pride. Edward was also impressed, but by the 'really splendid chapel'.

And so Fred embarked upon the happiest six years of his life. He was captivated by the school within days. 'Never in all his day-dreams had he conceived that [Marlborough] could be like this. It was not like a school, it was like some new and entrancing kind of home.'[22] A home, he might have added, blessed with the absence of a demanding father. Full of joy at this new beginning, he wrote to Truro for his books to be sent on, and his mother had to scold him for leaving them all over the place; Nelly had a difficult time finding them and packing them for him.

Minnie also felt the need to advise her son that he must henceforth be *manly* and not childish; he must respect regulations and develop a character which will grow wise. Above all, he must be *accurate*; this habit of decorating stories with fantasy, this 'aptness to describe a thing as one wants it to be, and not quite as it is',[23] must cease.

Fred's delight was evidently so intense that he redoubled his efforts to do well and placate his father. There was a foundation scholarship available to the sons of clergymen, to be sat only three months after his arrival. He took private tuition out of school hours to prepare for it, and gave up music (a deprivation he resented). Though he declared he fully expected another failure, there was no concealing his excitement when the list of winners was posted in December, and there among them was his name 'at a decent altitude'. With that hurdle behind him, Fred hoped that he could be left alone to enjoy all the splendours which this magical place had to offer, not least of which was the positive encouragement to indulge in sport and games for their own sake.

In this, Fred belonged to the first generation which was to benefit from a wholesale revolution in the attitude of educational theorists towards games-playing. The previous generation, which included Dr Arnold, Prince Lee, and Edward Benson himself, had held that every minute of leisure should serve some useful purpose and that idleness was a sin. God's earth should be studied and revered even on a ramble. Boys who wished to waste time playing games had been treated with stern disapproval, or at best made to indulge these bad habits out of sight. Games at school had been left to the boys to organise by themselves, and it had been unthinkable for a schoolmaster to notice them, let alone help arrange them or participate in them. The teacher's recreational time had been spent reading, by way of example.

All this changed in the 1870s. The legacy of G.G. Bradley's influence at Marlborough, during which staff had been recruited with the specific intention of finding good athletes as well as good scholars to instruct the boys, had begun to be felt. Bradley's view was that organised games helped create the habit of discipline and foster a spirit of co-operation, both important preparations for adulthood. Bradley was not alone in this reassessment (and at Marlborough he had had particular reasons to urge it, for the place had been near collapse through lawlessness), and similar reforms had been promulgated by others. The result was that the educational ideal changed from being set solely upon the goal of intellectual excellence, to acknowledge the moral usefulness of athleticism; also, in parenthesis, to celebrate its physical beauty. The salient characteristics of what has ever since been held to typify English public school education were in the process of being established. They included, in addition to this heavy reliance upon sport, the cultivation of Spartan habits and contempt for all that smacked of effeminate comfort; the exaltation of patriotic pride; and the conviction that intellectual accomplishment must take second place to the building of character.[24]

All of which now seems so obvious, as it has been the norm for one hundred years and echoes of it may still be heard in the last decade of the twentieth century. But in E.F. Benson's time it was all new, and he was destined to become one of the most perfect exemplars of this educational ideal for the rest of his life.

The Spartan side of the ideal was evident at Marlborough from the first, and it was no accident that the architect of the earliest buildings had previously been a designer of prisons. Fred slept in a draughty dormitory on a simple bed with no surrounding partitions. Privacy was considered childish. The bell rang at 6.30 a.m. for chapel at 7 a.m. and a first lesson, before a breakfast kept deliberately paltry to demonstrate that boys would not be spoilt. The day continued to be strenuous apart from a precious free hour around tea-time, and if they were lucky the boys might be treated to some hot buttered toast, out of the kindness of the head of house, before going to bed. The corridors and passages were stone, cold and unadorned. Fred never breathed a word of complaint about conditions. On the contrary, the fact that they were shared by all bred a spirit of *camaraderie* and gritty courage which he positively cherished.

Whatever the school denied in comfort and nutritional delights it compensated with team-games. Fred became addicted to cricket, played football and rugby, ran and jumped and hurdled in the athletics, and learned rackets. He was an instant recruit to every sport on offer, in fact, and excelled in most of them, growing rapidly into a handsome, well-built youth with exuberant energy and a winning smile. His sparkling blue eyes and sunny nature made him many friends; Fred was in his element, basking in achievement and popularity. Gregarious, yet he was not obsessive about company. He found time to wander alone in the Savernake Forest looking for butterflies, for his collection of which he was awarded a school prize; this forest, he tells us, confirmed his love of the solitary mood from time to time. Thus, when Fred went home to Truro for the Christmas holidays of 1882–3, he was fifteen and happy. Even his awkwardness in the presence of his father began to evaporate. This was just as well, for the news that Christmas was momentous indeed, and concerned Papa intimately.

A letter had arrived from the Prime Minister, Mr Gladstone. Edward read it alone, then shared its contents with his wife, and finally summoned the family round the fire to tell them that he had been invited to accept the appointment as the next Archbishop of Canterbury.

For a man still only fifty-two this was an extraordinary honour and eloquent testimony to the regard in which he was held in ecclesiastical circles. But it cannot have been, to him, an entire surprise. He had always coveted (in the most godly sense) the archiepiscopate and had been led to believe that others would promote him to it. The late Archbishop Tait, whose death had made the post vacant, was a friend of his and had been to stay with the family in Truro. Benson had in turn visited Tait within the last weeks when he knew he was near death, and Tait had told him that he hoped Edward would be Archbishop one day. (The close connection between Benson and his predecessor and successor is curious. One of Archbishop Tait's daughters, Lucy, was already a close companion of Mary Benson, and would eventually share her household and life; another daughter, Edith Tait, married Randall Davidson, who would be Archbishop himself in 1896). Nevertheless, it would have been more normal for Benson to wait until he was more senior in the hierarchy. The trouble was, Browne, the Bishop of Winchester, was now too old for the job, and there was nobody else. Browne was disappointed, for he had received no word that he might be passed over, but accepted the appointment of Benson with sincere approval.

Edward wrote to the Prime Minister that he needed a week to think. He also wished to consult other friends and consider how the upheaval might affect his family. If he wavered, on the grounds that he was untrained for a great office of State which would be largely administrative, all hesitation ceased when he received a personal letter from Queen Victoria. 'Heard that the Bishop of Truro felt himself overwhelmed at present by the weight of the office I had invited him to accept,' the Queen told her Diary. 'I shall write to him, to urge him to accept.' The amount of reliance she placed upon Edward's wisdom was far greater than has ever been acknowledged. Some of her letters to him are written, most unusually, in the first person, and signed 'Yours very affectionately'. She would learn to consult him on matters she kept from her ministers; 'my excuse is my great loneliness,' the Queen told him, 'my many heavy trials and troubles and the great need I have during my declining years.'[25]

Edward wrote to Mr Gladstone accepting the Primacy, and pointing out that the approval of the Queen, 'knowing almost better than anyone my earlier work, is a thought full of strength.'[26] Only Arthur wondered (in retrospect, admittedly) if it was not the only important mistake of his father's career. 'The most successful Archbishop is the man who does not only tolerate compromise,' he wrote, 'but believes in it enthusiastically as the best means of obtaining co-operation and loyalty. The note of the Primacy is sympathetic caution, and that was not by any means my father's ideal.'[27]

For the moment, however, the excitement among the Bensons was intense, and no one enjoyed their advancement more than Fred. He was, after all, at exactly the right age to savour the grandeur of their new status; the two girls and Arthur were virtually adults and able to affect indifference, while Hugh, not yet out of infancy, hardly noticed. Arthur was now a brilliant undergraduate at King's College. For Fred, the idea of one's own father being Primate of All England, and second only to the Royal Family in the precedence of the Realm, was heady indeed. The Archbishop came before the Prime Minister, before the Lord High Chancellor and all other Officers of State, before all the dukes, marquesses and earls, before everyone in Parliament. Fred was learning not to boast, but we may be sure he was also learning how to show off without appearing to boast, those very subtleties, in fact, which he would one day lampoon in his fiction.

One could hardly blame him. However lovely Cornwall had been, Lambeth Palace was by comparison an impressive abode, with large rooms and platoons of servants to look after them. There was a doorman at the imposing fortress-like gate, and a mediaeval garden, the largest in London, behind, which woodpigeons had made their home. Such was the ubiquity of soot in London that if you picked or smelt a flower you were liable to have fingers and nose blackened by the contact. The main palace itself was far from sumptuous; it was even rather austere and forbidding, with no allowance made for domestic comfort and very sparse, impersonal furniture. All the rooms gave off either side of a long, wide corridor, rather as in an hotel, so that there was precious little opportunity for privacy; the corridor was the single main artery of the building, along which all human traffic passed. Edward altered this, constructing connecting doors between all the rooms along one side. Thus he could walk from the library to the dressing-room to his bedroom to the sitting-room, all without having to show himself in the corridor. Benson's connecting doors are still there. The family ate in the huge so-called Guard Room with its timbered roof and chilly vastness, the dining-table reduced to doll's-house proportions in the centre, and uniformed flunkeys around.

With his passion for decoration Edward turned out cupboards and attics to discover furniture which had not been used for years, and transformed the Palace into a more richly furnished house than it had ever been. In one of the towers he found some old rusty pikes which had been carried in ancient times to precede the Archbishop in procession, had them cleaned, and hung them in a fan-shaped display on the walls either side of the entrance hall, where they are seen today. He also found the shell of Archbishop Laud's pet tortoise, and placed it in a glass case. Portraits of previous Primates he caused to be hung in a row along the corridor. Lambeth was very much the 'office' of the incumbent; there were very few rooms which could be considered 'spare', so that guests were more likely to be asked to the country home at Addington.[28]

The formality which attended an Archbishop's daily life appealed to Fred's burgeoning love of ceremony, and the scores of notables who passed through the Palace, all among the most important personages in the land, accustomed him to the society and glitter of the famous. It is fair to say E.F. Benson might have turned out quite a different novelist without this precipitate plunge into the highest reaches of London society. His frank enjoyment of it all echoed his mother's. For Minnie at last came into her own as the wife of the Archbishop of Canterbury. Though initially somewhat shy, feeling *gauche* and unsophisticated after years in the country, Minnie quickly adapted to the role of a hostess and mistress of a grand house. She controlled everything, from the stables to the kitchens, and with her witty conversation, her intelligence, and her endless interest in people and their problems, made every guest easy and every stranger welcome. Now forty-one years old, she was a different person from the bewildered and frightened little girl Edward had married. Only her private diary, written in plain little black books, revealed the anguish she still felt over the nature of her faith and the pain with which she fretted over her stubborn faults. (Minnie was predisposed to things small; her letters were mostly written on tiny pages only three inches high.) Outwardly, she was a lady of poise and irresistible charm. 'She revelled in the multitude of her engagements,' Fred wrote, 'she delighted in the froth and bustle and movement.'[29]

And so, of course, did he. Fred found he was able to charm the grown-ups with little effort, and engage in conversation which was superficial but entertaining without the need to shine or earn marks. Additionally, there was the glory of Addington Park, the Archbishop's country residence near Croydon, set in six hundred acres of rolling parkland the beauties of which could never be exhausted. Thus was he afforded the best of both worlds – bright dinner-table chat in London amid people involved in great events, and cosy family life at Addington, where the event of the day was the misfortune which befell the beloved collie, Watch, who snapped at a wasp and came howling into the house, tail down and head shaking helplessly from side to side.[30]

The greater part of the year was still, however, spent at Marlborough, where Fred's standing among the boys was measurably increased by his father's astonishing promotion. Tangible proof of this came when Fred was due to be confirmed, and Edward visited the school in his official capacity to conduct the service. Several other boys were confirmed at the same time, but the glory was all Fred's when a notice appeared on the board to the effect that His Grace had asked that the school should have a whole day's holiday in honour of his visit, and the request had been granted. 'I say,' said Fred's friends, 'do be confirmed again!'[31]

Life was indeed sweet for Fred from every point of view, and the one chore which had previously clouded the bliss of school, namely school-work, was turned for him into a joy by the intercession of one man, his favourite among the teachers, A.H. Beesly. Fred wrote that Beesly was 'one of those reserved demi-gods whom a boy obeys, reverences, and loves for no ostensible reason',[32] yet the reason can be found in the experience and memory of many a grown man who looks back on his schooldays with gratitude. For the gratitude is usually felt towards one individual, a teacher with that incomparable gift of being able to enthuse his pupil. Beesly was one such, and his influence upon Fred was crucial. He taught Greek and Latin, so opening for Fred a world of classicism and Hellenism which until then had been rather solemn and difficult. Beesly made the construeing of Latin texts amusing, creative and challenging. Moreover, it was a challenge to be shared, as he and Fred pondered possible translations and interpretations, honed them, and tried to put them into verse. (There were other students, but the nature of this peculiar gift is to fix a bond between teacher and taught which *feels* exclusive – it is as much an emotion and an intuition as a formal relationship.) So, imperceptibly, did Beesly manage to remain a figure to admire at a distance while becoming at the same time a partner in discovery, and thereby help Fred towards his intellectual maturity. Fred wanted to please Beesly, and worked well to this end, but he knew, without it being said in so many words, that Beesly also wanted to please Fred, wanted Fred to enjoy the things he enjoyed, and to understand why. In a sense, teachers like Beesly give of themselves in their lessons, and there is generally only one pupil in a year who can spot the gift and be willing to accept it.

A.H. Beesly epitomised the product of those schools which are dominated by the male ethic, for it was supposed he had never even spoken to a woman in his life. But he was austere with himself, and if he felt a fondness for his charges, as he must, he expressed it in pride and the sharing of rather recondite jokes. His love of ancient Greece infected Fred for ever after, and probably introduced, again without anything directly being said about it, that subterranean stream of homo-eroticism which was to flow, ever so quietly and secretly, throughout Fred's life. Beesly was also responsible (after O.C. Waterfield) for bringing alive to his pupil that pleasure in words, their origins and their meanings, their subtleties and development, their harmonies and allusiveness, above all their power when used with precision. Fred would never be a slapdash writer, and the structure of his sentences, with their balanced subjects and predicates, owed much to his years at Marlborough. Indeed, it was there that he first wrote seriously, assuming the co-editorship of the *Marlburian* (with his friend

Eustace Miles, son of a publisher) and devising much of its content from his own pen.

If A.H. Beesly gave Fred the opportunity of an intellectual friendship, it was wonderfully relaxed compared to the passionate affections which buffeted him, with both younger and older boys, throughout his career at Marlborough. These, too, were in the general run of things, and boys were expected to battle their way as best they could through the mysteries of powerful attractions to emerge sane and wise at the end. Whom one sat next to in class assumed an importance on which the whole of one's happiness might hinge. Who allowed one to look after his cricket bat, or to brew him a cup of tea, or simply to share a quiet, exclusive talk about nothing in particular, he would be the hero of the next weeks or months and all one's emotional energies would be bent upon seeing him or being seen by him as often as possible. Benson depicted the overwhelming nature of such hero-worship several times in later years, most notably in *David Blaize*, where he states that it is 'more complete and entire than is ever accorded by the world of grown-up men and women to their most august idols.'[33] In *Our Family Affairs* he conveys the intense pleasure that boys feel in being alive and being with one another; brewing their meagre tea together, 'you enjoyed the full fellowship of not quite enough to eat, scrupulously divided, and the romance of being fourteen or fifteen thickened and fructified.'

Romantic it certainly was, and fraught with the dangers of jealousy. 'We flamed into a hundred hot bonfires of these friend-ships, which were discussed with a freedom that would seem appalling, if you forgot that you were dealing with boys and not with men.' Fred was drawn to the masculine heroes of the sporting field, with their fine legs and handsome mien, and their effortless superiority to the common run of mankind. He confessed he was left cold by a mincing walk or 'softness of disposition', which at least indicates that mincing walks and melting eyes were not unknown at Marlborough, or he would not have had the chance to resist them. Favourites succeeded one another almost monthly. In the summer of 1882, for instance, Fred wrote to his mother of a new friend: 'A boy here, David Browne by name, has asked me to come to his home for a few days at the beginning of the holidays. Can I go?' Minnie did not think this a good idea; on the other hand, fully aware of the intensity of these couplings, she did not want to deflate Fred too abruptly. She told him it 'might be nice', which was neither one thing nor the other, the subjunctive conferring ambiguity on a matter which was urgent and terrific to Fred. 'Am I to understand by "*might* be nice" that I had better make this visit some other holidays when I have known the boy longer?' Poor Fred was crushed. 'I like him very much,' he said, a trifle lamely, adding what he hoped would be the clinching information, 'his father, who is dead, was a clergyman and lived at Cheltenham'.[34]

Mama was also gathered into the turmoil of schoolboy quarrels on occasion. Fred fell out with a boy identified only as 'S' and was desperate to repair the damage. He told his mother it had all been his fault. She replied by saying, in effect, don't tell me, tell *him*. 'I don't think you will effect a real reconciliation until you acknowledge *thoroughly* both that you were most to blame originally, and that you blamed him unjustly. Nothing short of *full* acknowledgement ever makes a thing up . . . So, dear boy, that is my advice.' She was evidently worried about him, for she began her next letter with self-conscious breeziness – 'How goes it, laddikins?' – and jocular references to her desire to see his 'dear phiz' before long.[35] Further evidence of Fred's distraction is that he had to be reminded even to reply to letters from his father, which were relentlessly stiff and exacting, and which he would rather not have. 'You should *always* acknowledge letters,' the Archbishop told him, while the Archbishop's wife took the gentler line: 'You will write to him next, won't you, dear boy, and thank him . . . write him longer and more interesting letters.'

As Fred became senior in his turn, so his affections fastened upon younger boys. First there was one Sheppard, followed by a long, turbulent flirtation with John Risley, which practically brought Fred to his knees. 'I am beginning to feel about Risley what I did about Sheppard,' he wrote in his Diary, 'but less hopelessly.' They quarrelled. 'It isn't nice to be in slavery to anyone. Yet it is pleasing.' Fred quoted Tennyson after the quarrel:

When we fall out with those we love
And kiss again with tears.

Still the bumps and jostles of affection tormented him. 'I feel dreadfully bad about Risley.' 'I must find out about Risley. If he feels as I do, I shall be happy.' 'I am feeling hopeless about Risley. What on earth am I to do?' Fred suffered considerable remorse and self-doubt over this affair, for there are four pages torn out of the Diary which purport to be 'the account of a dreadful period of frustration with its bearing on my friendship with Risley'. At about the same date he admits to 'yielding again several times to the old temptation; and it seems as hard as ever not to. God help me.'

Risley was succeeded by Alfred Glennie, a mere thirteen years old and the severest test Fred had yet encountered.

I have felt towards him as I have never felt towards anyone, infinitely more strong it has been than the other period . . . I have spent hours and hours in order to talk, even to see him. But it is not a healthy feeling and I wish to eradicate it from now. The only way will be to have no communication with him till I feel it has quite lost its power. What it might lead to if indulged I don't dare to think. But it is very sweet as it is . . . I hope sometime that Glennie will know all I have felt. I have been living in and for him alone up till now . . . Perhaps when he has grown older I can tell him.[36]

His abiding friendship, however, one that survived all the trivial upheavals of romance, was with Eustace Miles, one year his junior and a sportsman to surpass them all. When Fred was promoted to the Sixth Form, given a study of his own and a fag to fetch and carry and clean his shoes, he and Eustace became inseparable. Not only did they edit *The Marlburian* together, but they played rackets and tennis together, discovered the great classics of English literature together, and dropped History, Mathematics and French in order to concentrate on Latin and Greek, for they intended to go up for a classical scholarship at King's College, also together. To achieve this, Fred would need to stay on at Marlborough an extra year, and thus allow Eustace to catch up. It is odd that nobody appears to have objected to this plan, whose only *raison d'être* was an extension of valued companionship, for that is precisely what Fred was to do. In his last year he was head of his house and virtually free to adapt rules and customs to suit his whim. The attachment of Fred and Eustace bears all the marks of a mature and sensible alliance, based on more than physical beauty and the flutterings of a malleable heart. That they were to remain lifelong friends must lend support to this impression.

But what of all the others, the Brownes, the Risleys and the Glennies? Were they the recipients of Fred's serious and determined love, or merely pawns in the endlessly shifting game of schoolboy attentions? Fred went out of his way, later, to insist that there had been nothing improper in the affairs which galvanised him and his contemporaries at Marlborough. 'To suppose that this ardency was sensual, is to miss the point of it and lose the value of it altogether,' he wrote. 'That the base of the attraction was largely physical is no doubt true, for it was founded primarily on appearance, but there is a vast difference between the breezy open-air quality of these friendships and the dingy sensualism which is sometimes wrongly attributed to them.'[37] On the other hand, there are clear signs in the manuscript of *David Blaize*, which is entirely based on the Marlborough years, that 'dingy sensualism' was as much a factor of schoolboy life as was pure romantic yearning. And it is pretty clear that the feeling between the two protagonists was inspired by young Master Glennie.

The boy of the title is passionately attached to Maddox, the wise, clever, sophisticated older boy whose first quality is that he is 'damned good-looking'. As the friendship blossoms it becomes as important and consuming for Maddox as it is for David, who is blithely unaware of sensuality in any form ('his utter want of curiosity about all that was filthy'). When another boy, Hughes, is caught sitting on David's bed, Maddox furiously ejects him, and Hughes complains that David has turned Maddox into a saint. The implication of this is that Maddox has previously not been at all averse to boys sitting on each other's beds, and if he is now a saint, he must, in contrast, have earlier been a sinner with more to confess than mere sitting. Shortly afterwards there is a scene in which Maddox comes upon David unexpectedly after the latter's bath. He is naked but for a towel round his head. Maddox only looks and smiles rather stupidly, but David 'instantly has some sense of choking discomfort . . . He wanted to get away.' David runs down the corridor.

In the original unpublished version there is a little more to it than that. Maddox grabs hold of David, still naked, and holds him so close that their faces are almost touching and David has to break free of the embrace. It is unquestionably a love scene, and it makes more sense of the reconciliation a few pages later, when Maddox more or less begs forgiveness and makes it plain that he has threatened David's innocence with 'the miry road that had been in [his] mind'. As soon as one knows there was something to forgive, namely an attempt to seduce, the bringing together of the two friends at the end of the chapter is all the more touching. Also in Fred's original, David says to Maddox, 'I like you more than anything in the world, you know, but I expect I hate beastliness,' and so saying, lays his hand in the crock of Maddox's elbow. The first version of this fine story is altogether more tactile than the slightly sanitised copy that eventually went to press.

For the rest of his life, E.F. Benson looked back on Marlborough with an almost painful nostalgia. It was there that he learnt to give and accept love, to enjoy study for its own sake, to talk intelligently on a variety of subjects, to admire ancient Greece both in its artistic achievement and its ethical values, to welcome and cope with responsibility; in short, it was where he grew up. Lambeth Palace and Addington Park were not his, they were the décor of his parents' lives. His own territory was for six years bounded by the walls of that enchanted place, so that he could scarcely imagine living anywhere else. Whether or not he uncovered the mysteries of sex there as well is a secret he will not yield.

Curiously, brother Arthur was displaying similar signs of fastidiousness in the wake of a like experience. His first book was published in 1886, while Fred was in his last year at Marlborough, under the pseudonym 'Christopher Carr'. Entitled *The Memoirs of Arthur Hamilton*, it tells of an intense relationship which is terrified of physical expression. The hero had formed a devoted friendship with a younger boy during his last year at school. Such friendships, he wrote,

> are truly chivalrous and absolutely pure, are above all other loves, noble, refining, true; passion at white heat without taint, confidence of so intimate a kind as cannot even exist between husband and wife, trust such as cannot be shadowed, are its characteristics.

The fact that a modern paedophile could not put it better, and would approve the sentiment, cannot detract from the honesty of Benson's appeal. For the account is based upon truth, and the disappointment of this love drove Arthur to the first of his frightening mental breakdowns.

'Arthur' left school and went up to Cambridge, waiting three years for his friend to catch up with him and join him there. During this time they corresponded, and Arthur never suspected that the beloved had fallen into bad company. When he arrives in Cambridge, the revelation takes place, and Arthur is horrified. Writing in the third person, the narrator says:

> I can hardly picture to myself the agony, disgust and rage (his words and feelings about sensuality of any kind were strangely keen and bitter), loyalty fighting with the sense of repulsion, pity struggling with honour, which must have convulsed him when he discovered that his friend was not only yielding, but deliberately impure.[38]

Here are the same flight from ecstasy, the same conviction that physical tastes are brutish, the same antipathy towards 'sensuality' that we find in Fred's writing. Even at so young an age, the Benson children were already crippled, self-denying, prudish.

The Memoirs of Arthur Hamilton is undoubtedly autobiographical, despite Arthur's embarrassed protestations to the contrary. (There is a scene in which the hero, as a child, writes 'I hate Papa' on a piece of paper and buries it in the garden; this almost certainly happened at Wellington.) Mary Gladstone, the Prime Minister's daughter, easily identified the author and wrote to Arthur, who was quick to disown the book.

I don't in the least want to identify A.H.'s opinions with my own . . . as long as an *intime* book is the work of an unknown author, it may be read with interest, but as soon as he is known the interest becomes vulgar – I should feel as if I had made a sacrifice of decency for the sake of notoriety. But it is not an autobiography, though perhaps it might be mistaken for one; I rather wish it was.[39]

This last remark is disingenuous, to say the least. Many years later he admitted to Mr William Rees, a researcher, that he was Arthur Hamilton, and that though the book was a fiction, there were a good many real episodes in it.[40] It should also be noted, as it were in passing, that it is beautifully written, with a flow of narrative which is quite beguiling and which would one day stock row upon row of shelves with Benson output.

In Arthur's case, the crisis of affection coincided with (or perhaps helped to cause) a crisis of faith which all but unsettled his sanity. Throughout his childhood the role of the Church in ordinary daily life had been accepted without question, the facts of religion, the existence of a Deity, the divinity of Christ, all were as much a part of normality as breakfast. But undergraduates do not accept without question; it is part of their function to ask, wonder and ponder. And undergraduates at Cambridge in 1882 were prone to agnosticism. Arthur was thus subjected to influences which troubled him profoundly, and he placed the date of his breakdown to a specific event in November, when he attended a Revivalist Meeting and, while some in the audience made their way, eyes aglow, towards the stage, he, suddenly smitten with the awful truth, stumbled out into the night seeking shelter from his own thoughts. Weeks of deep depression followed, so emasculating that he feared he would go mad. He prayed, to no avail. He could not consult his father, who would not even allow him to dine with the actor Henry Irving lest he fall into bad company,[41] and he could not have it known that the son of the Archbishop of Canterbury was faltering. The burden of his parentage was a double booby-trap: his father's position placed on Arthur an obligation of silence about his own soul-searching; and his father's recalcitrant gene predisposed him to psychotic illness.

In his desperation, Arthur consulted the Roman Catholic divine, John Henry Newman, with no noticeable result, and finally sought solace with G.H. Wilkinson in London, the very man whom his mother had consulted ten years earlier in her own moment of crisis. There is a possibility that he spent some time in a mental hospital, but this is no longer verifiable.[42] It took many months for him to recover his equilibrium.

Fred must have heard what his brother had suffered, for the family was always together in the holidays, but he makes no reference to it. He was still too young to be involved, and still entirely intoxicated by Marlborough. It is tantalising to reflect how the family could assemble and not allude to the deep unhappiness of one of their number, simply because such conversation would hurt Papa. By the time all the Bensons were in Zermatt, Switzerland, for the summer of 1885, Arthur had resumed better spirits. He might never have needed to go through such torment had he but known that his omniscient, infallible father also had moments of doubt, however slight and ephemeral. Since becoming Archbishop he had begun to feel himself growing more distant from God. In a conversation with Minnie, pacing up and down the drawing-room at Addington one day, he said that he had a kind of fear that after death he would wake up and find God different. 'I am, so to speak, *at ease* with Him here on earth,' he said, 'I feel as if I might wake up there and *not* be satisfied with it.'[43]

And what of the others? Maggie, a young woman of twenty-three, accomplished, brilliant, with a stunning undergraduate career at Lady Margaret Hall already spreading her renown in academic circles, had as yet shown no sign of the morosity which would one day destroy her. Yet she was all brain and no feeling, able to love people in the mass, philosophically. 'Poor old Mags!' her sister Nelly wrote. 'You haven't anyone you *much* care about very particularly – and a sort of general philanthropy may be moral but isn't thrilling.'[44] As for Nelly, whose exuberant nonsense mirrored her mother's and was still not squashed flat by her father's threatening presence, she went on much as before, helpful, light-hearted, and also brainy. Unlike Maggie, she had made some close female friends during her undergraduate days, and did not merely discuss Descartes with them. 'Nellie is uncommonly jolly,' wrote her mother one day from Addington. 'She tries her "O Mama", but it has *quite* lost its power.'[45]

Hugh, now fourteen and at Eton, was spoilt, childish and petulant. Fred had little to say about him, or to him, and gave the impression he found him tiresome. Once more one has the feeling that Fred, though not indifferent to his family, is gradually establishing a separation between himself and their excessively claustrophobic ways, if only for self-protection. He is stubborn, too, and begins to insist on his opinion. In the summer of 1887 he is not quite twenty and about to embark on his own university career. First there was Queen Victoria's Jubilee, celebrating fifty years of her reign, to attend, for which he was given a day off from school, as his father was intimately concerned with the arrangements and conducted the service of Thanksgiving at Westminster Abbey. Fred tells a story which, for once, shows the Archbishop in an amusing light. Edward had forgotten his security pass to the Abbey, and found his way barred by a polite but firm policeman. With what Fred assures us was an engaging smile, he told the man, 'They can't begin till I get there,' and all was well.[46]

The family spent summer of that year in the Lake District, where they saw their old friends the Wordsworths. Fred and Eustace were due at King's in October. Throughout that holiday, Fred dwelt upon his last day at beloved Marlborough and the touching farewell he had been accorded by one person in particular. He had gone to the station alone, and was waiting on the platform for the train to pull in. There, by the bookstall, was his dear tutor, A.H. Beesly, pretending to be there by chance, and idly leafing through newspapers. He merely nodded to Fred. The train arrived, and Fred mounted. The whistle sounded. Only then did Beesly manage a word. Coming to the carriage door, he said, 'Just came to see you off. Don't forget us all.'

4 Dodo

E.F. Benson began his career as an undergraduate of King's College, Cambridge, on 4 October 1887. His father accompanied him and saw him into his rooms, obviously proud that he had become a handsome, confident young man with the brightest prospects. Writing to his wife, the Archbishop reflected 'with what awful reverence should I have looked at the said son as a "swell" if he had been about in the same flesh 30 years ago.'[1] An ironic remark, in view of the flighty social life which Fred would one day embrace with relish, making him rather too much of a 'swell' for Papa's taste.

Eustace Miles joined Fred four days later, and the two friends plunged into the bizarre, privileged, archaic atmosphere of Cambridge, in which young men were lauded for their youth and encouraged to do absolutely nothing at all with the greatest possible style and *élan*. The colleges at that time were packed with eccentrics so English and so peculiar that they scarcely seem credible to anyone not familiar with the strange evolution of a donnish life. H.M. Mozeley, a Fellow of King's, denied himself the light of day until three minutes before five every afternoon, when he would emerge from his rooms to walk across the lawn to the famous chapel. Fred, looking out over his window-box, whistled. Mozeley stopped briefly, then continued. He whistled again, and Mozeley again stopped. The charade was repeated, until the old Fellow gave up and turned on his heels, preferring to forgo chapel rather than risk exposure to such misery.

The dons were not always so reclusive. J.E. Nixon was quite the opposite, gregarious to the point of mania, full of ideas and inventions (how to turn envelopes inside out and use them again, how to cut pencils without getting lead on one's fingers), thinking and moving at such speed that undergraduates gave up trying to understand what he was saying or what he would be doing next. Just as sociable was Oscar Browning, of whom it can for once truly be said that he became a legend in his own lifetime; Fred left a brilliant portrait of him in *As We Were*. Browning taught history, but knew little. He had the supreme merit of being interesting, so that it mattered not whether he was accurate (a trait bound to excite Fred's admiration). Though obese and almost immobile, he was such a snob that, as soon as it was known that a certain undergraduate at Trinity, H.R.H. The Prince of Wales, played hockey, he attempted to do the same so he could be sloshed across the shins by royalty. And he had a fatal weakness for beautiful young men. His archives have since demonstrated that he formed close, intimate friendships with scores of them, writing (and receiving) letters which pulsate with passion yet appear to have done nobody any harm. That dons condemned to exclusively male society should occasionally fancy young men was not considered, in itself, objectionable.

As Fred said, King's was 'rich in variations from type'. He wrote to his mother about one such, a Fellow called Mr Baynes. '[Eustace] Miles and I came down to dinner first, we both dressed, which don't seem extraordinary. Next enter Mr Baynes, not dressed, in shabby clothes that looked as if he had been wiping his hands upon them. He remarked "what unnecessary extravagance!" alluding to our dress-clothes. After waiting about one and a half seconds he proposed going into dinner without waiting for Sinclair. However, I suggested he [Sinclair] might be making himself unnecessarily extravagant also, and waited.'[2] It must be admitted there is a tone of pomposity about this observation.

Another Fellow was J.K. Stephen, of the supremely gifted Scottish family which would include Sir Leslie Stephen, editor of the *Dictionary of National Biography*, and Virginia Woolf. Quite apart from his having been suspected of being responsible for the Jack the Ripper murders in London's East End,[3] and his having died insane in 1892, J.K. Stephen is interesting for his membership of the Apostles and his indirect influence, thereby, upon Fred's literary career. The Apostles were an exclusive group of undergraduates, very intellectual and aesthetic. Arthur Benson had failed to be admitted to the club, but his close friend Harry Cust was a member. Cust, a younger son of Lord Brownlow, was one of the most strikingly handsome men of his age and an incorrigible philanderer. It is said that more than a dozen of the aristocratic families of today are descended from Harry Cust's extra-marital adventures. The Marchioness of Londonderry had an affair with him, as did the Duchess of Rutland, who gave birth to his daughter, Lady Diana Cooper. It was either Arthur or J.K. Stephen who introduced Fred to Harry Cust, and through him to a set of fashionable people who would afford him the subject of his first novel.

Fred was not himself a member of the Apostles (it is more than likely that his father would have forbidden such society), but he did join a literary club called the Chitchat, which met on Saturday evenings and discussed matters of literature based upon a paper presented by one of their number, and, more significantly, the Pitt Club. Founded in 1835 in order to cherish the memory of its eponymous politician, the University Pitt Club had long since abandoned any political colour and was essentially an exclusive, slightly aristocratic gathering of undergraduates whose sole purpose in meeting was to encourage conversation. Its modest premises included a library and a smoking-room, with the bookcase in the former under lock and key to prevent pilfering, and a rule in the latter against 'promiscuous smoking'. The U.P.C. installed a telephone in 1888, during Fred's membership, only nine years after the first telephone exchange was opened in London, and shortly after he left they added an electric light. But the chief attraction of the club was not so much its amenities as an atmosphere which encouraged relaxed intelligent gossip, and as such it prepared members for the more sophisticated gentlemen's clubs of London. Undoubtedly the Pitt Club played an important role in shaping E.F. Benson's habit of confident convivial chatter. He was elected easily, as M.R. James (of whom more anon) was made President in 1887 and personally backed his candidature. James later reminisced, 'The Pitt, undisturbed as it was by politics and debates, was a delightful refuge, even with its very modest capacities for nourishing the bodies and minds of its members.'[4]

At the end of 1887 Fred won an exhibition at King's, which

alleviated the financial burden and released his ambition to write for pleasure. With Roger Fry he started a new magazine, the *Cambridge Fortnightly*, destined to survive only five issues but none the less providing an outlet for his literary energies. He persuaded his brother Arthur to contribute an article under his pseudonym of Christopher Carr; his uncle Arthur Sidgwick wrote a piece in Greek; Oscar Browning wrote an obituary, and Fred himself was in all probability responsible for the parody on Henry James. When the magazine folded, Fred turned his attention to the short book he had started at school and had published in extract form in *The Marlburian*, with the intention of making it fit to appear in book form. This he achieved with very little agony, relying on that fatal facility which was to be at once the advantage and bane of all the Bensons in their writing, and published it privately in Marlborough in 1888, using the printers who had produced the school magazine. Entitled *Sketches from Marlborough*, it is not only the first but the rarest of all E.F. Benson titles, and was probably limited to little more than one hundred copies. The book is obsessed with sport and jollity, and is utterly free from mawkishness or romance.

Fred purposefully did not inform his father that he had written the book, as he anticipated, correctly, that he would be reproved for wasting time on frivolities. When the Archbishop found out, he chastised his son as gently as possible, and Fred felt guilty. Perhaps for that reason alone he did not attempt to write anything more for three years, although one cannot entirely imagine the wilful Fred wilting beneath parental rebuke at the age of twenty-one. It was more likely that he was simply having a wonderful time.

He confessed later that, like thousands of students before and since, he did almost no work and attended few lectures. But he made another important friend in M.R. James, who had preceded him at Temple Grove and gone on to Eton and Cambridge, and Fred was present at what was probably the first reading of James's ghost stories. His latent interest in the supernatural was quickened by this encounter, which would eventually lead to his writing scores of stories in the *genre* himself. That the interest was determined genetically is a curiosity which will need to be explored later. We have already seen that one of Fred's Sidgwick uncles founded the Society for Psychical Research. It is not generally known that the Archbishop, too, shared a fascination with ghosts, which were taken quite seriously in the mid-Victorian period. In his day at Cambridge he had been a member of The Ghost Society dedicated to the discussion of such phenomena.[5] There is even a family tradition that some kind of black magic was responsible for his father's seeking refuge in the church. Edward senior is said to have dabbled with two heavy crystal balls for the purpose of summoning up dark mysterious forces. He succeeded all too well, and was said to have been terrified by the horror of what was revealed to him. The two balls in question are still in existence, as no one would have the courage to throw them away; they sit undisturbed in a cold cupboard, with a crucifix nestling between them for protection.*

Edward asked M.R. James to keep a watch over Fred, whose character was so much less grave, earnest or responsible than dear Arthur's, yet he appears not to have minded the ghost-stories at all. Fred pretended to be worried about Hugh, now nearly seventeen, who struck up a friendship with a man who played about with mesmerism. 'He has not been able to mesmerise Hugh,' he said, 'so no harm has been done, but it is a silly thing to meddle with, and wastes time.'[7] How absolutely would Papa approve of this sentiment.

Fred had been moving about since his arrival at King's, first in lodgings, then in E1 on the ground floor of Gibbs's Building, finally to F rooms next door, in an elegant and bookish ambience. This was a suite of rooms for two, and Fred's fellow-tenant was a young man called Vincent Yorke whom he had known for nearly two years already. Yorke would one day be known merely as the father of Henry Yorke, who wrote novels of a singular, individual style under the name Henry Green and was for a while considered

---

* The author has seen and handled both the crystal balls and the crucifix, which are in a private house. It is probably this to which E.F. Benson alludes in *As We Were*, 'My grandfather . . . convinced that he too by means of astrology had acquired such knowledge as was not proper for men to attain to, burned his books likewise and devoted himself to more legitimate investigations into white lead instead of black magic.'[6]

the equal of Evelyn Waugh. But in 1889 he was a striking, tall, slender youth with an aristocratic bearing and manner which Fred found utterly beguiling, allied to the usual ostentatious athleticism. Fred had briefly fallen out with Eustace Miles, whom he suspected of having slandered him – 'I do not think I care at all, because I am ceasing to like him altogether.' (In fact, their friendship was to endure.) Vincent was something quite different. He is not mentioned in letters home, but he does occur in Fred's Diary, and perhaps only the canny Oscar Browning would discern why. Fred was quite simply in love with his companion.

One may only surmise the turmoil and anxiety caused by living in such proximity to one who excited real longing. 'I have put Vincent's letter next Risley's,' he wrote. 'I feel perfectly mad about him just now, but I hope and believe it will soon be all right. Ah, if only he knew, and yet I think he does. It is happier than all others, for I have no reason to regret anything.'⁸ Whether or not Vincent reciprocated the affection is not vouchsafed to us. It is enough to know that Yorke held Fred's heart for a season; it was he who joined Fred in tormenting poor Mr Mozeley, and he the only companion to be referred to by his Christian name.

Another student who came up to King's in October 1888 and whose acquaintance would prove potentially very damaging was Robert Ross, the friend of Oscar Wilde. Ross is known to posterity as Wilde's most loyal companion, who stood by him after his disgrace with great dignity and admirable courage, and shouldered the responsibility of protecting Wilde's reputation. But that is long into the future. When Ross came to King's he was a fresh-complexioned youth of nineteen, with 'the face of Puck', short, boyish, and charming. The grandson of the Governor General of Canada, and son of Canada's Attorney General, Robbie Ross had been brought up in England by his brother following his father's premature death. Before coming to Cambridge, he had already met and seduced the much older Oscar Wilde, and the two were currently in the midst of their early passion. The young Robbie was not famous for circumspection, and would not have made any secret of his liaison. Moreover, his tutor was Oscar Browning, who would have encouraged him to reveal all.

Ross stayed at King's only for a few months, during which time

Fred was involved in the so-called 'Outrage' when Ross was set upon by six rowdies and dunked in the fountain. The affair caused heavy meetings to be called and careers to be discussed, for one of the dons at King's was in collusion with the offenders. The crime was publicly denounced as 'cowardly' and 'rank'.[9] Fred was said to have been one of the six hearties, but he was evidently forgiven by Ross, for we find them dining together in adult life. Fred would soon meet Oscar himself, and be drawn perilously close to that vortex of indiscretion which eventually exploded into catastrophe.

At least a dozen of E.F. Benson's books are nostalgic attempts to recapture and retain the sweet pleasures of those years at Cambridge – youthful exuberance, and that feeling of rapture in the proximity of uncomplicated young men:

> They had been together, of course, and none except a pair of boys under some bond of perfect comradeship could have come sauntering up, still together, in such intimate content. A boy and a girl couldn't have done it, and a man and a woman even less; sex would have intruded with its disasters and consummations and intrigues.[10]

Holidays were always spent with the family, at Lambeth or Addington, or occasionally abroad. The summer of 1890 was especially gruelling for the Archbishop, as he had a fearsomely difficult and abstruse point of ecclesiastical jurisdiction to pronounce upon; known as the Lincoln Judgement, it was of huge importance to the Church, and of none whatever to everyone else, and Edward's implacable sense of duty drove him to devote Herculean energies to the task. He took the whole family to a tiny hotel on the Rieder Alp in Switzerland. It was so small that the Bensons and Professor Seely filled it completely. Edward took all his books and papers and worked alone in a sitting-room which could have graced a large doll's-house, writing the Lincoln Judgement,[11] while Fred climbed the Matterhorn. With Nelly he also climbed a lesser peak, but he was bolder when alone. Majestic Nature enthralled him, and he was still attracted by, and skilled at, manly outdoor sports. There was something very hearty about the young E.F. Benson which now seems to sit oddly with the creator of Lucia and Miss Mapp, but Fred's generation saw no conflict between physical prowess and poetic flight of fancy.

One curious incident on this holiday has been preserved. Fred and Hugh went out for a walk with their father. Hugh was in skittish mood, treading on Fred's toes and generally making a nuisance of himself. Fred finally reacted by poking Hugh very hard with his umbrella. Edward faced Fred and asked him why he had done that. 'Because I chose to,' said Fred in his most stubborn tone, whereupon his father slapped him in the face, with the remark, 'And I chose to do that!' It is a pointless little drama, but it vividly conveys something of the characters of all three players.[12]

Fred was home at Addington in October. There were some house-guests, among whom one in particular, Ethel Smyth, left her mark upon the family's collective temperament. She was not yet acknowledged as the fine musician and composer known to history, nor the angry champion of women's suffrage, but she was already formidable, strong in will and firm in argument. Ethel first grew attached to Minnie Benson, whose talent as a solver of problems was fast prostrating before her many tormented souls. Ethel was not exactly tormented, but she was troubled, and Minnie was a careful listener and wise counsellor. Ethel and Fred were at ease with one another all their lives, probably because Fred seldom took anything seriously enough to warrant an argument, but such was not the case with either the Archbishop or Maggie.

Edward's discomfort in the presence of Ethel Smyth cannot be attributed to any archaic impatience with women who held strong views; he had bred one in Maggie, and his wife was growing into one. It was rather her masculine manner which irritated him and made her seem, in his eyes, an affront to nature. There was a frost between them which became so severe that Ethel was for a time more or less banished from the Benson household, and we have already heard her admission that she found him utterly terrifying. As long as they avoided each other, some kind of *pax* was possible. 'We all realise that you and the Head of the Church are *not* two dewdrops destined to roll into one,' Minnie told her.[13] With Maggie it was altogether more difficult, firstly because Maggie was nurturing that crucifying jealousy which would one day ruin her, and she looked upon Ethel's friendship with her mother as an intrusion; secondly, because Maggie herself had a powerful intellect allied to an intolerant nature, and expected everyone to acknowledge the inherent superiority of her opinion. This was an acknowledgement Ethel was not predisposed to give, and there were many heated discussions at Lambeth and Addington which ended in acrimony. There survives a letter from Ethel to Maggie which makes vividly clear that she is not prepared to place herself before a Benson tribunal to have her ethical values marked. 'You are at war with everything that does not fit in with your own conceptions,' she told her. 'You *must* change your attitude as regards the whole side of life you ignore, ridicule, or condemn . . . I love discussion and comparison of ideals, but deny in toto any sort of supremacy of your ideal.'[14] Maggie could be very trying.

On the other hand, there was often much laughter at Lambeth in these days, for all the Bensons had grown into wits and satirists of one kind or another, fond of paradox, eagerly iconoclastic, and Ethel Smyth enjoyed being among them on such occasions. Her closest relationship within the Benson household was, however, with Nelly. They had been brought together by a shared passion for cricket, and this was soon replaced by passion of a more personal kind. Nelly had always been the least complex of the children, adventurous, resourceful, full of fun and mischief, an enemy of solemnity. 'Nobody could be morbid or haunted or unduly fanciful in Nelly's company,' wrote Arthur. 'Her humour and common-sense, and a power of almost complimentary ridicule, swept cobwebs away very swiftly.'[15] She was enormously obliging and had a heart large enough to embrace every forlorn creature who crossed her path, to such an extent that, after coming down from Oxford she devoted her life to the comfort and care of the poor, the distressed, the destitute. Nelly was not merely moved to pity by the sight of deprivation; she was moved to action. A book she wrote about her experiences among the poor, *Streets and Lanes of the City*, was privately printed and published, at her request, posthumously; had her writing been available to the public, she reasoned, it might cause embarrassment to the people she described.[16]

All Nelly's close friendships were with girls her own age, and her archives are replete with letters from those favoured as well as those less so, remonstrating with Nelly that she did not love them enough. Ethel Smyth came into her life in 1889 when Nelly was twenty-six, and for a year the mutual attraction was intense. Nelly giggled, Ethel sparked, the Archbishop glowered, Maggie smouldered. As for Fred, he was not in the least censorious, and would not have thought it mattered very much. As it happened, that Christmas Fred found himself alone for a few days with Nelly, as the others had all disappeared early for various reasons – Mother and Maggie on errands, Father to Lambeth, Hugh to Trinity, Arthur to Eton. Fred recounts how they played old games with Beth, pretending to be children again, larking about and generally passing their time in fond amusement.[17]

Shortly after Fred's return to Cambridge, he received a telegram from his mother begging him to come home quickly. He checked with Hugh at Trinity, who had received a similar wire. Nelly had contracted diphtheria and was dying. That she, the most light-hearted and carefree of them all, even arguably the one who had quietly made most of her life so far, that she should die prematurely was a blow which at last shook the Benson brothers out of their chilly self-control. Both Arthur and Fred relate the last days of their sister with compassion. The diphtheria had almost certainly been contracted in the East End, where Nelly had selflessly mingled with the afflicted. She knew she was dying, and wrote notes to every member of the family on paper which was smothered in disinfectant before being passed on, urging them to love and be patient. She asked the nurse if there was anything she could do to help. With a smile she told her father she wondered what it would be like. As her mother began reciting 'Jesu, lover of my soul', Nelly breathed her last.[18]

Ethyl Smyth was notified by letter. Carrying the paper slack in her hand, she walked into her mother's room and told her, whereupon her mother burst into tears. 'O poor, poor Mrs Benson,' she said.[19]

The funeral was held at Addington, where Nelly was buried.

Fortunately, Edward was so busy with duties at Lambeth that he had little time to ponder, and so did not suffer as much as he had when Martin had so intolerably been taken from him. One of his brothers died a few days later, and he was still deeply embroiled in the Lincoln Judgement. To the Bishop of Rupertsland he wrote that he was distracted, 'losing the dearest of daughters, and the most helpful of friends to the poor, though with a courage and sweetness that must ever lift me – then immediately losing a loved and honoured brother, and all this in the midst of most anxious and laborious work.'[20] Arthur and Fred took it hard, though neither knew quite how to show it. They went for a long walk together along a country road, in those days a most unusual occurrence. It was, said Arthur, 'a horribly dreary time' when they both 'tried to be cheerful'.[21] Arthur felt that night that he was about to die as well; it was a visitation which would plague him with increasing vehemence and regularity as the years progressed.

Thereafter, the family drifted apart, as if Nelly's sweet and playful nature had been their glue. They abandoned the lingering habits of childhood and never again, for example, wrote a joint Christmas story to be enacted around the tree after lunch. Fred said, 'With her death some unrecapturable magic was lost.'[22] That Christmas Fred was given the collected poems of Matthew Arnold by his mother, while Papa offered a more robust volume of Sacred Latin Poetry.

It was also at this time that Lucy Tait, unmarried daughter of the previous Archbishop of Canterbury, moved in with the Bensons and made her home with theirs. It was a perfectly logical step to take, for Lucy had worked very closely on parish work with Nelly and was anxious to continue it alone. Why not from the base at Lambeth Palace? Besides which, she had known the Bensons for such a long time that she was already almost one of the family. The Archbishop expected Lucy to be a daughter to Minnie and himself and a sister to Maggie. Yet it was not to be quite so simple. This seemingly innocent and unremarkable event, slipped in between the death of Nelly and the Lincoln Judgement, was in the long term to have the most severe repercussions. For

Lucy knew that Minnie was in danger of being rather too fond of her, and of taking Nelly's place in her affections.

Back at Cambridge, Fred coped with the nightmarish realisation which sooner or later every undergraduate must face – that examinations are approaching, and that one has done no work whatever to prepare for them. With Eustace Miles he settled down to dreary belated swotting, consigning to memory as many facts and allusions as his essentially lazy mind could absorb. M.R. James took him on a walking tour of Normandy and Brittany as a refresher,[23] and for the last paper in the Tripos he sat up all night doing the work of three years. 'I can't tell you how I have done in the Tripos because I don't know,' he wrote to his mother, adding somewhat aloofly, 'I don't feel any unusual bitterness towards the Examiners, which is on the whole a favourable sign.'[24] His Diary, about to be abandoned for good, frankly admitted, 'I have been very anxious and dispirited all this fortnight about Tripos.'

No doubt he was surprised when, a week or so later, he was awarded a First Class Honours degree, as was Eustace, and was further congratulated on his masterful grasp of his subject. The Archbishop was very pleased and urged Fred to stay at Cambridge another year and take a second Tripos. What he most desired, of course, was that one at least of his sons should take a theological degree and enter the Church. Arthur appeared content to be a beak at Eton, so perhaps Fred was destined for ordination? It is doubtful whether the Archbishop entertained this hope for long, as he must have known Fred was not cut out for piety. He did stay on at Cambridge, though, and chose to study Archaeology.

It would not be fair to suggest Fred's archaeological work was half-hearted, as he genuinely found the subject fascinating, and it bore some relation, at least in principle, to his beloved Ancient Greece. Yet his mind was working in other directions as well, and he was moving towards the idea that he might, possibly, make his living as a writer. The *Sketches from Marlborough* had whetted his appetite, and Arthur's modest success honed the competitive side of his character. During long vacations he had imagined a story with a maverick, unconventional heroine, which he had worked on with his sister Maggie at intervals. The resulting manu-

script did not satisfy him, so he had put it away for future reference. Now he returned to it and tried to give the story shape; it
evolved from being an amusement to being a serious contender
for publication. Thinking that he ought to discover whether he
had any talent to appeal beyond the undiscriminating audience of
Marlborough, he wrote a short story entitled 'Some Experiences
of a London Doctor', which he sent to *Blackwood's Magazine*
with an accompanying note, resembling every other note ever
composed by a hesitant author. 'I venture to send you a short
story,' he wrote, 'which I hope may be found suitable for your
columns.' Notwithstanding that the note was sent from Lambeth
Palace, with instructions the reply should be directed to King's
College, Cambridge, surely an unsubtle attempt to impress by one
or other address, the story was not found suitable, and the editor
returned it to Mr E.F. Benson with regrets.[25] Thereupon, Fred put
the manuscript of his embryonic book away in a drawer and
concentrated upon archaeology.

Almost immediately, his studies were a pleasure to anticipate
more than a chore to be endured, largely due to the happy chance
of another total eccentric as tutor. Professor Middleton conducted
his tutorials in a dressing-gown and skull-cap, leaving books
unopened and untouched as he extemporised on the civilisation of
Ancient Greece and infected Fred with his unbridled enthusiasm.
Lessons were conversations, anecdotes, chats about this and that
as the Professor produced a statue from his mantelshelf or an
object from his pocket and the glory of Greece was transmitted
through shared experience. Fred was rapt, and smitten with unim-
peachable love for all things Greek, a love which had been initiated
at Marlborough and confirmed at Cambridge. Thereafter he never
lost his appreciation for what he called 'the supreme race of all
who have inhabited this earth'.[26]

Fred duly gained his Tripos in Archaeology and an Open Scholarship at King's. He then went to Chester for six weeks' field
work, undertaking excavations which produced new evidence of
Chester's Roman past. Fred's purpose was to find Roman tomb-
stones which would indicate which legion had been posted there.
The City Council gave its approval and offered the assistance of
the city surveyor. So successful was the enterprise that Fred was

the first to prove the existence of a Roman legion so far north, and thus contributed to the *corpus* of studies into Roman Britain which we have inherited. He was congratulated on all fronts, and summoned by Mr Gladstone to come to Hawarden to expatiate on his researches. (Gladstone was by this time a close family friend, his relationship with the Archbishop being based upon mutual respect despite political division.)

Edward was interested in his son's achievement, but only distantly, as he was once more plunged into another affair of importance which required his intervention. This was the Tranby Croft scandal, which implicated the Prince of Wales in a tawdry tale of gambling, cheating, and the trivial honour of the upper classes. It paralysed the Royal Family and the ripples of its disgrace are felt even today. The Prince was moved to write to the Archbishop a letter of consummate hypocrisy. 'I have a horror of gambling,' he said, 'and should always do my utmost to discourage others who have an inclination for it – as I consider that gambling like intemperance is one of the greatest curses which a country could be inflicted with.'[27]

Minnie's fiftieth birthday fell at about the same time, and to this event Edward did pay the most touching attention. He presented her with a leather-bound copy of *The Imitation of Christ* by Thomas à Kempis, on 21 March 1891, suitably inscribed and dedicated. The book still exists, and offers yet more insight into Edward White Benson's strain of Christianity by virtue of the passages which are underlined in pencil. Whether he brought them to the attention of Minnie, or she spotted them as recognisable echoes of her husband's philosophy, is but a detail. They certainly convey the notion of the religious life as a vigilant war against a powerful enemy, and the most oft repeated verb is 'fight'. God is forever offering us chances to fight, by allowing us the temptation of sin, so that we may conquer and be triumphant. It is the idea of salvation through self-inflicted hardship which rings loudest, and quite the most unpleasant couplet to be underlined is from Chapter XXII, *Thoughts of the Misery of Man*:

> And, save you act with violence,
> You will not crush your sin.

Having grown up with this rather suspect masochism, it is little wonder that Fred threw himself with such joy into the arms of the pagan Greeks, with their tolerance, their adoration of the beautiful, their psychological maturity. Many years later, as an elderly man of letters, he was to write a biography of Alcibiades, the opening paragraph of which sings with the intense lyricism of discovery and delight which he had felt in 1892:

If we leave out of consideration the moral wealth bequeathed to the human race by the founders and the prophets of religion, no other spiritual endowment can compare with that which we have inherited from Hellenic culture. The sciences of philosophy and criticism, the arts of literature in all its branches, prose, poetry and drama, of sculpture in all its forms, from minute gem to colossal statue, of painting, of drawing, and of architecture, are among the cosmic bounties of that many-sided genius which blazed for a century and a half on the shores of Greece. In some of these manifestations of knowledge and art, subsequent generations and individual creators may claim to have approached that noble illumination, but in none can they claim to have outshone it in beauty or in clarity, and for the most part later ages and renaissances can only measure their achievements beside and far below the standard then set up, which, to our human perception, still seems flawless in temper and in execution. What, above all, characterised this age was its intellectual curiosity, its lucidity of expression and its love of beauty; by these instincts, freely and fearlessly pursued wherever they led, were fashioned those heirlooms which are the chiefest treasures of the human race.[28]

Or, as Maddox put it to David Blaize, the Athenians had the perfect physical and intellectual life. 'Oh David, let's save up and go to Athens.'[29]

It had long been an ambition of Fred's to see Greece for himself – an ambition fuelled by Beesly and fanned by Middleton. His chance came when the Archbishop decided to take his wife, his daughter Maggie and Lucy Tait on a pilgrimage to Algiers and Tunis. Fred would accompany them and then separate to go alone to Athens. It was a pilgrimage for Edward in particular, as he had for many years been writing a biography of St Cyprien, a labour of love to which he could devote only rare days of his incessantly frenetic life, and wanted to see Carthage with his own eyes. Fred described the joy on his father's features as he walked over what appeared to everyone else barren land devoid of interest, and reflected upon it later when he experienced the same *frisson* on his first view of the Acropolis.

The trip to Athens was not merely a holiday. Fred was to follow a course of study at the British School of Archaeology and take charge of the excavations at Megalopolis for a few months. The best work had already been completed, but he did manage to make some contribution worthy of a real archaeologist. To imagine E.F. Benson at this point in his life is a curious exercise. Extremely handsome, with cornflower-blue eyes which would melt many a dowager, athletic, muscular, witty in conversation, self-assured but a trifle remote and aloof, he was the son of the Archbishop of Canterbury and an accomplished archaeologist; there was as yet no hint of the prolific, observant and rather subversive novelist we now know. He was collecting experience and personalities, and on this first visit to Greece he had opportunities for both. His father's position made him *persona grata* in the highest society. Fred found himself mixing with the Greek royal family fairly frequently, which was not likely to cause him much anxiety. His already noticeable snobbery was tempered by an ease in company which made the royals themselves feel more comfortable. What they did not realise was that he was noticing their every foible, marking down their mannerisms, storing their characters for the future. King George, for instance, had the habit of rising on his toes and rocking back on his heels, so that conversation was conducted as if in mid-Atlantic; Fred adopted the same see-saw motion, which made the two of them look perfectly ridiculous together, but the King seemed not to be aware of it. Queen Olga, very grand indeed (being of the Russian Imperial Family), pushed ladies down with a rather rough punch so they could sit in her presence, and assumed she was doing them a favour.

Fred brought back some naughty little statues of satyrs and gods, only two inches high and, who knows, possibly excavated by himself, which are to this day among his personal effects inherited by others. If the first trip to Athens confirmed Fred's loyalty to Hellenic ideals, it did not, it seems, convince him that he should seek a permanent career in archaeology. He hankered after a career with the pen, and back in London he found the raffish, artistic, self-conscious society of *literati* much more to his taste than that of diggers and sifters. Oscar Wilde's first big success, *Lady Windermere's Fan*, had occurred while he was in Athens. The famous first night on 20 February 1892 has passed into theatrical legend. This was the occasion when Wilde was summoned to the stage after the last curtain by cries of 'Author!' and jauntily, even insolently, told the audience:

> 'Ladies and gentlemen, I have enjoyed this evening *immensely*. The actors have given us a *charming* rendering of a *delightful* play, and your appreciation has been *most* intelligent. I congratulate you on the *great* success of your performance, which persuades me that you think *almost* as highly of the play as I do myself.'

It was the first time an author had addressed the audience while smoking a cigarette, and the first time Wilde sported the famous green carnation. The whole of London society was present, including Lily Langtry and Oscar's wife, but also including a clerk at the Bodley Head called Edward Shelley, with whom Wilde afterwards spent the night at the Albemarle Hotel, and who would be called to give evidence against him three years later.[30]

Though Fred could not attend the first night, he went the day after returning to London, and took his mother with him. 'We went to the theatre last night and saw Lady Windermere's Fan by Oscar Wilde and were both most awfully amused,' Minnie wrote to Maggie, adding that she would sit through anything with Fred anyway. 'Fred is the *dearest* person and so delicious to have in the house.'[31] A week after this she was noticing how restless he seemed, and concluded, 'he is a perfect dear, but London doesn't suit him and he knows it and gets demoralized, for he can't settle and doesn't take enough exercise. Bless the darling!'[32] With hindsight, it is relatively easy to divine why he could not 'settle', for he was twenty-five, bouncing with energy and ambition, anxious for a literary career, but circumscribed by filial duty. When all of the brightest of literary London scintillated at the Café Royal, Fred behaved himself in the decorous gloom of Lambeth Palace. It would not be seemly for the Archbishop's son to collude with the literate but *louche* world of the Café Royal. It must indeed have been acutely frustrating for him.

Fred rescued from the drawer the novel he had abandoned before going to Athens. With the best motives, his mother had shown it to one of her new and devoted friends, no less than Henry James himself (who had stayed at Lambeth Palace in 1890), and sought his opinion and advice. He cannot have been too pleased, for successful writers are forever having dumped upon them heavy packets of time-swallowing banality, and Fred's manuscript was in addition very untidy. He described it as 'a long and crabbed MS., roughly and voluptuously squirted on to the paper.'[33] He did not, after all, expect it to be read by so illustrious a critic. James replied to Mrs Benson with consummate grace. 'It is charming to hear you on so interesting a topic,' he wrote. Naturally he would look at the story, but he warned that he was 'deplorably fastidious'.[34] To Fred himself he wrote some long and 'brilliantly evasive' letters about the book, chiding himself with being 'corrosively critical' and praising the story, ever so faintly, as being 'lively'. 'Hew out a style,' wrote James. 'It is by style we are saved.'[35] Fred drew the unhappy conclusion that he needed saving, and years later confessed that 'never by any possibility could that MS. have seemed to [Henry James] worth the paper it was written on'.[36]

Following Athens, and with all London gossiping about Oscar Wilde's frothy confection, Fred felt the urge to try again, and this time asked his mother's friend Mrs Harrison, who wrote under the name 'Lucas Malet', to see if anything could be salvaged from his work. (It is interesting that Minnie chose the enormously highbrow Henry James, while Fred, who knew at what level his writing truly belonged, pitched much more correctly with Lucas Malet). She advised him to cut here and there, develop character, write a second volume, and be clear about his central theme, or *idea*. 'The idea should be like the thread on which beads are strung. It shouldn't show, except at the two ends; but in point of fact it keeps the beads all together and in their proper relation.'[37]

This was much more useful counsel, and Fred accepted it. He wrote his second volume, and honed the central character, a witty young woman in high society, beautiful, wilful, direct and utterly heartless, in such a way that her personality is revealed through her speech, thus obviating the need for too much analytic description. The finished manuscript was sent, at Lucas Malet's suggestion, to Methuen, who immediately accepted it for publication. In this way was *Dodo* born and E.F. Benson's life transformed.

While it is true that many people now find *Dodo* almost unreadable, that is not because it is badly written, but because the subject is unrecognisable to modern eyes. The characters seem arch and artificial, their manner ridiculous and their speech contrived. One wonders why the author should invent such preposterous people. This is entirely to misunderstand the historical context, for Fred was not really inventing people at all, but, as with all his work, observing them, and the atmosphere of privilege, of self-conscious posing, and of intellectual brittleness, was lifted from a very prominent group of friends known to themselves and outsiders as 'The Souls'. (In *Dodo* Fred calls them the 'apostles'). 'The Souls' were rich, aristocratic, sparkling, more interested in poetry than hunting and shooting, highly intelligent and well-placed. They included such eventually powerful men as A.J. Balfour and H.H. Asquith, both to be Prime Minister; George Curzon, future Viceroy of India; George Wyndham and Harry Cust, Arthur Benson's friend. It is almost certainly through Harry Cust that Fred knew about 'The Souls'.

The women of the set were Lady Desborough, mother of the poet Julian Grenfell, Lady Elcho, Lady Aberconway, and Margot Tennant, who would one day become Margot Asquith, then Lady Oxford. They were all vivacious, socially accomplished, smart and whimsical; not for them the dreary duties of a country housewife – all grace and no substance. These were brilliant women, able to hold their own in any conversation, and as likely to talk philosophy as fantasy. They were much talked of in their day, and their parties were considered an education in themselves. 'The Souls' rose to prominence about 1887 and remained a force in society until the First World War. Thus, when Fred was writing *Dodo*, they were relatively fresh and young. What he would have noticed most was their fierce anti-Philistinism, of which he approved, and the habits of speech which they evolved to distinguish themselves from the common run of boring aristocrats, which he found gloriously amusing if rather silly. The weather could not simply be fine, it had to be 'wholly blissfully ideally delicious'. A lady who was feeling miserable was described as 'utterly utterly'. There was the occasion when Lady Desborough asked her dour, unsmiling butler to telegraph an acceptance to an invitation. Though not effusive himself, he could adopt his employer's style when necessary, and so worded the cable, 'YES HOW PERFECTLY WONDERFUL LOVE LOVE LOVE'. Unfortunately the invitation had been to attend a meeting of the Thames Conservancy Board.[38]

There are pages of such extravagant language in *Dodo*. Mrs Vane tells Jack, for example, that Dodo 'is simply expiring to see you'.[39] Lest there be any doubt, Fred departs from his conversation-only rule to explain to the reader that his heroine was prone to contrived exaggeration, and we recognise immediately a description of Soul-speak: 'When she wished to do honour to a melancholy occasion, for instance, her vivacity turned any slight feeling of sorrow she had into hysterical weeping; when the occasion was joyful, it became a torrent of delightful nonsense.'[40] Though Fred's book was meant to be an entertainment, and succeeded as such, there is an edge of criticism in these remarks, of pointing the finger at hypocrisy, which was to cause Fred some difficulty when the great search began for the source model of Dodo herself.

While capturing and mocking Soul-speak (and after publication London was alive with the affectation of Dodo-speak, a kind of artless prattle combining the charm of a child with the wit of an adult, which amounted to the same thing), Fred also tried to emulate the style of the current literary hero Oscar Wilde, with pithy paradox and antithesis, balances and *bons mots*. For instance, Mrs Vivien says, 'My dear Dodo, I should never venture to be shocked at anything you did. You are so complete that I should be afraid to spoil you utterly, if I tried to suggest corrections.'[41] Fred would improve upon his Wildean fancies as his career progressed, but he never really acknowledged their obvious inspiration in the outrageous Irishman himself.

Fred went back to Athens for a further course with the British School of Archaeology, and was thus absent when *Dodo* appeared in May 1893. He clearly did not expect much attention, or he would have made an effort to be in London to enjoy his moment of triumph. Minnie wrote to him on the day of publication, *'Dodo is out!* Your father had the first copy and has positively read some of it!' She seemed as amused as anyone that Edward should give time to such frivolity, but a week later she wrote again, proving from the beginning that she was to be Fred's most implacable critic. 'I think it cleverer than I even thought, but I also am afraid the blots are more crude than I thought too.'[42] In private conversation later, she confided that the characters did not develop and did not always ring true.

Never mind. The public pounced upon Fred's first book, as they will sometimes for mysterious reasons which have nothing to do with either inherent value or publicity. *Dodo* sold out within a month. The second edition appeared in June, with an acceleration of three more editions in July, two in August and two in October. No fewer than twelve editions were published in under a year. Fred returned from Athens to find himself a celebrity, his book a sensational bestseller. Lord Halifax told the Archbishop that everyone was talking of nothing but *Dodo*, which must have perplexed him, especially as it was said to be 'most diverting'. The President of the Society of Authors welcomed Fred to their ranks and congratulated him on his achievement. 'People are all talking about it, which is the only proof, real proof, of success.'[43] At Addington Park, the whole family of Bensons celebrated with a rollicking party in which they dressed up as Indians, in warpaint, and danced like madmen. Even Edward joined in.[44]

If people were talking about Fred's book, more specifically they were speculating on the identity of its outrageous heroine, and within days the consensus view was that Dodo was none other than Margot Tennant, one of the striking daughters of Glasgow industrialist Charles Tennant. Margot was vivacious, quirky, electric, with an embarrassing habit of saying whatever was in her mind before weighing the consequences. Thereby she was liable to offend unwittingly, or at the very least amuse with repartee which threw up the most amazing metaphors and unexpected allusions. Just as Balfour was the male core of 'The Souls', so Margot was their undisputed female mascot, a woman to galvanise every company she joined with her maverick wit and intoxicating *badinage*. Moreover, she possessed such self-confidence that she was indifferent to opinion.

Fred had met Miss Tennant the year before, when his brother Arthur had introduced her to the family. Fred was entranced by her, and completely captivated by her wild, theatrical manner and apparently unconscious verbal tricks. She was unlike any woman he had ever encountered, a rocket soaring above the multitude. It was inevitable that she should inform his writing in some way, but was it true that the unconscionable, rather dreadful Dodo was an actual portrait of Margot? Clearly, Fred did not anticipate the huge success of his novel, and must have assumed in the ordinary way that it would sell modestly and hardly be noticed. Now that it had become the talking-point of the moment, he was deeply embarrassed by his pretty obvious impertinence, and absolutely denied that the character of Dodo had anything to do with Miss Tennant at all. To the end of his life, he could not bring himself to confirm the identification.

Dodo is described in the book thus:

Her method is purely to be dramatic, in the most unmistakeable way. She is almost always picturesque. She seems to say and do anything that comes into her head, but all she says and does is rather striking. She can accommodate herself to nearly any circumstances. She is never colourless; and she is not quite like anybody else I have ever met. She has an immense amount of vitality, and she is almost always doing something. She is beautiful, unscrupulous, dramatic, warm-hearted, cold-blooded, and a hundred other things.[45]

It would be difficult to imagine a more succinct, and on the whole flattering, depiction of Margot Tennant than this. But there were other passages which pointed up the arid selfishness of her emotions, and these were to cause Fred more trouble. Dodo has no understanding of love, except that it makes people do ridiculous things, like writing absurd sonnets. She admits that she likes wealth and success, society and admiration, and holds no higher ideals. She does know what ideals are, but is content to do without them, though she does not mind if other people wish to waste their time aiming for something better than self-indulgence.

> I cannot accept ideals that I don't feel [she says]. I can understand them, and I can sympathize with them, and I can and do wish they were mine; but, as nature has denied me them, I must make the best of what I have.[46]

Worst of all, Dodo's attitude towards the very idea of childbirth and motherhood is callous.

> Dodo had a deep-rooted dislike of ugly things, unless they amused her very much. She could not bear babies. Babies had no profile, which seemed to her a very lamentable deficiency, and they were not nearly so nice to play with as kittens, and they always howled, unless they were eating or sleeping.[47]

Moreover, Dodo made notes about people and passed them around her friends, in a kind of pre-Freudian game of character-analysis. So did Margot Tennant.

Miss Tennant's defenders were horrified. Years later Sir Henry Lunn chastised Fred for depicting Margot as a wicked mother and adulteress when she was in fact quite the opposite, and accused him of cowardice for not making a public announcement that his creation was no more than a caricature.[48] Lady Emily Lutyens opined that Mr Benson deserved 'a good kicking', and the Rev. Whitwell Elwin chided the author for letting the Church down. 'If I were the son of the Archbishop of Canterbury I hope that I should consider that my genealogy, in my father's lifetime, ought to keep me from proceedings in contradiction to the spirit of his office and teaching. Indifferent as I might be to disgracing myself, I would not recklessly discredit him.'[49] This was a view commonly held in the summer of 1893. The outraged cleric went beyond his brief when he further attacked the book's literary value. 'The author's knowledge of human nature is only skin-deep,' he wrote, 'and almost as limited in extent as in depth. There is some cleverness in the book, but to my mind it is of a low order, and of a kind so little desirable that the writer would be a more respectable person without it.'

At a ball, the Prince of Wales addressed Margot as 'Miss Dodo', and so closely did the identification cling that some years later, when Asquith was about to become engaged to her, Lord Rosebery felt obliged to warn him with the words, 'My dear Asquith – I advise you to read *Dodo* if you have not already done so – there's a great deal of truth in it.'

And what of Margot herself? Was she resentful, angry, hurt? She professed not to notice. A contemporary story held that Fred had written to apologise for the publicity which had pursued her as a result of his book, to which she replied, 'Dear Mr Benson, have you written a novel? How clever of you', which was a perfect Tennant rejoinder. To others, she was less controlled. To Betty Lytton she confided, 'If young Benson did but know the harm he had done me with that book – not that I mind what he says about my character, but I am so sick of hearing of it, it is so stupid and vulgar.'[50] When she married Asquith, he was the only person never to allude to Fred's heroine, as he knew she was secretly tired of being teased over it. In her memoirs, she passed over the matter in cursory fashion, pointing out that so accurate was the description of her sitting-room in the novel that Fred must have had her in mind, but she does not admit to being wounded. With splendid accuracy she wrote that Dodo was 'a pretentious donkey with the heart and brains of a linnet'.[51]

Such was the level of gossip in London two months after publication that Arthur Benson made a special journey from Eton to call upon Margot and apologise for Fred's indiscretion. On 12 July she wrote Arthur a gracious letter:

I do not like you to be so distressed on my account and you may be quite sure I shall never be tired of your family or not be anxious and happy to welcome you. As far as Dodo is concerned I find life so complicated that I could have wished this sort of accident had not occurred. If the book had had more intellectual merit I should get less tired of being talked to about it – but I am *not angry* with your brother, for I think many people might have done the same thing – it may even do me a good turn for perhaps the readers of Dodo of which there are many may find when they come to know me that with many faults I am not quite as selfish or irreverent as they had supposed.[52]

Gracious certainly, but at the same time a devastating comment upon the reputation Fred had so quickly earned for himself. It was clear that nobody thought *Dodo* had any intrinsic worth – it was a bestseller but not a literary event. Members of Margot's family confirm she found it bothersome to be calumniated by an essentially trivial book. Fred, they thought, had 'let the side down' in a distinctly unfriendly and silly manner.* Asquith himself appears to have harboured more serious resentment.

Fred had less trouble with the other most easily identifiable character. Edith Staines, who smoked after tea, who wore her hat rakishly pushed to the side of her head, whose hair looked as if hairpins had fallen out, whose boots were large, unlaced and dirty, whose hands were black with smoke and oil, this was the formidable feminist and musician Dame (though not yet) Ethel Smyth. The initials, the habits, the character, all left no room for doubt. Fred even dared to be sarcastic about her, through spiky comments made by Dodo: 'You know she's doing a symphony, and she has to smoke to keep the inspiration going.' Dodo teases Edith about her vanity. 'Did you ever play the game of marking people for beauty, and modesty, and cleverness, and so on?' she asks her. 'We played it here the night before you came, and you didn't get a single mark from anybody for modesty.' Fred went so far as to have Edith boast about her fickleness, which in view of her variously intense and difficult relationships with Minnie, Nelly and Maggie, was almost treacherous. 'You know I get frightfully attached to some one about three times a week, and after

---

* At the time of writing, almost 100 years after the publication of *Dodo*, there are two surviving sisters of Margot Asquith: Lady Wakehurst DBE (91), and Baroness Elliott of Harewood, DBE (88).[53]

that never think of any of them again. It isn't that I get tired of them, but somebody else turns up, and I want to know him too.'[54]

As it happened, Ethel trusted Fred and remained true to him in friendship all her life, so she was not at all hurt by the parody. On the contrary, so perverse was she, and so proud of being different, that she thought Edith Staines was the one decent character in the book. *Dodo* also earned for her an unexpected and not entirely welcome reconciliation with the Archbishop, of whom she had always been wary, and who did not approve of her 'style'. Ethel found herself summoned to dinner at Lambeth Palace, and as she entered, Edward himself rushed forward to greet her, put up with her irritating use of the adverb 'awfully' with every sentence, petted and spoilt her as he had never done. Minnie explained later that he was worried she might have been upset by the book, and wanted to apologise on his son's behalf for so lamentable a lapse in taste.[55]

Fred would have us believe that he did not think much of *Dodo*. He called it 'hideously crude, blatantly inefficient', claimed he had scribbled it out in a few weeks, and that there was no plot, 'merely a clash of minor personalities breaking themselves to bits against the central gabbling figure'.[56] That harsh judgement, however, was delivered by Fred the mature man of letters nearly thirty years later. In the year of his death he was to look back with yet more dismissive scorn. The success of *Dodo* had been a disaster for him; 'it made me think that all I had to do was to keep up my interest in life and dash off stories with ease and enjoyment.'[57] That, alas, was precisely what he was to do for a number of years. But at the time *Dodo* appeared and created such a fuss, Fred was naturally rather pleased with himself. He was justified in reflecting that he had scored a hit. He sent a copy to Edmund Gosse, the distinguished critic and essayist who had been Clark lecturer in English Literature at Trinity College when Fred was at Cambridge, and who would in 1907 write the seminal autobiography *Father and Son*. Arthur Benson had taken Gosse to stay at Addington the year before, so Fred was already an acquaintance. When he received a note of praise, his reply bubbled with happiness:

Your letter *was* encouraging, and it really is a great relief to me to find that you do not agree with all that has been said about it. And half the people who liked the book liked it for the wrong things, and it is wholly delightful to find that you not only like it, but like it for those things which led me to write it. I really intended when reviews of the book began to appear to try to digest them and profit by them, but I have given it up as a bad job . . . the majority misunderstood what I meant.

Fred returned the compliment, by buying a copy of Gosse's essays *Questions at Issue* and writing him a letter in suitably grave terms, as befitted the correspondence of one author with another. He discussed the work of Zola, the champion of Naturalism in France, averring that there were no limits to the scope of realism in literature. 'Surely beauty is capable of realistic treatment just as much as ugliness, with which Zola . . . is chiefly concerned. Can you conceive of anything beyond realism at its best; it is easy to say "mysticism", but what on earth is mysticism, except the realistic treatment of the emotional side of man?' This is confused, to say the least, and does not reveal much grasp of literary theory. At least it is an early indication of E.F. Benson's desire to describe people as they are and not as they would like themselves to be. Fred savoured his instant insubstantial success, as anyone would, yet he wanted to be an intellectual. Having thrown in another quotation from Pierre Loti, he finishes his letter to Gosse with an endearing apology. 'I wonder how foolish all this appears to you,' he says. 'Remember I am very young.'[58]

Later that year Fred accompanied his sister Maggie on a trip to Greece and Egypt. It was the second time he had been to Greece within six months, but he was still officially an archaeologist and had work to complete in Athens. He arranged his dates to suit Maggie, who was showing signs of peevishness and wanting attention. Throughout his life Fred would always be the one to come to the rescue, obligingly to subordinate his plans to others' if it made life easier. At Athens they were, as Maggie put it, 'quite hand in glove' with the Royal Family. Maggie and Fred contrived a farce called 'The Duchess of Bayswater' for an audience of English governesses and residents, with Maggie as the Duchess. Sailors from the British Mediterranean fleet joined in the audience, as did the entire Greek royalty. It was all quite ridiculous, but proved yet again that English satire does not export easily; the Queen asked Maggie if the British aristocracy really behaved like that. It also gave a glimpse of Fred at his most playful, for he was a superb mimic and not at all worried about making a fool of himself. The King told him he should go on the stage, preferably in broad comedy. 'Fred has made quite a reputation as a comic actor here,' wrote Maggie.[59] He also showed his petulant side when he and Maggie were kept standing while the Royal Family were engaged in private colloquy.

Fred spent many leisure hours with a new friend whose sense of fun matched his, Reggie Lister, a diplomat at the British Legation and only two years older than Fred. The third son of the third Baron Ribblesdale, Reggie was connected by marriage to the Tennants, as his brother married Charty (Charlotte) Tennant, sister of Margot. That may well have been the excuse for their meeting in the first place. Be that as it may, Fred was charmed by Reggie, whose enthusiasm about everything was infectious. The two men spent hours together in museums, dined together, went off in boats together, and Reggie was to become a lifelong friend, despite a career which took him to Berlin, Paris, Constantinople, Copenhagen and Rome. He would often visit the Benson family, who liked him unreservedly and gave him a roaring welcome.[60]

Another friend, and not one who ever visited the Benson family, was the worryingly handsome blond poet Lord Alfred Douglas, currently embroiled in his disastrous relationship with Oscar Wilde. He stayed for a week in Fred's rooms in Athens, but we know nothing of any outings they may have made together.[61]

Fred and Maggie went on to Egypt and stayed at the very grand Luxor Hotel. Among the other guests were Lord and Lady Albemarle; Lord and Lady Charles Beresford (with whom Fred would become especially close, writing about Lady Charles more than once in his non-fiction); Lord Alfred Douglas again; and a seventeen-year-old future novelist called Robert Hichens. They frequently all dined together at one long table, but during the day they went their separate ways. Tantalisingly, we know that the three young men – Fred, Lord Alfred, and Hichens – went off together up the Nile, but we do not know they discussed anything more than the Pyramids. It is impossible to believe Wilde and his habits did not come into the conversation somewhere; gossip about Wilde and Douglas was reaching its peak. Later in the holiday they were joined by Reginald Turner, the 'boy-snatcher', who would figure prominently in the scandal to come.

Hichens tells us that Fred was tanned and athletic, and already an accomplished skater (heaven knows why he should have noticed this – there cannot have been much opportunity for Fred to skate in Egypt). He envied Fred's success coming at such an early age; he seemed to have everything – fame, position, money, beauty. His conversation was more enjoyable than his books, said Hichens, and he and Lord Alfred 'got on marvellously together, the wit of the one seeming to call out and polish the wit of the other'. As for Maggie Benson, Hichens perceptively notes that 'I never met anyone else so quick to notice a flaw in an argument as she was.'[62] Brother and sister were both, in their different ways, argumentative.

By the time they returned to Egypt, Fred was an author with two books to his credit. The second, a collection of short stories entitled *Six Common Things*, enjoyed none of the *succès fou* which had attended *Dodo*, and it is not difficult to see why. The stories are moralistic, in that they are designed to make a point, to teach, to prompt reflection, and Fred was not a mature enough writer to attempt such a task. Some stories are directly lifted from Fred's own childhood memories; others seem preoccupied with death and deprivation. The Archbishop was said to have approved of this book most heartily, although he detected in one of the stories some dissatisfaction with the divinely-ordained class structure of England, which bordered on heresy.[63] He was thinking of the governess Miss Huntingford who dared to complain of her arrogant treatment at the hands of Miss Grantham. Much more important to us is the character of Miss Grantham, who dimly anticipates the kind of sharp female selfishness which E.F. Benson would make famous: 'Miss Grantham went on with an infernal sweetness of manner, unable to deny herself the pleasure of making a scene even at the expense of a governess.'[64]

Nevertheless, whatever else Fred would produce, for the generation of 1893 he would forever be the author of *Dodo*. Indeed, it immediately became his nickname, and many of his correspondents were still addressing him as 'Dear Dodo' some thirty years later. The Archbishop was sometimes irreverently called 'Dodo's Papa'.

5   Independence

Minnie was very happy to have Fred back home, frequently referring to how 'good' and 'nice' he was, how gently he behaved with
his father, and what jolly company he provided. He also looked
wonderful. When he went for a medical check-up, advisable after
exposure to Egypt, Mama reported that the doctor said 'what
magnificent health Fred was in, "like an Apollo" he said, in the
perfection of his muscles. Lor!'[1]

Within weeks, Fred renewed the acquaintance he had made on
the Nile with Lord Alfred Douglas, who introduced him to Oscar
Wilde in June 1894. Wilde presented Fred with a copy of his
very rare and controversial book *The Sphinx*, inscribed 'To E.F.
Benson, with the compliments of the author, Oscar Wilde'.
Limited to two hundred copies, *The Sphinx* needed to lurk in
obscurity, for its pagan and homosexual themes artfully mingled
with Christianity made it decidedly 'decadent' in the fashion of
the day, and appearing at the very time that mad Lord
Queensberry (Alfred Douglas's father) was being taunted to distraction by Wilde's impudent defiance, it would have been a
dangerous provocation had the book been widely available.
Shortly afterwards, Douglas gave Fred a copy of Wilde's even
rarer *Salome*, limited to a mere one hundred copies. Wilde had
written it in French and dedicated it to Douglas, who translated
it into English. With illustrations by Aubrey Beardsley to add to
the spice, *Salome* was soon notorious enough to be banned in
England. It is indicative of the relative closeness of their friendship
that Douglas signed his presentation copy with both their nicknames, 'To Dodo from Bosie'.[2]

There is a delicious piquancy in the juxtaposition of events, that
while Fred was enjoying the company of this amusing, intelligent

but definitely *louche* society, his younger brother Hugh, now twenty-two years old, was taking Holy Orders. Edward was relieved that at least one of his sons should join the Church, and it was wholly appropriate that it should be Hugh, the most innocent and naïve, the one who had been spoilt in compensation for the cruelly early death of Martin. The Archbishop had long surrendered hope for Arthur, old before his time, or Fred, apparently captive to frivolity. If Fred had felt any pressure to conform to paternal expectations, which had been unlikely since Cambridge days, the pressure was finally lifted when Hugh was ordained.

Minnie began to fret that Fred was lacking direction, that he needed a job or at least something to do, but to suggest he was leading a life entirely devoted to amusement is unfair. He produced two learned papers for the *Journal of Hellenic Studies* which were so well received they were republished as pamphlets; one was an archaeological and historical analysis of Aegosthena, the easternmost bay of the Gulf of Corinth, the other a study of a fourth century Head in the Central Museum of Athens. Both came out in 1895. Of far more interest to us is an article he wrote for the *Contemporary Review* in July of that year on a literary subject with strangely prescient echoes. In it, he starts by telling the reader that the attempts of biographers to illumine the work of artists by dwelling upon their personal habits is futile (a view he will overturn forty years later in his biography of Charlotte Brontë), then goes on to talk about the sad aberrant gene in the family of Charles Lamb:

> [Lamb's] sister . . . was liable to fits of madness, in one of which she killed her own mother. Later on these fits were preceded by some warning, and she would go voluntarily with her brother to the asylum before they obtained complete mastery over her. A friend of the Lambs has related how on one occasion he met the brother and sister, at such a season, walking hand in hand across the field to the old asylum, both bathed in tears.[3]

Quite apart from this being a rather moving image, it is also a personal one, and the first time, so far as I am able to discover, that E.F. Benson mentions the subject of inherited madness. It is another mark of Benson reticence that he would never use the word when referring to the misfortunes that befell his own flesh and blood, although he must have reflected upon their source and, when he was writing about Lamb, he would have witnessed the first distressing signs of them. His father had always been prone to melancholia, and we have seen that Minnie pleaded with him to seek the help of medical men to combat what she was certain was a disease. Arthur, though respectful in his diary, is initially much more hostile, ascribing his father's moods to sulking and petulance. Edward was 'unscrupulous, bringing in higher motives to make people do as he liked, and talking pathetically about other people's selfishness, when it was only a question of two alternatives, one of which he did not happen to care for.'[4] The Archbishop longed to be surrounded by love and joy, yet was unable to see that enjoyment could not be compelled, and when thwarted in his desire he was convinced that everyone was doing wrong. Thus justified, he would revert to his black moods of despair at the essential sinfulness of humankind.

Arthur himself was not free from the taint, and in 1895 began to feel renewed stirrings of that 'black dog' which would eventually make his life a misery. As yet it was faint and mysterious. He told his mother that he was suffering from 'a peculiar nervous condition the discomfort of which I can hardly describe'.[5] As the years went on the condition hardened, and he would expend much of his energy on the attempt to describe it.

Then there was Maggie, who suffered from pain at the temples and head and was liable to throw herself into a temper with very little provocation. In Athens she had suffered what was euphemistically called an 'attack', and it had befallen Fred to coax her back into self-control, a task he had undertaken with a ready heart. Minnie had written to him that he was 'a son who inherits his mother's propensities in some things',[6] a reflection which was looking more and more true as they stood together against the illnesses which threatened the rest of the family. To Maggie she wrote, with mock hilarity which in the circumstances was perhaps ill-judged, 'Oh *do* be *normal*,' and '*PUL-EASE* do what is best.' Maggie had been told by someone that she was a disagreeable sort of person, and had brooded upon an insult which she might earlier have dismissed as pointless. Her mother begged her not to distress her 'blessed little mind' over it; *she* didn't – 'I larf, I dew.'[7]

When Maggie returned to London she was sent to consult the eminent gynaecologist Dr Mary Scharlieb, which suggested her trouble might be more physical than psychological, but the diagnosis was vague – 'congestion, dilation, displacement'.[8] In her diary in 1896, Minnie confided that she had endured the anxiety about Maggie for three years, together with anxiety about Edward and, for good measure, irritation with Lucy Tait as well. Lucy worked hard among the poor, as had Nelly, and like many martyrs longed for her martyrdom to be acknowledged. She chided Minnie with lack of sympathy for herself or for the poor and, more ominously, began to show authority in the household at Lambeth: '[Lucy] was didactic and I was unkind and huffy,' wrote Minnie. 'She laid down the law.'[9] That was precisely the characteristic of Miss Tait which would eventually break the Benson family apart.

Pathetically, through all this Minnie is wont to blame herself. If only she was less self-indulgent, less fond of comfort, had more humility, and so on – 'oh how often would things have been better if I had held my tongue three minutes more.'

Fortunately, Fred gave no cause for worry, apart from an excessive fondness for whisky and wine; this gave rise to quarrels with the abstemious Archbishop which made Fred furious at first, though all was generally resolved in humorous fashion. When he went to stay with Lady Henry Somerset he had to conceal his bottle; he told Bishop Talbot 'how in that unalcoholic hospitality I secretly purchased a bottle of whisky for private consumption, and how Lady Henry shouted with laughter when in a conscientious fit I confessed.'[10]

There is no evidence whatever that the scandal which consumed Oscar Wilde and Fred's friend Lord Alfred Douglas in 1895 reverberated within the walls of Lambeth Palace, although it would be impossible to believe that they never discussed it. Minnie was no stranger to these delicate matters. Two of her closest friends were sisters – Adeline, Duchess of Bedford and Lady Henry Somerset, daughters of the redoubtable Lady Somers who was one of the fabulously beautiful Pattle sisters. Lord Henry Somerset, a son of the Duke of Beaufort, had been driven out of the country in

1879 when his interfering mother-in-law broadcast his love for a
seventeen-year-old boy. Ten years later his brother, Lord Arthur
Somerset, was implicated in the Cleveland Street scandal revolving
around the use of a male brothel in central London. Thus Wilde's
dilemma was not as novel as some of those in court liked to
pretend, and Mrs Benson would certainly have known what it was
all about. If she or her husband remonstrated with Fred about his
friendship with such people, all references to their discussions
have disappeared.

In later years Fred distanced himself from Wilde and his disgrace, managing deftly to express compassion and disapproval
with the same voice. Wilde's second trial was a 'savage stupidity',
since the man was already ruined after the first. His 'poor tortured
soul' produced one of the finest ballads in the language, yet his
prose suffered from 'tawdry glitter'. Wilde's tastes were not 'ordinary', his appetites 'uncontrollable' (is it fair to read into this
choice of word an implication that Fred's appetites were strictly
controlled?). And here the pious and the forgiving combine: 'the
slime of intemperance and perverted passions gathered upon him
again, till the wheels of his soul were choked with it. No decent
man can feel anything but sheer pity and sympathy for one so
gifted and so brittle and withal so lovable.'[11]

Immediately after the Wilde trials there was a panic of emi-
gration from the country by frightened or prudent homosexuals.
One such, who settled in Capri, was an interesting but indolent
poet called John Ellingham Brooks. He will bring a tangent upon
Fred's story a little later.

At the same time, Arthur was relishing his friendship with
Henry James, whose letters to him are maddeningly elliptical.
While it is possible to suppose their florid, perfervid style is
Jamesian rhetoric, some of the phrases he employs merit a stab at
bewildered reflection. 'I am divided between two sensations,' he
tells Arthur, 'panting for tomorrow p.m. or blushing for all the
hours of all the past days', and he signs off, 'Yours almost uncon-
trollably'. A couple of months later he is talking of 'an indestruc-
tible tenderness' and lamenting the passage of time which keeps
him and Arthur apart:

We are in truth both victims of our devouring age, and if I can pick your bones before the last scrap of you – and of me – is gobbled up, I suppose I shall be entitled to say that I have known friendship and intimacy in what they have of most intense and abandoned. *Pazienza* – there must be some quiet backwater stagnating for us (forgive the ungraceful image) somewhere ahead. I've got you on the shelf in other words – the little high-up dusky shelf, safe and obscure, of last resource or (what is it I mean?) supreme appeal. I'll respect you till I'm dying – then I'll grab at you.

He signs off with typical flourish: 'Farewell, noble ghost. There *is* no life, but I am if not for time at least for eternity yours.'

Shortly afterwards, James took the lease on a cottage with a view at Point Hill, near Rye (presaging his, and Arthur's, and Fred's eventual adoption of the town), whither Arthur sent him a photograph of himself which James received with 'a good conscience if not with mad rapture'.

The letters demonstrate, too, the evident pleasure James derived from his visits to Addington and his very warm appreciation of the 'noble courtesy and kindness' of Edward and Minnie. He also mentions Fred in flattering terms as 'your gallant brother, my illustrious colleague, or rather confrère. Please assure him of my watchful interest when you have a chance.'[12]

Maggie had gone to Egypt for the winter of 1895–6 to engage on what would be her most significant work, the excavation of the Temple of Mut, and had met a young woman who was not only to help her in the work and the eventual preparation of a book describing it, but also to be a lifelong friend. This was Nettie Gourlay, a quiet, introverted young woman who sat spellbound by Maggie's verve and crystal intelligence. The two women became inseparable, and Minnie, ever alive to the happiness of her brood and the unusual springs which might nourish it, made a point of asking after Nettie in every letter. She was also worried about Maggie's health still, and that she might have taken on too much in an inclement climate, so Fred went out to join her and pursue his own archaeological work for the Egyptian Exploration Fund. Minnie painted an endearing little vignette of home life when she reported his departure to her daughter. 'Beth had a hard time of it after seeing Fred off,' she wrote. 'I found her in tears because he hadn't had the sandwiches he asked for. They had been taken to her room and she had not seen them.'[13]

This was a very happy time for Maggie, and a correspondingly relaxed one for Fred, who delighted to see his sister at ease with herself, working well, achieving something, and annoying no one with her intolerant brilliance. They wrote their books in the evenings, and dined constantly with Nettie. Fred was, however, dissatisfied with his work, which produced poor results. His heart not in it, he left Maggie and Nettie in the summer and continued his journey to Athens. On the way back to England he stopped off, for the first time, in Capri, an island which he found enchanting beyond words (it was then perfectly idyllic and unlike anywhere else, and tourists had not yet discovered it). Capri had for centuries had an especial fascination for the bachelor, as it combined isolation with an almost feminine prettiness, wonderful flowers and the bluest of seas, and a population of beautiful, obliging men and women. There Fred saw John Ellingham Brooks, whom he had met in Athens at the British School of Archaeology. Brooks was a refugee from an England bound by post-Wildean moral rigidity, and there were on the island a number of other single men who were enjoying the sensation of being left alone. He determined he would return one day.

Coming home from Capri Fred found his father in good form, but obviously suffering from exhaustion. The load of the archiepiscopate was a punishing one, and Edward was not a man to shirk duty or dilute responsibility. He keenly felt the threat of post-Darwinian dissension, which called for perpetual vigilance on his part. He would not delegate. He could not rest. He had been taking too much on his shoulders for years. The family doctor by now was Ross Todd, an Irishman with a pre-Freudian knack for intuiting neurotic conditions. Dr Todd suspected something more tangible on this occasion, and sent Edward to a heart specialist. Minnie told her diary, 'Dr Douglas Powell is seeing Edward and of course I am rather jumpy. I don't really at bottom feel there is anything radically wrong, but I *fear*, that's no wonder. Dr Powell laid great stress on his heart being weak. They told him to rest before and after meals. He is furious and won't.'[14] In fact, Powell had said the Archbishop was unlikely to live more than two years.[15]

The Archbishop found time to discuss Fred's future with him now that grants and sponsorships for further digs looked unlikely. He recommended a job in the Education Office, but Fred affirmed that he intended to make his living as a writer. Edward did not approve. It may have been on this occasion that he summoned the energy to make a joke. Workmen were doing repairs at Addington and pointed out to His Grace that the banister at the top of the stairs was dangerously loose. Should they replace it? No, said Edward with histrionic thunder. 'When the heathen moves in here he will place his hand upon it and plunge to his doom.'[16] It always comes as a surprise when A.C. Benson, E.F. Benson and R.H. Benson separately refer to their father as a funny man, a wit and raconteur, for it ill accords with the brooding despot of his letters. 'His sense of humour was undeveloped', says one author laconically.[17] Edward was a raconteur by design, since he felt that his job included entertaining on a social level and he must be good at it. He kept a Commonplace Book in which he wrote epigrams, funny stories, after-dinner conversation topics, collected and bound under the title *Mores Dicteria*. When on 16 September Edward and Minnie left for an official tour of Ireland, with a gruelling list of engagements and most probably never a meal alone, he took his little bound book of epigrams with him. Fred and Maggie were at the door to wave their parents off. Edward kissed his son and said, 'God bless you and make you a good boy always.' It was clear he was sad to leave.[18]

The Irish tour, though arduous, turned out to be a great personal success, with Edward preaching eloquently to large and appreciative crowds. After three weeks they finished in Belfast, and crossed over to England where they had been invited to spend some days with the Gladstones. Edward and Minnie first spent a day in Carlisle, where they saw the beautiful red sandstone cathedral, much of it the original Norman, then journeyed south to Chester. They arrived at the Gladstone house, Hawarden, on the afternoon of 10 October. Edward had been looking forward to it immensely, for though Gladstone had frequently invited him to stay, this was the first opportunity he had been able to grasp. Benson and Gladstone talked all evening, before, during and after dinner, until midnight. Minnie said, 'I never saw him better, more active, serener.' It was as if Edward had decided, perhaps truly for the first time in his life, to relax. From his bedroom in the small hours could be heard some curious knocking, but nobody paid serious attention to it.

The next morning they had an early breakfast and all assembled to go to church. All, that is, save Edward, who was slow to prepare himself, so that Minnie had to go and fetch him. Minnie drove with Mrs Gladstone, while Edward walked with Mary, the daughter, who noticed that he was obliged to stop several times to catch his breath. In church, the Archbishop knelt in the pew for the Confession, with his wife and Mrs Gladstone near by. (Gladstone himself stayed at home.) Suddenly, while the Lord's Prayer was spoken, he sighed as the breath flew out of him, sank back, and was dead. As Fred movingly put it, 'he bowed himself before his Lord, as he met Him face to face.'[19]

A doctor in the congregation loosened Edward's clothing and attempted to revive him for an 'agonizing quarter of an hour', but to no avail. The rest of the worshippers assumed it had been an ordinary fainting fit, until the death was announced at the end of the service, and the organist played the 'Dead March' from *Saul*. The body was laid out on a sofa in the Rectory library, then dressed in episcopal robes. Fred was informed by telegram on 11 October, rushed to London and took the first train to Chester on 12 October. He found his mother in a state of shock, but behaving sensibly, and stayed with her until preparations had been set in motion for the removal of his father's body to Canterbury for the momentous funeral. The body travelled down by train, with clergymen standing at each station on the way to do him honour. Queen Victoria grieved genuinely for a man she had held in the highest regard for thirty-five years, and begged to be informed. 'He was such a friend of ours,' she told the Duke of York, whom she commanded to represent her at the funeral. 'He married you and your sisters and christened little David [Edward VIII, later Duke of Windsor]. A great loss.'[20] Mrs Gladstone wrote to the

Queen, 'Mrs Benson has just started for London, calm and patient, full of faith and courage. It was indeed a lesson to be with her.'[21]

Privately, Minnie was thrown by the cruel suddenness of her bereavement into an agony of remorse. All those years of trial, when she had struggled to make herself worthy of Edward and had battled in vain against a different kind of love, when she had fought to overcome their basic inescapable incompatibility, rushed into her consciousness as she thought what she might have said, what she might have done, given five minutes' grace. 'O Edward,' she wrote, 'is it possible that now in the bosom of God you see all the past, and understand that . did not choose before? and that you are *wanting* me to choose you – and choosing me afresh. I must have been a bitter disappointment. That is over.'[22]

To her close friend Adeline, Duchess of Bedford, she confided her 'wailings' and permitted herself some expression of loneliness. 'I didn't know how *utterly* my whole being was just him,' she wrote, 'and there is nothing left of me.'[23] Feelings of barrenness, of emptiness and desolation, are common to all bereavements, but in Minnie's case the pain was exacerbated both by Edward's powerful personality which, of a sudden no longer there, seemed to leave her meandering without purpose; and by the upheaval in her position. From being the wife of the Archbishop of Canterbury, with two palatial homes and about thirty servants, she was overnight a mere widow, with no special call upon the country or the church. In a way she welcomed this, but it also initially frightened her. 'I never had time to be responsible for my own life,' she told her diary. 'In a way I feel more grown up now than I ever have before. Strange, when for the first time in my fifty-five years I am *answerable to nobody*. No one has a right to censure my actions, and I can do what I like . . . one more widow who has come down from a really high position pitches her little tent.'[24]

Mary Benson's distress and loss of anchor had a profound effect upon E.F. Benson's life. Henceforth he would be expected to subordinate his preferences to hers, to be available when needed, to comfort and caress and cherish. It was an unspoken truth within the family circle that Fred was the only reliable member, that is the only one unlikely to take refuge in a tantrum. Arthur was increasingly reclusive and would feel a headache coming on if anything was demanded of him. Maggie had to be handled with care, or she might hurl accusations against all and sundry. Hugh surrounded himself with the aura of his own uniqueness. In fact, they were all in varying degrees sunk in selfishness. Only Fred was generous with his time, and they would all in due course come to lean on him rather too much. Small wonder, then, that Edward had turned to Fred for the promise that Minnie would be looked after, and little wonder again that Fred had given the promise with a whole heart and had undertaken to set up home with her. It was an obligation which he would live to regret, as it became clear that a gregarious, hedonistic, clubbable man had no business living with an ageing, cloying mother. The realisation would alter his relationship to Minnie and inform the narrative tenor of his books.

In the immediate aftermath of Minnie's widowhood, however, Fred was the perfect son, an angel of care. Minnie described him vividly: 'Fred was as tender as a child, as loving and strong as a husband and as sensitive as a woman. He only wanted not to disappoint me and he told me one evening that he could never marry [because] he loved me too much.'[25]

It was he, naturally, who undertook the removals from Lambeth Palace and Addington Park, for the Bensons were all now homeless in a flash, and the new Archbishop Temple must needs move into the official premises. Even the furniture, accumulated over three decades, had to be sorted, packed, and despatched. The strain would be too much for Minnie, so it was arranged that she should go with Maggie and Lucy Tait to Egypt, there to be joined by Hugh a little later, and, when all the work had been completed, by Fred himself. Thus it was that the family abandoned Fred to his wearisome labours. In addition, Fred had to prepare his father's manuscript of the St Cyprien biography for the press, which he did at Lambeth as the furniture crated up around him. The party meandered southwards in a gentle manner through Paris and Venice, and Fred caught up with them a few weeks later.

Arthur, meanwhile, stayed aloof at Eton, unwilling to risk the fuss and bother which might be injurious to his health. He did, however, undertake to write the official life of Edward White

Benson, which he could accomplish without too much shoulder-rubbing with human beings. In the event, this mighty labour would prove a serious mistake for Arthur, as he was made to face truths about his parents' marriage which he would rather had remained hidden. For Arthur, it was always simpler not to know; his curiosity about human life was theoretical, whereas Fred's was ebullient and amused. Arthur was inclined to look for the meaning of life, Fred for its comedy.

Not that there was much fun to be derived from those disastrous six months in Egypt in 1896–7, intended as a recovery from loss. One after another, the party succumbed to intolerable heat and insanitary conditions. Maggie had a heart attack, developed pleurisy and underwent a stupid operation to tap the lungs which caused her to lose consciousness. The family expected her to die, but she recovered, it was supposed through sheer willpower. Then Fred caught sunstroke from too much swimming and sun-bathing, followed by typhoid fever so severe he had to be carried off on a stretcher. No sooner did he show signs of recovery than Lucy was stricken with the same disease and seemed certain to die. Poor Minnie looked as if she might lose three of her dearest in one terrible month. It was with enormous relief that the party returned to England to face the lesser problem of finding somewhere to live. Those old family friends the Randall Davidsons (he was now Dean of Windsor at Queen Victoria's personal request conveyed to a compliant Edward) offered them temporary shelter at their home, Farnham Castle.

Meanwhile, Fred had published three more books, each progressively diminishing what reputation he had made. *The Rubicon* is best forgotten, and the evidence is that Fred tried to forget it. A melodramatic and preposterous tale which ends with a prussic acid suicide, it is not a Benson subject, nor is it written in the Benson style. Both subject and style would elude Fred for some time yet, and the critics were not going to wait. 'The worst-written, falsest and emptiest book of the decade,' wrote one, while another summarised it with brutal candour as 'a school-girl's idea of a plot, a nursery-governess's knowledge of the world, a gentleman's gentleman's view of high life, a man-milliner's notion of creating character.'[26]

Fred wrote to Edmund Gosse:

The Rubicon seems to be arousing a good deal of vehemence on the part of critics. Can you tell me exactly what it all means? When they say things so violent, it seems to me to discount all they say, unless it were better that I had never written a line, and that, to speak quite frankly, I consider absurd. I may say at once that I don't care the slightest, personally. I am so happily constituted that I enjoy praise immensely and don't the least mind abuse.

Which was just as well, and probably honest, too. Fred could not quite bring himself to ask for Gosse's august patronage, but he clearly admired the man and went on to declare that he could not help writing. 'It really is not my fault. That I don't take time enough is certainly true, but what is to be done? If a situation or series of situations occur to me, I want to write them down.'[27]

The Judgement Books is Fred's attempt to emulate *Dorian Gray*, and was published in the year of Wilde's disgrace (1895 also saw *The Importance of Being Earnest*). The hero, Frank, is an artist who believes that each time he paints he loses part of himself which is, as it were, kidnapped and absorbed by the picture in hand. He is now embarked upon a self-portrait, but is frightened by the prospect that he may paint himself as he really is – dissolute and depraved – and not as the good and decent man his loving wife Margery sees. For Frank, before he married, had been rather a cad and risks raising the ghost of that past life. Indeed, as the picture progresses, it grows more vicious and reveals a loathsome personality, which Margery flees from in fear. Eventually, Frank persuades Margery to help him, to rescue him from himself, and the painting is dramatically ripped to pieces.

Not only is the theme Wildean, but there is a Wildean principle at stake which Fred seems to question. The preface to *The Picture of Dorian Gray* makes the famous claim, 'There is no such thing as a moral or an immoral book. Books are well written, or badly written.' Benson has Frank make an analogous point about art:

You call one thing pretty, another ugly. Believe me, art knows no such terms. A thing is true, or it is false; and the cruelty of it is, that if we have as much as a grain of falsehood in our measure of truth, the thing is worthless. Therefore, in the picture I am now painting, I have tried to be absolutely truthful; as you said at dinner, I have tried to paint what I am, without extenuation or concealment. Would you like to see it? You would probably call it a hideous caricature, because in this terrible, cruel human life, no man knows what is good in him, but only what is bad. It is those who love us only, who know if there is any good in us.[28]

In other words, a portrait may be well-painted (honest) or ill-painted (deceitful), but it cannot be accused of evil. It can only depict what is, and not be blamed for failing to depict what ought to be. With the denouement of the story, however, it is clear that Benson is challenging this view. He does believe the artist has a responsibility towards his audience as well as towards his art, that there is evil in the world and the artist must neither glamorise nor excuse it. Fred's moral view is simple, and it occurs again and again in his work. It is this: evil can be banished by good, and salvation is always possible, but the struggle, the conflict, are unceasing. In *The Judgement Books* it is Margery who saves Frank; in the much later *David Blaize*, which we have already had cause to look at, it is David who saves Maddox. Since many of Fred's books are made of incidents in his life, stitched together in varying ways, or reflect moments in his intellectual and moral development, we are bound to ask, who was it who saved Fred from himself?

The Judgement Books was a dismal flop, so for his next Fred returned to King's College, Cambridge, and contrived a yarn about a young man who resists advice to choose a profession, gives his soul to art, and falls on hard times. Written after the discovery of Athens and Fred's complete surrender to the Greek ideal, *Limitations* has a hero, Tom Carlingford, who is in many respects drawn from Fred himself. At Cambridge he makes a virtue of loafing about and doing nothing in particular save dine at the Pitt Club, even boasting that to be totally idle requires some talent; getting a degree is a wretched nuisance, an interruption of life's pleasures. He is a breezy outdoor type, inordinately fond of cricket; he plays the piano reasonably well; he skates. All this is recognisably E.F. Benson as a young man. The parallels become closer as the story develops, and Tom goes to Athens rather than get a job. There he is smitten by the beauty of Greek sculpture and determines to become a sculptor himself. Art will be his religion.

The story departs from autobiography when Tom marries (and incidentally affords us one of the few successful love scenes in the whole of the Benson *œuvre*), but there are pages of discussion about the nature and purpose of art which mirror Fred's post-Athenian preoccupations, and there is even a heart-to-heart talk between Tom and his father which gives some clue to the interview Fred had with Edward about the lines of his future career. We only know that Edward recommended a job of some kind, perhaps in the Education Service, but from this and other Benson books we may safely surmise that when Fred declared his intention to be a writer he had to defend the artistic life against the remonstrations of a very sceptical father. Scenes in later novels, including *The Challoners*, support this supposition. *Limitations* was written in 1896, and published two months after the Archbishop's death.

The Babe, B.A., Fred's next book, is also set in Cambridge against a background of flippant undergraduate repartee. It is full of froth signifying nothing, bright inconsequential chatter at the Pitt Club wrapped in compulsive cheerfulness. There is a nice buoyancy about the book, but not the smallest attempt to delve into character. Fred admitted it had been written piece-meal, and it shows, each chapter independent of its predecessor and the whole devoid of plot. That stupendous facility of Fred's is not yet in harness – the book looks as if it was written over a glass of whisky in the early evening, and within a couple of weeks.

Deciding where the survivors of the Benson family should live was the main preoccupation of 1897. Arthur and Hugh were not much affected, the former living quite happily at Eton, the latter in the Rector's house at Kemsing, where he was curate. Thus the house they were looking for had to be home to a widow and three single ladies – Minnie, Lucy, Maggie, and Beth – plus a bachelor, Fred, who had promised his father he would live with them.

Queen Victoria was worried about Mrs Benson, and enquired of Randall Davidson, rather touchingly, whether she would be left well off. Mrs Davidson informed her that Mrs Benson would be all right, 'but certainly not rich. My sister [Lucy Tait] will continue to live with her, but where the home will be is not yet settled.'[29] The Queen promptly offered the use of Royal Lodge, Windsor, and Princess Beatrice wrote a personal note to Minnie in an attempt to persuade her, pointing out the comfort of having one of her sons so near[30] (Arthur was teaching at Eton). The Queen also summoned Minnie and Lucy to Windsor for a private chat.

The women considered the possibility of taking Royal Lodge and buying a small house in London as well, but when Arthur took a look at the Lodge on their behalf he advised against it, for reasons which are unclear.[31] In declining Her Majesty's offer, Minnie used Maggie's fragile health as the excuse, for Maggie had been suffering from rheumatism and had gone to Egypt partly in order to counter it. 'Of course your first thought must be for your daughter's health,' wrote Princess Beatrice. This was not the whole truth. It was Maggie's personality rather than her rheumatism which was giving most cause for alarm, and every decision relating to the move was taken with her interests paramount in view. Maggie's needs were gradually becoming dictatorial.

They settled for a handsome house in St Thomas Street, Winchester, for £4000. The expense would be onerous, but 'with Lucy at our back we shall do', as Minnie told Fred. That Lucy Tait's money should be necessary to see the family through would be one source of resentment in the great catalogue building up in Maggie's mind, yet it was Lucy's home as well, for better or worse, and it was perfectly in order that she should have a hand in the choice and contribute to the upkeep. Minnie asked Fred (who was still abroad) for his opinion. 'Of course I approve,' he wrote, adding mysteriously, 'and tell Lucy I think she is quite a nice person.' By the end of the year they were all ensconced.

For a variety of reasons, the Winchester period proved to be a deeply unhappy experience for Mary Benson. In the first place, the revelation of her husband's diaries, which Arthur was consulting for his *Life*, provoked in her some painful introspection. If Fred and Arthur, who pored over the diaries at Eton, admitted that they hardly recognised their father in them, Minnie certainly did, and they reminded her of the misery of those early years. She read that he had chosen her deliberately as a child whom he might educate, and that he used his betrothal to her as a means of self-denial ('he even wanted to preserve himself from errant feelings in love') – surely an extreme display of selfishness. Looking back, Minnie realised that she had been happiest when she could escape from him. 'The strain and pressure from that time till now – forty-three years – was such that every interval was to me a kind of holiday in which I drew breath and played, and so it came to pass that I *did not grow up*.'[32]

She further reflected how Edward had held such high ideals and toiled night and day to uphold them, while she did not sympathise with that austere part of his life. 'He used to say to me that I only cared about being comfortable and smooth, and he couldn't get me to enter into his struggles . . . How *blind* I have been.' Edward was still able to reprimand Minnie from beyond the grave, it seemed, and to make her feel guilty. Her guilt spread to the conviction that she had not been a good mother. 'I was *most* blameworthy when they were growing up, and I neglected them so dreadfully.'[33]

Minnie's feelings of inadequacy were compounded by the indifference of many of her husband's friends, who acted as though she too had died. 'I was not associated with him in people's minds,' she said. '*His* friends did not and do not seek me . . . I imagined they would take me as a *relic of him*. No, I was a pain, because I reminded them of him without being like. And yet I *toiled* to make myself agreeable to his friends.'[34]

And then there was Maggie, whose behaviour was a constant reproach to her mother. In the course of helping Arthur with the biography of their father, she seemed to absorb some of Edward's exigent, harsh personality, to wish to replace him, to keep his influence alive by *becoming* him. Like Edward, she began to organise everyone, to make peremptory orders for the running of the household, to shoulder the responsibilities he would have shouldered. As Fred put it, 'Insensibly she laid her hands on the reins, making the household to take its pace from her.'[35] Worse yet, Maggie further imitated her father in those black sulking moods which the whole family used to dread; now it was she who slammed doors and would not speak. Again Fred summed it up neatly: 'into her nature there passed as well something of his severity and of those moods of dark depression which sometimes obsessed him.'[36] In the old days, when Maggie sank into gloom Fred had been able to lift her out of it with a tease. 'Hump!' he would shout, 'Play the fool', and the atmosphere would lighten.[37] But in Winchester, the moods were too serious, too inaccessible, to be dispelled by any easy banter.

For poor Mary Benson, the effect was hideously dispiriting. She had to watch what she said and how she said it, for Maggie would imagine lapses in conduct or negligence of duties and add them up against her. Should a letter arrive which did not mention Maggie, Minnie would hide it rather than risk another sulk. She found herself behaving furtively, out of a 'dreadful *fear*, fear lest one should be displeasing her. There is in her displeasure, as there was in her father's, a power of bringing one into bondage. I catch myself acting as of old, in a sort of dull slave spirit. O God, what to do!'[38] Pathetically, she confided in her Diary that she had a 'fettered sense of a long vista of slavery'.

Maggie quarrelled with Arthur over the biography of the Archbishop, in all probability because Arthur wished to suppress her contribution. Minnie did not need this on top of everything else and sought to bolster Maggie's confidence by telling her bluntly, and dishonestly, 'Your chapters are going to be the redemption of the book.'[39] But above all else, plain jealousy was at the bottom of Maggie's misery. She looked upon Lucy Tait as an interloper who usurped what ought in all logic to have been her position within the family. For not only did Lucy provide financial assistance to Minnie, she also provided much of the affection. Following the Archbishop's death, Lucy moved into the large bed wherein all Mary Benson's children had been born (they had kept it since Wellington days), and the two women shared this bed for the rest of Mrs Benson's life. It would be a mistake to read too much into this, and suppose with late twentieth-century perceptions that Minnie and Lucy were lesbian lovers. But it would be equally ridiculous to deny that a very close affection – love, if you like – united them. Fred declared that 'it was impossible to think of them apart', and there can be little doubt that Maggie, observing this closeness, felt excluded.

'My mother's intimacies and emotional friendships had always been with women,' Fred wrote. 'No man, except my father, had ever counted in her life, and this long love between her and Lucy was the greatest of all these attachments.'[40] Lucy was the successor to, and supplanter of, the Miss Wordsworths and Miss Halls of yesteryear, and once established in Minnie's heart, her position was unassailable. They were by no means unique in Victorian times, and the phenomenon was widespread enough to excite comment among those whose business it was to ponder the human predicament. Ethel Smyth, for instance, elicited the following remark from Harry Brewster on the subject:

> You wonder why so many women prefer friends of their own sex, to the degree of being able to work up a much greater amount of excitement about them. Probably there are several reasons; among others this one, that these affections entail no duties, no sacrifice of liberty or of tastes, no partial loss of individuality; whereas friendships of equal warmth with men have that danger (and others) in the background.[41]

The dissemblance of that 'and others' is incidentally beguiling, but the implication here, and it is an important one, is that friendships between women, though sexless, were often more total and complete than the love a woman dutifully bore her husband. To Maggie's jealousy at Lucy Tait's intrusion into the house must therefore be added, in view of her unnatural and obsessive identification with her father, the more intense jealousy of the suspicious husband. Maggie began to prowl, to be ever vigilant, on the *qui-vive* for examples of Lucy's influence with her mother. She watched and listened furtively, taking every opportunity for a quarrel with her rival. 'Some sharp sparring with Lucy', noted Minnie in her Diary. Minnie had even to 'avoid too much companionship with Lucy', implying that Maggie would get angry merely if she saw them together. Often no words would be said, but the other would notice a look on the daughter's face – 'saw a shade come again over Maggie'.

In these circumstances, the atmosphere in the house at Winchester became almost intolerable, and if I have examined it at length, it is because Fred, as the only man in the house, had to witness it all and occasionally to intervene; the poison entered his blood and coloured some of his sharpest portraits of female vindictiveness (notably in *Pharisees and Publicans*). There is, after all, something quite nasty about Lucia and Miss Mapp, however amusing they may appear behind Fred's careful detachment.

The position grew so grave that Dr Ross Todd, whom Mary, with her passion for nicknames, called 'Toddles', was summoned to give Maggie a talking-to. Dr Todd figures more and more in the Benson story as the years progress. An Irishman, he had given up general practice in London some years before in favour of early retirement, but his reputation among his patients was such that he was frequently called back for consultation, with the result that he found himself working full time after all. Apart from his medical skills, Todd's real talent lay in an intuitive understanding of the mischances of human personality, of what could go wrong with the mind. Though he could not have used the word, he was what we would now call a psychiatrist specialising in the treatment of neurotic disorders.

Maggie was not very co-operative with Todd. She gave monosyllabic answers to his enquiries, then lapsed into morose silence. Eventually, his sympathetic persistence elicited something more than petulance from the patient. Maggie told him she felt neglected, that life was dreadfully dull and monotonous, and that Mama only made matters worse when she told her to go and spend a week with Nettie Gourlay, her own intimate 'companion'. It was obvious that motives and intents were being misconstrued, tangled up into a knot of incomprehension. Maggie was bored. She kept harping on the need for 'change'. Mary, wanting to help, suggested she visit Nettie. Maggie interpreted this as a desire to get rid of her.[42] Though there had long been latent danger in Maggie's arrogance and sententiousness, it was not until the spice of jealousy entered her soul that her long descent into madness began.

Hugh, too, gave cause for anxiety. He possessed a similarly arrogant nature to Maggie, but his found expression in stubbornness and foot-stamping rather than sulking. Mary thought he was 'getting curious and difficult and rude' on the rare occasions he visited Winchester. Then he announced his intention of leaving his curacy to take a step nearer the absolute discipline he craved, and join Canon Gore's rather dubious sect at Mirfield in Yorkshire. His mother tried to get him to feel filial, as Edward would not have approved his 'flying out of the diocese to please himself . . . he has acted so hastily that to do anything [to prevent him] is almost impossible now . . . I feel that we mustn't give him the idea of a wilful boy thwarted.'[43]

It is scarcely surprising, with this wretched confluence of adverse stars, that Minnie should tell her Diary she was '*an utter and absolute failure*. Maggie ill, . . . defeated and undone. I can't pray. I can't offer anything. I can't live. I don't care.'

The one bright spot on the horizon, to which she would cling with ever more desperate and devouring need, was her dear son Fred. Fred had not been keen on Winchester but was determined to make the best of it, despite the claustrophobic atmosphere created by the women, and from the first treated it as his home. The neighbourhood was replete with the folk whose company he enjoyed, the titled and the amusing, and he frequently entertained. Reggie Lister, for instance, passed through the week before Christmas, on his way to similar sojourns with the Marquess of Salisbury at Hatfield House and the Duke of Devonshire at Chatsworth, and Fred made sure his pal was treated just as well in Winchester. Lister wrote afterwards, 'I look back to those two days as the happiest and most satisfactory in all the course of our friendship.'[44]

The trouble was, the house in St Thomas Street was not really large enough to warrant much entertaining, and Fred still wanted to carry on as if he were at Addington Park. The women ganged up on him and asked him not to keep inviting people down. Not unreasonably, Fred was distinctly peeved. His mother wrote to Maggie (who was away on convalescence), 'I am *awfully* sorry about having made Fred low . . . I *hate* not falling in with any plan of his, but it's *economy* that sits beside me at bed and board – and so I fear our staff couldn't do it (and perhaps a secret thought that we can scarcely afford more guests than the ordinary spare room).'[45] Faced with this attitude, Fred glumly absented himself from the house as often as he could, sometimes playing golf (his latest sporting craze) all day long rather than be in the way. Of course, this too was misinterpreted. 'Fred is staying away from golf to be at lunch,' said Minnie. 'There's glory for you!'[46] She imagined her famous novelist son was getting above his station, which was entirely unfair, and the squabbles normally restricted to the ladies of the house spilled over into his lap. One frequently finds his mother calling him 'contradictious' and 'captious' during this fraught period, and she is so concerned about his tiresome selfish little ways that she eventually realises that 'his life here' (i.e. in Winchester) is to blame:

It is all on so small a scale. He is awfully nice to me, but we run dry in a few minutes, and in the drouth I hear my own silly words ringing in my own sad ear. I think the only thing would be to live with him, *alone*, for two or three months. I can't do it, and if I tried I shouldn't last out, but he can't tell you himself by words, and if there was more than one person with him he would leave them to each other. Clearly this points to WIFE. Will it be?[47]

It seems Mary Benson was not the only member of the family to see marriage as the solution to Fred's *cafard*. Arthur, too, had a go at him on the subject. 'I implored Fred to marry: he is the only one of us four likely to. We are the only Bensons of our line left . . . we have struggled into a certain position and it would be pathetic if we died out just now.'[48] It is interesting that Arthur has at this early stage given up all idea of marriage himself. Thirteen years before, at the age of twenty-two, he had felt he 'might' have fallen in love with Miss Erna Thomas, the sister-in-law of his father's friend Canon Dalton, but Dalton had ridiculed the whole idea of Arthur's being married to anyone, and Edward, of all people, warned him against the perils of marrying too young.[49] So Arthur lost heart and pursued Miss Thomas no farther. In time, he would admit to himself that he was not marriageable, and settle for the less trying pleasure of watching naked young men cavorting by the river, which afforded him 'an indescribable thrill of romance and desire'.[50] That he should now 'implore' his thirty-year-old brother Fred to save the family genes by getting a wife, and that Fred did not disabuse him, points to the lack of candour then existing between the two men. For Fred, though eligible and in his good-looking prime, never once gave marriage a thought.

His mind wandered farther afield, to Athens and to Capri, and as by the spring of 1898 it was clear life in the oppressive Winchester house was no longer tenable, he decided to escape. His excuse was afforded by Maggie, whose convalescence had made no appreciable difference to her persecuted frame of mind, and who was ever more loudly braying the need for 'change'. Dr Todd proposed that she be humoured, that she needed wide open country, a garden with trees and fresh air, that to be cooped up in a town house was hopelessly bad for her. And so the family began looking for somewhere else to live, and decided that it would be best to have a country house (for Maggie) and a small house in London as well (for the others). Fed up with it all, Fred went off to Athens. Arthur summed up the position in March with, incidentally, a vivid assessment of Fred's character:

> At the crucial moment EFB flies to Greece. His motto is anything to save trouble. Now MB and Lucy propose a London house *and* a country house. I doubt finances, Lucy to run town house, we country . . . I beg them to calculate. I fear I don't really want it. I don't think I should do to live at home; we are all too much alike – too critical – too clever – all see what everyone is going to say before they open their mouths – I always get depressed there. Fred by golf and avoidance of all responsibility prolongs insouciance of youth longer than most people – and moreover he understands women which I don't do . . . Fred can give way in trifles, is very companionable, easily amused, seldom depressed.[51]

The journey to Athens was not entirely for amusement. Fred had undertaken to do some work on Greek refugees from the Turks, and to write it up in *The Times*. Nevertheless, there is no mistaking the lightness of his heart as soon as he is there. 'I enjoy it all the more because last year I was still rather tottery after typhoid, but now I sing in my bath for joy.'[52] His mother innocently remarked that 'he found a little boy to play with – a nice young officer,'[53] but we need not necessarily suppose that this contributed to the joy. At the end of May Fred left for Capri, staying for ten days at the Villa Ferraro, where he realised once and for all that this special island felt more like home to him than the grim little rooms in England with their moody inhabitants:

> The vineyards, olive groves, uplands, cobbled alleys, shining waters and sun-soaked sands put out a magic that ensnared him completely. Every part of the day, from dawn to dusk, brought its own special spell. He bathed and basked, climbed Monte Solaro, wrote another novel, played the piano, gossiped with feminine relish, ate and drank what he described as the food of the gods, and was as happy as he had ever been.[54]

At such a distance, the problem of where to live evaporated into the royal blue sky, and it was with some indifference that he wrote recommending 'a nook in London and a house at Winchester' as the best solution. So relaxed was he that he spoke about the book he was working on, *The Money Market*, with cheerful derision. 'I rather think it is twaddle,' he said, 'but it's hard to judge till one sees it in print. I think so because I see no reason why I should not go on with it till it is as long as the Encyclopaedia.'[55]

The Bensons looked at houses in Haslemere and Basingstoke, but it was Lucy who found the magnificent pile which would be their last home – Tremans. She also bought the lease of a small house in Barton Street, Westminster, not far from the cathedral, and by the time Fred arrived back in England it was all settled. Minnie felt guilty about arranging everything without allowing proper consultation with Fred. 'I feel deeply heavy-hearted,' she wrote, 'for down at bottom lies the deep sadness that Fred is not with us in all this. What is he to do? No one about, and no amusement, and no employment. Here [Winchester] he is never with us, but also a great deal with others. How is it we are so far apart? And yet Fred loves, and I love.'[56]

In September Fred was alone there, very much annoyed about leaving (wrote Arthur).

> It is very hard on him. He did not like the idea of Winchester, but was always kind and nice, made the best of everything, wanted no amusing, always good-humoured, fell into the ways

of the place and people, and just when he has got rooted, it is all pulled up and he has to begin again. The whole thing is very unsatisfactory. The entire decision has been really made by a hasty doctor humouring Maggie in a nervous and fanciful mood. And the painful sense remains in everybody's mind that all their wishes have been sacrificed to this. Either MB could have averted it by decision, or M herself by consideration.[57]

Fred wiped his hands of the whole miserable affair and let them get on with it. The day before they moved out, Minnie and Lucy spent the entire morning rummaging around in Fred's room, presumably because he had left them to do the packing, and found 'treasures' – letters from Queen Victoria and other members of the Royal Family addressed to Edward. It is not clear what they were doing there, as Arthur should properly have had them with him at Eton. Perhaps it was Fred's innocent snobbery at work in so far as he saw himself as the natural curator of such gems. Beth, who was by this time very old and in need of care herself, was much distressed by the upheaval, and begged Mrs Benson not to leave her behind, but arrange for all of them to leave together. 'When you are away,' she said, 'I wake in the night and keep on waking and thinking, but when you are here it is all right.'[58]

By the spring of 1899 the family was established at Tremans, a beautiful seventeenth-century manor house with mullioned windows, high chimneys and a lead-topped cupola, which they leased initially for a year. The house and its surroundings were enchanting, quintessentially English, set in one of the finest corners of Sussex near Horsted Keynes. A long avenue of Scotch firs led to the house, and the grounds included everything that a country house should have – bowling-green, fishponds, brooks and streams, farm buildings and barns, a cherry orchard, and in the distance, gentle soothing views of rolling hills studded with hamlets. It was a scene to delight a painter, and the house seemed designed to create and sustain happiness.

'Fred hates it,' exclaimed Minnie in dismay. He did not so much dislike the house, as resent the reasons for taking it, and he displayed his feelings in the most unmanly sulks. He refused to work, or to bestir himself. He complained of draughts. The truth was, he missed the charm of social life. 'Fred is a Sphinx,' said his mother. 'One day's loneliness makes him captious.' Eventually she faced the fact that her son would not be happy, even at such a place as Tremans, imprisoned with four inquisitive women, his wings clipped and his need for a private, not to say secret, life unsatisfied. 'Poor Fred fled from Tremans to go and play golf,' wrote Arthur. 'I found him in bed at Barton Street with influenza, flushed and miserable and in a great rage. He ought I think to be living more independently, and immersed at Tremans he is a prey to moping devils.'[59] After only four weeks at the house Mrs Benson decided to release him from his promise to live with her. She told Maggie of 'Fred's depression, culminating in such awful gloom that it gave me the courage of despair to write to him an exhaustive letter setting him free, body and spirit and financially.'[60]

Fred promptly rented a bachelor flat at 395 Oxford Street in London, visiting Tremans at weekends, and his life of independence may be said to have begun with the advent of his thirty-second birthday.

6 Society's Pet

London life at the turn of the century suited Fred perfectly. He was famous, and he was courted. He added to the vast number of his 'society' friends during this period, and from now on we hear of Ladies Galloway, Radnor and Charles Beresford unendingly. There was no kitchen at the flat in Oxford Street, so he regularly dined out, except when he had a meal brought in from the Italian restaurant round the corner. He went to concerts, theatres, galleries, keeping up with the latest cultural events and generally devouring all that a great cosmopolitan city has to offer to the successful and the fashionable. He went to Bayreuth and fell captive to the lush sounds of Wagner, who 'welds into one harmonious whole, the ugliness of sin and the beauty of holiness'.[1] He also read widely in compensation for his rather desultory studies as schoolboy and undergraduate, and went to the skating rink every day to maintain fitness. It comes as a surprise that E.F. Benson should pass every grade of the National Skating Association and rise to the rank of gold-medallist, but it is so.

If his mother complained of Fred's secretiveness, his unwillingness to say whether he was coming to Tremans for the weekend or not, and his inability to know in advance whom he was bringing with him, she did not understand the tribulations of a young man in society. Fred was not being furtive – he had nothing in particular to hide – he just wanted to keep his options open in case something better should turn up. Yet she appreciated how much he wanted company. 'Fred comes tonight,' she said, 'oh poor boy how dull he will find it. He's had a very jolly time in London and done mighty little work – Charles Beresfords, Ribblesdales, and just that set.'[2]

The pretensions of London social life really did go to his head, thought Minnie, when he announced the engagement of his own personal servant – a gentleman's gentleman – to look after him. 'A footman! My! that's his Lady Charles,' she exclaimed in mock horror. Her distaste for the idea was, however, genuine. Ostentation was a vulgar trait, and she had never encouraged her children to 'show off' in any circumstances. 'Oh if only he could know what people think!' While Fred was in London, she at least would not have to witness her son making a fool of himself, but then he brought the man, called Sidney, with him to Tremans, and maternal discomfort was almost tangible. 'I can't tell you how queer things are here,' she wrote to Maggie. 'First Fred arrived, *with Sidney* (he hadn't been mentioned so I hadn't expected him) . . . his little servant is nice, in his way, but I have to mind my p's and q's and I'd much rather he didn't come – and it costs – and our estimates are somewhat tight. But Mum's the word . . . I had to explain that it didn't do to smoke in the servants' hall with the door open.'

Fred prevailed upon Mrs Moss, the cook, to teach Sidney some simple breakfast dishes, which offers an interesting glimpse into the Sidney episode; for, if he were hired as a gentleman's gentleman he would surely have been skilled in the duties of his profession, and since he was not, one is justified in wondering on what basis he was selected in the first place. Minnie did not wonder – she merely seethed. '[Fred's] manservant sticks in my throat,' she said. 'It now appears he is going to take him about to places and *bring him here*, and I squirm a little at that, though of course I have not said a single word. A strong young man with all his income to make should scarcely go about with a man, do you think? But Peace! time will shew.'[3] One must not allow Minnie's choice of words to mislead: she is not here concerned with Fred's having a man with him all the time, but with Fred's having a servant with him all the time.

Despite his mother's promise to say nothing, Fred certainly knew she and Beth and Lucy would all disapprove. They were not likely to surrender the chance of a squabble, and Fred responded by being difficult himself. When Reggie Lister was there, in that first summer, all was well and cheerful, but otherwise Fred was downright rude to guests. One rash lady declared, in the midst of a heated discussion, 'I have not time to instruct everybody,' to which Fred acidly replied, 'then we are the exceptionally lucky people.' Minnie had to point out that women disliked *rudeness*, but secretly smiled at Fred's witty rejoinder. In her turn, Minnie berated Fred for not *working*. It is a frequent complaint of writers that everybody else assumes they have no proper employment, but in Fred's case it was probably true. Writing presented no hardship for him – he did not have to hew words out of a recalcitrant brain, they flowed easily straight on to the paper. Mary Benson pounced on this fatal facility at every opportunity. Her comments on Fred's books invariably gave the impression she thought he had not worked hard enough at them.

She told him, for instance, that when writing about character one must needs suppress abstract ideas of personality in favour of observation as to how people actually *are*. 'Fred read me a lot of his book, which has some *very* good things in it, but still wants depth and body. O how he DID want to bouleverse me, and see me in great emotion and laugh and cry – but it couldn't be.'[4] *The Money Market*, which Fred himself had described as 'twaddle', elicited much the same verdict from his mother.

And oh! Maggie! [she wrote] such a shock about Fred's book. The early part is very well-written and very amusing, tho' light, and I was going swimmingly along, when suddenly a thumping impossible incident (of the usual worst order) cuts clean across all the weavings of character and is followed by equally impossible mawkish sentimental Christian forgiveness – (I put it strongly). It rings all false and seems to me not only quite untrue to human nature, but to the nature and the history of the people he has sketched . . . his knowledge of human nature with regard to mothers and babies is incomplete as you might expect . . . for the life of me I don't know what to say to him . . . I am rather tired of smart people and should have liked him to have struck a deeper vein. I wonder how far his conception of a speculator is drawn from knowledge or other books or imagination.[5]

From knowledge, as it happened, for Fred was at this time speculating somewhat recklessly on the Stock Market. Arthur spotted that the character of Percy Gerard was highly autobiographical, and dismissed his 'shallow philosophy' as something which 'would vanish in mist before a prolonged stomach-ache'. He did, however, think the character of Blessington, based on Beth, 'delightful'.[6]

Shortly afterwards, he tried his hand at two novels based on the Greek War of Independence, and using his recent experience with Greek refugees from the Turks. These were *The Vintage* and *Capsina*, written in very unDodo style, obviously in an effort to find the depth and body his mother demanded. As historical novels they fall short of adequate, and *The Vintage* is downright soporific. '*Capsina* has turned out as I hoped,' Fred wrote, 'and is certainly a street or two higher than *The Vintage*.'[7] Maybe so, but Minnie was critical of it for quite other reasons, and she wrote him a schoolmistressy letter chiding him with what we should nowadays call obscenity. Fred had tried to describe lust, and he just wasn't up to it. Mother pointed to specific pages – 'the blood and flesh of her' on p. 258, 'the fever of her love-sickness' on p. 274, 'her love-fever' on p. 275. 'Things of this sort seem to me an unnecessary kind of sensationalism,' she told him, 'they pull it down a moment and suggest images much lower than the great swing of the whole . . . quite another class of people, of rather nasty minds, will read into them things which you certainly don't mean.'[8]

Oh, but he did mean them, only they were born of poor imagination rather than rich experience, which explains the risible artificiality of these images. Minnie should have recalled her own advice to stick to observation and eschew theory.

That Fred was earnestly and honestly trying to turn himself into a more serious writer is attested by his brief foray into political journalism with *The Imperial and Colonial Review*, a new magazine which he was invited to edit. The first issue contained an article by Sir Charles Dilke, which Fred sent to Lord Rosebery with the request he should contribute to the second issue. The request was politely declined, which did not deter the editor from publishing a fulsome review of Rosebery's own *Napoleon*, written by Fred under a pseudonym. He worked on the journal entirely from the flat in Oxford Street, in a state of extraordinary happiness, according to Arthur: 'he is greatly excited'. The magazine failed only because it did not have the backing of good distribution and expensive publicity.[9]

With the next book, *Mammon & Co*, Fred returned to a society theme, with happier results. Lady Conybeare is a frivolous and heartless beast of the kind he would perfect in his more mature fiction, while Lord Comber is the first portrait of that vain and vapid male sub-hero who would achieve his finest incarnation in Georgie Pillson of the *Lucia* series twenty to thirty years later. Comber repairs to the lavatory of his club to apply a little rouge to his make-up and considers the mirror his only uncritical friend. Here at least Fred is relying upon observation for his characterisation, and one can only speculate which of his friends might have been used as model. To suggest, as some have, that this kind of effete individual gave expression to a self-portrait is utterly ludicrous.

Mrs Benson was indubitably a worrier, and it must be significant that Fred gave her no cause for anxiety if we except the current ubiquity of his Sidney, and his poor showing as a novelist. Arthur was being awkward about pictures and furniture left over from Addington, which he wanted for himself and which she was holding back until she knew what Fred, the favourite, required. One visitor had a son who was in Arthur's house at Eton and who doted on him. 'He told me Arthur goes round every night and *tickles* all the boys, and shows them too how strong he is.' It says much for the climate of the times that she did not find this in the least objectionable. 'Doesn't it sound funny?' was her only comment.[10] He composed poetry, but had not yet begun that long series of reflective quasi-philosophic essays which would bring him a huge readership in excess even of Fred's. Hugh, always content and childlike, was, however, lurching closer to the ultimate authority he yearned for, and his mother correctly diagnosed that he would one day find fulfilment in the bosom of Rome. He, too, was writing a book, causing Minnie to make the beguiling observation, all too prescient, that writing was 'the one solace of a Benson under all difficulties'.

It was again Maggie over whose fragile welfare Minnie fretted endlessly. The move to Tremans, undertaken entirely for her benefit, was initially successful. The challenge of a beautiful garden to maintain and improve exhilarated her and satisfied all her love of nature. Arthur, who felt slightly responsible for the change in her character, as it was he who relied upon her 'incalculable' work for him in preparing the *Life* of their father, was relieved to find her 'wonderfully well – tranquil, industrious, cheerful, able'. On a visit to London, Maggie and Arthur met for tea at Fred's Oxford Street flat and tried vainly to recapture old nursery days. 'Fred was at his best, bright, hospitable, contented. Maggie said it was an odd contrast a few minutes later when Lady Charles Beresford, painted, her eyebrows put on wrong, screaming and calling Fred 'Dodo', flew into the room. 'I suppose there *must* be something attractive about Lady C.B.,' mused Arthur grudgingly. 'Fred calls her "the soul of honour".'[11]

A further cause for rejoicing was the publication of Maggie's own book about the excavations at the Temple of Mut, which she wrote in collaboration with Nettie Gourlay, provoking from her mother a quite disproportionate degree of elation. 'Your beautiful child is born,' she told her. 'I bless you, my own, in the name of your Father, and with a very full heart.' Fred's books were never accorded such rapturous welcome. Minnie obviously thought her daughter's every effort needed to be greeted with applause, or her confidence might evaporate, whereas Fred was quite stable enough to do without it. There is evidence that she was wrong in this, that her obsessive worrying over Maggie did more harm than good. 'I am going to take a Total Abstinence Pledge from Anxiety', is a promise from mother to daughter which indicates some tension, as does Maggie's undertaking in return that 'I, Margaret Benson, in full possession of my faculties, do hereby declare that for the future I will go to bed at an earlier stage of a really bad cold, especially if influenza is about – and this I acknowledge to my wise and doting mother and in conjunction with her.'[12]

Whenever they were separated, Minnie bombarded Maggie with letters of admonition or care, sprinkled with girlish squeals and bubbling with excitement at the prospect of reunion. 'Now I find you are coming home EARLY IN MAY. Oh Lorks! What an idiot I feel! I danced around and shrieked to Beth and sent for nurse and made a fool of myself in general.' Maggie was too fierce and proud to put up with this nonsense for long, and frequently scolded her mother for her excesses. Her latent jealousy of Lucy sometimes surfaced, as when she elicited from her mother another promise, this time to make herself free from the other woman's influence. Yet these easy promises lacked weight and the underlying conflict steadily grew worse. Late in the year Minnie went to join Maggie in the garden and there ensued one of those terrible unpremeditated encounters when truth and honesty come pouring out unhindered by politeness.

Maggie began by saying that their former mutual understanding was extinguished, to which her mother replied that 'there were certain temperamental developments of late arising in her . . . ' That careful remark was like a match to paper, and Maggie flared. Those were the exact words Lucy Tait had used! Why did Mother not think for herself? Why parrot Lucy? Why always get Lucy to face difficulties for her? Minnie told her she was all too quick to sit in judgement on people when the shadow of depression began to fall on her, 'when I began instantly to feel it'. Maggie retorted that she was tight with money, which was irrelevant but true and served to spark the release of the real cause of antipathy in both women. Minnie told her daughter that she was getting so much like Edward she was in truth 'falling in love with her father'. Maggie objected to Lucy's constant presence, laying great emphasis on her being with Minnie *day and night*, at breakfast, all the time and everywhere. Could they not go to Brighton for a weekend, with Fred but *without* Lucy? Surely Mother would prefer to be with *her own kin*? Minnie said it had been so difficult for her since Edward's death, to which Maggie replied that she wanted to help her, but that Lucy was prising them apart. 'You don't trust any of us,' she said. She had good relations with both Arthur and Fred, but not with her own mother.

They then began to reminisce, and only made matters worse. Minnie had always wanted harmony in domestic life, and had never achieved it, whereas Maggie interpreted this, exactly as her father used to, as a weak desire to be comfortable and unchallenged, to be not really alive. The conversation left poor Minnie depleted and despairing. 'The long years in which my whole desire was to soothe her, and please, and make her sad ill life as sweet and cherished as possible have hidden from her me, myself (if there is a me!) I feel very sad and downhearted tonight – the new hope of strength and joy seems very far off – and the morrow brings – what?' She kissed Maggie with more warmth that night than ever in her life, because she felt, once again, that she had failed, that she could not be the strong person Maggie wanted her to be but would always have to seek the support of Lucy. In short, Maggie was too demanding; she wanted to swallow or submerge her mother just as Edward had done, to deny her the power of choice.

Four days later Maggie attempted to make amends. More promises were made – not to pick on a sentence and thrash it to death for days, not to make her mother feel guilty and uncomfortable about Lucy, and so on. But they were just words. Maggie's fate was determined by her genes, not her vocabulary, and as the new century began there was a real sense of foreboding at Tremans. Mrs Benson decided for once not to share the discussion with Lucy. 'I keep all this to myself. Lucy knows we have talked but no more.'[13] It was significant that when the memorial to Edward White Benson was unveiled at Canterbury, all his family attended save the one member who was most likely to appreciate it; Maggie, begging ill-health, stayed at home alone at Tremans.

'You have before you as a principle that you won't and don't judge,' Minnie scolded her, 'but in actual practice I never knew anyone judge more rapidly, promptly and without appeal, and you won't linger, or wonder, and get the people to explain themselves or be ready to learn and understand.' This was the old, peremptory, unyielding Maggie which Ethel Smyth had discerned fifteen years earlier, and of which she was herself painfully aware, in moments of lucidity and introspection. It cannot have been easy for her – a gifted, intellectual woman – to recognise that she was a torment to others, and it is with pathos we read of her apologies to her mother and to the immediate trigger of her agony, Lucy Tait. 'You and Lucy don't make me feel you are sacrificing yourselves,' she says, 'though it must be a pretty considerable tie.'[14] This exchange of letters occurred when the companions had gone to Strathpeffer in Scotland, ostensibly in order to encourage diet, for Mrs Benson was by this time getting stout and could not stop eating, but in reality to recover from the strain of dealing with Maggie's moods. Quite possibly the strain was the oblique cause of the over-eating in the first place.

The escape from Tremans continued to afford Fred a glorious sense of renewal and to instil in him an energetic determination to do serious work. He began to find London life too full and exhausting even for him, and decided to return to Winchester. *Mammon & Co* (1899) and his next, *Princess Sophia* (1900), had both sold well and presented Fred with a prosperous year, enabling him to afford both to keep Oxford Street and to rent a house at 3 St Cross Street ('3' was not a number but a name, he said), taking Sidney with him plus two maids. His investments on the Stock Market were healthy, but he gave up speculation because he found he was thinking about it all the time. He wrote two more books and a play for Mrs Patrick Campbell, of which he had high hopes. Minnie went to see him in Winchester for a few days and found him productive and full of life. He had built himself a tiny garden with a trellised shelter where he sat and worked all day and took tea ('Dark and cheerless is the morn Unaccompanied by tea', was his extempore couplet which amused Arthur very much). 'It is a good wholesome life,' Minnie wrote to Duchess Adeline, 'and full of very good work. The house is really charming – it only needs a wife – but one must wait for that.'[15]

Apart from the play for Mrs Pat, which opened in New York to the most frosty reception and was deemed neither amusing nor a suitable vehicle for the famous actress, Fred also wrote some short stories for *The Onlooker* on the subject of 'social criminals'. If nothing else, they indicated that he knew his way round the Almanach de Gotha and considered the legitimacy of titles a matter of grave importance. But his best professional success since *Dodo* came with the publication of *The Luck of the Vails* in 1901, a hybrid novel – part social satire, part horror story – based on a chilling tale Arthur used to tell his little boys at Eton. It is appropriately dedicated to Arthur, and elicited ungrudging approval, for once, from Mama. 'It rises steadily in interest and horror,' she said. 'I got quite creepy and felt as if I could kill anyone who opened the door.'[16] (The poor woman had to sit through a reading of Hugh's sermons immediately afterwards.)

Some of the critics were less than generous, and seemed to delight in knocking E.F. Benson with a relish they usually reserved for the absurd Marie Corelli. 'We believed that in *The Princess Sophia* he had reached the lowest literary depths possible in a man of breeding and education,' said one, 'but he has now condescended to write a story which has all the characteristics of a shilling shocker.'[17] Never mind; *The Luck of the Vails* remains one of the dozen or so books by E.F. Benson which is remembered with respect to this day, and boasts a brilliant melodramatic conclusion. 'I'm rather pleased with the yarn,' wrote Fred.[18] Next came *Scarlet and Hyssop*, a society novel in which Fred mischievously mocked the kind of folk who had been the principal *dramatis personae* of his social life for the past five years and began to show that special talent for acerbic satire which would eventually become the Benson trademark. Perhaps too acerbic – Fred has yet to develop that wry smiling tolerance which will make his characters endearing despite their foibles. Here they are little short of hateful. *Scarlet and Hyssop* sold 8,000 copies within a few weeks, and it was said to be the only book King Edward VII had read in six months ('Much good may it do him!' commented Arthur).[19]

Fred was perfectly conscious of the limitations of his talent and was still groping for its strengths. Arthur had begun the Diary which would eventually rank as one of the longest ever written, and brought it to London to show Fred one day in 1902 when it had reached the sixteenth volume. It is odd that something normally so private should be offered like this for comment, especially between people who were unassailably buttoned up, but it must suggest Arthur always intended the Diary to be published. Fred read the little brown volumes and immediately spotted how different was the style and approach compared to his own. 'I think you have got the knack of making common things full of distinction,' he told him, thus encapsulating the trick which would sell A.C. Benson's books in their thousands to earnest ladies who sought their philosophy in small sugared lumps. 'Personally, as my chief faculty lies in teasing the gilding off things which appear to be distinguished and are really common, I envy you.'[20] It would be difficult to imagine a more concise description of the essential quality of *Secret Lives* or *Lucia in London*, but they were far into the future and Fred had yet to find his way of 'teasing the gilding off' gently.

Arthur was busy editing the letters of Queen Victoria (at whose funeral all the Bensons had been present, seated in the nave) and continuing with his poetry, or perhaps verse would be a safer word, at the same time. One of his commissioned pieces was a Coronation Ode to celebrate the accession of Edward VII, which was set to music by Edward Elgar and was due to be given its first performance in a Gala at the Opera House on 30 June 1902. This would not normally warrant a mention were it not for the fact that Arthur's words have since become part of the national heritage, boomed out every September on the last night of the Henry Wood Promenade Concerts as 'Land of Hope and Glory'.*

It comes as a surprise to learn that when Sir Edward Cassel asked Fred to play bridge with the King, Fred politely refused. Cassel was not pleased, and said rather gruffly, 'I think it is almost a command,' to which Fred made the quick reply, 'Not from you!' It was a triumph of genial rudeness, yet also the surrender of a chance to hob-nob with the great. It was a fact that Fred was less easily flattered than he used to be, and though he cherished his titled friends, he was past believing that a title automatically bestowed interest, still less intelligence, upon its recipient. *Scarlet and Hyssop* was, after all, an attack against the worst moral excesses of high society. Fred told Arthur quite frankly that he did not want to get mixed up with the King's set.[22] He preferred people who were gregarious rather than grand.

There was another, more personal, reason for Fred's reluctance to become embroiled with the King. His close friend, Lady Charles Beresford, nicknamed The Painted Lady owing to her

---

* The exact sequence of events is as follows: *Pomp and Circumstance March No 1* was first performed in Liverpool on 19 October, 1901, and two days later in London. At that stage, no words were envisaged. In 1902 Elgar was commissioned to write a Coronation Ode for Edward VII's coronation, and it was due to be premiered at Covent Garden on 30 June; the concert was cancelled due to the King's illness. This ode was eventually heard for the first time in Sheffield on 2 October. The finale of the Ode is an adaptation of the trio section of *Pomp and Circumstance*, and it was the King who suggested it should have words set to it, proposing Arthur as the author. Arthur's words have been roared out with thrashing Union Flags ever since.[21]

extravagant make-up haphazardly applied (a little boy in a pram had once tried to snatch her eyebrow, thinking it was a butterfly), had been socially ruined by the then Prince of Wales twenty years before. Lord Charles, one of his nearest cronies, had had a mistress, Lady Brooke, known to history under her subsequent name of Daisy, Countess of Warwick. Lady Charles became pregnant by her husband at the age of forty, and Daisy had been so indignant she had accused him of infidelity and broadcast her fury all over London. She wrote a jealous and angry letter to Lord Charles, which Lady Charles opened and circulated. It was a fight to the death between the two women, each determined to banish the other from Society for ever more. Daisy went to the Prince of Wales with her distress, and promptly became his mistress instead. Lady Charles gave birth to a daughter, but thereafter she was never again invited to balls and dinners patronised by royalty. She had effectively been frozen out.[23]

By the time Fred knew her she had long since put the scandal behind her and determined to create her own alternative society. She dressed outrageously in pale pink taffeta more suitable to a twelve-year-old, which made her obesity quite laughable, and her face-powder flew off in clouds as she moved. She had become a gloriously manufactured creature.

Fred would not wish to hurt her by acknowledging acquaintance with the monarch who had served her so ill, and his disinclination to play bridge with the King doubtless helped to cement his relations with the Beresfords. (It is also typical of his caution that when he came to relate this story in *Mother* he referred mysteriously to 'a row', giving no names or details.) They took him to Bayreuth for the second time, and he went on alone afterwards to spend time skating and mountain-climbing in Switzerland, practising on the ice for six hours every day.[24] On his way back he called in at Paris to visit Reggie Lister, recently appointed Second Secretary at the Embassy, after which he positively welcomed a few days at Tremans. Now that he was not obliged actually to live there, he found the place a delight to visit, and family reunions a pleasure to anticipate, at least in small doses. Everyone was relaxed when they were engaging in simple communal enjoyments. One evening Maggie read out an amusing paper on Lucy, for once without rancour, while Fred composed spoof advertisement copy and a parody on Keats. Lucy read a poem of her own composition, Hugh a series of nightmare adventures he made up, and Mother a shrewd and funny essay on growing old.[25] It was also on this occasion that she poked fun at Fred for his addictive smoking habit. Though she would sometimes have a quiet smoke with Fred or Hugh after dinner, usually in another room away from Lucy's disapproving scowl, Fred was far more renowned for being furtive and surreptitious with his cigarettes. On returning to the dining-room for coffee, Minnie presented him with a rhyme she composed in his absence:

> Mysterious, secret, dark as night –
> The names of all his friends.
> He only says 'I go to write',
> And there my knowledge ends.
>
> I pry not, I – I only feel
> Whenever he comes back O!
> That through his letters loudly peal
> The pleasures of Tobacco.[26]

No wonder Gertrude Bell said of the family, 'That's one comfort about all of you. You are not in the least like children of Archbishops.'[27]

It was when earnest intellectual debate replaced family games that Fred felt less comfortable and grew impatient to leave for London. Arthur felt sure he wasn't up to it, that his mind lacked rigour and depth. 'Fred doesn't like the Tremans atmosphere,' he said. 'He likes to rattle away to an admiring throng – and hates the eager, critical and metaphysical discussions which rage here; he gets slowly more depressed and his face looks gloomy and irritable; but he tries hard to be nice.'[28] A little of this is true. Fred certainly did love an audience, especially one which encouraged him to perform and be witty. But he was also capable of dialectic, sustained sequential thought, logical argument. The reason he avoided them at Tremans was because he knew what they might lead to – Maggie's fierce and dangerous absolutism, Hugh's petulance, Mother's anxiety. He was simply more sensitive than Arthur, which is why he 'tried to be nice', to soften the atmosphere. Despite his intelligence and perception, Arthur was curiously blind to the inflammatory possibilities of hard debate when Bensons got together. Fred sometimes preferred to leave and play the piano for hours on end. His playing, sneered Arthur, was 'coarse and loud'.

Arthur was also irritated by Fred's habit of spoiling a good story by embellishment, that old want of accuracy for which he had been chided since schooldays. 'I never feel quite sure whether credence is to be attached to anything he says . . . All his stories are wildly inaccurate and yet he is absolutely positive as to details.'[29] The schoolmaster in A.C. Benson was frankly appalled by his brother's wilful mendacity. When he gets on his high horse his Diary gives us the most vivid impressions of Fred's presence and allure:

> He is much too desultory a talker for me. He likes to skip and leap about – now I like to *go on at* a thing and hate dropping it. I want to squeeze and squeeze it . . . This is the first time I have ever observed traces of advancing years in Fred [He was thirty-six]. He is less agile in mind, and I think his mind beats in a narrower circle. He tends to tell the same stories and to revert to the same rather small stock of subjects. His ignorance on certain points rather surprised me. He had no idea, e.g., that the Virgin Birth of Christ had ever been questioned except by quite desperate infidels. But he is brilliant too – very quick and brisk – lively in judgement.[30]

Again, it would not occur to Arthur that Fred thought the Virgin Birth a tricky subject for Bensons to gnaw at, and sought tactfully to deflect attention to a safer topic. One of his favourites was the invention of 'Gosses', that is dreadful *faux pas* in the manner of Edmund Gosse. Arthur thought this monumentally frivolous.

In 1903 Arthur left Eton to become a Fellow of Magdalene College, Cambridge and enter the bookish, unhurried ambience which would sustain him for the rest of his life. Also in 1903, on 15 July, the ceremony of consecration of Truro Cathedral took place in the presence of the Prince and Princess of Wales. Minnie and Fred were also invited, then separated – Fred placed, to his

Edward White Benson.

Mary Benson

Edward White Benson as Archbishop of
Canterbury. Oil by Sir Hubert von
Herkomer.

Mary Benson with Fred, Hugh and Arthur,
1884.

Fred at nineteen.

. . . . at twenty-six.

. . . . in his thirties.

E. F. Benson at his desk in Oakley Street. Sketch by Bernard Gotch.

Tremans, Horsted Keynes.

The Bensons at Tremans: Maggie, Arthur, Hugh, Mary,
Fred and Beth.

SPORTING AND COUNTRY HOUSE SUPPLEMENT

THE AUTHOR OF "DODO" AT VILLARS

On the left is Mr. Wilfrid Coleridge, who on the day our photograph was taken passed the gold skating test. In the centre is Mr. E. F. Benson, the well-known author of "Dodo" and many other novels, discussing the contents of his luncheon packet. On the right is the Hon. Gilbert Coleridge, brother of Mr. Justice Coleridge and father of Mr. Wilfrid Coleridge

The Tatler, 1910.

Lamb House, Rye, with the Garden Room on the right.

Charlie Tomlin when young.

Fred and Taffy at Lamb House, early 1930s.
Photograph by Charlie Tomlin.

With Francis Yeats-Brown on the Garden
Room steps, April 1931.

Greeting Queen Mary at the door of Lamb House, 1935.

E. F. Benson at his desk in the mid 1930s.

chagrin, behind a pillar. At the town hall afterwards he was further seated at the distant corner of the remotest table.

Truro may well have put him in mind of the family drama which was gradually unfolding in the course of this year and which would have driven the first Bishop of Truro to apoplexy. The Bishop's youngest son, the one who replaced Martin and was consequently spoilt, and the only one to enter the Church, was slipping by easy stages into the arms of the Antichrist. Hugh was becoming a Roman Catholic.

There had always been in Hugh a child-like craving for certainty; in this he was as absolute and unyielding as Maggie, but his absolutism took a different route. He could not bear to be interrupted, and dissent from his view provoked many a violent row. He simply had to be right about everything, or there would be a tantrum. He had written a book of short stories centred around a Roman Catholic priest which clearly expressed the direction his mind was taking. Entitled *The Light Invisible*, it is quite the best of R.H. Benson's many books and it deservedly won him a devoted readership. In July of 1903 Hugh put himself under instruction for the Roman Catholic Church, and in September he went to the College of San Silvestro in Rome where, incidentally, he met the Pope. It is not recorded whether or not the Pope rejoiced in the capture of an Archbishop's son, but we do know that when Hugh returned to England in June 1904, having been through the second ordination of his life to become a priest, Arthur was decidedly sniffy:

What grieves me about it is the lighthearted and self-absorbed way in which it is all done, like a child flying a kite; he goes to Rome like a person getting out of a shabby third-class carriage into a smart first-class; and has no thought for the wayfarers who have been with him . . . The one thing Hugh wants is authority and the luxury of not having to make up a confused and not very profound mind . . . I hate the thought of my father's son doing this – and I hate the thought that his conversion will, from that very circumstance, have more weight than the adhesion of Hugh's very light mind ought to give any cause or principle. I don't think it is the smallest grief or pain for Hugh; instead of looking like a man who has been struggling

and wrestling, he looks like a person with a comfortable cheerful
secret . . . the idea of all the old cords snapping, all the tender
associations cut adrift from, are nothing to him by the side of
satisfying his childish whim.[31]

Arthur was not worried lest the Anglican faith be questioned
or betrayed; he was himself quite happy in doubt. No, it was a
matter of good manners and motive. He could not help noticing
that Hugh loved dressing up and wore the biretta all day long.
(In Rome he had been dotty about both the splendour of the
Vatican and the hugeness of the soldiers.) Fred, too, was probably
a sceptic, though as secret in this as in everything else, and bore
no grudge against Hugh for his choice. He was more amused than
upset, finding it ticklingly funny that Hugh had to break off
croquet and rush indoors at the precise minute that God required
him to say his prayers.

Minnie was the very soul of tolerance and comfort. She made
no objection when Hugh commandeered the little room at Tremans used for Anglican prayers and transformed it into his own
private Catholic Oratory, not even when he added arrogantly that
without it he regretted he would be unable to visit her. Nor did
she flinch from facing a Prioress who had invited Hugh to say
Mass: she thought her 'an old darling'. The letter she wrote her
son to congratulate him – 'it has happened' – is full of decency
and love tinged with only the tiniest fear of severance:

We know you are ours still, and nothing will ever shake that
fundamental blessed reality of love. And we know too that in
all that we hold most dear we are at one, as ever. For the rest,
you know now where your heart feels you can be truly loyal,
where it finds its home, where you deeply feel God has led
you . . . only *let us in*, always, whenever you rightly can – my
heart cries out for that.[32]

There is a post-script which might almost have been dictated, with
a mischievous twinkle, by Fred: *'Tell me your proper address and
style.'*

Minnie did not forget her own struggles with faith, far more
severe than anything Hugh seems to have endured, which almost

destroyed her when the children were little and her exigent husband was too lofty in certitude to help her. She may well have reflected since on a prediction by one of the friends of her early marriage, that her children would grow up to cause her vexation in one way or another, but they would never be dull.

For all its attractions, Winchester was too far away from the vortex to satisfy Fred for long – 'it's no more like life than a duck pond is to the river in flood'[33] – and he bought a house in Oakley Street, Chelsea, in 1904. He demolished the wall of the hallway so that the front door opened directly into the dining-room, and equipped the house with furniture and pictures borrowed from Tremans. Here he worked daily, pouring out books at the rate of two a year, and entertained with equal assiduity.

Arthur grew more and more censorious both of his brother's character and way of life. 'I never felt so little near him,' he said. In the first place, Fred's evident happiness rankled not a little, added to the consciousness that he was successful, 'gone to the top like a cork in water'. Arthur deplored the quiet complacency, which he attributed to a kind of natural aristocracy in his brother's bearing and view of the world, compared to the plebeian attitudes of the rest of the Bensons. 'When he came to see me I felt a little as if he were a great man visiting an almshouse.'[34]

There was a paradox in this, however, as Fred's behaviour was not always aristocratic, but often rather peremptory and impatient. Arthur likened his manners to wickerwork, 'showing the nature through; they betray him', and thought that it was when he was not on show that his shrill and sour personality revealed itself. 'It is odd how Fred, who believes himself to be, and is in a way, a light of society, has such gruff, abrupt, rude manners. It is when he is at home, mostly, I think. When he is on his own dunghills he crows too lustily; abroad he is suave and brilliant.'[35]

In the summer of 1905 the whole family were together at Tremans, affording Arthur the opportunity to observe Fred in comparison with the others. It ill became Arthur to talk of sourness when he could, after dinner, repair to his room and the little volume he used for a Diary to dissect his family with cold detachment. Yet we must allow that his portraits of Fred are the nearest we can approach him, for they were penned in the immediate aftermath of a conversation and are much more vibrant than the considered essays written by Fred himself years afterwards. Arthur thought his brother was too fond of comfort – nice house, good cook, servants, whisky and soda – what Fred himself called 'the things which supply the wadding of life'.[36] 'He enjoys luxury and material comfort very much – all the things that I find, to my pleasure and relief, seem to weigh less and less in the scale.' Worse than that, Arthur was convinced that Fred still hankered after wealth and rank, that, in short, he was a snob.

It cannot be denied that Fred was easily seduced by the rich when he was a young celebrity. They wanted to gather him in as a jester at their tables, and he offered little resistance. But he was older now, nearly forty, and more discriminating. His posh friends were those who were distinguished by talent or interest or, as in the case of Lady Charles, rejection by 'society'. Besides which, he was fascinated and amused by eccentrics, and there were more of those among the aristocratic families than within the middle-classes. Nevertheless, the impression persisted that Fred was an egregious snob; Edmund Gosse, than whom there was scarcely anyone more snobbish, called him so, and Arthur said they were as bad as each other.

'The world in which he lives, peopled by dim aristocrats, is mysterious to me,' wrote Arthur. 'Evie and Algy and all the rest of them. I can't help feeling that he would not find them so interesting if they were not swells.'[37] Faith Compton Mackenzie referred to Fred witheringly as 'a worldling'. So, are they right? E.F. Benson himself frequently wrote with scorn about social climbers who confuse title with merit, and what are the *Lucia* books if not a glorious send-up of snobbery in all its petty manifestations? The social climber, he said, never has a moment's rest, and in New York she cannot climb at all, but can only stand on tiptoe! On the other hand, Fred is honest enough to admit that 'most people have a touch (just a touch) of the snob innate in them, if they will only take the pains to look for it.'[38] He would not deny, if pressed, that there was a touch innate in him, too, but it was not the vulgar self-promoting kind of snobbery which Arthur appears to detect. Frankly, he said, interesting people are more interesting than uninteresting ones, and if the people with brains have a title as well, they should not be dismissed for that alone. To prefer brains at your table is simply good selection, and 'if this is snobbishness, it is a very sensible and intelligent quality'.[39] Here he is talking more about élitism than idiotic people-collecting, but it was as easy then to confuse the two as it is now.

One example may serve to settle the issue. From 1905 onwards Fred spent several weeks a year staying with the Dowager Countess of Radnor at her house in Venice. For Arthur it was perfectly clear from the beginning that he would not have gone had she been the widow of a draper. Even five years later Arthur was still muttering, 'Old Lady Radnor is a nice old pussycat but very silly – and I can't understand Fred being so much with her. She is just the sort of person one would think he would not tolerate.'[40] Arthur simply could not understand, did not *feel*, the pleasure which a naturally gregarious man derives from easy and trustful social intercourse. He assumed Fred was blinded by her rank, flattered by her attentions, and more or less sold himself for a luxurious holiday at which he could show off whom he knew.

'Old Lady Radnor' was emphatically not an empty-headed crone. Born Helen Matilda Chaplin, the daughter of a clergyman, she had married the 5th Earl of Radnor and been widowed in 1900. Her niece was the formidable Marchioness of Londonderry, last Tory hostess, and she was descended through her mother from Georgiana, the delectable Duchess of Devonshire. After Lord Radnor's death she bought an apartment in the Palazzo da Mula, with a garden on the Giudecca, where she spent at least half the year. The guests from England who flocked to join her elegant house-parties included writers and musicians, politicians and diplomats, people distinguished by achievement rather than rank. For the essence of Helen Matilda was her creative spirit. The absorbing passion of her life was music. She not only played the piano but wrote music and some of her compositions to words by Kipling were performed publicly and professionally. She formed and conducted a famous amateur orchestra, known by her name, and did much to help the foundation of the Royal College of Music. In Venice she trained a choir to a very high standard. A year or so later, Arthur was visiting Fred at Oakley Street when

Lady Radnor was invited to dinner. He found her then 'a dear old goose . . . with just the touch of despotism one finds in count-esses,' and he noticed that when Fred played the piano at the end of the evening, she suddenly joined in from the sofa with a rich soprano voice. Yet he did not relent in his judgement that Fred worshipped her for the earldom rather than for her companion-ship. That there were many who cherished her as a friend he would find frankly suspect. He was crudely wrong. Fred's own tribute to her, written long after her death, is among the most graceful compliments a man can pay to an elderly maternal figure: 'To be with her was to sit in the sun.'[41]

In contrast, when E.F. Benson described those aristocrats who carried arrogance and condescension in their bones and had nothing to offer but their names, he was ferocious in his condem-nation. He scorned the notion 'that on one of the days of the Creation – that, probably, on which the decree was made that there should be Light – there leaped into being the great landowners of England.' And his portrait of one such landowner in the character of Lady Ashbridge can leave no room to doubt his sincerity:

> No idea other than an obvious one ever had birth behind her high, smooth forehead, and she habitually brought conversation to a close by the dry enunciation of something indubitably true, which had no direct relation to the point under discus-sion . . . she belonged heart and soul to the generation and the breeding among which it is enough for a woman to be a lady, and visit the keeper's wife when she has a baby.[42]

The other kind to earn Fred's derision is the hard-up aristocrat who hires herself out to snobs anxious to have a titled person at dinner and are prepared to pay for it. She is typified by Lady Mackleton, who has a regular tariff, 'two guineas for dinner, or dinner and theatre, and one guinea for lunch and her taxi-fares. Or if you engage her for a series of six, she pays her own taxi. She is well worth it, I assure you.'[43] Fred understood all about snobbery, far too much to remain a victim of it after the first glow of youth had left his cheeks. It is strange that Arthur could not see the truth.

Arthur tended also to look down upon Fred's lack of academic stature, his proud amateurism. Because he took no real interest in politics and disdained men of influence, he kept himself ignorant of important affairs of the moment. Nor, to Arthur's horror, did he read anything fresh. When asked if he knew any of the modern writers, Fred replied 'No, thank God! as if he could not be tainted by the professional mud.'⁴⁴ As a result, Fred had virtually no conversation as far as his brother was concerned, because he could not follow a subject through. He preferred repartee to discussion. 'He delights in a kind of brisk and lively persiflage, which he really does very well, playing it like lawn-tennis with many dexterous strokes,' commented Arthur. 'Personally it bores me to extinction.' When Fred was present, conversation was always diverted towards the snappily humorous, the personal reminiscence, the anecdotal. When he was in high spirits he dominated the scene effortlessly. 'The talk became a rattling on, from person to person, subject to subject, all really funny, but one simply gets tired of it . . . His idea of a successful conversation is when you don't know at the end what you have been talking about.'⁴⁵

For Fred, the purpose of conversation was to entertain, for Arthur it was rather to inform. Fred could not bear solemnity, the ponderous satisfied tones of the expert. If talk lacked sparkle, his face assumed 'a dark, crucified kind of expression'⁴⁶ and he would be eager to get away. Of his own contribution it is difficult at such a distance to extract a flavour, though everyone (even Arthur) agreed it was amusing. It relied a great deal upon paradox and irony, and relished the neatly balanced rejoinder. Fred himself tells of his response to Arnold Bennett, who had declared that E.F. Benson did not know how to write. Much chastened, he said, he decided to write no more, but to read instead, and with this determination he went to the library and took a book by Arnold Bennett. To his great consternation, he discovered he could not read either! One can imagine at how many tables was that story repeated. In similar vein was the fierce complaint made by the Archdeacon of Natal about a harmless little parody Fred had written, to which he said that since he had only intended to amuse, but had annoyed, and the Archdeacon had intended to annoy, and had only amused, they were quits.[47] There is something feline in this kind of snappy reaction.

For the most part, Fred's sallies were as ephemeral as the decorations on an ice-sculpture, witty trifles that were not fashioned to be remembered. We do know that he repeated himself, and that he stole stories from other sources, including Wilde, and passed them off as his own until one of the family, generally Maggie, spotted the filch and challenged him. There is also evidence that he could be supercilious in the company of lesser competing anecdotalists, betraying a little of that arrogance inherent in all Bensons. Faith Compton Mackenzie, who knew Fred in Capri, said 'there was always that faintly superior bearing which made one's own little quips and aphorisms seem rather faded and old-fashioned. Hardly worth going on with.'[48]

On the other hand, Fred could be serious when it came to a matter of moral conduct. There was a discussion one evening at Tremans about the behaviour of schoolmasters who set traps for boys with the intention of catching them out. The idea was that a 'good' boy would not fall into the trap and was therefore safe, whereas a 'bad' boy would reveal his moral vulnerability by lying or stealing or doing whatever he had been surreptitiously encouraged to do. Arthur thought this was a perfectly proper way to proceed and frequently resorted to such tactics at Eton, claiming, quite rightly, that Edward White Benson would have thoroughly approved. Fred was outraged and said so. That a defender of morals should resort to the methods of an *agent provocateur* disgusted him.[49]

Arthur conceded that Fred worked hard and was impressively prolific. Not only was he writing novels by the dozen and short stories and articles when asked, he also collaborated with his old friend Eustace Miles on books of advice – how to keep a body healthy through diet and exercise, how to skate; he also edited a book on how to play golf. Some of the novels were deservedly dismissed, but with *The Challoners* E.F. Benson wrote his best book to date, and one which seared with personal commitment. It is a story of conflict between generations and ideals, based almost entirely upon the author's pained relationship with his father.

The Rev. Sidney Challoner and his son Martin are locked in mutual incomprehension. The clergyman, an exact portrayal of Archbishop Benson, is stiff, unyielding, austere, with a heart imprisoned by the habit of dogma. 'Nothing in the world could be sadder to me than that my children should not think of me as their friend,' he says, all unaware that they are terrified of his displeasure and seek to avoid him. So faithful is the portrait to the original that Fred includes a scene at mealtime which corresponds with his recollection of childhood at Wellington. The two children, Martin and Helen, suppress an innocent giggle and are severely reprimanded by their father who tells them it is exceedingly vulgar to exchange glances; Martin's merriment is thereupon struck 'as dead as beech-leaves in frost'. Silence descends upon the meal, until Challoner chides the children for not speaking to him. It was all so familiar, but one wonders if Fred ever answered his father as Martin does in the book. 'I tried to tell you what I have been doing, but you stopped me. You said it was unsuitable.'

Martin is a musical genius whose talents should be displayed on the concert platform, but father will have none of it, as music is a reprehensible waste of God-given energy. Martin, though dutiful, is stubborn in adhering to beliefs which are in direct contradiction to his father's. Again, it is likely that Fred is here being covertly autobiographical, and that somewhere in the past lay an argument with the Archbishop which clarified their irreconcilable differences. When Challoner describes Martin as 'purposeless, desultory, without aims or interests, and so utterly unlike himself in every point of character that he could scarcely believe he was his son,' it is not altogether fanciful to hear Edward talking about Fred.[50]

Fred would not have dared write such a book while the Archbishop was alive, especially since it ends with the son dying in his father's arms – a fate which would have too cruelly recalled the death of the real Martin in 1877. Indeed, it is fascinating that Fred should have called his hero by this name, as if in some indirect way he was seeking to make amends to his father for the disappointment he knew he must have been, by fusing the beloved, the perfect Martin with the dunce, the imperfect Fred. Fred would have liked to have earned his father's love as Martin had done, but Martin, had he lived, would have needed to escape his father's love as Fred had done. Whatever the case, *The Challoners* is undoubtedly a very personal book. He completed the manuscript of 308 foolscap pages in just three weeks, from 18 February to 10 March 1904.[51] By Christmas that year sales had exceeded 10,000 copies.

Arthur, acknowledging that it was the strongest book Fred had thus far written, flew to the defence of their father, who he thought had been treated superficially.

> Fred fails purely from lack of sympathy with and knowledge of what really could be inside the mind of a man like that. All the real work of the world, whether religion, teaching or politics, is *dull* to Fred, because he does not know anything about it. His only idea of life is of people who bathe and play golf and smoke cigarettes and bang the piano.[52]

Thus saying, Arthur adopted, for a moment, the role of apologist for the father traduced, forgetting that he shared much the same opinion of Edward White Benson as Fred did, especially with regard to his capacity to shrivel a child's enthusiasm, and would say so in *The Trefoil*. Fred could not be a great writer, he said, for this lack of sympathy and imagination restricted him. 'But I suppose that to have a sharp cutting-edge a chisel must be *narrow*.'

Notwithstanding fraternal strictures, Fred's reputation was such that his next book, *Angel of Pain*, sold 8,000 copies on the day of publication, and his adaptation of *Dodo* for the stage was performed at the Savoy Theatre on 8 March 1906 to rapturous applause (Arthur remarking sourly that there were no calls for the author). 'I am besieged with congratulations,' Fred told his literary representative.[53] He gave a private reading of his next play, *The Friend in the Garden*, after dinner at Tremans to a company which included Mary Cholmondeley, author of the best-selling novel *Red Pottage*, and rather too gushing a personality for Arthur. Miss Cholmondeley declared the piece to be very fine, which for Arthur meant it must be poor to warrant *her* praise. Afterwards, he was driven to solitary fulmination. 'I am afraid I thought it essentially *common* and pretentious from beginning to end,' he wrote. The central character was 'one of the hard brilliant rattling intolerable women whom Fred loves,' and the play itself 'one of the most terrible and humiliating things I have ever heard . . . it seems to me like Dodo trying to write like Maeterlinck.'[54]

There is a harshness in this judgement which sounds close to bitterness. The fact is, Arthur was at this very time undergoing a trial of self-examination which left him fragile. The Headmastership of Eton was pending. To many people, A.C. Benson seemed the most likely candidate, as his House had been hugely popular and his personal standing among the boys secure. There were, however, two factors combining against his appointment. He had made enemies with the staff, some of whom were, in the manner of common-rooms, furtively acting against him while professing comradeship in his presence. And Arthur himself felt he had been a failure at Eton. Once that feeling has taken possession of the soul, no amount of facts or persuasive arguments can shift it. Arthur went through the motions of being interviewed, but let it be known that if the Headmastership were offered to him, he was not sure he would accept it. To his mother he wrote, 'I am not in the least morbid about it. But if one has been handsomely and wholesomely snubbed, one doesn't desire to see the place where it was done, or the people who did it.' He further reassured her that though there was a certain glamour in the post, he did not at heart desire it.[55]

Beset as he was by the conviction of his failure, almost by a self-inflicted longing to see it confirmed, it is little wonder that Arthur looked upon Fred's undeserved and uncomplicated success with envy bordering upon malice. He, Arthur, was serious and reflective, a man who suffered for his thoughts and his contemplation of human destiny. To his mind, Fred was shallow but ridiculously happy, and making a fortune from writing rubbish. It simply was not fair. It is in this light that Arthur's misprision of his brother's worth must be understood. It would take many years and two severe breakdowns before he was able to revise these judgements.

There was more. Within the same year Hugh made the most unfortunate friendship of his life, with Frederick William Rolfe, who styled himself, without a scintilla of justification, Baron

Corvo. Rolfe was a thoroughly nasty piece of work, treacherous, deceitful, and above all clothed with an impregnable vanity. He had for years coveted the honour of being a Roman Catholic priest, but had so consistently been denied his prize that he nursed a hatred for all the officers of the Church which was little short of manic. The people who tried to help him, for his talents as a writer and artist did not go unrecognised, were rewarded with spleen, spite and bitter revenge. Rolfe turned upon the world because his tortured personality needed enemies to feed his hatred, and if there was none, he would manufacture them. If priests were swindlers, friends were secret slanderers. Rolfe had written a book, *Hadrian VII*, which flopped badly with the public but was noticed by a small band of admirers for its unusual theme and the passion of its prose. *Hadrian VII* was the story of a neglected priest who, to everyone's surprise, is elected Pope. The tale clearly enabled Rolfe to write out his frustration, but it did not entirely banish it. He was still a dangerous man to meet.

R.H. Benson was ripe to be a Rolfe victim. Since his absorption into the Roman Catholic Church he had become smug, and insufferably pontifical in his pronouncements. He confused logic with rhetoric. In a family discussion Hugh would wriggle away from philosophical or doctrinal challenges presented by Maggie and Arthur with the bland statement that he *knew*, and they didn't, and that was that. His was precisely the kind of ecclesiastical arrogance which drove Frederick Rolfe apoplectic, and whole armies ought to have been ready to keep them apart. Hugh, alas, was a very poor judge of character. He read *Hadrian VII* and was entranced. He wrote to the author. Rolfe, who would not have trusted the Virgin Mary herself, was distinctly wary of fulsome praise from this well-known priest; he had heard it before; everyone let him down; he would treat Benson's overtures with lofty scorn. What worried him most was Hugh's fame – his book was a bestseller and all good Catholics were reading *The Light Invisible* while barely a few had even heard of *Hadrian VII*. Still Hugh persisted, and Rolfe relented. They met and were friendly. They contemplated a collaborative work, and Hugh brought Rolfe down to Tremans to meet the family. It was not a happy occasion.

Rolfe embarrassed everyone with his conceit and his vanity. Beringed and boastful, he was indifferent to the impression he was making, thinking it proper that a genius such as he should be welcome among pygmies. Hugh obviously thought he was a genius, too, and promised him that as soon as he was elevated to the bishopric, he would ordain Rolfe himself. Mary Benson was polite, as always with the friends of her children, and Fred was diplomatic. Privately, he thought Rolfe was 'picturesque and depraved and devil-ridden',[56] but if he was less than frank with the family it was because Rolfe knew some of the people he knew in Venice, and also because he was not especially fond of his brother Hugh and was happy to watch the disaster develop around him. Arthur was the most censorious. He called Rolfe 'the infernal exorcist' and deplored the fact that he was not a gentleman. Rolfe told the family that he had written *Hadrian VII* no less than eleven times. 'When one thinks a book thoroughly bad,' commented Arthur, 'it is rather depressing to hear how much pains have been spent.'[57]

The catastrophe which befell this ill-matched friendship was yet to come. Of far more immediate concern to all Bensons was Maggie's health. After a period of relative tranquillity, her appalling illness was about to recur with a vengeance and plunge her into the mirror-world of insanity.

7 Capri and Other Discoveries

Tremans was meant to be the salvation of Maggie Benson. For some years it appeared to work, rescuing her from the double scourge of aimlessness and introspection. She created a lovely garden in which she and her brothers rejoiced, she nursed her very few friendships, with Gladys Bevan, Beatrice Layman, and especially Nettie Gourlay, and she was writing a new book on a philosophical subject which properly stretched her analytic brain, *The Venture of a Rational Faith*. Alas, the cure of Tremans did not last.

One morning her mother went to see her as she breakfasted in her room, and found her spiritually flattened by a familiar Benson depression. She asked what was the matter, and Maggie replied, ambiguously, 'Oh, I am killing it.' She did not explain whether she was killing the depression or some other black demon which caused it, but Fred remarked that 'the first skirmish of a mortal struggle had begun'.*

For the next few months Maggie gradually sank into hopelessness, as she fought with a terrifying menace and saw that she would lose, for she had the self-knowledge and honesty to recognise that which nobody else would articulate, that she was slipping into insanity. With herculean strength she made herself finish the book, even so far as to write a second draft, and went to Cornwall for a month's holiday. From there she sent light and easy letters to her brothers, but Arthur responded with egocentric musings upon

* She had tried strangling herself with a piece of string and setting her room alight by burning the curtains, both signs more of psychosis than fever.[1]

his own moods of misery, an insensitivity which would later cause him much chagrin. On her way home she called upon Fred at Oakley Street and confided in him her terrible fear that the depression might prove unconquerable. Ominously, she said that she wanted to see him again 'first'; she knew that some catastrophe was imminent.

On the day that her cousin Stuart McDowall, son of the Archbishop's sister Ada McDowall, was married, Maggie fell into the grip of final despair. She had misused and lost and wasted all her opportunities, she said; worse yet, she had lost her soul. Beth noticed she was walking around the house with a fixed and deadly gaze, which worried her. She imagined in ordinary people nefarious intentions and desires, the masks of saints concealing the viciousness of devils, and assumed she was to be their victim. The doctors diagnosed a mild liver upset, and assured Mrs Benson that as there was no cause for anxiety, she and Lucy Tait should proceed with their plans to take a holiday in Venice. This was, of course, symbolically the last straw which toppled Maggie over the edge; it was an abandonment, a betrayal, a desertion, a confirmation of that jealousy which had been consuming her for years. Mother preferred to go off with Lucy rather than look after her own daughter. They were in league against her.

One day after a drive she took the whip-thong from the leading-rein of the carriage and embarked on a frenzy of self-flagellation. She said she had wanted to see what pain would do. Later, she tied her own hands together and said she was frightened she might lose control. Her mother seemed to assign all this to hysteria, which was foolish in the light of her lifelong experience of the Benson mind. She ought to have realised what was happening.

The night before Minnie (or 'Ben' as she was now called) and Lucy were due to leave, Maggie could not sleep. Before coming down in the morning, she sent for Lucy and told her solemnly that it was 'all over'. She was afraid she might kill herself or hurt someone else, and she would have to be restrained. As Arthur said, it was horrible to think what agony she must have been going through, but he did not notice the significance of her making this declaration to Lucy, of all people. She was saying, in fact, that if she did anything silly, it would be Lucy's fault, for Lucy had stolen her mother. At last the women were sufficiently alarmed to summon Dr Ross Todd from London, on Friday May 3 1907, and ask him to stay the night at Tremans. He arrived in time for dinner.

As if on cue, Maggie duly displayed to the medic the damage that had been done to her. Throughout dinner she uttered not a word, but stared glumly, threateningly, at anyone who did speak. Obviously imprisoned by her thoughts, she placed her head in her hands and rocked and bowed low until she rested her forehead on the table. Then she slowly slipped from her chair to the floor. Dr Todd took charge as the others looked on in disbelief. He persuaded her to leave the room only by promising that he would tie her hands and feet as she requested. She appeared to imply she could not trust herself and could not persuade the others how bad a state she was in. More than anything she wanted to be put under restraint, held down, prevented from doing harm. As she was led from the room she broke into loud awful sobbing.

At eleven o'clock that night Lucy and Dr Todd went to her room and heard her cry out. They found a scene of Dantesque horror, Maggie delirious and struggling and bent on doing herself harm. Fred was later to call her attack 'homicidal', and it has often been supposed that she went for her mother, but on the evidence it seems far more likely she was trying to kill herself when she was discovered, for the nurse and three servants (Beak, Hendon, and Ryman) were immediately summoned, came running, and spent the next four hours trying to hold her down, until eventually, at three in the morning, she collapsed into an exhausted sleep. The next day she almost boasted that it had taken six people to control her, as if to say, 'I told you so, none of you would listen, none of you noticed'. The little parish nurse took the brunt of it and was steadfast throughout. She tied Maggie's hands together as bidden.

Dr Todd was most alarmed that Maggie should keep repeating that she was 'lost', yet, as Arthur pointed out, the notion was part of their official creed, and it was wrong that as soon as someone expressed his conviction of the Fall he should be declared mad. Todd sent for two extra nurses and two more doctors, Dr Alban and Dr Savage, then despatched a telegram to Arthur in Cambridge

which he received Saturday morning. Arthur was under the mistaken impression his mother and Lucy had gone to Venice two
days before and he did not understand how Todd came to be at
Tremans. He dressed in frantic haste, caught the 9.38 to London,
and spent the hour before there was a train from London Bridge
to Horsted Keynes sitting in St Saviour's Church, Southwark, as
every possibility raced through his mind. He knew enough about
himself and his sister to suspect the worst. When he was told he
was overcome with pity. 'The pathos of all the flowers and walks
and seats here, all of Maggie's planning, is almost too much for
me . . . that Maggie put such love and gallant care, making the
place so sweet and beautiful, kept on piercing my heart . . . Why
could she not be allowed to have a better time? She did not ask
very much of life, and has been disappointed in everything, or
nearly everything.'

Mary Benson and Lucy had been spared the ordeal of watching
a suicidal and raging woman held down in her own bedroom. Mrs
Benson wrote to Fred that they were 'in very deep waters', and
he left for Tremans immediately on receipt of this letter, Sunday
morning. Meanwhile, Dr Alban had arrived and diagnosed cerebral
meningitis, in his opinion 'with a fatal ending almost in sight'.
The nurses maintained that it was largely a case of hysteria, a
desperate scream for attention. Maggie passed a better night on
Saturday. Arthur mused again on the heartlessness of beauty. 'The
thought of the way poor Maggie has been used by the world or
God makes me wonder how we continue to be so happy as we
are or to have any confidence in God at all.' He also reflected
how mean he had been to answer her letters from Cornwall with
such mournful replies and blamed himself for her present distress.
'If I could have been offered death myself at any moment in the
last 24 hours, I would have chosen it – but that is because I am
radically timid.' And invincibly morbid. That strain of self-pitying
pessimism so inherent in the Benson character, from which Fred
alone seems to have escaped, was never more evident than at times
of crisis.

By Sunday afternoon Dr Alban was beginning to have doubts
about the meningitis.[2] Arthur determined to stay at least a week
'or at all events for as long as I can stand it. A few bad nights and

such pleasant reveries as mine of this morning would soon embark me on the same course . . . what a beautiful, desirable, sad, treacherous, unjust world it is, little things punished so heavily, big things left alone.' After lunch Fred arrived in the company of the Archbishop of Canterbury, their old family friend Randall Davidson. Arthur and Fred walked together in the garden. Fred 'looked and was very anxious', but for Arthur it was a blessed relief to be able to talk to him. Fred did not record their conversation. Arthur merely said that 'at least we were all brought closer and nearer together'. Maggie stayed in bed all day.

On Monday she was restless, with sudden impulses to get up and go to the window, which could not be allowed. She said she wanted some air. The nurse told her, 'Yes, I want to get you out of doors. Could you go out without making a scene?' 'No,' said Maggie, 'I fear I should make a scene.' Yet despite this, she repeatedly tried to get up and had to be controlled by the nurse, who told her, 'You have been behaving very badly and have given me a headache.' 'I am very sorry,' Maggie said. Nurse told Arthur and Fred it was a bad case, but not so bad as a *silent* case, which was the worst. She wanted to argue with everyone, and purposefully did what she should not in order to provoke reprimand, like a child. 'I won't, I won't,' she kept saying. Gladys Bevan turned up unexpectedly on Monday afternoon, all worry and busy-ness, was intercepted on the drive and persuaded to go home.

Arthur frankly recognised that Maggie's symptoms echoed the morose behaviour of his father and wondered why God should visit such wrath upon their family, should be so unutterably cruel and horrible. No worse calamity could have been devised for them. Standing by the stables with Dr Alban in the dusk of late evening, Arthur heard the doctor's view that his sister could not live long, and was unlikely ever to recover her reason. When Dr Savage came to add his opinion, it was determined that Maggie would have to be removed to an institution for the insane, as the nurses could not cope at Tremans. There was a danger, moreover, of heart failure. Arthur lamented that he had never had such a day of suffering in his entire life – 'how does one go on?'

It was Dr Todd – 'Toddles' – who gave the news to Maggie

that she was to be sent away. She brightened immediately; was she going to get better? She asked only that one particular nurse, whom she did not like, should not accompany her, but the idea of departure itself was evidently an enormous relief. Todd gave instructions that the servants and family were to keep out of sight when she left. On Wednesday morning at 9.15, 8 May 1907, Mary Benson and Lucy Tait went for a walk, while Arthur kept Beth busy helping him pack. Maggie spent her time writing farewell letters to her friends, and asked for some hat-pins so she might look tidy. After a while Arthur looked out of the window and saw that the carriage had left, taking Maggie away from the house she loved so much. When he told the aged Beth, who had nursed Maggie from infancy as well as all the other Benson offspring and Minnie and her brothers as well, that she had gone, Beth burst into tears. 'To think that the dear should have gone off without my saying goodbye,' she sobbed.

Maggie was taken to a home for the insane, St George's Convent at Wivelsfield, not far away. It was run by the Sisters of Mercy. As she arrived, the nuns knelt down and said a prayer for her. The crisis was over.

Arthur said that Dr Todd had been like a brother to them all, that Mama was amazingly brave and calm, with a fortitude and tenderness which was incredible to him, and Lucy 'is simply beyond words'. They had been spared the worst of it, yet they had endured all the tension of the preceding weeks and their hopefulness was a lesson to all. Arther said that if God returned Maggie to them, he would try to be a better, more unselfish man.[3]

Fred had evidently returned to London after his initial visit at the beginning of the week, and now that Maggie had been removed, he sent a telegram to say he was coming down again. Hugh did the same. All three brothers visited her at the retreat on Thursday. With Arthur she shared her fears that the demons would return, fears she knew he would understand, fears she even might have wanted him to absorb, to be planted within him as a source of torment. With Hugh she was serene, seeking those words of comfort which the Roman faith alone could offer. With Fred she was distant; he said there grew a gulf between him and the bed in which she lay which could not be bridged. All agreed that poor Maggie was in fine hands with the nuns, and they left to set about retrieving normality from a life suddenly laced with misery.

Maggie did not make the recovery they had hoped for. As she could no longer feel persecuted by her mother, she felt persecuted by the nuns. On his next visit, Arthur learned that she was convinced the Sisters of Mercy were out to poison her. The realisation that his sister was truly mentally flawed edged Arthur ever closer towards his own breakdown. He was not assisted by the quarrels with Hugh over expense. Later in the summer Dr Todd recommended Maggie should leave the convent to take up residence at the Priory in Roehampton, which was, as it still is, a convalescent home for the mentally afflicted. The fees were £550 per annum. As Maggie's own money had been depleted, and Fred and Arthur had borne the brunt of her costs at Wivelsfield, it was agreed the Estate of Edward White Benson should pay the greater part, and Fred and Arthur would each contribute as before, Arthur rather more than Fred since he had the greater income. 'Ben' and Lucy would contribute what they could. Hugh, however, refused. It would ruin him, he said, he would have to sell up all he had. Some time later he was shamed into relenting, but the episode illustrated his meanness, often a trait of the spoilt child, and did little to endear him to his brothers. When the scandal erupted over Rolfe, it was Hugh's parsimony that Rolfe most gleefully exposed.

Before the move to the Priory, Arthur paid Maggie another visit which upset him profoundly. More than ever certain of her impending death at the hands of the wicked nuns, she made him promise never to come to the convent again. As he departed, he heard a terrible scream coming from the basement of the building as an inmate cried out in despair; Arthur concluded that this was indeed an abode of Hell, and with the scream reverberating in his skull, he brooded upon the fate of the poor woman who uttered it, as well as the deluded condition of his sister, for the whole of the next day. He knew that if he continued like this he would be on the precipice of grim clinical depression himself, and decided he must consult Ross Todd without delay. 'Something seemed to crumble in my brain,' he said, 'and clutch my heart. I thought I was going to die.'[4]

Todd recommended a change of scene, an enforced relaxation, so Arthur took a brief holiday with Fred at Seaford which did indeed revive his spirits for a while. But the 'black dog' was in pursuit, and it was not long before Arthur grew frightened that he might fall victim to the malady which afflicted Maggie. Significantly, his breakdown coincided, to the very week, with Maggie's removal to the Priory. Dr Todd sent him to a specialist, Dr Blaikie, who immediately saw that he needed treatment. A.C. Benson was admitted to a nursing-home in Mayfair in the autumn of 1907.

For the next two years Arthur coasted precariously on the surface of life, frequently gazing into the abyss and drawn back by doctors, family and friends. He tried drugs, hypnosis, foreign travel, country houses. He went to Rome and Florence and hated it. For a month he lived as a boarder in Hampstead at a house for the mentally ill and defective, a fearful, humiliating ordeal for a man who shunned the proximity of people and loathed the idea that his unhappiness could be visible, the subject of comment and dissection. It was also, of course, a miserable descent for a famous author and member of a Cambridge college. As his Diary testifies, Arthur's sufferings were so acute they all but saw the end of him. 'I ache and hunger for life and its sweetness,' he wrote, 'and hold out ineffectual hands from my dark cage . . . oh, if I could but die!' 'If I were given the choice of swift and painless death as against the chance of getting well, I should choose death, though I *want* to live with all my heart and soul. I *love* life.'[5] Once, on the train going towards Horsted Keynes, he mused how easy it would be to lean out of the window and be obliterated by a bridge; he saw Balcombe Tunnel approaching and wished he could do it, but he lacked the physical courage.[6] With Fred he discussed the likelihood of survival after death, convinced that though the memory might not endure, the personality would. Fred countered with the sensible argument that personality without memory was inconceivable (a view, incidentally, supported by neurologists). Robbed even of this comfort, he was 'simply filled with a strong and fruitless despair'.[7]

From our point of view, Arthur's long debilitating illness is important for the profound change it effected in his understanding of his brother Fred, who, more than anyone else in the family, went out of his way to help him and keep his mind occupied. We can watch, fascinated, as Arthur's appreciation of Fred develops in the course of 1908 and he comes to regard him in an entirely different light.

At first, there is the familiar contempt for Fred's style of life and values, his 'breezy materialism', his complacency. Fred is almost bound, thinks Arthur, to become a club bore, telling the same stories over and over again with glib and empty charm. 'He is so pleased with himself and his work and his little bits of silver and his friends and everything.'[8] Fred knows too many Jews, who are not quite gentlemen, and, again, is too servile towards the titled. And yet, his positive approach to life, refusing despondency and rejecting failure, is a contrast with Arthur's own which he gradually finds refreshing. Observing Fred, he wishes he had some of the same energy and extrovertism, and comes to 'the melancholy conclusion that I have been living too inactive and contemplative a life with my mind turned in upon itself'. He begins to worry lest Fred should spoil his good health and follow him down the path to morosity, drinking too much whisky at lunch, more at tea, wine with dinner and more whisky afterwards. 'I can't help fearing that it will end in overstrain, and he would find depression even worse than I find it.'[9] When Fred returned from a skating holiday in Switzerland, 'longevity written on every feature' and brimming with high spirits and jokiness, Arthur felt flat by comparison, and envious. Fred was still, at forty-two, the picture of vigorous, sunny health, despite going grey rather earlier than his mother would have liked. 'Who am I to talk,' she said, 'when I was SNOW WHITE at his age.'[10]

Fred gave his brother an open invitation to call in at Oakley Street whenever he liked, to relieve boredom, to seek company, or merely to chatter. For a man who cherished his routine, this was magnanimous indeed. Consequently, Arthur was frequently an additional and unexpected guest at dinner, and every effort was made to give him welcome and cheer. It was on one of these occasions, already referred to, that he ran into Old Lady Radnor. Another time he arrived an hour too early, when Fred was still working, and sat reading a book rather than disturb him. At 8 p.m. in walked Lady Evelyn Lister, a relation by marriage of

Reggie Lister, bearing a gift of lilac for Fred. The three of them
dined together, after which Arthur remarked, 'They seem great
friends . . . why does he not marry her?' Again, he was beginning
to envy Fred these cosy, easy relationships, and to rue the fact
that he had no close ties with anyone. 'It is too late now; and in
any case I think that our stock ought not to be perpetuated. It is
unsound. Indeed, after my late experience it would be criminal of
me to beget children.' He seemed to imply that, though the Benson
gene was poisonous, his brother Fred appeared immune to its
destructive power, and that he, alone of all of them, could safely
procreate.

Arthur also went to Tremans a great deal more often than he
had been used to, almost invariably finding Fred there at the same
time. Family disputes were at their worst when Fred and Hugh
collided. Once at dinner Hugh again adopted the irritating
omniscience of the Romans and said, 'One isn't anxious about
anything when one is in the Church – when one happens to belong
to something eternal.' Fred suggested that since the Church had
not managed to chalk up two thousand years yet, it could hardly
be called eternal, to which Hugh replied that he had to fall back
on *knowing*. Arthur held on to the table and said nothing, though
boiling with rage, while Fred looked twenty years older in his
sullenness. All the more odd it is, then, that Arthur should persist
in maintaining that Hugh was more intelligent than Fred because
he was able to understand ideas.[11]

When an argument was in full spate at the Tremans table, Lucy
Tait was the most positive and aggressive, Mary Benson looked
pained at the flight of harmony, Arthur was voluble and vehement,
Hugh smug, and Fred 'silent with suppressed wrath'. Arthur began
to notice during this time that it was Lucy who added the
combative element. Despite being 'a wonderful creature, so strong,
cheerful, useful, and so totally free from meanness', she was self-
satisfied in her saintliness, making it clear that she forgave people
for disagreeing with her, as if hers was the only approval worth
seeking. She said exactly what she thought and would be deflected
from her opinion by no knowledge or fact, and as she did so much
selfless work for the poor the others were expected to defer to
her goodness. She had a habit of interrupting someone else just

after he had begun to speak, and as for 'Ben', she was repeatedly silenced by Lucy's peremptory interventions and bore it all gracefully. Arthur concluded:

> The fact really is that Lucy, who is very strong and unimaginative and good-humoured, has a subtle effect. She has been *everything* to Mama, and I am everlastingly grateful to her – but I think she has really rather broken us up as a family. She *disapproves* of us all, for various reasons, and is quite unable to see another point of view. It is she, I think, who is really the provocative element.

> She is the evil genius of the family. I think it is she who has done most to disintegrate us. She doesn't assert herself, she just goes her own way.[12]

In which case, poor Maggie had been not so misguided after all.

Arthur remonstrated with Lucy for reading the Bible to Ben at 7 a.m. in such a loud voice that he could hear every vowel in his bedroom. Even in church she responded as if she were talking into a telephone, whereas Ben had two distinct voices in prayer, 'one as if she were telling a ghost story, the other as if she were wheedling a cat'.[13] Lucy did not take to these strictures very kindly; she smiled and forgave, almost contemptuously.

It might appear that family gatherings were not all that recuperative for Arthur as he slowly dragged himself up into the light, save for one ingredient: it became clear to him that his happiness actually *mattered* to Fred, and with this realisation there grew, ever so tentatively, the experience of fraternal love rather than the mere discussion of it. 'He has stuck to me in this bad time,' Arthur wrote, 'has put himself to much inconvenience to come down here and cheer me up, when he doesn't like the country, or the atmosphere of Tremans either.' He confessed to being touched by Fred's willingness to chuck everything and go to Tremans simply to be with him, 'because of my unhappy and lonely self', and after some weeks of getting used to his visits, he would ask after Fred and suggest he be called. He came slowly to rely upon him. When Arthur looked like sinking into suicidal lethargy once again, Mary Benson would summon Fred and Fred would come.[14]

It is wonderfully engaging to see these arid, untactile, enclosed and cerebral men inch towards one another with arms ready for embrace, Arthur speaking openly, for the first time, of 'brotherly love'. At the end of his illness he is ready not only to acknowledge Fred's kindliness, which had never been in dispute, but his solidity. 'I sicken to think how lately I thought of him as a sort of easygoing mundane creature. Now I realise how far ahead of me he is in every respect – courage, will, effectiveness, kindness.' 'I have sometimes thought Fred elementary and childish. I now realise, in this dark hour, how infinitely stronger and better he is than I am.'[15]

One day Arthur received a telegram saying that Fred was too ill to come down to Tremans, and immediately took the train for London and hurried to Oakley Street. Fred was sitting in an armchair by a glowing coal fire, a large lunch and an empty bottle of burgundy on a tray beside him, his face enveloped in bandages and much flushed with wine and drowsiness. In answer to Arthur's imploring look, Fred in a deathbed voice said 'Streptococcus', and turned down the bandage to reveal a pimple, said Arthur, the size of half a dried pea. The next day he turned up at Tremans in time for lunch, hale and hearty. 'The doctor says I have great recuperative power,' he announced with a grin.[16]

Quite often Fred would arrive with a young man nobody had seen before as his guest for the weekend, giving Arthur cause to ponder why these people should choose to spend so much time with a man twice their age. One such was called Daukes, 'one of Fred's mysterious young friends', a twenty-year-old junior at the Foreign Office whom Arthur thought charming, clever and industrious, but 'why is he such friends with Fred, and what, I wonder, do the talk about?'[17]* Arthur was not so naïve as to miss the point that the young men were also very handsome and unselfconsciously flattered by the attentions of a famous novelist. He also noticed that there was usually an undercurrent of suppressed eroticism in the relationship, never admitted and generally disguised

---

* We are in 1910, and this is almost certainly the same Major Archie Daukes who married and lived in Egerton Crescent, within walking distance of Brompton Square. He was a life-long friend to Fred. See C. and T. Reavell, *E.F. Benson Remembered and the World of Tilling*, p. 48.

as 'sentiment'. It was especially noticeable when Fred brought Wilfrid Coleridge, eighteen years old and just out of Eton. 'He is a cheerful creature,' said Arthur, 'not very attractive, with an odd rather assured manner; he admires Fred devotedly, and Fred seems to have an affection for him, half paternal half sentimental. He is always with him and yet seems to snub him a good deal in a jovial way.'[18] Wilfrid was the son of Gilbert Coleridge, grandson of Lord Chief Justice Coleridge, and a descendant of the poet. He came across Fred's path because he was a keen skater, and by this time Fred was a judge for the National Skating Association. He may well have coached Wilfrid, for two years later we find them both in Switzerland where the young man passed his gold medal test.

These attachments satisfied the need of the older man to watch the younger grow to maturity in physique and social graces, in the cosy warm knowledge that he had contributed to that maturity by example. That is why Fred's affection for Wilfrid Coleridge was, as Arthur observed, half that of a father and half that of a lover. This is a long way from suggesting that the affection was ever given expression beyond a slap on the shoulder. Men in this kind of situation often derive an essential *frisson* from the knowledge that the friendship is bound to be sterile, that it must be denied and frustrated in order to be pure. In the case of the Benson men, this universal truth is exaggerated to the point of exquisite parody, for they inherited, whether they willed or no, some of the self-punishing puritanism of their father. None of them could bear to be touched, and there is certain evidence that they went out of their way to avoid physical contact altogether.

Arthur, for example, was witness to a funny scene at Magdalene when his two guests embraced each other. They were the novelist Howard Overington Sturgis and a former pupil of Benson's at Eton, Percy Lubbock, who would one day be the first to edit his Diary. In the morning, Sturgis and Lubbock 'parted with a long and loverlike kiss'. Sturgis apologised to Benson for this display of 'sentimentality', but Lubbock said that such behaviour must be excused at moments of emotional crisis. Arthur wrote that evening, 'to me it is very distasteful. After all, it is only a symbol, but I don't want that kind of symbol.' He went on, and the shudder of his body is almost palpable on the page, 'He said afterwards he would have kissed me if he had dared. I am glad he did not, tho' the fact that he could rather relieves my perpetual sense of physical repulsiveness. Indeed, to hear Howard talk, one would have thought I were handsome!'[19]

Similarly, there was little likelihood of Fred's involving himself in any mischief while in Venice, which he visited once a year to stay with Lady Radnor. Percy Lubbock and Arthur discussed the Venetian scene, 'the life which Fred leads so mysteriously and of which he says nothing', and wondered what it all amounted to. Arthur berated 'the silliness of it, the idleness, the sentimentality about bronzed gondoliers etc, with I daresay a nastier background', but Lubbock maintained that there was nothing wicked about it; 'there is no passion about, it is all too trivial and light for that'.[20] Lubbock was right. There could be some gawping, some tittering, some passing of admiring comment, and no doubt some 'favourites', but no serious liaison. The worst thing Fred did in Venice was to write some execrable verse for his Dowager Countess, which we forbear to reproduce here. In speaking of a 'nastier background', Arthur may well have heard of the activities of Hugh's friend Frederick Rolfe, who made ends meet in Venice by procuring boys for visiting Englishmen. Nothing is more certain than that fastidious Fred would steer well clear of him, for every possible reason. With his coarseness and his paranoid distrust, Rolfe would not have fitted easily into Lady Radnor's salon, and if there was one rule which Fred upheld all his life, it was at all costs to avoid social embarrassment.

It is also interesting that Fred should have taken the trouble to copy out in longhand the whole of Oscar Wilde's *De Profundis*, in a notebook heavily inscribed PRIVATE and stretching to eighty foolscap pages. He included all the passages which had been expurgated in the 1905 edition, and it obviously mattered to him that the record of this masterpiece should be complete. Nevertheless, it was risky, the name of Wilde was in the pit of disgrace even after death, and the people who would own to an admiration for him were a mere handful.[21]

One of Fred's most enduring friendships was formed around 1905, with Philip Burne-Jones, son of the artist and an aspiring

painter himself. Philip was an amiable fellow, but hopelessly in-
effective, condemned to having enough talent to make him clever
and not enough to make him brilliant. He was undisciplined, and
therefore did nothing memorable. Yet for Fred, he was the most
perfect companion, for they shared the same sense of humour and
looked at the world and its parade with a cheeky, perky icono-
clasm. Arthur encountered Philip at Oakley Street more than once,
and liked him more than any of Fred's other friends, largely
because they were rich and important, while Philip was always
penniless and did not cut a figure in society. He called him 'a
pathetic, elf-like, feeble, sparkling, dabbling, affectionate, absurd,
loveable little man . . . He was quick, and amusing, but somehow
infinitely sad and even tragic to me, as being conscious everywhere
of a sort of failure to be anything in particular.' Arthur added that
he could sympathise, presumably because he also felt he had done
nothing, which was patent but unshakeable nonsense.

The three of them played bridge while Arthur looked around
and noted with distaste how the house was filling up with 'things'
– silver, china, bits of carving – which he considered oppressive.
Then came the games, the practical jokes, the amusement, Philip
suddenly pulling a burning cigar from his pocket to the mock
consternation of Fred and genuine alarm of Arthur, who, on
discovering the cigar to be made of wool and tinsel, pondered
how it was possible for a grown man 'to put such things gravely
in your pocket when you were going to dine out'.[22] There was
nothing in the least grave about Philip and Fred, for the essence
of their friendship was fun, mostly of the schoolboyish variety
which seeks to puncture the pompous and turn a frivolous light
upon so-called serious matters. They were jesters and iconoclasts,
their purpose to amuse, their intentions benign.

Together they compiled a scrapbook entitled 'Episodes in the
Life of Lord Desborough', properly bound in full leather with a
title in gold beneath a gold coronet. Lord Desborough was a very
serious man indeed. A Tory MP before his elevation to the peerage
in 1905, he was the epitome of the English gentleman, hugely
accomplished in every sport, a member of one hundred and seventeen different committees, handsome, noble, and extremely boring.
He was known to Fred because his wife Lady Desborough was

the leading hostess of 'The Souls', whose mannerisms Fred had mocked in *Dodo*, and their son Julian Grenfell had been a pupil of Arthur's at Eton. Ettie Desborough was a sparkling, vivacious, happy woman, whose bright conversation made her husband's rock-like silence even more obvious. Mabell Airlie told her, 'He may be a little dull, but after all what a comfort it is to be cleverer than one's husband.'

Desborough had run a mile in 4 min. 37 sec., a record unbroken for sixty years. He rowed from Oxford to Putney in one day. He climbed the Matterhorn three times by three different routes, was champion punter on the Thames for three years, wrestled, swam, played cricket, and represented England in fencing at the Olympic Games. Twice he swam across the foot of the Niagara Falls, once during a storm. Margot Asquith called him 'a British gladiator'. But if he was as strong as an ox (and he enjoyed killing those too, along with everything else which ran, swam or flew), Lord Desborough's mind was as flaccid as lukewarm stew. His conversation was dire. Conceiving a passion for bimetallism, the proposal to combine gold and silver currencies in the economy, he proceeded to bore anyone who was polite enough to approach within earshot. His other great interest was the Thames Conservancy Board. It is important to bear all this in mind when seeing what Benson and Burne-Jones did to the poor man without his knowledge. To his great credit, Desborough knew he was tedious. 'I sometimes wonder that I have a friend left,' he said, 'as I am apt to bore my acquaintances with the number of gallons which go over Teddington Weir.'[23]

The Desborough scrapbook consists of letters mostly from Philip to Fred, adorned with very witty pen-drawings, and pointing out news items from the daily press from which he has laboriously extracted the reported name and substituted Desborough's. All the extracts are chosen to mock his lordship's well-attested strength and solemnity. 'The Royal Train will be drawn by Lord Desborough. He will be decorated in crape and will be in charge of Mr Armstrong, chief of the locomotive (GWR) department. On the arrival of the train at Windsor at 12.30, he will be removed to a gun carriage waiting in the station yard.' There is a picture of Lady Desborough as a Swiss teenager with flowing tresses, and another of Lord Desborough aiming a hose for target-practice. 'Spectators in the Stadium on Saturday saw a remarkable exhibition of wrestling by Lord and Lady Desborough. Lady D is marked with a cross.' 'Last night at the Crystal Palace Lord Desborough created a world's record by swinging a heavy blacksmith's hammer for twelve hours without stopping. Lord D is a variety artist; he was born in Brixton but spent his early years in France.'[24]

And so on. It is impossible to detect malice in this innocent fun. Another album he compiled was called 'The Book of Fearfuljoy', replete with malapropisms, misprints, bad verse à la William McGonagall, and stories bordering on the bawdy. There is a press-cutting about a Siamese twin who gave birth; 'the inseparable sister, Josephine, expressed great surprise at the unaccountable occurrence which made her an aunt.' A copy of an unlikely magazine published in Connecticut, *The Uric Acid Monthly*,[25] is juxtaposed with an announcement that 'A handsome widow has been unveiled in memory of the late vicar'. Fred is especially fond of clumsy translations from the French, of which one suffices to give a flavour: 'Visitors are kindly invited to brought your boots self to the shoemaker, then they are frequently nagled by the Portier and that is very dammageable for boots and kosts the same price.'

Fred is beguiled by the absurdity of beauty contests, which he collects for his album, and records for posterity the truly dreadful epitaphs which Queen Alexandra penned every time she lost a close friend. By far the most interesting component of the book, and the most extensive, is the collection of cuttings, pictures and letters relating to Marie Corelli. Miss Corelli was the best-selling novelist of her day, enormously popular with the public and totally derided by the literary establishment. She claimed to be descended from the Venetian musician Arcangelo Corelli (who had no offspring), but her real name was Minnie Mackay, the illegitimate daughter of a well-known Scottish poet, Charles Mackay. So certain was she of her brilliance that she went to live in Stratford-upon-Avon to be close to the other genius of English literature, and imported a gondola complete with gondolier to glide her on the River Avon. The townspeople tried vainly to get rid of her. Fred and Philip visited her more than once at her house,

Mason Croft in Church Street, behaving like schoolboys, tossing hay in the paddock and having a jolly time of it. Miss Corelli liked Fred because he was 'quaint and clever and says original things spontaneously', and she valued Philip because he was an artist. She had recently conceived a middle-aged passion for the artist Arthur Severn and saw herself as a discriminating patron. Philip wrote fulsome letters of thanks to her after every visit. Fred pasted pictures of her in his 'Book of Fearfuljoy'.[26]

The reason this contact assumes importance in E.F. Benson's life is that Marie Corelli is the inspiration for more than one of his finest creations. She is the substance for Susan Leg in *Secret Lives*, and the source of all the silliness and pretension of Lucia in the 'Lucia' series of novels which came in the 1920s and 1930s. She claimed to speak Italian, and did so with few words ill-placed, changing the subject if the meagreness of her knowledge risked exposure. She spoke in baby-talk when she wanted to be coy, her letters to Severn representing the most embarrassing examples of ridiculous language from a woman of advanced age. She claimed to be in her twenties when she was well over fifty. And she went to inordinate lengths to make sure she was seen in all the right places, complaining to newspaper editors if her name was omitted from the list of those present. All this is pure Lucia. Thus when Fred cut out pictures of Marie, writing 'unauthorized' or 'authorized' beneath them, and collected nuggets of information about her activities, he was storing up the raw material for one of the most glorious heroines of twentieth century fiction.

The only uncomfortable note is struck when one reads Marie's letters to him. It is clear she regarded him as her friend, and had no idea she was the subject of mockery behind her back. But then that was her fate with most people she knew; Fred was by no means the only one to be fascinated by her eccentricity and laugh at her foibles.

In the midst of all which Fred could turn his hand to a serious piece of research at Alcote Park, Shrewsbury, and at Tunbridge Wells, for an article on Salopian pottery made by Thomas Turner at Caughley from 1772 to 1814, the originator of the famous Willow Pattern design. Benson had wider interests than he has sometimes been given credit for.

And the books came piling out of him, every year, helter-skelter. *The Relentless City* (1903) satirised, in none too subtle a fashion, the vulgar behaviour of American society, so gauche, uncouth, uncivilised. *An Act in a Backwater* (1903), set in Winchester, is sentimental, slushy, mawkish, too sweet. *The Image in the Sand* (1905) is set in Egypt and is a proper novel with a good, long melodramatic story, centring on the need of the hero, Sir Henry Jervis, to communicate with the spirit of his dead wife. (The publishers objected to its original title, *Things Under the Earth*, so Fred rather petulantly proposed *The Terror By Night*, *Out of Egypt*, and *Graven Image*, before settling upon the final choice.)[27] In a disguised form, the novel is another variation on one of Fred's favourite themes, that of salvation by the forces of good, and it dwells heavily upon his flirtation with the occult, always a source of fascination for a Benson. Two collaborations with Eustace Miles were quite unlike one another: *The Mad Annual* is a collection of parodies and humorous pieces, while *Diversions Day By Day* (1905) celebrates the pleasures to be derived from indoor sports (of the ping-pong variety). The authors were paid £20 each, which Fred dismissed as paltry, loudly complaining that he had not seen a *single copy* of the latter on the bookstalls.[28] *The Angel of Pain* has already been mentioned. In the same year appeared another story of salvation, *Paul*, in which the eponymous hero has an affair with a married woman, murders her husband, repents, and finally saves her child from being squashed by a train.

The next book, *The House of Defence* (1906), proved to be one of E.F. Benson's bestsellers, although it is not much read today. Its subject is Christian Science, a pet obsession of Mrs Benson and a frequent theme of discussion and argument at Tremans. Fred is open-minded, leaving the reader to suppose that faith-healing, the supernatural, occurrences which we do not understand, are all none the less possible. He will return to the position of the tolerant enquirer many times in later years; he is prepared to suspend belief, even occasionally to embrace occultism as one who needs to believe. *Sheaves* (1907) tells the story of a marriage which appears happy yet conceals distress, and ends with typical

Benson sentimentality – a consumptive death. The title, replacing the original *Indian Summer*, is taken from Psalm 126.

The *Blotting Book* (1908) is much shorter than any of the previous novels, being in fact a long short story, and it is quite different in style and purpose. This attractive little book, still available nearly a century later, is a clever piece of detective fiction with the obligatory surprise ending. It cannot have taken Fred more than a weekend to write, which was just as well as he had another novel to deliver the same year. This was *The Climber* (1907), his best so far and the one of which in later years he said he was proudest. The central figure, Lucia Grimson, is a recognisable Benson heroine, hard and brittle, determined to grab what she can from life, using her charm and looks to entrap people into serving her interests. This time, however, Fred does not merely allow us to observe and laugh at the creature, but to judge her, for the story has a strong moral flavour, with Lucia Grimson's fall and disgrace matching on every level the vertiginous scope of her earlier rise. It does not pay, says Fred, to be a social climber and nothing more.

English Figure Skating (1908) is a textbook timed to coincide with the first Olympic skating events, which were held at the Princes Skating Club in Knightsbridge, London, in October 1908. As a member of the National Skating Association since 1900, a gold medallist and a renowned exponent of the 'English' style, Fred helped set up the special committee to organise these Olympic events, and was himself a member of it. His book explains the technique of the English style, which is quite unlike the acrobatic displays we have become used to in international ice-skating in recent years, though there are still those who perform it. Captain Richardson described the English style in these words:

> with its insistence on poise and pure edge-running, the importance placed on shoulder-control in executing all figures, and the elimination of all superfluous movement, it is a very difficult and pure form of figure skating . . . The English stylists have no stunts, no shows, no applause, and no professionals.[29]

Holding a natural position was more important than assuming an impossible one, and if one were to find parallels in the ballet world, one might say Fred's skating was more akin to the elegance of Balanchine than the fireworks of Petipa.

A Reaping (1909) is not a novel to shine, and again ends with Bensonian drama, a likeable lad falling from his motorcycle under the wheels of a bus, and being brave withal. And *Daisy's Aunt* (1910) is so cloying it is like having toffee stuck to every tooth. It was after this book that the rival novelist Hugh Walpole, about twenty years Fred's junior and a friend of both his and Arthur's, accused Fred of being a fraud. 'E.F. Benson is a charlatan in literature,' he said, 'and writes solely for money; but I write for art's sake and am going to be a great artist.' Fred retorted that Walpole was swollen with wind, and ought not to seek invitations to dinner at his house if he intended saying such rubbish afterwards. Arthur had to pacify Fred, who was truly stung, telling him not to confuse good company with bad opinion. 'If I were to refuse to meet everyone who thought me a literary charlatan, I should dine alone constantly.'[30]

Fred was then earning up to £3,000 a year from his fiction, and it would have been foolish of him to pretend that most of it was written for any other reason. But Walpole was pompous to say so, and Benson was ever alert to pomposity.

It was a sadness, not a tragedy, when Beth's aged body began to wind down, and a beautiful circle was made as, at the end of her life, all those she had cared for with perfect selflessness were now called upon to care for her. She was bedridden and incapable of work. She had her own nurse. Her mind could no longer grasp facts and realities, and it was merciful that she should be unaware of the real cause of Maggie's absence. Mary Benson read to her in bed as often as she could, and all the brothers made straight for her room whenever they came to Tremans. Not one of them ever had anything but the sweetest recollections of her, her solicitude and pampering, her unadmitted conspiracy with the children to make life more jolly despite an abnormally stern father, her wish to serve and provide. There were men and women over seventy who had been brought up by her, like Mrs Benson's brother, Henry Sidgwick, who always recalled her 'smiling and making subjunctive observations'.[31] She died in Minnie's arms, at the age of ninety-three. All the family save Maggie was present at her funeral. In so far as any of the Benson men loved without thinking of themselves, or dissecting and analysing what love might do to them, they each loved Beth unconditionally.

'She judged people wisely,' wrote Arthur, 'but she never tried to interfere with them, or to make them do what she wished; she never triumphed over them, or glorified herself.' The dignity of the funeral was spoilt, he thought, by Fred's lightness and triviality in regaling them all with stories of Marie Corelli.[32] Beth would not have minded.

Fred's attachment to Capri blossomed in the years before the First World War, and he tried to spend some time there every summer. The homosexual population was spreading effortlessly as more and more men sought the beauty and isolation of the island to soothe their persecuted souls. Italy had legalised sexual relations between men as early as 1891, which was a powerful attraction additional to the charm of the place. Fred was a total hedonist in Capri, swimming, sun-bathing, quaffing wine and gossiping. He always returned with a deep russet tan which made his blue eyes look paler and more beguiling than ever. There was certainly the feeling that Fred, 'the Sphinx' who would tell nothing, may have disported himself on the island with that abandon which accompanies the certain knowledge that one will never be found out.

He had much to gladden the eye, for Caprese youth was, at that time, astonishingly unselfconscious and free of inhibition. Something of the delight he felt in contemplating untrammelled beauty found its way into one of his books years later. *Colin* has scenes set in Capri wherein the author dwells with sensual pleasure upon the charms of young Nino, whose 'black hair grew low on his forehead, the black lashes swept his smooth brown cheek'. Fred then allows himself to be carried off by rapture tinged with envy:

How attractive was the pagan gaiety of these young islanders! They believed in sunshine and wine and amusement, and a very good creed it was . . . Love was a pleasant pastime . . . They were quite without any moral sense, but it was ludicrous to call that wicked. Pleasure sanctified all they did; they gave it and took it, and slept it off, and sought it again. How different from the bleak and solemn Northerners! These fellows had charm and breeding for their birthright, and, somehow, minds which vice did not sully.[33]

And one of the poems Fred wrote when staying with Lady Radnor at the Palazzo da Mula in Venice extolled such youths as: 'Nude white pillars of manhood beneath the night.'[34]

Fred placed roots on the island by sharing the lease on a villa with John Ellingham Brooks, who had lived permanently in Capri since 1895, and was to die there in 1929. (He 'came for lunch and stayed for life,' he said.) Brooks had the better deal, therefore, since Fred would be there only for a few weeks a year, and as he became more territorial about the villa, he began even to resent Fred's visits. Later, Somerset Maugham also took a share in the villa, he and Benson paying for the lease, but never staying there at the same time, Brooks living from their joint generosity all year round. The house was called the Villa Cercola.

Brooks was an unusual man, possibly the very definition of an aesthete. He had an eye for beauty, perfect taste, a discerning ear, but he was not in the least creative. In his instinct for excellence he chose the best of everything and had perforce to rely on others to pay the bill. Maugham cattily said Brooks appreciated beauty, but had to have it pointed out to him, a remark which should not be taken too seriously, for the two men had once been lovers, and Maugham was ever afterwards uncharitable towards the effete and useless poet whose influence had revealed that part of his sexuality which he would have preferred to have kept secret. Where Fred fitted into this ménage is not at all clear; but he would certainly have run a mile from any involvement. Faith Compton Mackenzie does say of Benson and Brooks, somewhat archly, that 'they had tastes in common besides literature'.[35] When Maugham took up with women and threatened to introduce one to Capri, Brooks went into a fantastic tizzy. 'I don't know what I shall do if Maugham brings a wife to the Cercola,' he wailed, adding, 'I don't think Benson will like it at all either.'[36] What makes his panic all the odder is his own bizarre marital status. In 1903 he had married the American artist Romaine Goddard, and separated a year later when they both belatedly recognised the idiocy of the arrangement. Romaine was one hundred per cent lesbian, and thereafter lived in Paris with her lover but under her married name of Romaine Brooks.

Comically, Fred and Brooks deplored one another's work with parallel zest. Brooks was enormously lazy, spending the whole of a lifetime translating the admittedly difficult sonnets of Hérédia from the French (the translation was never published), which gave Fred, whose industry was truly appalling, the edge in probity. 'Happily the gods in their mercy had withheld from him the perception of his own incompetence,' he wrote icily. 'I prayed that they would never grant him that disastrous boon.'[37] Brooks did not regard prolixity as the test of merit. 'One thing I do hope,' he said, 'is that I shall not have to read his new novel. Fond as I am of Benson I *cannot* read his stuff. It seems to me – hm – hm – deplorable trash. I turn the pages, but, upon my soul, I can't do more.'[38]

Benson took exquisite revenge with a short story, entitled *The Poet*, which belittled Brooks in true feline fashion. The poet of the story is called Godfrey Freeland, and he lives on the Isle of Alatri, where time seems a non-existent dimension. Freeland 'moved with the lissom, careless carriage of a youth,' wrote Fred. 'Youth lingered also in his dress', but there was a sarcastic suspicion that all this clinging to fruity adolescence was for nefarious purposes – 'the mouth with its full sensual underlip suggested that the victory over the flesh was not yet decisive.' As for Freeland's work, that too earns some very tart observations from the author. 'Twenty-five sonnets would be an ample achievement for a lifetime,' he wrote, 'if each was flawless.' The sonnets were polished so slowly and laboriously that they never appeared in print, and the poet might read one to assembled friends who would recognise it as identical to another he had read ten years earlier. Freeland was perfectly contemptuous of the little talents of all his friends on the island, compared with his own total commitment to the artistic life, but he was hurt when they failed to resent his derision. 'Their indifference humiliated him in the sense that he no longer counted for anything.'³⁹ Fred's essential good nature rescued the story from unkindness, for when Freeland dies at the end, a package arrives from the publishers, and the friends join in pretending that it contains the proofs of his sonnets, so the poor man may die happy, whereas it is the returned, unwanted manuscript.⁴⁰

Far more important a friendship than Brooks's was Fred's new alliance with a young man whom he met at Lord Stanmore's castle of Paraggi in 1909, after a sojourn with Lady Radnor in Venice. This was Francis Yeats-Brown, a twenty-three-year-old officer with the Bengal Lancers who had served three years in India. He was striking, handsome, and exotic. He also had ambitions for a literary career, which meant Fred could indulge that pleasure which befell him with the young – giving advice. Francis was wildly excited by the thrill of meeting a real author, and one moreover who looked boyish and spoke cleverly. The two men were left alone at the castle when Stanmore returned to England, and enjoyed themselves hugely, rising at 6 a.m., writing for three hours, talking about literature, trekking over the hills. It was a perfect companionship, and it would one day bear fine fruit with Yeats-Brown's book, *Bengal Lancer*, published in 1930, a best-seller in its day and now a classic, adapted as a one-man show for the stage by Tim Pigott-Smith, and still collecting admirers. It is without doubt that Fred had a hand in this, as his new friend was not slow to acknowledge.

That they retained a fondness for each other well into the future is attested by Yeats-Brown's relaxed presence at frequent intervals in Fred's home. In 1911 they were both at Portofino, Francis returning with Fred to Oakley Street, and the following year Fred would journey out to India with him. Francis found Fred a 'remarkable' man, with perfect manners, a love of work and of the world in tandem, for whom he felt a mixture of fear, awe and love.⁴¹ Fred admitted, in his usual elliptical manner, that their mutual attraction was immediate: 'The tentacles of friendship instantly shot out from his side and from mine.'⁴² Moreover, *Bengal Lancer* was still being worked on in the garden of Lamb House some twenty years later, and it was Fred who found a publisher for it. Whether Fred's emotions were aroused by those tentacles of friendship, he would consider as not a matter worthy of our enquiry.

8   David Blaize

E.F. Benson's literary career sped along in the pre-war years, earning him popularity, wealth, but very little critical respect. Within less than two years (1910–11) he produced *Daisy's Aunt*, *The Osbornes*, *Account Rendered*, and *Juggernaut*, of which only *The Osbornes*, which he wrote while on holiday at Portofino with Francis Yeats-Brown, shows some maturity of characterisation. The story hinges, once more, on the power of good instincts to neutralise and emasculate evil in others (Claude, beautiful but apparently vacuous, saves his intelligent but wicked brother-in-law from ruin by an act of pure selflessness). There were still too many contrived climaxes, too many leaden characters, too much superficiality, as if the author were afraid to get to grips with his subject. However, Fred was changing as an artist, and there were signs that the authentic Benson voice was beginning to make itself heard. This is not merely the wisdom of hindsight – contemporary reviewers also hinted that E.F. Benson had something to say, if only he would sweep away the debris of bad habits in order to say it.

Typical of the notices he was getting are those which greeted *The Weaker Vessel* (1913), whose characters include an alcoholic playwright, a temperamental actress, and the stock clergyman's wife stuffed with nauseating piety. *The Gentlewoman* wrote, 'They are essentially Bensonian creations. They might quite possibly be copied from life, but they do not live.' The reviewer went on to lament Fred's 'surface polish, the Benson Brilliantine', because it obscured the talent beneath. *New Age*, having depicted Fred as 'a servile scribbler', wondered whether he was not, in fact, a satirist in disguise, which was true though not generally acknowledged. Similarly, the *Western Gazette* remarked that 'Mr

Benson attacks no problem, but merely paints portraits remorse-lessly; but the problem nevertheless peeps through between the lines.' With *Mrs Ames* (1912) there emerge more of the qualities which would eventually constitute the Benson cocktail, namely a rich capacity for inventing farcical situations, and a compassion to replace the cynicism of the earlier books. *Mrs Ames* contains two gloriously funny scenes, of the kind which in the *Lucia* books keep the reader smitten with a continuous grin: the Fancy Dress Ball, spoilt by the appearance of three separate Cleopatras each with her much embarrassed Mark Antony; and Mrs Ames's pro-test at the election meeting of the local Tory candidate, when she chains herself to a table-leg *à la* suffragette, only to have her moment of fame thwarted by the lifting of the table-leg leaving her forlornly dangling an empty chain.

Though we are invited to laugh at the absurd posturings and pretences of little people like Mrs Ames and her neighbours, we are not permitted to gloat triumphantly or to snigger vindictively. As Lloyd and Palmer have aptly put it, now that Fred was in his forties, 'middle-aged people were beginning to capture his sympathy rather than his scorn'. The author felt something for his characters – he no longer stood aside and looked upon them with sardonic detachment.[1] Fred was not really changing his out-look, but allowing it to show through the previously bland coating of his style. He had always been compassionate and tolerant, but his literary self had smothered his true self in bright, spurious hardness.

His brother Arthur did not yet perceive the admittedly con-cealed workings of Fred's heart, and continued to regard his obser-vations of life as shallow, his witty rejoinders as 'little maxims with an air of originality – such funny frozen little things'.[2] Arthur ponders Fred's character with increasing frequency and mounting exasperation. He chides him (yet again) with being a snob, boast-ing how he was so much at ease with Duchess Adeline that they were on first-name terms, the while claiming that snobbery no longer held any sway in England; and with being selfish, in so far as he interrupts conversation and will not bear criticism (i.e. Arthur's). 'You have to be amused, or else he rolls himself in a cloud of gloom which sparkles with restless irritability . . . the Tartar is *close* underneath.'[3]

Arthur dwelt much upon Fred's earnings, which exceeded £3,000 a year, with the definite implication that they were undeserved. There is something unpleasant in Arthur's constantly nagging the negative, in his remorseless determination to find fault and examine it, which makes many of his most engaging and lively portraits very suspect. If one were to know E.F. Benson solely through A.C. Benson's Diary, one would have a peculiarly unbalanced picture of a man consumed with trivia and self. Fred's most beguiling characteristics – his kindness, his generosity, his sense of fun, his pity for humanity – would be entirely absent, because Arthur was not the sort of person to notice them. Not yet, anyway. A little incident which concerned Philip Burne-Jones illustrates the point well.

Burne-Jones started to bewail his penury within the hearing of his friends, to wonder what would become of him and how he would ever learn to make ends meet. A. C. Benson's response was heartless and cruel. 'He is the kind of man who begins as an elf and becomes a gnome,' he wrote.[4] Marie Corelli exhorted him to pull himself together and do some *work*, though she knew the advice would not be taken. '*He hasn't the necessity on him*,' she told Fred, 'and in the long sunshine of his father's genius, I'm afraid he hasn't the *ambition*.' All very true, but not very helpful. What did Fred do? He sent some money, unsolicited and unexpected. Burne-Jones was deeply touched and not a little ashamed of himself. In a letter declining to be helped, he referred to Fred's 'kind heart', and the faithfulness of his friendship, and excused himself for the silly habit of 'talking poor' when in reality he had enough to be comfortable.[5] The truth of his situation, and the figures involved, are unimportant now. What matters is Fred's spontaneous response, and the expression of love which he elicited, where Marie Corelli's bitter distrust could only summon scorn, and A.C. Benson's arid fastidiousness earned him some pity.

Fred considered meanness to be self-defeating and injurious to joy. *The Miser*, a cautionary tale he wrote some years later, traces the history of a little boy who put his shillings in a piggy-bank and would let nobody touch them; he grows into the youth who will not afford a wife and the adult man who cannot afford a friend.[6]

At the early age of forty-five Fred's health began to deteriorate. Following a bad fall when skating, he was increasingly attacked by rheumatism; once it was so painful that he forbore all company and had to leave Cambridge, where he was staying with Arthur, to take the waters at Bath. Then something worse developed. In 1913 Fred went to India to stay with Francis Yeats-Brown. While there he suffered periodic but excruciating pain in the kidney. Having consulted a doctor in Bombay, who overhauled him and told him he was perfectly all right, and having found that professional optimism of this sort did nothing to dilute the pain, he returned to England and was again examined, this time by Dr Ross Todd, the family physician. 'Toddles' diagnosed congestion of the kidney, derived from drinking too much fluid, allied to a nervous disposition. The attacks would decrease in severity and frequency as long as Fred followed a rigid diet and took great care of himself. The diet, alas, did not include whisky. 'Todd finds him a very awkward patient,' said Arthur, 'petulant and neurotic.' For once, Arthur was not being hypercritical. Like many a vigorous, athletic man, Fred did not take to invalidism with good grace; he was not used to it, and it annoyed him. Arthur went to see him at Oakley Street, where he was being tended by the mysterious young friend Daukes. 'Poor Fred without wine or tobacco, slipping on and off his sofa, was melancholy.'[7]

A week later, the predicted improvement had not taken place. The kidney had swollen dangerously, due to a stoppage of some sort, and when it did not subside, the decision was taken to operate. Fred's child-like fear and anxiety to be reassured were touching to behold, but when he resorted to daily visits from a man called Hickson, all the Bensons, with the exception of Mama, were alarmed, for Hickson was notorious (or famous) as a spiritual healer.

The operation took place in May 1913, with Dr Todd in attendance, and lasted one hour and twenty minutes. Fred's kidney was in such a bad way that it had to be removed, and he was keen everyone should know it was a *severe* operation. However, he was able to withstand a visit from his mother in the afternoon, which cheered him much. Arthur, ever careful to steer clear of difficulties, stayed away, and with breath-taking egocentricity told his Diary that he was in a very depressed state while the operation was in progress; the depression lifted at 11 a.m., just as Fred's ordeal was over. Shortly afterwards, Fred was moved to a nursing-home in Wimpole Street, where he showed so few signs of feeble-ness that Arthur felt fate had somehow been cheated. There was his brother sitting up in bed and receiving his clutch of dowagers with their grapes and their gossip, even smoking after dinner, when he ought to be laid low with post-operative misery.

'The Benson mind naturally thinks that anything which concerns itself is of the nature of a national crisis and a local convulsion,' wrote Arthur. 'It is all lit up in a kind of golden glory, and the actors have tongues of fire in their heads.'[8] This is less true of E.F. Benson than it is of his siblings. Though argumentative, even combative, he was not self-important.

Convulsions among the Bensons there were aplenty, and they nearly always derived from an excess of that egocentricity which Arthur identified. Worst of all was the unabating calamity of Maggie's mental illness. After she had lived at the Priory in Roehampton for four years, and there had yet lingered some hope of recovery and eventual return, she relapsed into worse disorder than ever, forming the conviction that her mother was her direst enemy and had been conspiring with Lucy Tait to keep her incarcerated. She saw Lucy as the Devil and Mother as a vicious hypocrite. She refused to accept visits from either of them, and wrote the most disgusting letters home, accusing Mary Benson of all manner of Machiavellian intrigue. These letters were later destroyed by Fred, but some of Mary's replies have survived, and they offer an insight into the painful emotional tempest which mental illness may cause in those close to the sufferer.

Dearest Child [she wrote]. Why do you write me such unkind letters? You know they can do nothing but give pain, and all is so untrue. When you feel it would be a pleasure to see me, you must write and say so – I believe you love me deep down, but you have allowed these poisonous thoughts with all their false-ness to take possession of you. I love you, as I always have, with my whole heart – and you can imagine therefore what a letter like this is to me. Always your Mother.[9]

Maggie could not be coaxed into rational or affectionate behaviour. Her illness had devoured her heart, and left her with a cautious, distrustful eye, alert to treachery. So misanthropic did she become, that she managed to turn every remark into a hidden sneer, and every expression of concern into a desire to get rid of her. She told Arthur, for instance, that he was indifferent to Fred's illness as he had always been to hers. 'Maggie's ingenuity in saying unpleasant things is satanical,' he wrote, and that was as good a word as any.[10] The doctors might say that Maggie suffered from chemical imbalance; the psychiatrists might say that her mental equilibrium had been disordered. They both beggared the question of who or what had created disorder out of order, imbalance out of balance. To a family brought up on biblical views of human imperfection, there was no mystery – Maggie was possessed.

It was decided the invalid should be moved from the Priory to a private house in Wimbledon, where she would stay as paying guest to a Dr and Mrs Barton. The Bensons squabbled, as usual, over the cost of the arrangement, which was £800 a year. Arthur guaranteed to contribute £225, and Fred £175, figures which were roughly commensurate with their respective literary earnings; Mary Benson and Lucy Tait would together find another £300, though Arthur suspected they could afford more. Hugh was typically uncooperative, saying his sister should stay where she was, at the Priory. The move did, however, take place in October 1913, when the saintly Bartons took on a chore which the worldly Bensons could not contemplate. In fairness, had Maggie returned to a Tremans which had Lucy Tait in it, the outcome would surely have been catastrophic, and no one appears to have considered for a moment that Lucy should leave. What the Bartons were taking on filled Arthur with acute horror. He wouldn't do it for £10,000 a year, he said. 'They give up their house and their time to Maggie – and her presence, her exactingness, her censoriousness all day long, must be awful! Her incessant grievances, her desire to find fault with everyone must be very depressing.' She was, he reiterated, 'demoniacal'.[11]

194

For her part, Maggie complained to Fred that Arthur had not visited her for more than a year. He admitted to lack of courage, as he attributed his own illness to that terrible interview at Wivelsfield shortly after her collapse, when he had heard fearful screams from the dungeon; the onset of his own trouble had occurred the very next morning. Therefore, he told himself that he could do her no good by seeing her, but might well do himself a great deal of harm.

Eventually Arthur was persuaded, probably by Fred and Mama, to take the plunge, and his account of Maggie's conversation and obsessions is so detailed it deserves lengthy quotation:

> She was full of strange delusions of conspiracy and evil influences, and complained that everyone was trying to obliterate her and misrepresent her . . . 'I can't be sure', she said, 'that anyone is quite the same – Fred, you, Hugh, all seem a little different, as if some other element had come in – it is horrible, horrible! Even I am changed. There has entered into me something that is not myself. I don't want to go back home now, it has all melted away, like snow in a thaw. I made the mistake of not thinking enough things beautiful.' She said that Fred was dead, she was sure, she had come away from seeing Fred, and knew that he was being accused of murdering her. 'There were people in the garden, I thought, and I knew that if I could only show myself at the window, they would know he had not killed me, so I kept opening the shutters and pulling up the blind.' She was like a child wanting to be comforted. She kissed me repeatedly and wished that I had not got to go . . . she evidently desires affection very much.[12]

That this last remark should carry with it a sense of surprise says something about the disastrous aridity of Benson emotion – the obvious was hidden from their bright and lively intellects as surely as a pane of glass means nothing to a trapped bird.

On another visit the following year, Maggie told Arthur about her illness in terms which are vividly recognisable as the symptoms of depressive schizophrenia. 'I am restless,' she said, 'I move about and try to get out and open the windows [this is a few months before the transfer to the Wimbledon house]. They call more and more people in, they hold straps across me, they hold me down, they take everything out of the room, they even sit on me.' Arthur gave her some stationery, but she said she was afraid to use it. 'Each piece I used might bring disaster – a chimney might fall down at the nursing-home – to put out envelopes might be like pulling out bricks.'

Arthur thought his sister did not realise how ill and abnormal she was. 'She spoke bitterly of Lucy, as having ousted us all one by one, and rather bitterly of Mamma, as never having cared for any of us.' Sometimes she would stop herself in mid-sentence, and ask if what she was saying sounded in any way wild. If Arthur told her she was like her old self again, she immediately interpreted that as a prelude to relapse. Most interesting of all, she insisted that Fred had much to bear, but never spoke of it. When Arthur argued that their brother was naturally most cheerful, Maggie sighed, 'Ah, that's what I call courage.'[13]

It is a commonplace in our more enlightened age to see the mad as having a closer insight into truth than the sane; R.D. Laing built his reputation on this very notion. There is a sense in which Maggie may well have been more percipient than her siblings, though she could not be trusted to discern motive with the same acuity as she could observe results. Of course Lucy had taken over their mother's affections almost to the point of monopoly – 'Ben' was subservient to Lucy's decisions and desires. But that this had happened through malevolent intent was nonsense; the Bensons were no less victims of life's erratic dispositions than anyone else, but the mad cannot allow for accident or the merely contingent. Maggie's mind inhabited a world in which cause and effect were necessary, not occasional. When she spoke of Fred's courage in coping with his own misery (she said much the same of Hugh), she may have been transferring her own confusion on to him. On the other hand, it is at least possible that she discerned the efforts Fred made to be free of trouble, and by extension concluded that the troubles must be great if they required such effort to contain them. There is a beguiling logic in the insane mind. Fred spent more time talking to Maggie than did Arthur, but, alas, he left no record of their discussions.

After the move to Wimbledon, Arthur visited Maggie again, and regretted it immediately. She was, he said, 'like a cross, naughty, perverse child, determined to give pain.' They went for a walk in the countryside, and after more than an hour Maggie lay down on her back on the grass and refused to return to the house. Arthur was beside himself with anxiety as to what she might *do*, and in panic called out for help. Dr Barton was not at home, but an unidentified woman came running out, and Maggie, deeply suspicious, said, 'Did you know all these people were coming? Had you arranged it?' She went on to declare that she *knew* how much her mother hated her. The strain of this encounter was very nearly intolerable to Arthur. 'It's horrible to see her misery,' he wrote, 'but I think there is a touch of malignity about it too.' In conversation with Lucy Tait the next day, Arthur learnt for the first time that Maggie's jealousy had been festering as early as 1897 in Winchester, and that Lucy had told her then that she must be mad.[14]

Maggie tried to apologise to Arthur, but he would have none of it. 'It seems to me *nonsense* just to sue for forgiveness. She meant to give trouble and she knew quite well she was giving trouble . . . I am *not* going to pretend that I don't mind.' She thereupon turned once more on her mother, addressing her the most vitriolic letters which we know only by second-hand. Mrs Benson poured out her heart to her youngest son Hugh, who she thought understood the religious life better than any of them. 'She surpassed anything she has ever said before in bitterness and dislike and reproach and fulminations,' she told him, 'so I have passed into silence again. Oh how I wish one could find the source of this poisonous hatred! Bless her.' The poor woman tried to find refuge in meditation, to empty her mind of all worry and be still, but it would not work. Her mind was twisting and seething, 'and in my ears one deep throb is always going on, Maggie, Maggie, Maggie, – and what it all means.'[15]

Arthur had a pretty shrewd idea of what it all meant, namely that the Bensons were a family ineradicably stained. 'Mamma's spirits are wonderful,' he wrote, 'in spite of what she suffers. We are a tough lot, I think, below our sensibilities. But the knowledge of Maggie's weakness, and how certainly derived it was from Papa, and my own tendencies make it clear to me *why* we are coming, as a stock, to an end – and I don't think it would be *right* to prolong it.'[16] The only one of the Benson offspring who could have married, and who in former days both Mary Benson and Arthur had hoped *would* marry, was Fred, and he showed no inclination to oblige. Now, in the light of Maggie's harrowing condition and his own nervous inertia, Arthur is clearly convinced that none of them should beget children even if they wanted to. What he does not admit is the sadness such a reflection causes him; one has to look at the care with which he traced Benson ancestry, in notebooks preserved by descendants of a collateral branch, to realise that he was by no means indifferent to a sudden termination of the line.

Maggie managed to recover sufficiently well to be permitted a visit to London with a nurse. Arthur came down from Cambridge to meet her, and they toured museums before calling upon Fred. 'It was understood that Tremans was to be a *republic*,' she complained, 'but Lucy was dictator!' Then she laughed. She did not brood upon whether or not she would be alive within a month, as she generally did, but behaved with simplicity and charm. Arthur went with her to catch her train back, and stood on the platform before it left. Maggie put her hand out of the window, and he kissed it.[17]

Perhaps it was the relative ease of this outing which persuaded the family that Maggie could join them for a nostalgic visit to Lambeth Palace. It was a dreadful mistake. Once more Arthur came down from Cambridge to meet Maggie at St Pancras; waiting at Lambeth were Mrs Benson, Lucy Tait, and Mrs Davidson (wife of the current Archbishop and sister to Lucy Tait). Fred, still convalescing, was briefly with them, but Hugh did not appear. Very quickly there brewed an unpleasant and embarrassing scene, with Maggie talking bitterly about motherly love. Mrs Benson tried vainly to change the subject. Suddenly Maggie took off the necklace which her mother had given to her and held it out. 'Please take it back,' she said. Mary refused. Maggie then placed the necklace on the table between them and stared at it. Later she passively allowed it to be clasped around her neck again, but the threatening drama unnerved them all, and Mary Benson told Arthur to take her away. Maggie repeated her conviction that both

Fred and Hugh were sufferers, who did not enjoy life, and as she parted company with Arthur, she spat out probably her most wicked remark of all. 'Well,' she said, 'when Mamma has manoeuvred us all into our graves, perhaps she will be content.'

While Arthur consigned his record of these appalling interviews to his Diary, Fred distilled some of them into characters for his novels, and with a crucial difference. For Arthur, his sister's behaviour was the effect of pure malevolence. 'One doesn't wonder at the idea of *possession* – indeed the phenomenon has got to be explained, for the credit of God . . . the devilish nature of the things she says to Mamma is almost incredible . . . she is only capable of using her faculties to hurt others.'[18] Whenever the shade of Maggie turns up in an E.F. Benson story, however, it is always disguised, and nearly always treated with sympathy, pity, or dismay. A short story he wrote, entitled *The Hanging of Alfred Wadham*, warns against heeding too seriously any communications from the dead during a séance. Alfred Wadham has been hanged for a murder he did not commit. The real killer has confessed to Father Denys in the safe knowledge that his confession is protected by the Church. Thereafter the hapless priest is tormented by visions of the dead Wadham, but they are counterfeit, says Fred, – voices from the Devil. Such voices must never be trusted, and the distortion they attempt to wreak upon normal, good human behaviour must be resisted. Fred writes, 'We all do wicked things constantly: the life of all of us is a tissue of misdeeds, but he alone of all men I have ever met seemed to me to love wickedness for its own sake.'[19]

Fred is suggesting that only the Devil himself can embrace evil wholeheartedly, and that any of us who are occasionally cruel or wicked, as Maggie was, are victims of human fallibility at the mercy of diabolical influences. The pity of Maggie was that her suffering was so protracted and the pain she inflicted so acute. This is not to say, of course, that he did not admit the flawed Benson gene which lay at the root of Maggie's illness – his writings about her and their father amply demonstrate this. But he does imply that the Devil may work through the genetic inheritance as efficiently as by any other route.

It was not easy for Fred to dodge Maggie's shafts and abrupt clouds of persecution; he told Arthur that he always had a bad fit of indigestion following a visit to her (which Arthur termed 'neurotic'). But he did not try to avoid visits, as Arthur sometimes did; he was capable of abnegation of self. In a discussion with Percy Lubbock, Arthur confirmed that he was beginning to realise he would always go to Fred in distress rather than to Hugh, for Fred was ever ready to make sacrifices.

In April 1914, Maggie walked out of the Bartons' house in Wimbledon and took a train by herself. Hours later she turned up on the doorstep at Tremans and caused a flurry of telephone calls to be made. Arthur hastened down from Cambridge, Fred from London. Meanwhile, Maggie confronted her mother in a tense scene in the latter's bedroom. On the sofa was a whip. Maggie picked it up and exclaimed, at once gloomily and fiercely, 'What is this?' Her mother told her it was the whip which her pet parrot, Joey, liked to bite. 'It's the whip I used on myself,' said Maggie menacingly, eyes ablaze. 'Did you put it out on purpose?' Mrs Benson tried to deflect her daughter's attention by showing her little objects and talking down to her, as to a child, but Maggie continued to look 'old, tired, thin, and in the morning light dark about the eyes, and very angry.' When the doctor and nurse arrived, Maggie flew into a terrible rage, shouting and screaming and begging not to be taken away. 'Why shouldn't I be at home?' she implored, as the two of them manhandled her and led her forcibly to the car. It was a pitiful, painful sight, and it was to be the last time Maggie would see the home that had been bought with a view to her happiness. The episode also throws a slightly different light upon Mary Benson's behaviour and sensitivity; how could she, in all conscience, allow the presence of the very whip which her daughter had employed in her mad suicidal terror some years previously? Would it not all the time remind her of that terrible scene? To leave it as a plaything for her parrot lends credence to the idea that there was something wanting in her love, something less than whole with the Sidgwick side of the family as well as the Benson side.

Fred was at the Villa Cercola on the Isle of Capri, with John Ellingham Brooks, when the Edwardian world came to an abrupt end at Sarajevo in 1914. So many millions of words have been devoted to the theme that the world was irretrievably changed by that sole event and the war which followed, that there is no need to add to them now. It is curious, however, to see with what resigned nonchalance E.F. Benson mentions the event in all of his published memoirs, especially since he was a man who belonged wholeheartedly to Edwardian society and flourished therein. One would expect him to view the outbreak of war as the slamming down of a great iron dam, whereas he sees it rather as the gentle drawing of a curtain. In *As We Are* he contrasts the ways of the modern post-war world with those he knew before, without loud lamentation because he did not realise how much there was to lament. He observes and records an annoying shift in manners, but little more.

Arthur was right; his brother took so little interest in politics, in the discussion of important issues, that the war took him genuinely by surprise. He noticed the news of Sarajevo in the local newspaper, as he munched an olive and watched the lizards basking on the whitewashed walls of his villa, as of a distant and somewhat tedious rumpus. That was not an altogether blameworthy attitude to adopt while one was on Capri, for nothing that happened in the world seemed to be relevant to that sun-blessed island. He was even buying furniture to ship to Capri in August 1914. It was not until Fred returned to England and found his country gripped by patriotic fever that he realised the significance of the Balkan assassination.

Still, of all the Bensons Fred was the only one to be touched by the war, albeit tangentially. At forty-seven he was too old to enlist, but he was able to make himself useful in other ways. Arthur, six years his senior, constantly under the threat of debilitating neuralgia and imprisoned in academe, felt appallingly superfluous. 'I was made to be of use in peace,' he wrote. 'I am useless in war . . . I feel today an embarrassed loiterer on the fringe of life.'[20] Fred received an anonymous letter from a woman who berated him for not being in khaki – 'No Benson ever did anything for anyone else.' Arthur agreed with her. 'We are individualists and require both money and applause.'[21] The conviction of his pointlessness made him more than usually irritable and waspish.

'Whenever I have a free day someone pounces on it,' he said, referring to his unsolicited mail of thirty letters a day and ghastly flow of visitors. A clergyman called upon him without warning, saying that he must 'grasp the hand of a true man'. 'He little knew of the boiling tide of execration rising to the true man's lips,' Arthur wrote to his mother.[22]

All of which is ironic when one considers that Arthur's lyric 'Land of Hope and Glory' was probably in the end more effective in promoting morale than any amount of propaganda or exhortation; as David Newsome has pointed out, it became virtually a new National Anthem, and Arthur was asked to write additional verses for it.

Fred's contribution to the war effort was more direct. In common with every other writer in England he was summoned to Whitehall for a conference called by C.F.G. Masterman, who was in charge of Information, which meant, as it usually does in wartime, misinformation. The department was so deeply secret that only now, seventy years later, has there been a proper study of its work, and this has been hampered by the destruction of all obvious records. Masterman's purpose was to harness the talents of the country's writers in order to excite and enthuse the populace at home, if necessary by telling lies, and to demoralise the enemy. Almost all those approached agreed to be part of this dubious enterprise and to jettison one of the most prized principles of a writer – namely to employ words in the service of elucidation and truth – and replace it with the tawdry toil of the propagandist. They included John Galsworthy, H.G. Wells, Arnold Bennett, G.K. Chesterton, Hall Caine, Arthur Conan Doyle, and Robert Bridges. None of them felt, nor were they regarded as, shameful; they were swept up by the same tide of nationalism as overwhelmed the rest of the country, and genuinely wanted to be of service. Only two refused – Bertrand Russell, whose uncompromisingly logical mind perceived the danger of deception, and George Bernard Shaw, whose passion dissected the folly of it. Shaw's *Common Sense About the War* created a furore, not only among the politicians and military, but in the ranks of ordinary folk. Surprisingly, A.C. Benson was briefly allied to Shaw and Russell for having written an article in a church newspaper which warned readers not to accept news of German atrocities in Belgium at their face value.[23] This was picked up by the national press and Arthur was vilified for his temerity. (It was established long afterwards that the British propaganda service under Masterman invented many such stories.)

Fred's job was to write about German activities in and intentions towards Turkey. At the same time the Foreign Office sent him on a mission to Rome, to report on the morale of the Italians and, more important, to ascertain whether or not the Pope was as neutral as he claimed, or secretly biased in favour of the Germans and Austrians. This suited Fred very well indeed, for he was afforded a special pass enabling him to travel without hindrance to Italy and to write the report on his beloved Capri. Brooks had a new young friend with him called Giovanni, back from the Front for a brief spell; a year later he was dead. 'It may be decorum but it is certainly not dolce for dear boys like that to be slaughtered for their country,' said Brooks.[24]

Benson's message to the Foreign Office was divided into two parts. In the first place, he pointed out that the middle and upper classes in Italy were hardly touched by the war, and that the burden of suffering was borne by the people. They were about to enter what was likely to be a bitter winter (Italy was not so warm a country as the English supposed, said Fred), and it was imperative that profit-taking in coal be stopped, and public food kitchens be established throughout Italy. Furthermore, forests should be cut down 'ruthlessly' to supply wood and charcoal for fuel. On the second point, Benson told the F.O. that the power of the priests throughout Italy was controlled by the German and Austrian embassies to the Vatican, who had been entertaining cardinals 'on a vast scale'. The Vatican's neutrality was false and dissembling, and moreover insulting to the Italians, who could do nothing to prevent the Pope's undermining of Allied efforts. 'It is an intolerable position for Italy that there should be a nest of intrigue in the very capital of her country . . . Its facilities for propaganda among the clergy are enormous.' Fred therefore recommended that the German and Austrian Legations should be cut off from communication with the Vatican altogether.

The career diplomats at the Foreign Office were not a little perplexed by Fred's proposals. In a covering note sent from Rome Sir Henry Lyson called them bluntly 'preposterous'; they were calculated to infuriate the Italians and alienate the Roman Catholics at one and the same time. As for censoring communications with a neutral State, that was 'even worse. I confess I am surprised that Mr Benson should think it worth while to put forward this kind of stuff.'[25] So much for Fred's lone experience as a political *guru*.

He was on much safer ground with his work for the Propaganda Department, where his advice was not sought, and his talents as a novelist would not interfere with his purpose. The book on German involvement in Turkey was duly published, was followed by another on 'the crimes of Germany for circulation among neutral countries' and a third on Poland. Masterman was delighted with Fred's work, which was naturally unpaid, and wrote fulsomely to express the gratitude of a nation for his 'unfailing readiness' to contribute towards 'the great task of enlightening foreign countries.'[26]

Unfortunately, Fred imagined himself far more a man of influence than he really was, and made dark hints to his mother and brother that he held in his breast some privileged information which he was not at liberty to divulge. He dropped names, then retracted them as if he had foolishly let down his guard, and spoke mysteriously about his sources. Mary was amused by it all, and spoke of Fred's 'brightest shining OPTIMISM aglow like the Kaiser's silver armour'.[27] Arthur, on the other hand, was not so readily impressed, and more or less said so. Fred was 'crusty and testy, the sort of man (I fear) who would get his way in his own house, because it would be worth his relations' while to keep him appeased.' When Arthur contradicted him concerning a point about the war, Fred took refuge in silence behind his newspaper, replied five minutes later, then sulked behind the paper again.[28]

It is none the less the case that, two years after the cessation of hostilities, E.F. Benson was honoured with the MBE for his warwork; he had additionally run a charity for the wounded in hospitals and convalescent homes, from an office at 4, Buckingham Gate, and this may have had something to do with it. Arthur called the award 'a generous offset'.

Lucy, too, was much appreciated for her efforts on behalf of children orphaned by the war, and rejoiced in hard work. She received a proposal of marriage from an Archdeacon whose career ended in scandal owing to a boy he lived with. Lucy presumably declined the offer, as we hear no more of the suitor, but it turned out he was not the first. An elderly parson had sought to woo her with the priceless remark that he always judged by the ear and not the eye, and an Armenian bishop had sat forlornly on her doorstep for days on end until he was carted off to appear before the magistrate. He said he intended to marry Lucy, was told to behave himself, continued to sit in the porch, and was eventually sent to an asylum. 'Lucy's suitors seem to end ill,' commented Arthur.[29]

The war years were a period of recurrent sadness for Fred for reasons quite unconnected with politics: no fewer than three members of his family died between 1914 and 1918. The first was the youngest, Hugh, barely a few weeks after the outbreak of war. He had complained of chest pains while preaching at Salford Cathedral, and consulted a local doctor who could find nothing which required diagnosis. The pains, however, grew worse until, as he was preparing to return to his beloved home in the country, called Hare Street, he found he was physically unable to move, and returned to the Rectory at Salford for a few days' rest and quiet. Ross Todd was sent for and declared the trouble to be 'false angina'. Hugh unwisely took a walk in the garden when he should have been in bed, as a result of which pneumonia developed and death looked over his shoulder. Telegrams were sent to Arthur, who hurried to Salford in time, and to Fred, advising him not to make the journey, as the presence of too many family members would alarm the patient. Accordingly, Arthur went alone, which was entirely appropriate, as the brothers were closer to each other than either was to Fred at that time.

Hugh knew what was beckoning. 'I don't feel like dying at all,' he told Arthur when he arrived. The next day he called for Arthur to come to his bedside, announced 'This is the end!' and asked for his love to be given to all the family. 'Make certain I am dead,' he added.

Then he said to the nurse, 'Is it any good resisting, making an effort?' She said quietly, 'No, Monsignor, it is no good.' He closed his eyes at this, and his breath came quicker. Then he opened his eyes and seeing I was looking at him he said gently, 'Don't look at me, Arthur,' and to the nurse, 'Stand between me and him.' The nurse moved round and I saw his face no longer. Then at one point he said, 'I commend my soul to God, to Mary and Joseph.' Sharrock went on quietly reading. Twice Hugh drew up his hands to his chest – but there was no struggle. I heard him moan a little very faintly, but more like one who was tired out than in pain – and the nurse kept feeling his pulse. I heard his breath no longer, and she said, 'It is over.' Then I saw his face, fallen forwards, the under lip dropped, very pale and helpless, but looking very young. The nurse laid his head back on the pillow. I kissed his hand which was warm and firm.[30]

Hugh's loss was felt very keenly by the Roman Catholic Church, for whom he represented not only the supreme catch of a convert from the very arms of Canterbury, but a proselytiser of genius and a preacher with fire in his voice. There is no doubt that his influence from the pulpit was enormous. Whenever Monsignor Hugh Benson was due to preach one could be sure the hall, no matter how big, would be sold out months in advance. This was as true in America as it was in England, for Hugh gave a *performance* in the pulpit as certainly as Sarah Bernhardt gave on stage. The present author has heard from a Monsignor of the church that he was converted to Catholicism overnight, when he was a young boy, as a result of hearing Benson preach. Robert Hichens confessed to being utterly amazed by what he saw, which he described thus:

In the pulpit he was startlingly sensational. His changes of voice were so abrupt as to be almost alarming. But even more surprising were his movements of body. Sometimes he would suddenly lower his voice and simultaneously shrink down in the pulpit until only his head and face were visible to the congregation. Then he would raise his voice almost to a shriek and, like a figure in a Punch and Judy show, dart up diagonally and lean over the pulpit edge until one almost feared that he would tumble out of it and land sprawling among his fascinated, yet apprehensive hearers below. I have in my time heard a good many preachers . . . but Father Benson surpassed them all in exaggerated emotionalism of manner and voice . . . he almost stupefied me on that occasion. He seemed an entirely different man from the charming and unaffected visitor with whom I had conversed a few days before. I have heard him called dramatic. I thought him melodramatic.[31]

Fred also paid tribute to his brother's 'tumultuous eloquence' and the 'flawless, flame-like' delivery of his sermons,[32] but there was no secret that he was entirely out of sympathy with their content and was constantly irritated by Hugh's monumental certainty, which caused as many of the arguments in the family as did Lucy's subtle tyranny, and, as we know, 'the family required little provocation to be argumentative'.[33] At Tremans with his family, Hugh was infuriating as he stammered out his *dicta*, but in the pulpit, not surprisingly, the speech impediment disappeared. Preaching was his medicine and his pride. So, too, were his books, overtly propagandist and written, as Fred said, 'in furious haste' with a 'terrifying fecundity'.[34] The most famous of these are *Come Rack! Come Rope!*, *The Light Invisible*, *The Necromancers*, *A Winnowing*, *The Conventionalists* and *Confessions of a Convert*. It is probable that Hugh could beat both his brothers in speed of conception and composition, because his content was predetermined. It was this quality, partly, which was responsible for the breakdown of his most famous friendship, with Frederick Rolfe, 'Baron Corvo'.

The unlikely pair had agreed to collaborate on a biography of St Thomas of Canterbury, as co-authors with royalties divided two-thirds to Benson and one-third to Rolfe. On the face of it this was a sensible arrangement, for Rolfe was good at research and scholarship, and Benson could polish off the text in a few days. But Rolfe was a slow worker, a plodder, who took himself seriously and would not be pushed; Benson grew impatient. Then he was advised that it was hardly suitable to have his name coupled on the title-page with a Venetian pimp and procuror of boys, and he became frightened. He told Rolfe that the financial arrangement could stand, but that the Benson name alone should appear as author. Rolfe interpreted this, not without reason, as another in the long line of betrayals which had ruined his life, and turned upon Hugh with vicious ferocity. He bombarded the priest with letters and recriminations for years, finally satirising him cruelly in his *Desire and Pursuit of the Whole*. Rolfe was convinced that the entire Roman Catholic clergy were in league to prevent his advancement.

Hugh had written to Canon Lonsdale Ragg that the conspiracy idea was simply silly. 'Rolfe apparently thinks it is a conspiracy for his friends to refuse to support him indefinitely under circumstances which they entirely disapprove of. It is not a conspiracy for them to agree to keep him; it is one for them to refuse conditionally.'[35]

This painful episode had come to an end with Rolfe's death in poverty in 1913, just a year before Hugh's; it is symptomatic of Hugh's naïvety that he should have blundered into the web of this frightful man so blindly. Not all the fault had been on Rolfe's side. Hugh was certainly hard and avaricious – it was difficult to squeeze pennies from him even for his sister's board and lodging at Wimbledon. He was also weak and feared contamination instead of fighting it. There is even a view that Rolfe was, at bottom, more engaged in spiritual life than was Benson, for all the latter's prefabricated fervour.[36] The truth was that Hugh, hopelessly spoilt as a child, had remained child-like in his perceptions and judgements despite the buffetings of experience. Maggie said, 'Of all the people I know he is the most permanently youthful,' adding that she was not sure whether this was defect or quality.[37] Arthur called him 'the imperishable child', and he retained all his life the humour of boyhood. When once he missed a train and arrived late for a sermon, he drew the most endearing and captivating caricatures of himself, cassock blowing in the wind and stared at by bewildered alley-cats, which he sent to Arthur who roared with laughter.[38]

It fell to Fred to look through his brother's things at Hare Street for a last Will and Testament. What he found was so astonishing that it has become the one salient fact which is remembered about Monsignor Benson when his books and his sermons have been forgotten. Like many of the Bensons, Hugh was riveted by the occult and believed wholeheartedly in ghosts. But he had no intention of being one himself. His instructions were that he should be buried in his garden in a sunken brick vault accessible by a flight of steps. The vault was to be closed with an iron door which could be unlocked from within, and the coffin should be lightly made 'so that in the event of my being buried alive, I could escape, and that a key (of the vault) should be placed in the coffin'. The vault should not be closed and sealed until a month after his death, just in case! Further, an artery in his arm must be opened as an insurance against any mistake. These instructions had been written two years earlier, which indicated that Hugh's terror of finding himself shut in a wooden box was of long duration. Indeed, he had been thinking about it ever since, in Rome in 1903, he had been to the Catacombs of St Callistus and beheld the statue of Santa Cecilia sixty feet below ground, in the reclining position in which her body was supposed to have been found. Her neck bore the wounds inflicted by a soldier sent to behead her, but she died three days after he abandoned what he thought was her corpse.[39] Fred made sure that his brother's wishes were followed to the letter.[40]

Hugh left no heirs save the Roman Catholic Church. His house, Hare Street, was given in perpetuity as a private residence for all future Archbishops of Westminster. Numbers of women were distraught at his death and besieged both Fred and Arthur with letters about him. A Miss Lewis, for example, claimed that Hugh's spirit in Paradise had turned to her in love and that she had thereby a right to be buried beside him. She put her soul into the wound on Christ's left hand, she said, as Hugh had put his soul into the wound on Christ's right hand. 'What *awful* language these Roman Catholics use,' said Arthur.

Hugh had jealously guarded one part of his life from the other, and protected himself from the contagion of love from any quarter simply by becoming an icon, to be admired and applauded but not embraced. He left no *close* friend, male or female, to bewail his departure. Arthur and Fred, in separate assessments, agreed that he recoiled from tactile human contact, and had known no sexual experience. 'He did not know the need of human beings for each other,' said Fred, 'and no one ever really took possession of his heart.'[41] What even Fred did not know was that, in Rome, Hugh had repeatedly dreamt of being arrested by Italian police and treated brutally![42]

Within six weeks Arthur had completed his *Memoir* of his brother, as usual evasive, a book in which he contrived not to mention Frederick Rolfe once. An official biography was commissioned from Father Martindale, whose task was rendered difficult by the reluctance of some people to speak at all nicely about Hugh. Edmund Gosse told Martindale bluntly that he would not help with his book, claiming, 'It appears to be a matter of general conspiracy to present him now as a miracle of genius and virtue,' an aim with which he would have no part.[43] When Fred came to write about Hugh in *Mother*, matching Arthur for brilliant avoidance of anything which might be uncomplimentary or prying, Ethel Smyth told him off sharply for making Hugh more attractive than he really was.[44] Hugh finds his way into Fred's fiction in the deathbed scene of *Mike*, published two years later, wherein Lady Ashbridge recognises her death is near and accepts it with quiet dignity. 'It isn't lonely or terrible,' she says; such is Fred's tribute to the decency and modesty of his brother's departure, and it is more touching than any amount of humbug about his character.

The following year there came to Arthur probably the most extraordinary offer ever made to an author. For years he had been plagued by correspondence from admirers of his gently reflective books – what they lacked in profundity they compensated in elegance – and he nearly always answered every letter. 'I realise that, in spite of my critics, my books have made me friends,' he had told his mother in 1911.[45] Such works as *The Upton Letters*, *From A College Window*, *The Leaves of the Tree*, *The Thread of Gold*, earned him a veritable army of women who hoisted their banners in defence of his wisdom. It irked Arthur somewhat to be a sort of tea-party author, when he wanted most of all to write a big and beautiful book, but he accepted the burden of fame with a good grace. With one correspondent in particular, a wealthy American lady called Madame de Nottbeck, he formed an agreeable epistolary relationship. Then she wrote a letter with an astonishing proposal:

Here is the strangest birthday present I ever had [he told his mother] – a bona fide offer – so far as I can make out – from an American admirer of my books, of a gift of *forty thousand pounds* for my personal use and benefit . . . I wonder if an author ever received such a testimonial before! I would rather that you would not mention the great offer to *anyone, not even to Lucy.* I shan't take it, I need hardly say, but I would like to divert a little to Magdalene.[46]

He did not yet know how difficult the refusal was to be. Three times he wrote to decline, and three times Madame de Nottbeck pointed out that the money was not needed by her family, so if he didn't take it it would serve no purpose at all; that the gift was unconditional – he could do what he wanted with it; and that it was meant as some kind of return for the intense pleasure he had given in his writings over the years.

Eventually, Arthur did accept, and immediately became a man with a fortune. It had taken him twenty years at Eton to earn the amount which was now offered to him for nothing. He felt he had not earned it, but was finally satisfied that neither had she, and Magdalene would be the ultimate beneficiary. Oddly, he thanked her for her 'motherliness' (he was fifty-five years old); yet more oddly, the donor and the recipient were never to meet, as neither of them thought it was such a good idea.

After 1913 Fred found a new home in Brompton Square, Knightsbridge. No. 25 was a beautiful Georgian terrace in what was for London a remarkably secluded spot, at the far end of the square in the shadow of a church spire and overlooking an old graveyard. This was to remain his London address for the rest of his life, and to still be part of his estate as recently as 1967. Fred fell in love with the house, as one is supposed to do, and immediately terminated his lease at Oakley Street. With a friend, archly unnamed but possibly Daukes or Yeats-Brown, he spent four weeks decorating and furnishing the house and was hugely pleased with the result. Readers interested in colour-schemes and removal problems may find details of both in more than one of Fred's books, notably *Up and Down*, of which 25 Brompton Square may be said to be the hero. Arthur was among the first to see the house finished, and was most impressed. 'It is comfortable and delightful,' he said, 'and the boy-footman very competent and eager.'[47] There is no clue as to who the boy-footman was, nor how long he lasted.

Brompton Square injected Fred with a tonic of inspiration and he wrote three books within his first eight months' residence – *David Blaize*, *The Freaks of Mayfair*, and *Mike*. Of these, the first two have been reprinted. We have had cause to discuss *David Blaize* in earlier chapters as its source is quite clearly Fred's own schoolboy experiences. But its subject, the romantic friendship between two adolescent boys, came so close to identifying one of the Benson 'problems' that it unnerved Arthur, who would rather the book had been more distant and detached. In fact, it was moving, it was emotionally engaged, and that, to Arthur, was its most threatening aspect. The subject 'either ought to be handled as a problem or else skated over,' he told his Diary. 'But he doesn't handle it scientifically – he treats it romantically, and this isn't convincing to me.' Besides, 'Fred is a caricaturist really, that's the part he does best.'[48]

Well, for once he was not going to be a caricaturist. *David Blaize* pulses with the life of real people who have genuine feelings for each other. It was an entirely new departure for Fred, and an (almost) final break with those talking robots who prattle away to no effect in so many of his early novels. David and Frank Maddox have red corpuscles in their veins, they become the reader's companions and their fate actually matters. The book was an immediate critical success (*Punch* and the *Daily Graphic* in particular giving fine notices), and placed E.F. Benson's name for ever among the great practitioners of the school story. The romantic treatment is nowadays commonplace and no longer surprises, but in 1916 it was entirely, and dangerously, new. As it became clear that the book would be famous and attention towards it could not easily be deflected, Arthur was sufficiently alarmed to write to Fred expressing his disquiet at some length:

this particular subject is *tacendum* . . . not as a rule written *truthfully* . . . even George Moore can hardly hint at it, though he is outspoken enough. Tom Brown entirely shirks it, even

Sinister St shirks it. You have gone further than any of these . . . The question rather is whether you want to raise it *as a problem*. I think this book might do so . . . Personally, I should *not* wish to raise it as a problem because I don't think it is a thing which can be fought by talking. The more openly talked about the more likely to be experimented in. Why I think your book is risky is because you speak in those pages very plainly, and though you face the fact, you don't discuss the question. My experience is that it is a thing which varies singularly both as to sets and generations – I was at Eton for seven years in a bad time, but it never came near me in any shape, except vague gossip – it lay in streaks and patches. Well, your book rather gives the impression that it was general and a regular sort of thing to be expected by any boy . . . there is a chance of talk and criticism of an unpleasant kind . . . Of course I think it would be *most* unadvisable for you to open the whole subject – it could only be done by a fanatical medical man, with a knowledge of nervous pathology.[49]

To make his point even clearer, Arthur listed those pages which he thought ought to be modified if Fred was not going to omit 'the thing' altogether, and they are all pages in which the sensual pleasure of male companionship is manifest, passages where Maddox and David all but fall into an embrace, passages where the current of sensuality is at its strongest. For example, Arthur objected to the scene in which the boys are lying side by side on the grass prior to Maddox's departure from the school, when they would 'lose each other':

'The chances were millions to one against our ever coming across each other at all. So buck up, as I said.'
David had rolled over on to his face, but at this he sat up, picking bits of dry grass out of his hair.
'Yes, that's so,' he said. 'But it will be pretty beastly without you. I shan't find another friend like you – '
'You'd jolly well better not,' interrupted Frank.
David could not help laughing.
'I suppose we're rather idiots about each other,' he said.[50]

Arthur was doubtless aware that this was in all essentials a love scene, and ought for that reason especially to be suppressed. Fortunately, Fred's readers had other views.

Mary Gladstone (Mrs Drew) thought that Fred had 'just the right combination of technical skill and genuine irresponsible youthfulness' for the task.[51] Letters of appreciation poured in, notably from women. A mother with three teenage sons said she read the book aloud to them and to her husband, and they all declared it to be wholesome and heart-breaking. A man wrote to say it was 'gloriously young and fresh and clean-smelling'.[52] Old Marlburians were affected by nostalgia. 'It *is* the place, in all its essentials,' said one. 'How on earth did you manage it? It's a possession for ever. Other school tales can hide their dishonoured heads.' A Major Hesketh Prichard wrote from the Front to tell the author that his book, 'the best school story yet written bar none', was a source of inspiration and courage to his soldiers – 'The lads in the trenches are sharing it and passing it around.'[53]

Inevitably, a few of the fans claimed *David Blaize* as their own for reasons Fred would genuinely abhor, and he would not have been pleased to learn that the novel is still on the list of homosexual book clubs. Clearly, it does not belong there, for it contains nothing overtly erotic and, indeed, bases its theme upon the purifying power of goodness. Yet the undercurrent is so strong that men who found it awkward to admit their emotional needs felt liberated by the novel, and in complicity with its author. An eighteen-year-old American wrote to say it was 'the most beautiful book I have ever read', and went on to seek Fred's help in a very personal enterprise. 'Have you yet discovered an English boy with whom I may correspond? I hope so. I enter Harvard next month, but I'm a terrible kid still.'[54] It was not, after all, common for a novelist to be asked to procure in such a flirtatious manner. An anonymous admirer in Norwood, South London, sent Fred a simple square piece of paper in the centre of which was written 'I know your secret'.[55]

Fred was consequently circumspect when discussing the degree of authenticity in *David Blaize*, but he was immediately aware that he had achieved something different and worthwhile. In answer to Mary Gladstone's effusions he said that he knew the book was more true to life than any other he had written, but thereafter he deflected enquiry and attempted to avoid too close an identification with his heroes. Some twenty years later, however, only four years before he died, Fred finally ceased prevaricating. In reply to a scholar whose interest was obviously academic, he wrote a letter which was, for him, fairly candid, and in which he admitted his personal investment in the story:

The idea of writing a school story which without being sentimental had much about the strong affections between boys, which can amount to a sort of passion, had been in my mind for years before I wrote David Blaize. I tried it once, got all the values wrong, and then after a long period of internal simmering began it all over again and wrote it in a few weeks, because I imagine it was already written in my mind. My reason for writing it was because it was a subject that, as far as I knew, had never been frankly treated before. The scene and the general mode are those of my own private and public schools, Temple Grove and Marlborough, with a certain dash of Winchester thrown in with regard to certain members of the staff. There is a good deal of autobiographical stuff boiled into it, and whether the book was bad or good, it was pretty well what I meant. It is selling in smallish but steady quantities twenty years after its publication. I wrote it, in its final form, here [Brompton Square] during the first year of the war. I have had more correspondence about it than about any book I ever wrote. That I think has been because there was no 'book-making' about it, but because it was a genuine piece of self-expression.[56]

9   Enter Lucia . . .

The relationship between Fred and his sister Maggie deepened considerably in the closing months of her life, and to him must be given much of the credit for her return to peace and serenity before the end. Fred made the journey to Wimbledon with increasing frequency, often more than once a week, fully realising that he was her only visitor and thereby her one source of affection. He told her about his improvements to the new house at Brompton Square and about the success which had greeted *David Blaize*, and they reminisced over childhood memories. Quite apart from being joyful, these nostalgic journeys offered Maggie a route to discovery of self and were thereby of great benefit to her troubled mind. She recalled, for instance, that she used to practise tying knots on Hugh when he was little, and had once tied him to a tree and abandoned him there. Now, she said, she repented, and was prepared to admit that she had a devilish power to put everyone in the wrong.

Her sense of humour was restored by Fred's presence. Before Christmas 1915, she prepared an elaborate spoof called 'Summer is Icumen In', which she claimed was a hitherto unknown mediaeval manuscript, as her careful analysis demonstrated. She knew it was the sort of whimsy which would appeal to Fred. In more serious vein, she gave him a copy of their brother Hugh's *Spiritual Letters of Monsignor R.H. Benson to one of his Converts*, and an edition of Shakespeare's *Sonnets*.[1] There was no doubt that she eagerly anticipated his visits and in a curious way looked to him to secure her salvation – thus Fred found himself in life playing the role of many of his fictional characters, that of healer and reconciler. His efforts were rewarded by a meeting which in recent years had become unthinkable, a friendly visit from both Mother and Lucy entirely free from recriminations.

During her final week Maggie suffered no delusions and her mind was clearer than it had been for years. She was, however, dropsical, and knew perfectly well that she was dying. She told Fred he was a miracle of kindness and gentleness and asked him to place around her neck an Egyptian charm – a hawk – which he had given her years before. 'It must never be taken off again,' she said. On the last two days her misery was totally lifted; it was as if the illness had never occurred, and she behaved towards her mother with normal, ordinary love. Realising time was short, Fred got in touch with Arthur and asked him to get to Wimbledon as quickly as he could. Arthur reacted swiftly, leaving by the first train the next day, 12 May 1916, but when he arrived he was told that Maggie had died in her sleep that morning. Her last words to Fred had been, 'Well I *have* had a jolly day,' after which she had slept well and stirred only once, at 4 a.m., with a sigh. She died at 6 a.m.,[2] aged fifty-one.

No one was prepared to deny that Maggie Benson's death was anything less than a blessing. Arthur said it put an end to nine years of Hell. The blazing intelligence which had been so disastrously distorted could never have been restored to sufficient equilibrium for her to realise her talents, so there was little need to lament the waste – the time for lamentation had long since past. But her miraculous renewal of happiness in the last weeks and days lifted a terrible burden of guilt from the shoulders of Mary Benson and Lucy Tait. Lucy was almost childishly pleased to find herself once again included by Maggie, and one can virtually *hear* the release of pressure in the ecstatic letters which Mary sent to her son Fred, who she thought had been entirely responsible for the transformation. She 'thought of her [Maggie's] Freedom, and Life, and Joy, and all those nine years either wiped away, or perhaps more truly and better still, *understood*. How one's heart revels and is *satisfied* . . . O BLESS YOU. A mother may bless her son, I suppose, just for the pure joy of *what he is*. I'll take the risk anyhow.'[3]

With Arthur it was quite otherwise. Predictably, he reproached himself for having neglected Maggie for his own self-protection.

'The fact remains that *Fred* has done everything for her of late – quite *splendidly* – he saw her every week and often more.'⁴ Fred received a fulsome letter of tribute from his brother, in which the Benson emotion strains to be contained rather than to escape:

> I think you have been most wonderfully kind, good and patient in all you have done for Maggie in these last months. I must blame myself for not having done more and I am punished by not having seen her before the end . . . I cannot be sad, when she was allowed to show her old self once more to Mamma and Lucy. Yet I want you to know how deeply grateful I am for all you have done for her. Your visits I am sure have been her chief joy of late, and you have shown yourself truly unselfish and kind, as indeed you always are. I didn't wish you to think I did not realise and admire this – for I do so with all my heart . . . those last hours of Mamma with Maggie have taken away all the bitterness of the long estrangement.⁵

All the Bensons knew perfectly well what had been at the root of Maggie's illness, but they kept it tightly to themselves. Those outside, even those as close as Dame Ethel Smyth, professed to having been mystified. 'No storms are more terrible than those that rage in high altitudes,' she wrote, 'and I often wonder exactly what inner conflicts brought about the final clouding of that wonderful brain.'⁶

Two weeks later Fred was summoned to jury service at Chancery Lane, a chore which could not have come at a worse time, for he began to be anxious about his brother's state of mind. He was right to be concerned. Just as Arthur's collapse in 1907 followed the onset of Maggie's insanity, so the return of the nightmare was a direct sequel of her death. It took a little longer for the depression to grasp its victim, but it was to cling viciously for much longer too, more than five years of what he called 'a breath from Hell'. Arthur was Executor of Maggie's estate and had to cope with funeral expenses and debts to Dr Barton. Very unwisely, he also undertook to produce a Memoir of his sister, which would be published under the title *Life and Letters of Maggie Benson*, and by this means more or less obliged himself to dwell upon her madness, its cause, their father, and the possibility of his own descent into the pit. It was for this reason, allied to the customary Benson secrecy, that he intended the book should be a 'half-told tale', only hinting at the nature of the illness, a plan with which his mother was entirely in agreement. Interestingly enough, in view of the reticence of his own books of memoirs, Fred held out strongly for the whole truth to be told in a frank statement on the nature of mental instability, rather than concealing it beneath euphemistic references to 'invalidism'. Fred did not win this argument.[7]

It was Fred, again, who would have to come to the rescue. Arthur felt the shadow threatening with increasing menace until one day, 'I had an access of horror and wretchedness so *awful* that I became aware that I was becoming actually insane, as Maggie did.' Two days later, while on a walk along a country path, he sat down with his head in his hands 'as utterly crushed with misery and despair as I have ever been in my life'.[8] He knew then that he must go to see Ross Todd at the earliest opportunity. The doctor sent him forthwith to a nursing-home for the mentally ill, St Michael's at Ascot, where he spent several weeks under sedation.

Arthur was concerned that he might never again recover clarity of mind, so he prudently wrote out for Fred 'some directions which I know I can trust you to see carried out if they prove necessary . . . I don't honestly feel sure what will happen to me.'[9] The instructions included what to do with keys, what bequests to leave to the caretaker and his wife at the Old Lodge, Magdalene, and to the chauffeur, to return Queen Victoria's letters to Lord Esher, and to lock up his own Diaries. He also wrote out his resignation from the Mastership of Magdalene, but did not send it.

To his mother he wrote letters of such alarming despondency she feared for his life. 'Not only does my heart embrace you all the closer for all your misery,' she replied, 'but because I lay claim as to say being your mother to a certain responsibility in it all . . . *I am your Mother*, and I know the Beast from within . . . I pray for you often, in these words – "Bring his soul out of prison, that he may give thanks unto Thy name".'[10] The same day, she confided her anguish to Fred, who responded by sending her a letter of comfort and wisdom, which, though unfortunately no longer traceable, elicited this from her:

> Dearest, was there ever such a dear letter by a Son to a Mother, in a great common anxiety! *Bless* you. It told me more, and gave me *much more* strength than Todd's, which has come by the same post. And I put my hand in yours and have patience and Hope. I am so glad you will go and see him ... Thank you, thank you, my own dear Son, for all you ARE.[11]

Although she could not bring herself to talk of her own need, the sorrows of Mary Benson's life weighed upon her in old age and Fred's ever more frequent visits to Tremans were a great solace to her. Not only did he bring news of and reassurance about Arthur's condition, but he brought back some of the laughter which they had shared when they had been able to avoid intellectual arguments. No less than four times Fred relates the occasion when he, Arthur and Hugh had gone off into separate corners each to write a page in the style of one of the others, mockingly of course, and unsparingly accurate, with the result that their mother, hearing them all send one another up, rocked with mirth and giggles. Like Fred, she was fascinated by the comedy of life and the absurdities of human behaviour, and her letters are sprinkled with wide-eyed exclamations at the antics which are beyond 'umin langwidge' to unravel. But unravel them she did, for her first role was as a curer of souls, a listener and a counsellor of wisdom. She quite enjoyed having people come to her for advice, like patients queueing up outside a psychiatric clinic, and she was an excellent dispenser of it. 'If you love anyone too much,' she once said, 'it is no good trying to pull back. You must go on and come out the other side, trusting to life to restore the balance.'[12] In an unpublished memoir of her life and character Arthur wrote categorically, 'I do not hesitate to apply the word genius to my mother's power of dealing with people.'[13]

Ready and eager as she was to help others, she would not seek help for herself, and the last year of her life, when she grew deaf, and was stout, and slow, calling herself 'a tottering tortoise',[14] was marked by sterling resilience. She did not ask for sympathy and preferred to keep quiet about her increasingly tiresome ailments; she, too, possessed a goodly share of that purposeful reticence which her sons elevated to an obsession. It is significant that in all the volume of her correspondence, from early womanhood to grieving old age, she rarely talks about herself, save for that one occasion when she reminded Maggie how bruising was her hostility. (Her private Diary was another matter.) This caution was less a token of evasiveness than of tact, the obverse side of it, in fact. Fred intuited her need and went warmly to meet it.

Twenty-five years earlier, Ethel Smyth had written to her in effusive vein:

> The reasons for which I love you are unshakeable; here are some of them; your truth, your fire, your intensity, your power of sustained effort, your extraordinary grip over other souls, your intellect, and above all, in the words of a prayer I like, your 'unconquerable heart'.[15]

Those words remained true to the end. She died without fuss and without pain in June 1918, aged seventy-six, and was buried at Addington next to her two daughters. Arthur and Fred were chief mourners, and among others present were Lucy Tait, Adeline Duchess of Bedford, and Ethel Smyth. Arthur wrote of her, 'my mother's temperament and mind were not in the least degree malleable. She had the strongest individual bent I have ever known, a very clear, critical and intelligent judgement, and a perfect knowledge of her own limitations.'[16] Fred's own memoir of her, which was published, ends with a much simpler tribute. 'I thank God for her dear love, and her shining life, and her swift death.'[17]

Fred shelved the immediate headache of what to do with Tremans until he might know whether Arthur would recover sufficiently to use it as a retreat from Cambridge. Lucy certainly did not want it, and moved out quite soon. The house was too big and unwieldy for her, besides which its pregnant emptiness held memories which made her shiver: nearly thirty years had passed since Lucy first made her home with the Bensons. So, while Tremans was left alone with its ghosts, Fred went on with his writing – as Mama had said, the solution to all difficulties for a

Benson. He did not care to be idle, and had always one book in preparation while another was going to print. It is instructive to see what he was writing about in those years of deprivation which covered the death of a sister, the debility of a brother, and the death of his mother.

Mike had appeared before Maggie died, and was written during those months when he was visiting her every week. Their many discussions covered aspects of their peculiar family history and the overwhelming influence of their father, to whose brooding personality Maggie had finally succumbed while Fred had mutely fought against it. In *Mike* Fred returns to the theme of a brave son asserting his individualism in the face of tyrannical and obtuse paternal authority. Michael Comber (Lord Comber) is the son of Lord Ashbridge, and thereby predestined to the life his forebears had mapped out for him. Ashbridge is a powerful landowner, so powerful that a train can be made to stop as it passes through his estate, merely to allow him to alight. (Fred took this from reality: the Duke of Beaufort dictated just such an arrangement at Badminton, and moreover it continued until the early 1960s.) His existence is its own justification. His wife is stately, elegant, and lifeless. She does what is expected of her in graceful but mechanical fashion. Lady Ashbridge 'had her convictions. She had a mild but unalterable opinion that when anybody died, all that they had previously done became absolutely flawless and laudable.' Michael, the son, was 'an uncomfortable sort of boy . . . he had the inconvenient habit of thinking things out for himself, instead of blindly accepting the conclusions of others.' What he thought was, that his parents were puppets and that his life and liberty depended upon his thwarting their intentions for him.

Michael resigns his commission in the Guards in order to devote himself to music. Lord Ashbridge finds all this beyond his capacity to understand, and Michael (it irks to call him Mike, as Fred does with dated bonhomie) resists his father's strictures with the only weapon left when reason is rendered impotent – humour. 'All dignity is funny, simply because it is sham.' Humour was similarly Fred's own defence. At a Lieder recital given by Sylvia Falbe, with her brother Hermann Falbe as accompanist, Michael realises that he has done the right thing. At the same time, he falls in love with Sylvia.

The love scenes which ensue are, alas, utterly unconvincing, and bear no comparison with the tender scenes of *David Blaize*, published not many months before. But by making Sylvia and Hermann half-German, Fred is sticking his neck out and making a point which few would want to hear in the middle of the war. Michael goes to Bayreuth to hear Wagner and is enraptured. Englishmen of Lord Ashbridge's ilk considered German music as filth and Germans as uniformly verminous. Fred shows that independence of mind must be made to prevail against the corrupting tide of ignorance and nationalism – 'there was no Germany apart from music' – but he nevertheless timidly dilutes his message by including several passages about the nastiness of the Hun, as though he were afraid his patriotism might be in doubt. The climax is pure Bensonian melodrama: Michael marries Sylvia, then rejoins his regiment to do his duty by his country. Hermann returns to Germany to do his. They meet, by chance, at the Front, where Michael kills his friend, whose dying words on recognising the enemy are, 'Good morning, old boy!'

Fred's understanding of the emotional conflicts aroused by the war is superficial, but his determination that art and beauty and loyalty should not fall victim to it are at least brave in the circumstances. Readers could not know, however, to what extent the author's private life and regular visits to a reduced sister found their way surreptitiously into the book. Chapter XI recalls Maggie's supposed attack upon her mother, which in reality had been an attack upon herself.

An Autumn Sowing (1917) shows E.F. Benson at his very best, the satirist with insight and the stylist with sparkle. It is every bit as perceptive and amusing as the *Lucia* books, and it is with good reason that this delightful romp was republished in 1988. Fred has realised that the story must be subservient to the characterisation, if his sharp and saucy view of human follies is to be allowed room to flower instead of being constrained by too rigid a plot. Thus, what happens in *An Autumn Sowing* is not memorable and aims at no compelling point of view. But its characters are glorious, drawn with wit and precision, especially Mrs Keeling and Mr

Silverdale. As one might expect, their glory resides in their being perfectly insufferable.

Neither this nor Fred's subsequent three books reflect any of the cares which then afflicted him (nor, for that matter, did they seem to notice that the country was embroiled in a vicious war). It is not so much a matter of escapism as of chronology. *Mike*, which does contain such echoes, was composed at the time of Maggie's final suffering. *An Autumn Sowing* and *Mr Teddy* (1917) owe their genesis to a period of relative calm, before the death of Mary Benson and before Arthur's breakdown. *Mr Teddy* is not such a happy invention as its predecessor, for it reverts to the necessity of plot, people falling in love for no obvious reason and developing incurable diseases. The central character, Edward Heaton, is a painter approaching middle-age whose salient features are a fierce adherence to what remains of his youth and an inability to complete any job of work. In both respects he is another incarnation of John Ellingham Brooks, with something of Philip Burne-Jones thrown in, but because his creator treats him with indulgence he is not nearly so effective as the Mrs Keelings who would proliferate within a few years.

Up and Down (1918) and *David Blaize and the Blue Door* (1918) were composed during and after Arthur's committal to a mental home, yet they are innocent of any reference to it, even by implication. This was probably quite deliberate, for both books are an evasion, a denial of the real and the important. The hero of *Up and Down* may be said to be 25 Brompton Square, for so many of its pages are devoted to the difficulties of decoration and furniture removal. One wonders why Fred should think that any reader would find interest in such banalities, but by now publishers accepted everything from him, and Arthur had for years sprinkled his books with like vapidities and suffered no apparent damage to his readership. There is a 'friend' in the book, called Francis, who on the evidence is probably not Francis Yeats-Brown (if only because the cautious Fred would have given him a pseudonym), who dies of cancer at the end in what are probably the worst pages ever penned by a Benson. *David Blaize and the Blue Door* is a book of fantasy for children, in the manner of *Alice in*

Wonderland. It enjoyed much success in its day, but now seems contrived.

When Methuen proposed to bring out a new edition of *The Rubicon*, Fred wisely refused permission, declaring that he would, on the whole, prefer it to remain out of print. At the time, he had just finished a new story set in an English village which had as its central character a lady of ferocious social ambition called Mrs Emmeline Lucas. She would become the ultimate Bensonian heroine and the foundation of his enduring popularity. The book was *Queen Lucia.* In the meantime, while Lucia waited at the printers to be sprung upon the world, her creator had tiresome chores to undertake.

First, there was the disposal of Tremans, which became urgent when it was clear that Arthur would never want to live there and was still shut up for long periods in the Ascot nursing-home. There were rooms full of furniture to sell, cupboards full of objects to disperse, and desks stuffed with papers and letters dating back nearly seventy years. Fred was helped in this task by Francis Yeats-Brown, and it occupied several weeks of unrelenting labour. The easiest decision was to send some of Edward White Benson's belongings to the Cathedral archives in Truro, which he knew would have pleased Minnie. The rest was overwhelming in its quantity. Both he and Arthur had enough furniture of their own at Brompton Square and Cambridge, so very little of it was retained, but the revelation of his parents' early letters to each other, and especially his mother's heart-rending Diaries, caused him to see their lives in a perspective which had hitherto been denied him. He showed the extensive archive to Arthur, and together they ruminated upon the personalities which had made them what they were.

When Arthur read Minnie's Diary, and promptly locked it up, he admitted that it was 'very painful to me because it shows how little in common they had, and how *cruel* on the whole he was'. Both brothers drew upon this and the letters in their autobiographical writings, though understandably only obliquely. In private discussion, however, they were more frank in assessing the marriage and its consequences. Arthur sat upon his thoughts for many months while he was convalescing, and only later felt up to a proper analysis.

I have been present at talks at Addington [he said], when Papa's hard displeasure, about some trifle, was intolerable. On the other hand I used to think at the Addington meals that Mamma was not always dexterous in reverting to subjects which *always* rubbed Papa up the wrong way. It was, as you say, a case of real natural incompatibility. Mamma was an instinctive *pagan* – hence her charm – with the most beautiful perceptions and ways. Papa was an instinctive Puritan, with a rebellious love of art. Papa on the whole hated and mistrusted the people he didn't wholly approve of. Mamma saw their faults and loved them. How very few friends Papa ever had . . . he disliked feeling people's superiority. His mind was better and stronger than his heart and his heart didn't keep his mind in check. It was a *fine* character, not a beautiful one. He certainly had a tendency to bully people, as he believed from proud motives. Mamma never wanted to direct or interfere with people and I think was the most generous and disinterested character I have ever known.

Fred agreed, though he maintained that the marriage had worked very well, despite the incompatibility, because Mary preferred not to stand up to her husband but, for the sake of peace, to serve.[18] Arthur referred to her being 'in bondage'. Further, Fred maintained that Edward White Benson had fundamentally been a deeply affectionate man. Yes, said Arthur, but the affection was nearly always hidden, and he left little of it behind:

Papa was a very difficult person to deal with, because he was terrifying, and remembered things, not very accurately, because he remembered the points which were in his favour and forgot the points which were not. Mamma forgot everything, or if she remembered, forgot the sense of resentment. Then he wanted, as you say, obedience and enthusiasm. Mamma never claimed either exactly, but got both. Papa cared intensely about details, and details never interested Mamma. And one must remember, as you also say, the other side – and Papa's affection, when it rose to the surface, was very rewarding indeed.

Fred's pondering upon these matters was fruitful. For the first time he felt able to deal with his family life in literary terms, not to conceal rebellion against his father within a fictional character, but to bring the man forth into the (relatively) open air of honest scrutiny. At the same time, he wanted to celebrate the girlish yet dependable personality of his adored mother. Her death and his discussions with his brother released these possibilities, enabling the first of Fred's many autobiographical writings, *Our Family Affairs* (1920) and *Mother* (1925), to appear soon afterwards.

Houses were still very much on Fred's mind. He had recently lost his eighteen-year-old manservant to the army, conscripted in the closing weeks of the war; at the same time, sixteen-year-old Charlie Tomlin, who had been employed at Tremans for three years, was suddenly without work. Fred offered him the place of manservant, to live in at Brompton Square and accompany Fred on his travels, which Charlie eagerly accepted. He was to remain in his service until the end, and be the one lingering link with E.F. Benson to survive into the 1970s. At the same time, Fred was involved in a move to a house in Sussex which, tentative and half-hearted at first, was gradually to lead to a new home and a new role in public life. This was Lamb House, one of the most beguiling Georgian houses in the delightful country town of Rye, and formerly the home of Henry James.

James, who had been a friend of the Benson family virtually since Fred was a schoolboy, and had, it will be remembered, been the first reader of Fred's first manuscript, lived in Rye for the last sixteen years of his life. He had initially rented a cottage near by in order to work undisturbed, and was so enchanted with his first sight of Lamb House that he moved in before the end of the century. Fred visited him there in 1900, and would call in whenever his journey took him within reach. That Henry James was always glad to see a Benson is confirmed by an abject letter, decorated with customary Jamesian flourishes, which he wrote to Fred on one occasion when they missed each other. 'Please believe I would have surrounded your advent with every circumstance of welcome had I been here,' he said.[19] Fred had stayed at the house as James's guest for a few days, when he would hear the great man dictating his novels to a secretary all morning long, in a room privately apart from the rest of the house, and at right-angles to it, called the Garden Room. He had never then suspected that he would one day live there.

Henry James died in 1916, leaving Lamb House to his nephew, who rented it to an American widow, Mrs Beevor. She grew tired of the harsh winds which could afflict Rye in winter, and offered it to an artist called Robert Norton, who was a friend of Benson's. Norton then suggested Fred and he share the place, which seemed a very congenial idea, so Fred began to spend weekends in Rye, returning to London by train on Monday morning, an arrangement which lasted a few months. Norton was then obliged to go to the United States and suggested Fred might like to take on the whole lease by himself. As he still paid towards the Villa Cercola in Capri and had every intention of spending as much time there as possible, the rental of a third home would have been an immodest and uneconomical luxury. He declined, and Lamb House was let to a stranger.

In the event, Capri was soon lost to Fred, for the owner of the Villa Cercola declared he would no longer rent it out and that Benson and Brooks would have to buy it if they wanted to go on using it. This did not suit Brooks, as he had no money, or Benson, as he did not wish to tie himself to property abroad which he would *have* to visit regularly simply because he owned it. At the same time, the new tenant of Lamb House, finding the climate as inimical as his compatriot Mrs Beevor, offered the lease back to Fred. This time he was ready. Although the house was furnished to some extent, Fred determined to bring in many of his own things and some of the left-overs from Tremans, which he had only just finished emptying. Thus did Fred spend much of the year 1919 in transporting large objects from one place to another. The famous piano which had got stuck in the hall of Brompton Square was brought down from London and once again proved obdurate in Rye. 'There was an awful morning when I thought I should have to get the permission of the Town Council to build a shed for it in the street outside.'[20] They managed, somehow; today the piano is in Wiltshire, and will probably never again be submitted to the indignity of scraping its nose on the floor.

Fred did not give up Brompton Square; on the other hand, he

could not have known to what extent Rye would increasingly become his home. Significantly, he thought less of Lamb House being a refuge for himself, as being a salvation for Arthur. The first thing he did, having ensconced himself with the help of Charlie Tomlin and made the place comfortable, was to invite Arthur to come down and spend several weeks there. It takes a moment to realise just how altruistic a gesture this was. Fred had never shared a house with anyone. Nor had Arthur. They were independent bachelors, set in their ways, and unwilling to adapt or compromise on trifling domestic arrangements. Apart from weekends at Tremans, which had generally ended in heated argument, they had not spent prolonged periods together since childhood. Nor did they entirely approve of one another, Fred deeming Arthur's life to be circumscribed and solemn, Arthur convinced that Fred's was meretricious and trivial. Added to which, Arthur was seriously ill, likely to prove a burden upon the most obliging of nurses. All in all, it was positively saintly of Fred to submit himself to what might well be a blistering ordeal, but he did not hesitate. It is speculative, but justifiable, to suggest that he thought of their mother's intense worry during the last year of her life, and her reliance upon Fred to look after his older brother; this is what she would have wanted. She may even have asked him to do something. Anyway, he wrote to Arthur inviting him to stay as an experiment, a possible antidote to melancholia, and Arthur accepted.

They adapted brilliantly. Fred made sure that Arthur was not left alone to brood and ruminate, that they shared meals and went for walks together every afternoon. Arthur started to rediscover pleasure in what he did, and to write once more. Every morning he received a bundle of letters, which he answered immediately, the same day, sitting in an armchair and dropping them on the floor as he dealt with them. Again in the evening, he would write his essays, poems, reminiscences, pouring words on to reams of paper which he would shovel into an envelope, unread and unrevised, for his secretary to type out. Gradually Arthur came back to life under this regime, for Fred's company was the reward for his effort to conquer misery, and, moreover, it was reliable, constant and unwavering. Arthur well knew that he owed his recovery to his brother, and once he had returned to Cambridge, wrote frequently to give voice to this realisation. The fact that his letters sound more like the polite expressions of a patient merely testifies to a lifetime's control of the emotions, but it is possible to discern the stream of feeling running beneath them:

> You have been wonderfully good to me all through this bad time and I only wish I could do something to prove how grateful I am. I am afraid I have caused you great trouble and anxiety and I shall never forget all your patience and kindness . . .
> . . . another instance of your *unfailing* kindness, and it has moved me very much indeed to realise it. I don't seem able to do much at present except express gratitude for all that you have done for me – but it's very real, though singularly ineffective, I fear.[21]

It was still important that Arthur not be left alone, so Percy Lubbock went to stay with him in Cambridge, where he was even yet undergoing specialist treatment for depression, and either Lubbock or Geoffrey Madan would accompany him to Rye.

As the 'experiment' appeared to succeed, the Bensons took on a joint lease of Lamb House for three years, it being understood that they would stay there at different times if they so wished, or together, according to the fates. Lamb House would be an inspiration to them both, for while A.C. Benson wrote some of his last books there, E.F. Benson was to produce the very best of his work, in an astonishing burst of creative energy and stylistic aplomb over a number of years. It was also there, oddly enough, that he began developing his technique as a writer of ghost stories. It was not that Lamb House was especially haunted, though Fred frequently told visitors in old age that he had met one ghost there, but that if any house should be, this would be it. More than a few of his stories, of which he wrote over seventy, are recognisably set in or around Lamb House.

We have had cause to notice earlier that the Bensons and Sidgwicks were all, to some degree or another, seduced by aspects of the supernatural; it was the fashion of the age, and not peculiar to this family alone. Edward White Benson may well have embraced the church as protection against the black magic in which his father had unwisely dabbled, but he could not prevent his three sons from flirting with the occult. Hugh, the most religious, was the most obsessed, bent on avoiding being buried alive lest he encounter the devils on their own ground. He firmly believed in diabolic possession and visited haunted houses in order to cast out their loathsome invisible inhabitants. Arthur also came to the view that their sister Maggie was possessed. For his part, Fred was fascinated by spiritualism; he turned tables, summoned spirits, consulted mediums, placed himself in the hands of a faith healer at the time of his kidney failure.

While all three Bensons wrote ghost stories, Fred's were the most numerous, and the most horrid. He did not shirk the consequences of his vivid prose style, which gloried in descriptions of flies and loose eyeballs, malformations and dismemberments, and knew he could make the reader's flesh creep. In *Final Edition* he more or less said that it presented no great difficulty, so he did not value his horror fiction at all highly. Which is a pity, because nearly all his stories are uncomfortable and powerful, and should be rated alongside the best. *Caterpillars*, for example, tells of a vile dream in which millions of the insects are crawling in through keyholes and covering the floor with their writhing mess, which on waking turns out to be a presentiment of cancer.[22] M.R. James, the master of the *genre* and an old family friend, ranked Fred's supernatural writing very high. However, he criticised his 'stepping over the line of legitimate horridness', and pointed out that it was relatively easy to be nauseating.[23]

Caterpillars is such a long way from the arch humour of Benson's English village novels that it scarcely seems credible they were written by the same man, but the bridge between them can be crossed at various points where he dwells upon the nature and function of evil. In the horror stories evil is incarnate and terrifying; in the *Lucia* books it is emasculated by silly women who do not realise the harm they are up to. But they are both, in the end, about the same thing, and demonstrate that E.F. Benson, for all his irresistible light humour, has a serious point to make.

A story called *Lady Massington's Redemption* is one such bridge. It was a story which mattered intensely to Fred, who wrote to his agent several times imploring him to place it well. Lady Massington is dead and buried, but shows up for lunch with her husband and goes out to a concert. She remembers she was buried in her own body, so is certain the coffin cannot be empty. The coffin is disinterred, and within it is found a little body fast asleep, wrapped in a bride's veil. An obligatory clap of thunder accompanies the opening of the coffin. As the tale develops, we discover that Lady Massington was a selfish woman and consequently, when she died, found herself in Hell, where she was visited by God and offered salvation. The little baby is her redemption, for it represents 'utter forgetfulness of self . . . a soul had been born to her as well as a child'. She tells her husband that either she or the baby must die, and she has chosen to die again herself. 'The child is my redemption, for at last I have cared for something not myself,' she tells him. Underlining the point, Fred terminates with, 'her redemption was accomplished, for she had loved'.[24]

Benson's central ideas are contained in this not altogether successful story – that the powers of Good are capable of conquest over Evil; and that salvation is possible through abnegation and love. The original title of the story was *Lady Massington's Resurrection*.

Fred's experiments with mediums were by no means secretive; at his request, Oliver Lodge arranged a sitting immediately after Maggie's death, on condition he should be anonymous – 'names do no good, they spoil evidence'.[25] His mother's ridiculous sprawling hand-writing when in the grip of some unearthly spirit is preserved at Oxford as testimony of their games. Mary Benson had left a mysterious packet for him to open after her death. He consulted a medium who told him that 'direct voice' and 'automatic writing' revealed the contents as a lock of hair. In *As We Are* and *Up and Down* Fred is at pains to defend this interest from the suspicion of quackery. 'Francis' indulges in eastern-style meditation and earns the author's approval, not denigration. Towards the end of the book there are five pages explaining that spiritualism is not essentially to do with the supernatural, but is a perfectly explicable extension of natural law. An essay entitled *Demoniacal Possession* explores this theme further. What is regarded as superstition in one age, he says, becomes scientific knowledge in the next, as happened with the wireless (what we now call radio). As for the medium and his/her trance, all this does is to bring the subconscious to the surface and allow, by telepathy and thought-transference, other consciences to plug into it.

On the question of Evil, Benson is somewhat more troubled and less didactic. He accepts that there are two principles in the world, and can discern no intrinsic reason why prayer and devotion to Evil should not produce active intervention on the part of the Devil. He adduces evidence of diabolic cunning in taking over control of a mind when its guard is down, as when perfectly respectable people say the most indecent things when chloroform is administered to them (Freud would say the Id is surfacing – Fred says it's Satan; they are in practice saying the same thing). Fred's meditation on the subject then comes up against a block which he finds impossible to shift; Evil must be created by an omnipotent God, who created everything, and who is also all-loving, absolute God, and cannot therefore create Evil. This is the problem, which it is dishonest to shirk. The Christian Science people avoid it by denying it, by saying there is no such thing as Evil. 'Though it may be a comforting notion to those who cannot think, it never brought the smallest consolation to those who can.' Fred will not avoid it, but is prepared to accept defeat in attempting to understand it. The origin of Evil, he says, is one of those things, probably in fact the only one, about which thought leads nowhere. The prayer – 'from all unprofitable speculation on the origin of Evil, Good Lord deliver me', is a wise one, which we should all adopt. We should immensely like to know, but we are aware that we cannot.[26]

It is fortunate that E.F. Benson was not a philosopher, as his surrender to the insoluble would have earned him many a stiff rebuke. But as a novelist he is ready to grapple with it, and to spotlight its manifestations in a gallery of genuine, recognisable, and increasingly funny characters. What he is not prepared to do is to tolerate charlatans, who cheapen what is a profoundly worrying subject with their antics. In *The Freaks of Mayfair* (1916) he makes the casually dismissive observation that 'spiritualism for some obscure reason almost invariably causes people to lay on flesh'.

As for the Christian Scientists, with whom Mary Benson had consorted, he finds their self-importance and their self-absorption thoroughly objectionable. 'One of the strongest characteristics of Christian Scientists,' he writes, 'is their inhuman disregard of other people.'[27] This is, in essence, his view of Daisy Quantock, the rabid mystic and Christian Science fanatic of *Queen Lucia*, but by the time that book appeared, Fred had realised that his talents ill-equipped him to carry his message in persuasive prose, for he was defeated by logic and the point he was making was not expressed with sufficient intellectual rigour to impress and convince. When, however, he concealed the point in wickedly funny farce, he won through and made converts by the thousand. Thus it is that the carefully controlled essay in *The Freaks of Mayfair* merely describes a Christian Scientist, whereas the portrait of Daisy Quantock depicts the species so uproariously, with such relentless mockery, that no reader is left in any doubt where Fred stands. By hiding serious arguments inside hilarious plots, he would be able to achieve an influence far wider than he had ever hoped or even intended.

The means of this influence was nearly always the exaggerated portrait of an outrageous woman – outrageously stupid, or pompous, or ambitious, or selfish, or cruel, or an amalgam of all five. Benson's first book, *Dodo*, was such a portrait and nothing more; because it lacked depth and compassion, the character excited our hostility rather than our mirth. His next, *Six Common Things*, contained the genesis of his snobbish ladies in the stories 'Poor Miss Huntingford' and 'The Defeat of Lady Grantham', but once again the author's eye is less than indulgent and our sympathies are not engaged; these are still essays disguised as fiction. Fred relished stories of appalling women making fools of themselves, especially when there are two rivals for supremacy, but until he was older he failed to see that they must be allowed to enlist our understanding or they are as flat as propaganda. An early tale of 'pestilent upstarts' shows how the vain must tumble; Augusta Plaice and Alethea Frink are rival snobs who have not met. Mrs Frink turns up at Mrs Plaice's party uninvited, and Mrs Plaice has the delicious pleasure of telling her to go away. She does. Later, Mrs Plaice realises she has insulted the wrong woman, for the recipient of her triumphant snub was no less than Lady Cynthia Matcham, a close friend of the Prince of Wales.[28] It is a slight story, which of itself does not deserve to be remembered, but one may clearly spot in Mrs Plaice and Mrs Frink the precursors of Lucia and Miss Mapp.

So, too, one of the first incarnations of Georgie Pillson turns up in *The Freaks of Mayfair*, but he is again painted with unkindness more than humour, thereby sacrificing the reader's interest. Many of the social faults which Fred loves to hold to ridicule are adumbrated in this book – snobbery, faddism, gossip, slavery to routine, effeminacy – and they will all find their place in the *Lucia* novels. One who makes no further appearance thereafter is 'The Spiritual Pastor' – the purveyor of literary pap who is based on A.C. Benson himself:

> For Mr Sandow never fails you; his fund of mild and pleasant reflection is absolutely unending, and if from a mental point of view the study of his works is rather like eating jam from a spoon, you can at least be certain that you will never bite on a stone and jar your teeth. And if you do not by way of intellectual provender like eating jam, why, you need not read Mr Sandow's books, but those of somebody else.[29]

The identification was so obvious that a rumour spread to the effect that the Benson brothers had fallen out over it, and Arthur felt obliged to assure Fred that he really didn't mind:

> I was much amused to hear this morning on good authority that you and I had had a serious quarrel (I rather think that Hugh Walpole is at the back of this). It is said that in the Freaks of Mayfair you satirised in the essay about the parson my style of writing and that a rupture of relations is the result... I was wholly and entirely *amused* and even rather flattered, to speak the truth... [it is] a good description of my essays, not at all unfair.[30]

It is in *Mrs Ames*, published in 1912, that one may best discern the evolution of style which would gleefully erupt eight years later in *Queen Lucia* (1920). Harry Ames, the hopeless son, like

Georgie Pillson is rather too keen on his appearance and fatuously unaware that everyone else knows the trouble he has taken. 'It was difficult to arrange his hair satisfactorily. If he brushed it back it revealed an excess of high vacant-looking forehead; if he let it drop over his forehead, though his resemblance to Keats was distinctly strengthened, its resemblance to seaweed was increased also.' Major Ames is similarly smashed in a few bold strokes: 'Major Ames was not really an untruthful man, but many men who are not really untruthful get through a wonderful lot of misrepresentation.' And Mrs Ames, naturally, enjoys the author's most acid observations, as when she 'raised the pieces of her face where there might have been eyebrows in other days'.[31] The style which emerges is sharp, succinct, witty and cleverly reticent, for it is this use of understatement, permitting the reader to fill in with his own imagined gloss, which recruits so many admirers. This new style, quite absent from Fred's earliest books, broke into joyous expression with *Queen Lucia*.

The story is simplicity itself. The village of Riseholme, a more or less genuine Elizabethan treasure with a few studded front doors for added authenticity, lives entirely for gossip. The emotional sustenance of its inhabitants derives from knowing who is having whom to dine, and which weekend guest presents the best opportunity for showing off. 'The hours of the morning between breakfast and lunch were the times which the inhabitants of Riseholme chiefly devoted to spying on each other.' Of paramount importance to the exclusive set is the pleasure of observing the excluded, and so the ultimate misery is to know something is going on and not to be invited to witness it. The next worst experience is to be the subject of a conversation which is less than adulatory, and as everyone is bent upon impressing everyone else, the risk of this happening is very high indeed. 'Humour in Riseholme was apt to be a little unkind: if you mentioned the absurdities of your friends there was just a speck of malice in your wit.' Benson based the physical features of Riseholme upon the Cotswold village of Broadway, but the personalities of the villagers were composites of all the most garrulous and risible women he had known.

The arbiter of taste and director of destinies is a lady of vast pretension called Emmeline Lucas, who prefers to be known as 'Lucia' in deference to her mastery of the Italian tongue. In fact, she can manufacture only a few pointless sentences, which she has to rehearse in private, but the whole village offers her the admiration they might reserve for a polyglot. She plays the piano, but it is always the same piece – the first movement of Beethoven's 'Moonlight Sonata', the second two movements being, in her view, vulgar and uninspired; in truth, they are too difficult for her, and it has taken her years to manage the first. Her pretty garden is called 'Shakespeare's Garden' because every flower in it is mentioned in one or other of the Bard's plays, and her guest rooms are named after Hamlet and Othello, for Lucia is also a mistress of literary values and must needs educate the rest of the village by example. When in her most cunning and dangerous mood, she resorts to baby-talk, on the grounds that this is the nearest route towards getting one's own way. 'Me vewy sowwy! Oo naughty, too, to hurt Lucia,' is among her least offensive effusions in this vein. She believes in God in much the same way as she believes in Australia. When she is satisfied, or triumphant, or inspired by music and literature, Lucia is fond of adopting 'the farthest-away expression ever seen on mortal face'. In fact, she is the most crashing hypocrite, and would be utterly deplorable were she not saved by her creator's wit and compassion.

Thus far, Benson's most famous character is based almost entirely upon his contemporary and sometime friend, concerning whose life and career, as we have seen, he collected a scrap-book full of press cuttings, the best-selling novelist Marie Corelli. She, too, attempted to speak Italian and professed even to be descended from the (childless) Venetian musician Arcangelo Corelli (her real name was Minnie Mackay). She, too, relapsed into embarrassing baby-talk with men, and wrote letters in the style to the painter Arthur Severn. She, too, kidnapped Shakespeare for her own, electing to live in Stratford-upon-Avon in order to protect his memory from the ignorant townsfolk who knew little of literature. She, too, played the piano with pitiless sincerity. Marie Corelli was a monster of pretension who would have ruled the lives and manners of Stratford people given half a chance, and Fred pounced upon her every weakness with victorious glee, distilling them all into the awesome Lucia. Whether Marie Corelli also drew as much pleasure as Lucia from spoiling that of others, is open to doubt; Fred may well have thought he spotted this trait among his own siblings.[32]

Lucia has a husband, idiotically called 'Peppino', totally under control. There is no suggestion that he has ever demanded carnal relations or would get very far if he did. Her loyal henchman is Georgie Pillson, a slightly effete bachelor whose principal accomplishment has been to decorate his cottage with his own embroidery, and whose toupée he fondly imagines is a secret from everybody. Georgie joins Lucia in small-talk, or pidgin Italian, or piano duets (he always taking the bass notes, because Lucia says he is more suited for them, thereby reserving the melody for herself), always when bidden. He is better at obedience than initiative, and supports the throne upon which Lucia, as Queen of Riseholme, appears to be immortally placed.

Daisy Quantock represents the faddist. Like Uncle Davey in Nancy Mitford's *The Pursuit of Love* she has been the happy victim of every fashionable fad in sight, has eaten all the right things and done all the right exercises. Her flirtation with Christian Science led her to the knowledge of her own perfection and the gloomiest views on all her friends. In the course of *Queen Lucia* Daisy is twice bamboozled by a fraud. First she boasts her own in-house eastern guru, to the envy of all save Lucia, who annexes him, and he turns out to be a cook in an Indian restaurant and a burglar to boot. Lucia craftily contrives to blame Daisy for the guru's faults. Then Daisy discovers a Russian princess who is marvellous at a *séance*; mercifully, when the princess is arrested Daisy and her husband manage to conceal their shame by burning the muslin drapes which the spirit wore when summoned by the jumping table, and buying all copies of the daily newspaper which contains the law report. Daisy subscribes to a magazine with the unlikely name of *Uric Acid Monthly*: in fact the Connecticut journal which Fred had pasted into his scrapbook.

Mrs Weston is another glorious type, the eyes and ears of the village, she who misses nothing, and embellishes her narrative tale with a hundred tangents and non-sequiturs about the fishmonger's son and the Thursday before the Tuesday of the full moon and so on. It is essential to Mrs Weston's happiness that she be the bringer of the latest news, a trait Fred found in the London hostess Sibyl Colefax, of whom Margot Asquith once said that one could not talk about the birth of Christ without she would claim to have been there in the manger. Another Colefax marker was her illegible handwriting, which meant her letters had to be thrown on the floor in the hope they might release their secrets by accident; this Benson lends, in muted form, to Daisy Quantock.

In one form or another, the Riseholmites are all lying to themselves or to each other, and in every case for reasons of self-aggrandisement and vainglory. 'It is hitting below the belt to appeal to unselfish motives', might be the motto of them all. Even the loyal Georgie, content to glow but dimly in Lucia's benevolent shadow, can be seduced away by a more glamorous protector. Such, indeed, is the plot of Fred's story, for into this tiny sizzling cauldron of self-interest comes Olga Bracely, the famous opera singer, who is so enchanted by what she takes to be a quaint, charming, quiet little backwater that she takes the lease on a house in Riseholme and is immediately transformed from a welcome catch to an unwelcome rival. Lucia tries to look down upon her as a vulgarian, making due allowance, of course, for her quite pleasant voice, and allows it to be known that she will give Miss Bracely the benefit of her superior social standing to eliminate that touch of 'the footlights' about her. Olga is in no need of Lucia's help, and to the latter's acute discomfiture, manages to outshine her without even trying, thereby throwing the balance of Riseholme into a spin – 'all the known laws of gravity and attraction were upset'.

The trouble is, Olga is genuine and Lucia a fraud. Daisy Quantock very kindly attempts to point this out to Lucia, who is impervious to sarcasm because she affects not to notice it, but secretly she 'cloaked her rage in the most playful manner'. Lucia's exposure comes with the advent of the great Italian composer, whom Olga thoughtfully seats next to Lucia at dinner, thus making it impossible for Lucia to disguise that she knows nothing of music and speaks nothing of Italian. The last straw is Georgie's defection to the newcomer, with whom he appears to be in love, but more as a brother than a suitor.

Lucia is miserable in her wrath and turns bitchily upon everyone. It is a measure of Benson's skill that he can parade before us such a platoon of hypocrites without arousing our antipathy. Despite Lucia's ridiculous posturing and her ignorance, we feel sorry that she should be so laid bare. So does Benson, who remarks (through Georgie) 'how she must have suffered before she attained to so superb a sourness'. It is Olga herself who saves the heroine from utter neglect by making Georgie return to her and butter her up with some flattery and attention, enabling Lucia to 'queen it' over Riseholme society once more. Benson does not require she should see the error of her ways, or apologise, or repent. She is simply forgiven and understood. Olga finds it easy to achieve this magnanimity because she is urban and sophisticated and never intended to upset the delicate filigree of village pretensions. Yet she has learnt to appreciate their potency. 'I never knew before how terribly interesting little things were,' she says. 'It is all of you who take such a tremendous interest in them that makes them so absorbing, or is it that they are absorbing in themselves, and ordinary dull people, not Riseholmites, don't see how exciting they are? . . . And to think that I believed I was coming to a backwater.'

Queen Lucia afforded Fred his biggest success since *Dodo*. Critics and public alike were entranced. 'One of the best he has ever written,' wrote one. The *Athenaeum* cleverly pointed out that Mr Benson's humour had gone, not to the dogs, but to the cats. The reviewer for the *Westminster Gazette* was complimentary but mistaken:

> *Queen Lucia* is studied with a concentrated vindictiveness unusual in Mr Benson's treatment of his central character . . . all her shoddy detestableness. Those people who have grown a trifle tired of the kind but rather machine-made tale which he has written a little too often lately will be glad to know that something as efficacious as and rather less sweet than sugar has been dropped into the novelistic champagne this time.[33]

Like so many readers since, this critic has enjoyed all the manifestations of petty malice, and ignored the forgiveness which accompanies them. If the author is represented by any one of his characters, it must be Olga Bracely, who recognises the pain that humiliation may cause and concludes that no amount of sin warrants that degree of retribution. Lucia is silly and selfish, but she is not wicked, and it is important to distinguish between the two.

Is it fanciful to hear the voice of Mary Benson behind this, with her wisdom, her tolerance, and her sense of fun all combining to look upon the follies of humankind with a benevolent eye? Never before had Fred sounded so like his mother as he does in *Queen Lucia*. She had died in 1918. He wrote the book at 25 Brompton Square not long afterwards, finishing it on 31 December of that year. There is no doubt she would have both relished the book and approved of it. She had always lectured him on the need to make his characters intrinsically logical, true to themselves, believable, accurate, and would have been pleased that he had finally heeded her advice. It is not at all impossible that Fred wrote *Queen Lucia* for his late mother.

10 ... and Miss Mapp

Our Family Affairs was published in 1920, the same year as *Queen Lucia*, but it enjoyed nothing like the same success. The public now expected E.F. Benson to be funny, and were presented with an E.F. Benson who was solemnly concerned with the importance of his own parentage and the surface details of his own life. The book is an autobiography disguised as chronology, taking the reader from Wellington to Lincoln, to Truro and on to Lambeth Palace. It struggles manfully to be honest about Edward White Benson, is protective towards Mary Benson, and is tantalisingly evasive about Fred Benson himself, so that the writing, for all its elegance, has a quality of concealment. It lacks liveliness and indiscretion.

Maurice Hewlett's review may be said to be representative of critical response:

> the smallest of all the seeds has produced this vast amount of leafage ... 340 pages chiefly about himself, with photographs of himself at nineteen, twenty-two and twenty-six, read like a rather heavy joke. The heart faints in the contemplation. One wonders not only why, but how, Mr Benson managed to do it. Most people find it pretty difficult to talk, much more so to write, about themselves at all. To do so at such extraordinary length is a serious matter. For, observe, he has only so far reached his thirtieth year. Something must have happened to Mr Benson momentarily to eclipse his sense of humour.[1]

Hewlett was right. Fred's sense of humour was eclipsed by his inherited pervasive need to divert prying eyes, with the result that he appears far more respectful than his iconoclastic nature would normally permit. His brother Arthur was still alive, and Arthur, we know, was even more circumspect than Fred; it is likely that the style and mood of *Our Family Affairs* was influenced by this consideration.

Arthur had continued to spend a great deal of time at Lamb House, and his depression persevered with its toll of gloom. Even when Fred went out of his way to bring laughter, to include Arthur in amusing conversations, the effect was sometimes to deepen his brother's sense of isolation. Fred invited his old friend Archie Daukes to stay for three weeks, and presumably to share some of the burden. Arthur was stricken by their *bonhomie* and his own relative futility:

> Fred and Daukes like each other's company and neither of them care for mine. I am perfectly certain I am going to break down altogether in the next few days; and I have *no one* to say a word to . . . It's a strange experience to take five years in going out of one's mind, as I am now doing . . . Two brisk and cheerful people . . . terrible to be here with them . . . dumb and impotent horror. I felt that some help *must* come, or better still, death. But neither came . . . I am in utter fatigue and despair, abandoned by God and man, and harrowed by incessant wretchedness . . . I don't see how I can emerge from this tangle of misery . . . I feel a wretched incubus here, but in these moods I can neither behave decently nor efface myself.[2]

One is bound to wonder how on earth Fred coped, playing chess, taking walks, going out for drives, with a man who was most of the time morose and negative. Added to which, Fred was by this time in some discomfort himself, for arthritis, which had attacked him when he was still in his forties, now gave him more or less constant pain and severely restricted his movements. Like his mother, Fred was not a complainer; he bore his cross cheerfully and stoically. Besides, it would hardly have been much use to his brother had he competed with him in moping. Arthur's comment was, 'You walk so much better than I do, and you are altogether so good-natured and seemingly unconcerned about it.'[3]

Seemingly, indeed! In fact, Fred was obliged to take medicines to alleviate the pain, and had been advised to take the waters in Bath on more than one occasion, counsel he declined for fear of abandoning Arthur. (Months later, he did recuperate in Bath, with the very old and very stout Lady Radnor as his only companion.) Arthur's Diary demonstrates that his awareness of Fred's trouble grew gradually as his self-absorption decreased; probably the one helped to promote the other. 'Fred is undoubtedly very lame and stiff,' he wrote, 'thighs much shrunken, and pathetically anxious to get well. He swallows strange concoctions and applies unpleasant souches. He seems hopeful, but I don't expect he obeys rules as to diet and drink. "As a treat", he says. But he is very good-humoured, infinitely more so than I was when ill.'[4]

Much more touchingly, something else grew in Arthur as the danger of madness slowly receded. He was coming to realise, for the first time in his life, that he was very fond of his brother. 'I have never found Fred in such a wholly gentle and sympathetic mood,' he wrote.[5] It would be truer to say that he had never before been in the mood to notice how sympathetic and gentle Fred was. But he was noticing at last. His Diary contains a moving passage of such simplicity and ingenuousness that it is possible to miss it entirely. After several weeks of looking after Arthur, Fred arranged for Percy Lubbock to come down to Lamb House and keep him company while he took a respite in London. Lubbock was in all ways the best possible choice, being both trusted by Arthur and acquainted with his problems. But there was not, in the end, an adequate replacement for a brother. On the day of Fred's departure, Arthur went for the daily walk which they had fallen into the habit of taking together. This time he went alone – Lubbock was due to arrive later. He walked down to the level-crossing at Guldeford and watched Fred's train pass as it sped towards London. Peering into each window, hoping to catch a glimpse of him, hoping to wave goodbye, the sixty-year-old man stood forlornly with his stick as the train disappeared into the distance, and he slowly returned to the house. All he can bring himself to say is, 'I did not see him'.

One day, when they were reunited at Lamb House, the two bachelor Bensons fell into a chat about marriage, celibacy, and attraction towards one's own sex. Arthur tells us little about it, Fred nothing at all. 'We discussed the homo sexual question,' wrote Arthur. 'It does seem to me out of joint that marriage should be a sort of virtuous duty, honourable, beautiful and praiseworthy – but that all irregular sexual experiences should be bestial and unmentionable. The "concurrence of the soul" is the test, surely.'⁶ Does this imply that Fred *did* maintain that they were bestial and unmentionable? Arthur presents his case as if it were an argument he had needed to defend. Elsewhere he remarks that 'Fred cannot be so borné as to think that a ceremony before a registrar makes the difference between morality and immorality . . . it only shows how patchy and streaky his mind is.'⁷

Quite possibly Fred did argue the narrow-minded view, for there is a paradox, an ambivalence, at the heart of his attitudes towards sensuality, which he considers at one and the same time a liberating influence – an avenue towards self-expression – and a dangerous toxin leading to perdition. He is able to reconcile these opposites only by the intercession of romanticism which idealises the one and falsifies the other. Further, this reconciliation was essential to his equilibrium, for he was deeply afraid of the sexual impulse. There is a passage in *Mike* wherein the hero is depicted as paralysed in the presence of the loved one: 'There had been the cabalistic question of sex ever in front of him, a thing that troubled and deterred him.' Later, Mike is able to relax with Sylvia, not because their sexual natures are free from inhibition, but, on the contrary, because the inhibition has triumphed and sex has been banished: 'The two were lover-like, without the physical apexes and limitations that physical love must always bring with it. The complement of sex that brought them so close annihilated the very existence of sex. They loved as only brother and sister can love, without trouble.'⁸

Trouble, limitation, deterrence, these are not words of liberation or joy, but of fear, and they occur again and again in Benson's fiction. We have already seen how *David Blaize* looks with repugnance even upon sexual curiosity, which the author calls 'filth', while the love between the two boys is celebrated precisely for its purity and control, as if self-denial were the high road to ecstasy. For Benson, it almost certainly was, and we have had cause to point out more than once how securely his heroes march towards salvation with, in their wake, a convert whom they have snatched from the jaws of sin. When love is spoken between Martin, the pianist, and Karl, his teacher, in *The Challoners*, Benson is quick to make clear that he does not mean anything 'beastly':

Martin looked at him with that direct lucid gaze Karl knew so well, level behind the straight line of his eye-brows. His smooth brown cheeks were a little flushed with some emotion he could not have put a name to. Slight injury was there, that Karl could possibly have supposed him bestial, the rest was clean modesty.
'I am not beastly,' he said, 'if you mean that.'
'I did mean that,' he said, 'and I beg your pardon.'
Martin stood up.
'I think you had no right to suppose that,' he said.
'No, I had none. I did not suppose it. I warned you, though.'
A tenderness such as he had never known rose like a blush into his old bones, tenderness for this supreme talent that had been placed in his hands.
'I only warned you,' he said. 'I looked for burglars under your bed, just because – because it is a boy like you that this stupid world tries to spoil. Aye, and it will try to spoil you. Women will make love to you. They will fall in love with you, too.'[9]

The ambivalence is manifest also in Benson's comments on the disgrace which enveloped Oscar Wilde. He regards Wilde as a man who forsook the nobility of self-control and surrendered himself to the beast. 'With the removal of discipline, the slime of intemperance and perverted passions gathered upon him again, till the wheels of his soul were choked with it.' And yet Wilde is not wholly to be condemned; he is perceived as a victim, as one abandoned. He was denied that saviour who would have led him into the light of a good love. 'No decent man can feel anything but sheer pity and sympathy for one so gifted and so brittle and withal so lovable.'[10] Fred's views on such matters were surprisingly inflexible. He shows no sign of being prepared to consider that, perhaps, there could be an alternative to his rigidly Manichean understanding of sensuality, nor that his attitude might have been blighted by an uncompromising moral education at home. Arthur, in contrast, admitted to Geoffrey Madan that 'I have suffered by being brought up to regard all sexual relations as being rather detestable in their very nature: a thing *per se* to be ashamed of.'[11] E.F. Benson was, in short, a prude.

There is a sadness about Fred's self-denial which he only allowed to show, obliquely, in his fiction. We have already seen his admission to a correspondent, whom he did not know and would never meet, that *David Blaize* was a genuine piece of self-expression. Maurice in *The Inheritor* is as close to a genuine piece of self-portraiture as we are likely to find, at least in select paragraphs where Fred's guard is down. 'Maurice had always avoided intimacy,' he wrote, 'keeping round himself some sort of thorny zareba where he entrenched himself. And yet always from boyhood he had longed and starved for close contacts, but he retreated from them when they threatened to approach, in a panic of reserve and shyness.'[12] He once asked Spencer Lyttelton if he had ever kissed a girl.[13]*

Arthur was chaste throughout his life, and his pupils at Eton testify to his exquisite moral influence upon them.[14] He was able to admire the beauty of young men and enjoy the *frisson* of their company without ever wanting to upset the delicate balance of friendship by a clumsy gesture or an unseemly approach. What he felt for the boys and undergraduates in his care was a love uncontaminated by lust. David Newsome explains this pedagogic love (which Arthur would not regard as 'homo sexual' at all) in a passage of uncommon clarity, already once lifted by Richard Ollard in his *An English Education*, which deserves further quotation here:

Love is a noble passion; and no less noble for being the bond

---

* According to a ribald story told by Hugh Walpole, Arthur actually attempted to do so on one occasion, with farcical results. Three (unidentified) friends who thought he was in need of some education kidnapped him and took him to a brothel, where they stripped him and abandoned him to the attentions of a whore selected because of her passion for *The Upton Letters* and *From a College Window*. 'Followed Horror of Victim, Seduction by Siren, Victim gradually tempted into bed, Siren quoting *Upton* and asking questions à la *Church Family News*. Victim gradually forgets where he is, is slowly and skilfully beguiled, finally as he enumerates with high-voiced pride the number of subscribers to *Church Family News* and the virtue of Reginald Smith unexpectedly falls.' (H. Montgomery Hyde, *Henry James At Home*, p. 47.) Henry James apparently relished this story too, but it is certainly apocryphal.

which may unite two persons of the same sex or of different ages. Such love might, at certain stages of history and civilisation, be considered unconventional, but in itself it is neither unnatural nor immoral. Indeed, the propensity to feel such a love, in a schoolmaster or a don, can often be the particular gift which he brings to his calling; and if such emotions were branded as ignoble or base, then it would remove from these professions the inner commitment or vocation which so often inspires them.[15]

This is A.C. Benson's view precisely put. As a teacher he was alive to his duty to guide by precept and example, to offer counsel and wisdom, but he did not think it part of his task to talk the young into orthodoxy, as if all love but the standard was to be banished from human experience. 'Isn't it really rather dangerous,' he said, 'to let boys read Plato, if one is desirous that they should accept conventional moralities?'[16] Oddly enough, it is Fred, the more worldly brother, who would say boys may read Plato as long as the naughty bits are excised from the text. Arthur thought that paramount among the teacher's many offices was the duty to be honest, and it is perhaps significant that Fred, who never taught, is demonstrably less than honest in his dealings with his readers.

A few years later, one of Fred's most enjoyable novels was published under the title *Paying Guests*. In it, the conflict which buffeted his moral stance was vividly exposed, for he has a pinched, desiccated, downtrodden young woman called Florence, who is brought to life and released from subservience to the conventions by her not-quite-spoken love for another woman, Alice:

How amazingly Florence had expanded in the warmth of her own emotion! A fortnight ago, in spite of her sturdy and manly appearance, she had owned a squashed and middle-aged soul; now though she was still essentially the same, all that had been repressed and nipped in her had opened like a flower. Self-expression had vivified her . . . [17]

Such is the fate which Benson reserves for all his favourite heroes in his non-farcical novels, that of blossoming into freedom and casting off the smothering blanket of parental expectations.

(Florence has heretofore sacrificed herself to her father; there are echoes from *The Challoners, Mike,* and many more in this.) Having given his creature her freedom, Benson proceeds to set conditions upon it – she must be decorous, oblique, circumspect; though her joy be as explosive as from an uncorked bottle (Fred's image) she must not come out and speak it plainly. Unforgivably, Fred even nudges the reader into thinking there is something slightly amusing in this hesitant passion. One scene shows how impossible it is for him to reconcile all these jostling motives:

> They kissed and then neither of them knew what to say next in a situation which was new to them both. In slight embarrassment Alice, still holding Florence's hand, began out of habit to warble something.
> 'Oh sing something or play me something,' said Florence. 'Sit down at the piano and make something beautiful. Improvise.'
> It was a relief to do something, and Alice went to the piano.
> 'Shall I?' she said. 'Just anything that comes into my head?'
> 'Please, and may I sit where I can see you as well as hear you?'[18]

So he settles for concealment behind manners. It is ironic that Benson should use a sentence to describe Florence's achievement which is not only untrue but accurately denotes his own problems in this area. 'Florence had come out from behind all curtains,' he wrote. Fred, one might add, contrived to remain behind all his. Radclyffe Hall and Una Troubridge, the celebrated lesbian couple who were anything but reticent in the promotion of their sexual needs, knew Benson during his Rye years and disapproved of his deception. They thought he ought to be more open and honest. He thought they were vulgar and tasteless, not real 'gentlemen'.

Fred was always wary of being known by anyone, save society dowagers and clubmen (he was a member of the Garrick, where one talked endlessly and amusingly but rarely bothered to ask anyone's name, and the Bath, where you were left in peace). Arthur can admit to his Diary (admittedly in the knowledge no one would read it in his lifetime and for long afterwards), 'it dawned on me how much I had fallen in love with him, so to speak [Dadie Rylands] – the old flame. How pleasant to be really liked, for oneself, by an ingenuous and beautiful youth.'[19] Fred never admitted anything of the sort. One may rehearse the clues which point to a life of sorts – in youth, the holidays with Lord Alfred Douglas, acquaintance with Wilde, the laboursome copying of *De Profundis*, his sister Maggie's remark that if she wanted to be surrounded by young men she need only stick with Fred,[20] his predilection for pretty young manservants, not to mention all those holidays in homophilic Capri. The poems to which he refers in *As We Were* are all 'Uranian' in style, the kind of sentimental verse which celebrates the love of an older man for a younger (though, characteristically, he does not vouchsafe this information to the reader).[21] One piece of his own composition which some-how escaped the various conflagrations of papers contains the lines:

> And every bed had bitter words to say –
> You stirred beside me, and your sundered arm
> While yet I feigned to sleep slipped round my breast
> And on mine your head was softly bent.[22]

He also owned a copy of an openly paederastic book by the pseudonymous Sydney Oswald called *Epigrams from Anthologia Palatina XII*, privately printed and publicly banned.[23]

Fred was still acquainted with his undergraduate enemy Robert Ross long after Wilde's death, when Ross was a lone voice in his defence, and we find him lunching with Ross in 1914. In more mature years he had lasting friendships. One of them, the American artist George Plank, who designed his bookplate and illustrated *The Freaks of Mayfair*, he contrives not even to mention once in his own reminiscences. Yet they were close friends, and Plank stayed both at Tremans and at Lamb House. Mrs Benson was also fond of George Plank, and it is evident from her letters to him that she was well aware of the close affection that existed between him and Fred. She even, in a slightly meddlesome way, tried to encourage it. Inviting him to Tremans, she found the excuse to say, 'it will be so nice for Fred, who will be here four nights anyhow *by himself* – and no one else here.' On another occasion, she tried to elicit some confidence about his low spirits.

'Is it unhappiness, dear man, is it? Or is it any kind of misfortune? Has it anything to do with Fred? Anyhow, in the name of Friendship, that delicate, sacred and fundamental Reality, TELL ME ALL.'[24]

Plank's total exclusion from Benson's memory is suspicious, but of course one can draw no conclusions from it, as Benson made sure one would not.

Nevertheless, there have survived a few letters to Plank which obviously strain not to reveal too overt a fondness. George Plank was in his early twenties when Fred met him, a handsome man with blue eyes and a perpetual blue pullover to match. He was blessed with a cosy fireside manner which encouraged people to confide in him, and he made many friends, paramount among whom was Lady Sackville, Vita Sackville-West's flamboyant mother. (He designed the dust-jacket for Vita's long poem *The Land*.) George knew virtually everyone on the London literary scene, as well as the indispensable Rosa Lewis of the Cavendish. Even more attractive to a man of Fred's age, he was full of promise. Born in a poor mining-town in Pennsylvania, he had taught himself to draw and design, eventually rising by his own efforts to compose covers for *Vogue*.

Fred addresses George as 'Plankino dear', and signs off 'best love', a salutation not granted anybody else. There are clear signs of affection, even of pining. 'For what reason don't you mean to write me long letters?' he asks. 'What have I done? I walked by your home the other day and whistled but nothing whatever happened.' Again, Fred confesses his letter 'carries with it a great many wishes that you were not away, and when the telephone bell rings, I miss your voice.' One page closes with the plaintive cry, '*Come back. This is my wish.* I shan't sign this, and I don't believe you know who wrote it.' It is safe to say Fred's heart was touched, and just as safe to speculate that he did not know quite what to do about it. The struggle to be true, yet restrained, led him into tentative declarations which merely befitted a gentleman; 'and I send you my love, if I may make so bold'.[25]

Throughout his life Fred was captivated by the ideal of ancient Greece, and not least by its revered custom of open friendship between men. Had he the choice, he would have lived then, and would have felt no need to obscure his preferences. He comes closest to an avowal of them, at one remove, in his biography of *Alcibiades*, wherein he proclaims his long-hinted view that love is traduced by carnal expression:

> [In Athens] every good-looking youth had a man who was in love with him (indeed it was a reproach to him if he had not)... This Athenian love was by no means as bestial [that word again] as we are prone to think it. It would, of course, be quite idle to deny that it was accompanied by a vast deal of unnatural vice, but it would be equally idle to deny that it also gave rise to blameless and noble friendships, untainted by physical indulgence... The Athenian lover, as defined by Plato, was no carnalist, but one who filled the mind of his beloved with all manliness and noble aspirations. He was not, as Socrates the arch-lover of youth is never tired of insisting, the lover of the beauty of his body, but of the beauty of his soul, which he discerned and adored through the fair veil of the flesh.

Fred admits that Alcibiades 'had the morals of a Satyr' but is at pains to emphasise the idealistic aspects of his love throughout.

In short, while Arthur asserts that 'the concurrence of the soul' does not preclude sexual expression, Fred would argue that the pleasures of the flesh disqualify love from its aspiration to belong at the pinnacle of human selflessness. He was wary of sex, distrusted it, feared it, and probably in the end avoided it. To him, self-control was all, and disinterested affection the noblest of the instincts.

In his fiction, he continued to enlarge a gallery of characters for whom disinterested affection was such a useless concept that they barely acknowledged its existence. More and more, Benson concentrated on the monsters of selfishness who were driven by that most ignoble of instincts – the competitive. In 1922 he published *Miss Mapp*, and presented us with a woman for whom we relish a kind of envious contempt. If Lucia was absurd in her pretensions to intellectual and social superiority, Elizabeth Mapp is positively odious, with an unconquerable need to spy upon everyone and take mendacity to new depths. Fred refers in the novel to 'her malignant curiosity and her cancerous suspicions about all her friends', and the 'acidities' which well up in her fruitful mind. She goes about her destructive tasks wearing 'a practically perpetual smile when there was the least chance of being under observation'. So fixed is this smile, and so poisonous, that Benson has much fun describing it at every opportunity – 'Miss Mapp's smile was frozen, so to speak, as by some sudden congealment on to her face', and when she was at her most waspish she was not afraid to smile as far back as her wisdom teeth. In tandem with this badge of insincerity she spoke with 'horrid wheedling tones' whenever she was sloping towards some deception, and when she wanted to be haughty she affected a voice 'as icebergs might be supposed to use when passing each other by night in the Arctic seas'. In short, the woman is another wretched hypocrite.

The fact that she is also hilariously funny is a tribute to the quality of Benson's heart, for as he chuckles at his creature's absurdities he also forgives them. 'It was very inconvenient that honesty should be the best policy,' muses Miss Mapp. The source of the humour is in watching the woman think; she is not actually a very good liar, and the purposes to which she turns this doubtful talent are among the silliest obsessions of village life. In her iron determination to guess what everyone is up to, and work out what might be their motives, she is a sort of manic and trivialised Miss Marple. Fred openly admitted that he set the novel in his new home town of Rye, and had Miss Mapp watch the world from the bow window of her garden room, at right angles to her house with an untrammelled view down the street before her. This is Lamb House, and that is Fred's window. 'As an external observer I had seen the ladies of Rye doing their shopping in the High Street every morning, carrying large market baskets, and bumping into each other in narrow doorways, and talking in a very animated manner.' Which is not to say that he had observed anything of the *personalities* of these women. Benson was too tactful a man to suggest there was anyone in Rye remotely like Miss Mapp; or Godiva Plaistow, who talked in staccato phrases shorn of unnecessary prepositions, like a telegram; or Quaint Irene, the invader who clomped about the place in most unfeminine manner and mocked the little ways of the more established inhabitants. (He did, though, let slip to Compton Mackenzie that there were some extraordinary women in Rye.)[26] These people are 'fussy and eager and alert and preposterous', but the atmosphere of the town in which they move, its self-importance and narcissism, is palpable.

In another letter to George Plank, Fred is less guarded about his mockery of Rye and its inhabitants.

Just now all the ladies of Rye are sitting in the streets painting the church, as there is a local picture-exhibition in a few weeks. It is curious how *differently* the church strikes them. In some sketches which I see as I pass by the rows of easels, a towering edifice *pierces* the sky (you would think the angels could step on it without flying); in others it crouches among the red-roofed houses. A favourite observation point is the step of Lamb House; when there are so many artists collected there, so that I can't get out, I play the fugues of Bach on my piano, and then they go away. But really the streets are full of these old tortoiseshell butterflies flapping about, rather the worse for wear, in the sunshine. Their hats – I wish you could see their hats. I never saw such funny hats, with buckles and birds' eggs and bandana handkerchiefs to decorate them.[27]

Benson summed all this up in one figure:

I outlined an elderly atrocious spinster and established her in Lamb House. She should be the centre of social life, abhorred and dominant, and she should sit like a great spider behind the curtains in the garden-room, spying on her friends . . . Of course, it would all be small beer, but one could get a head upon it of jealousies and malignities and devouring inquisitiveness.

Once again, Fred plundered the antics of Marie Corelli to provide some of his material. It was Corelli who grandly ignored daylight saving time and kept her grandfather clock permanently adjusted to 'God's Time', thus causing guests to arrive or leave early or late. Benson uses this as an eccentricity of many Tilling residents, but notes that they make exceptions when it comes to catching buses or trains. (Corelli turned up at Stratford-upon-Avon station to welcome Mark Twain at a time God would have considered one hour too early.) In 1917 Corelli was convicted of food-hoarding and fined £50 with £20 costs, much to the delight of the newspapers. Benson turns this into an embarrassingly farcical scene to reveal Miss Mapp's dishonesty.[28]

Not the least beguiling of Mapp's qualities is her infuriating obtuseness. 'Quaint Irene's' sardonic mockery of her is utterly lost, for Mapp is impervious to subtlety and only knows Irene does not behave *comme il faut*; she returns with impotent hatred masked behind a treacherous smile. Self-confidence will always protect her from defectors and rebels. She was 'the centre of the Tilling circle, and if any attempt was made to shove her out towards the circumference, she always gravitated back again.' Only once in the book does she appear to wobble. When the Italian contessa comes to Tilling with her sophisticated ways and civilised behaviour, above all with her quite inappropriate sense of humour, Miss Mapp is momentarily bewildered. The Contessa is honest and forthright, which is hideously irritating to Elizabeth Mapp, who has shaped her dominance upon the twin principles of dishonesty and dissemblance. As soon as she realises that the foreign countess just does not know how to do things, Miss Mapp bounces back happy and exultant.

Fred could not but help notice the implications of *Miss Mapp*'s resounding popularity – that his financial future might very well depend thenceforth upon his creation of monstrous women. On seeing that one hundred and ninety-three copies of *Queen Lucia* were unaccounted for on his royalty statement, he complained to Hutchinson's and was told they had been lost, 'due to damage by water, vermin and damp'. To compensate for the bad news they also informed him that plans were afoot to bring Lucia to the cinema screen, with Gloria Swanson playing the title role; this failed to placate Fred, simply because he had never heard of Miss Swanson.[29] *David at King's*, a sequel to *David Blaize* which carries the eponymous hero to manhood and Cambridge, came out in 1923 and elicited from Ethel Smyth a rapturous if slightly breathless explosion of praise. 'I think it's frightfully well done,' she said, 'the sort of thing no one but you can do. The balance between . . . oh well, all moods, is so truly and well kept I think. Congratters.'[30]

Arthur's final depression lifted at the beginning of 1923. To

Edmund Gosse he wrote of a 'dragging melancholy' and in a pathetic response claimed 'your letter has given me the only moments of happiness I have known for months'. He averred that he could only just hold on from day to day.[31] Yet when Dr Todd pronounced him cured in March, he knew he was right, and celebrated his release with a furious burst of energy. As David Newsome has written, 'It is characteristic of the manic depressive that he can do nothing by halves. Emerging from a state akin to living death, Arthur Benson bounced back into life with all his powers renewed.' He formed an engrossing infatuation with an undergraduate of easy good nature and flattering charm, George 'Dadie' Rylands (whom he took to Lamb House), followed by another attachment to the handsome and intellectually inquisitive Noel Blakiston. His work at Magdalene kept him busy, and he began work on yet more books. Fred, on the other hand, was an increasingly valiant victim of arthritis, and together they reflected what a pitiful pair they had become, the last of the Bensons, two old men progressing ponderously through the day in an elegant house in Rye.

In his last year Arthur was placid and happy in Fred's company, no longer critical and at last fully aware how fond of one another they were at root. 'Had a long morning finishing up letters and sitting with Fred,' he wrote. 'He walked to the station with me and I felt that we meant more to each other than we have ever done.' They spent Easter together, when Fred invited Lady Maud Warrender to meet his brother. 'She and Fred on very easy terms. She is more male than female.' Christmas brought them both to Rye again. 'Fred is tremendously cheerful. What a difference it all is from our old times here, I so distracted and miserable and he so miserable about me.' The last Diary entry pays generous tribute to Fred's influence upon his spirits. 'It has been a delightful time,' Arthur wrote, 'Fred more cheerful and companionable than I ever remember, falling in with everything, no irritations. He has written nothing here, but done a good deal of music. He is very lame.'[32]

The following summer Arthur suffered a massive heart attack while sitting in his armchair at Magdalene. He lingered for another six days, with no hope of recovery. In the first minutes of 17 June 1925, with most of the Fellows of the college around him, he died.

Fred told Edmund Gosse how happy Arthur had been during the last year at Rye, and one knows, without the need for emphasis, that Fred drew comfort from this reflection. Lamb House had turned out to be the last family home. From now on, Fred would be the solitary survivor of a once-illustrious clan, and he would have increasingly to struggle with the loneliness of one bereft of blood connections.

'There is one loss incident to advancing years which is irreparable,' wrote Fred in an unpublished first draft more than a decade later. 'Friends (with care) may be retained, new friends may be added . . . but nobody can take the place of near relations who have gone.' Usually, there would be children to redeem the isolation, be they nephews and nieces, but the fact of the Bensons all being celibate meant that none of them had a home in the domestic sense at all. Fred had a house, but 'I cannot warm my hands *with* anybody at its beloved fireside; if I sit by its logs, and with the bellows of memory blow them into flame, I have always to sit alone there. Yet I can hardly think of this as sad. Sad indeed it would be if the bellows produced no warmth, or if instead of the fragrance of burning logs there was the odour of bitterness or even, in a way, regret.'[33] Fred was not so much lonely in the last years as unshackled, with all the strings of attachment hanging loose. In truth, he had always enjoyed being alone for long periods, from his earliest childhood, and as old age beckoned and he passed the sixtieth year, he more and more took refuge in communion with the birds and silent ruminative observation of nature. 'The man who cannot spend a day or a week alone without feeling lonely is to be deplored rather than pitied,' he wrote.[34] And again, 'It is a mistake to think that solitude means loneliness. Loneliness is the regretful and often bitter consciousness of solitude, but solitude does not necessarily induce it, nor is the sense of it to be dispersed by continuous cocktail parties.'[35]

For the last time Fred was called upon to sift through a Benson archive and decide what should be left for posterity, and more important, what not. In *Final Edition* he would admit to having burnt 'a packet of letters of very dangerous stuff' and another so explosive it had to be destroyed unopened. Arthur left a great deal of material, the accumulated debris of years of epistolary labour, and the survival of thousands of letters makes one pause in wonderment at Fred's toil in obliterating perhaps thousands more. Even when he knew that there would soon be no one to embarrass, he was fearful of private matters getting into 'the wrong hands', and was faithful to the precept, 'when in doubt, burn'. The innocent parodies, when Arthur, Hugh and Fred had all written stories in the others' style, causing their mother to fall sideways with merriment, were also consigned to the flames. 'I would sooner piously annihilate such things myself,' he wrote, 'than leave them to cause amazement subsequently at the notion that anybody could have kept such rubbish.'[36]

As for Arthur's huge Diary, the burden of decision was taken from him, as Arthur had made his intentions perfectly plain. '*My Diaries are to be read by no one,*' he had written from his bed at St Michael's, Ascot, when under an attack of gloom. 'They should all be put under lock and key, and eventually dealt with according to the terms of my Will.'[37] In a codicil to the Will, Arthur stated that only Percy Lubbock should be permitted to see the huge document, and that he should 'undoubtedly' destroy some volumes. Fred is specifically excluded from this trust despite his being an Executor. Lubbock may publish short extracts from it, if he should wish, after which it should be kept at Magdalene and seen by no other eyes for the next fifty years. This is precisely what happened, and the one missing volume is presumably that which Lubbock decided to suppress. The rest are now in the care of the Pepys Librarian, and much more of their content has since been published, due largely to the herculean task, undertaken by David Newsome, of reading the lot.

The total value of A.C. Benson's estate was £121,000, which made him the equivalent of a double millionaire today. His first bequest was £10,000 to Fred, followed by £300 to Dr Todd and £300 to Percy Lubbock. There were smaller legacies to his college servants, and a ring for the elderly Lucy Tait. All the royalties from his books went to the Fellows of Magdalene College, while all the property – pictures, books, furniture – were inherited by Fred, with the exception of his library chair, previously the property of J.K. Stephen; this was bequeathed to Magdalene. The money which had derived as a gift from Madame de Nottbeck was to be divided three-quarters to the College and one-quarter to the Royal Society of Literature. After some donation to Truro Cathedral, there still remained a sizeable sum which was left to Fred, in trust for their counsins the McDowalls, descendants of the Archbishop's sister Ada, whom neither Arthur nor Fred could claim to know with any degree of familiarity. This trust stipulated that on Fred's death the residue should be divided three-quarters to Fred's children, one-quarter to the McDowalls, and in the event of there being no children to Fred, it was all left absolutely to the McDowalls. At the time of Arthur's death, Fred was a few weeks short of his fifty-eighth birthday, with nary a bride in sight.

The effect of Arthur's death was to make Fred more than ever aware of the tyranny of self-absorption which had to some degree afflicted all his family, to regret the limitations it imposed, and to determine that it should be put to good account. He knew well enough how he and his family were regarded in the world. 'A very odd brotherhood,' said George Lyttelton, 'so clever, and humorous and self-conscious and ultimately rather futile ... a tragic family really, ending, actually as well as figuratively, in nothing.'[38] There is evidence that Fred resolved to spend his remaining years conquering this futility and avoiding the awful legacy of nothingness. He needed to effect certain changes in his life and in his writing if he was to achieve this, to spend more time amid the peace of Rye and less in the hurly-burly of London (an aim rendered all the more desirable by his debilitating arthritis), to turn away from fiction and concentrate his energies on the more austere discipline of biography. Hence all the finest non-fiction he produced came during those meditative years as the sole surviving son.

Looking back, Fred was quite candid in his appraisal of his status as a writer. That early success of *Dodo* was a curse, a 'disaster', because it made him feel that, as long as he was enjoying himself, he could simply go on writing as much as he liked. Now, to his horror, he could hardly remember what most of his books had been about. 'Unless I could observe more keenly and feel more deeply, I had come to the end of anything worth saying ... I made my people bustle about [but] they lacked the red corpuscle ... I had often tried to conceal my own lack of emotion in situations that were intended to be moving, by daubing them over with sentimentality.'[39] Writing of Arthur, Dr Newsome has declared, 'One cannot actually live a full life until one is prepared to abandon the spectatorial role, to descend into the arena and become actively involved.'[40] The same could be applied to Fred. If it was true that he was an observer more than a participant in life, he would find the way to make his observations useful rather than merely amusing. But not just yet.

In a sense, of course, he had already been involved, if only to the extent that he had lately been the consoler in the family, the one to rescue a wounded brother or sister. He had grown into a kind and generous man. From the greedy socialite of his twenties, when he would visit his mother as long as nothing better turned up, and be irritatingly secretive about what that something better might be, he had become one ready to subordinate his immediate interests to the needs of those close to him. Benson has frequently been saddled with the reputation of a 'cold fish' simply because he was not demonstrative or extrovert. He was not one to fling his arms around people, and his reserve efficiently deterred anyone from flinging arms in his direction. That is not to say, however, that he was insensitive. He was a man of deep, silent compassion. At the very beginning of his career he had written, 'it is in the small unnoticed sorrows of average people that I realise most deeply the infinite pathos of human life,' and 'the old do not shed tears very easily; they have learnt that it does no good.'[41] No contemporary recalls Benson revealing emotion, though many are the testimonies of his kindness. Additionally, there were some who noticed that Fred did not like to be thanked. He gave help willingly, but would almost have liked it to be anonymously as well, in order to avoid that obeisance of gratitude which made him wince with discomfort. Gratitude as a form of human contact veered dangerously close to the intimate. One cannot but notice the striking disparity between his eulogy of Arthur in *Final Edition*, respectful and detached, and the heart-rending account in the same book of the death of his dog Taffy, which is among the most touching and emotional passages he ever wrote:[42]

One evening, carrying the paper, he tried to get up the stairs of the garden-room where he delivered it, but he could not manage them. He put it down, barking to show he had done his duty, and crept back into the house again. The June weather was very hot, and all day he lay for coolness on a rug in the hall, very polite, with a languid thump of his tail for his friends, and he did not seem to be in pain. When the sun was off the garden he shambled out there to lie on the lawn, but one evening he could not find strength to walk, and he was carried out on his rug. He sat up for a moment and looked about, then lay down panting a little and stretched his legs out and moved no more.[43]

In the days when he was living in Oakley Street, Fred had written a play called *The Friend in the Garden* which, like *The Monkey's Paw*, is eerie and unsettling. The 'friend' of the title is Death, who is welcomed at the end as the solution of all ills and the confirmation of all goodness. Yet there is a determinism in the story which is sad and pessimistic, totally devoid of the ebullience, the twinkle, which inform the most joyful of Benson's novels. The hero of the play, Jack, makes a woeful remark in which one is bound to hear a personal note from his creator. The very opposite of Sartrean, Benson's philosophy is passive and responsive; he suggests that man is imprisoned in himself and can expect no release except in death. 'There is neither Heaven nor Hell except what a man carries about within him,' says Jack. 'If I could only weep! If only the ice round my heart could melt! However cold death is, I think that she would thaw it.'[44] The bleakness of this passage shocks at first reading, and reminds one that, though Fred managed to be free of the crucifying depressions which tortured other Bensons, the awkward gene lurked there within him, turning grey to black more readily than to white. Fred's heart was intact, and true, and alive, but the ice which had protected it for so long was as solid as armour.

Plenty were those who tried to give Fred as much in friendship and consideration as they received from him, from old Lady Radnor to Francis Yeats-Brown and Charlie Tomlin, his faithful and finally indispensable manservant. Everyone wanted to cherish the man if only he would let them, as they saw the chink of feeling and wanted to encourage it. Sir Steven Runciman, for example, has a vivid memory of Fred reproaching him for having said something unkind about someone (which, from the creator of Miss Mapp, is a telling *vignette*). He also received offers of friendship from total strangers, to whom he replied politely and rather frigidly. A nineteen-year-old from Bournemouth, clearly out for advantage, enclosed an attractive photograph of himself with his letter. 'I have stalked and captured a specimen of your "rare heart". I found him in a Southampton bookshop,' he wrote, though it is not immediately clear to what he refers. He then goes on to reveal that he is out of work. 'If you know of anyone needing a bright, adaptable youth with an accentuated sense of honour and a positive hunger to make himself generally useful, would you please recommend, yours very sincerely, Ronald H. Riggs.'[45] Fred actively tried to help another young man called Reddie 'who got into trouble a year or two ago and finds it difficult to reinstate himself', by asking people he knew to send him some typewriting work.[46]

Fan letters came in abundance, sometimes seeking not merely an autograph but pronouncements upon a variety of topics. These irritated him rather, and brought out his most laconic mood. 'Dear Sir,' he replied to one, 'when I first saw the sea I thought it flat and disappointing. Now I like it better than the land and prefer it flat.' Another correspondent invited Benson to join a 'symposium of terminological hatreds', which elicited this waspish response: 'I may say that I particularly dislike the word symposium (which means a drinking party) being used to denote an arid nosegay of literary opinions supplied by sober and sundered gentlemen.'[47] To a woman who boasted of having known him, and could not prove it, he wrote, 'Dear Madam, This, I hope, will thwart your friends. Yours truly, E.F. Benson.'[48] In view of Benson's popularity today, it is interesting to learn that the first E.F. Benson Fan Club was founded in 1931 by Professor Getchell, to whom Fred wrote a suitably humble letter of appreciation.[49]

The question of Benson's alleged meanness has to be addressed, if only because it runs counter to all we have learnt thus far of his generous help towards friends in need – Eustace Miles, Philip Burne-Jones, and so on – and their frequent attestations of his loyalty and reliability. The rumour begins with the famous female couple Radclyffe Hall and Una Troubridge, who, as we have already seen, disapproved of Fred for being buttoned-up. They broadcast their opinion that he was also stingy, and said Lady Maud Warrender had told them he had 'one-way pockets'. Further, they thought he drank too much and they said so. Dropping into Lamb House one hot August afternoon in 1931, the ladies were offered tea 'grudgingly'. Fred explained that he had already taken two teas that afternoon, one with Vincent Marrot (who had introduced him to the ladies in the first place). Una did not believe him. She told her Diary, 'Shrewdly suspecting that the earlier teas had lived in a bottle and been drunk with the aid of soda-water, we left.'[50]

It is more than likely that Una Troubridge missed the point. Fred could not abide vulgarity, and he would consider strident lesbianism as intrinsically vulgar. He would have disapproved of Evelyn Waugh and Cyril Connolly for allied (not identical) reasons, and would probably think even Harold Acton a trifle too *outré*. Fred had restraint, Hall and Troubridge despised it. Not only that, but to turn up unannounced, even to tea, was simply inconceivable to a gentleman of the Edwardian era. Fred may have felt like a fossil by this stage, but he was an elegant fossil whose exquisite manners were never tarnished. He was sometimes severe about people who did not behave with decorum, and it is not at all surprising that his gentle rebuff to the girls should be entirely misinterpreted by them. With a quiet chuckle, he enjoyed himself at their expense (not to their faces) when he wrote a jokey song about them to be sung by two female voices in canon. It began,

> My Troubridge have my heart, and I'm her Hall,
> By just exchange the one to the other given.
> She is my True, and I'm her Hall in all,
> There never was a better bargain driven.[51]

On the other hand, he was thrifty, checking his royalty statements, pointing out gaps and anomalies, making sure that the pennies were accounted for. For twenty years his books were typed by Mrs Gill, whom he congratulated for her knack of always deciphering his handwriting. When once she placed a surcharge on her fee, he remonstrated with her, pointing out that some of his manuscripts were so clear and free of corrections that they should not be subject to surcharge of any kind.[52] Similarly, when he had earned a total of $21,000 from sales of his books in the United States, he quibbled with the income tax demand from that country and managed to reduce it to $59.78. He commonly received an advance of $1500 on the American sales of his books, and pushed up his royalty share on British editions to twenty per cent. He would refuse to compile an index to his biographies, adding to the publisher's costs. Even then, having squeezed the publishers for as much as he dare, he upbraided them for not spending more on advertising and distribution. To Hutchinson he wrote complaining that several of his friends (a standard euphemism for oneself in authors' parlance) had been unable to find *Lucia in London* in the shops, that Bumpus (a bookshop in Baker Street, now no more) had ordered a mere twenty-five copies and not restocked, and worst of all, that he had seen no advertisements anywhere. 'I always welcome criticism and suggestions,' Hutchinson said in a letter to the agent A.P. Watt, 'and naturally have no objection to E.F. Benson's letters, but I should be very sorry for him to think that we are not doing the best that we can for his book.'[53]

This is not so much meanness as good business sense. Benson was a rich man. He did not become rich by accident, and no one gave him capital until he inherited a portion of the Archbishop's estate. As he knew his income might dry up at any moment, should his eyesight fail, or he have a stroke, or his capacity to earn be in some measure impaired, he must needs be careful to insure against an uncertain future. He kept his servants on low wages. When a magazine was four months late in paying for a short story he had written, Fred instructed the literary lawyer, William Morris Colles, to kick up a fuss. 'Insist on payment,' he wrote. 'Otherwise, County Court. It is only a wretched little £8, but I *won't* be "done" by anybody.'[54] On another occasion he advised demanding payment with threats. When it came to his livelihood, Benson was a capitalist through and through. 'The whole thing is a matter of business, *not* sentiment really, or love for small booksellers,' he wrote. 'I am perfectly willing to take a good offer from The Times as a retaining fee, so long as it is good business for me. I hate the oily rot about publishers being lovers of literature!!!'[55]

Fred could be tetchy at times. 'It is *never* any use saying violent things,' he wrote, adding 'I often do.' He always regretted loss of control, however brief, and his most peremptory and imperious letters are those wherein the temper is honed to a literary instrument and not left to wander into formless spleen. Typists, proofreaders, type-setters, these aroused him to indignant fury by reason of their inexplicable habit of adding hundreds of inverted commas to his text. The 'infernal stupidity' of the American edition of *Limitations* especially drove him mad, as someone had changed the order of paragraphs. 'I never saw such a hash in my life . . . who is responsible for this? Such tragic rot as this is really too much.'[56]

Benson produced three novels in three years. The first to appear after Arthur's death was in many ways one of the most important – *Pharisees and Publicans* (1926). It is significant in that it epitomises the *idée maîtresse* which we have seen in much of Benson's work so far, namely goodness resides in self-sacrifice; that it is the most severely anti-clerical book he had produced; and that it contains a character of hideous hypocrisy who, devoid of that humorous lens through which the author generally viewed the follies of mankind, is positively hateful. Moreover, there can be little doubt that Fred meant the reader to hate this woman, and that she represents everything he most detested.

Her name is Edith, the daughter of a clergyman. 'Bristling with Christian hostility', she makes hurtful remarks and schemes selfishly to undermine her husband Ronnie, while claiming to be acting for everyone's good and to her own disadvantage. She is a liar, 'clothing falsehoods with piety' and seeks every opportunity to appear meek and suffering. In short, Edith is Miss Mapp with all the fun removed. She and Ronnie have two children, Michael and Priscilla, although it is made clear that their marriage had never known any real love. Michael is close to Ronnie, and therefore easy-going, good-natured, honest and upright. Priscilla is in the image of her mother and will soon grow into another loathsome prig. Edith and daughter conspire with the clergyman father against Ronnie to turn his study into a chapel. Ronnie meets another woman, Violet, who has all the decency and love which Edith lacks and whose husband languishes in a mental hospital. Violet and Ronnie fall in love, but are not sinful. Edith, meanwhile, is in love with another clergyman, Tobit, but is too dishonest to recognise the fact.

Violet tells Ronnie that they must not meet any more, as her husband is to be released from hospital and her first duty is to him. Were their love to continue, it would hurt someone else and thereby be polluted and poisoned. Thus honour and true love must be revealed in abnegation, as good, when embraced with clarity, is necessarily stronger than evil. It is the theme of Frank Maddox being saved by David Blaize again. All of which makes a violent contrast with Edith's appalling selfishness. It is important that Edith should be the religious one, and Violet the non-professional Christian, for Benson suggests in this book more clearly than before that the God he knows should not be sought in the Church at all, but in the good acts of human beings.

In the final argument between Ronnie and Edith, he tells her what Benson has been telling his readers through comedy and farce for a number of years:

'Can you be sincere?' he asked. 'I don't want you to be what you tell yourself or Tobit that you are, nor what you ought to be, nor what you wish you were, but what you actually happen to be . . . You can't stand the truth, that's what ails you.'

Pharisees and Publicans is an intense book, and a personal one. There are passages written with rapid pen in fierce anger. It is a book which reveals Fred's true opinion of the silly creatures of his imagination, what he would really think of the Mapps and Lucias of this world if they were not protected by his irrepressible sense of the ridiculous.

Furthermore, the scenes in which Ronnie and his fifteen-year-old son share banter and back-slapping *bonhomie* are also personal, showing an ease in filial relations which Fred had never enjoyed with his father, and which he could only picture to himself as an ideal. Not only that, but they are so arch, so unlike the real father-son relationship, that they resemble more the close ties of adolescent friendship, or the fondness of a man for his younger companion. Consciously or not, Benson imbued these scenes with a gentle erotic undercurrent which adds force to his ferocious attack upon Christian marriage elsewhere in the book, simply by contrasting the feelings inherent in both.

Nevertheless, Edith plays the dominant role. '*Pharisees and Publicans* shows Mr Benson in his most acid mood,' opined the *Saturday Review*. 'He is a good hater, perhaps too good; his venom makes a monster of Edith, the admirable Ronnie Everton's selfish sanctimonious wife.' There are some who claim to discern Mary Benson in the character of Edith, a view to which the present writer cannot subscribe. Lucy Tait, perhaps, with her relentless authority and goodness, may have been a model. Certainly Fred was periodically obsessed with the notion of people who are the epitome of evil while bearing the appearance of consummate good. *Colin* (1923) was just one such, a man whose brilliant talent to dissemble is depicted with relish. Fred vaunts his 'sheer exuberance of wickedness'[57] and appears almost to envy it. Where did he see evidence of such pitch-black souls, people who can smile and smile and be a villain? It is not his father, nor can it be his mother. The show of kindness and selflessness which conceals a Machiavellian heart may just possibly be the essence of Lucy Tait, whom Arthur, we remember, pointed to as the ultimate cause of dissension in the Benson household. Fred had little contact with her after the sale of Tremans. She bought a small house in Horsted Keynes which she shared with her sister Edith, the widow of Archbishop Davidson.

Following *Pharisees and Publicans* came the second of Lucia's adventures, *Lucia in London*, written at Brompton Square in six weeks between 27 November 1925 and 14 January 1926.[58] The incorrigible snob inherits (or rather her husband inherits, but that was a mere detail) a London house, naturally enough in Brompton Square, and is encouraged by this to conquer London as she has conquered Riseholme. To the amazement of the giddy reader, who can scarcely credit Lucia's preposterous manoeuvres, she is triumphant yet again and in no time at all has collected so many titles and royalties that on one evening she is bound to curtsey six times! (In this Fred obliquely recalls his own experience thirty years before, when he had gone to a ball in Portman Square to discover that he was the only non-royal person present; he had mistaken the house, but all the princes and queens were too polite to allude to the fact.)[59] Benson attached no importance to this book, now among the favourites of his admirers. It had no more to do with serious fiction than had a game of marbles, he said.[60] These were the kind of books he raced through, enjoying himself the while, as he prepared for what he called *real* work. Quietly and methodically, he was at the same time researching for his first ventures into serious biography, the fruits of which were published in 1927 and 1928.

Sir Francis Drake was lauded by that venerable old man of letters Edmund Gosse, to whom Fred had written in breathless wonder at the very beginning of his career. 'You are the critic whose praise I most covet,' he wrote now, 'and to have it given me so generously makes me very proud.'[61] It was not, however, as important a work as the next.

The Life of Alcibiades is an astonishing book to come from the creator of Lucia, for it is scholarly, disciplined, and thorough, calling upon Benson's wide experience of classical literature and taking him back to sources he had not consulted since his days at Cambridge. Plato, Plutarch, Xenophon, Herodotus, Aristophanes, Thucydides, they and many more are properly plundered for the facts, while Benson's own insight and elegant style add flesh to a character of antiquity both well-known in reputation and relatively unknown in detail. It is a splendidly written portrait (provoking Ethel Smyth into one of her most enthusiastic fan-letters), and represents a turning-point in E.F. Benson's career. Still, it is recognisably a Bensonian subject, not only for the obvious attraction of Hellenic moral freedom and male beauty, but also for the inspiration of Alcibiades' extrovert personality. It is clear Fred admired his mischief and self-confidence as much as his charm. Alcibiades dared to do the unexpected, dared to be hedonistic, dared to subvert convention, all traits which Fred would have liked to possess and did not. Also irony intrigued and entertained Fred, and his *Life of Alcibiades* is a succession of ironies.

On the strength of this much-praised biography, Cassell

approached Benson with an offer to write a new *Life* of his father. For reasons undisclosed, nothing ever came of the project, but there would soon be other similar opportunities which he would not resist, for he found that he valued both the labour and the result. In the meantime, he could still indulge in some frivolity. *Paying Guests* appeared in 1929. It had no Lucia or Miss Mapp, but a fresh gallery of dotty English eccentrics all staying at the same guest-house in a country town. This is also the only novel of E.F. Benson in which the author shows some unkindness.

Fred knew something of these little hotels, having been annually to Droitwich to lie in mud and to Bath to sink in water, all in a vain effort to cure his arthritis. Staying at such places he would sit in the corner of the dining-room, observe, listen, conclude. *Paying Guests* is the result. There is Miss Howard, who 'suffered from the essentially middle-aged disease of fabrication'; Mrs Oxney 'who always said the agreeable thing'; Mrs Bliss, whose valiant attempts to neutralise her lameness by denying it remind one of Lady Desborough's 'stubborn gospel of joy'; and various other men and women bent upon showing off to one another or hiding the truth from themselves. It is a funny novel, yet slightly uncomfortable, for Fred is relentlessly critical of all of them and heartless towards their frailties. (The one exception is probably poor Florence, referred to earlier.) His usual forgiveness has evaporated with the promises of the doctors, and there are times when one feels that, not content to explore and expose pretension, he gloats over the misfortunes of little people who know no better, and has no sympathy for their small triumphs. There is a new kind of snobbery in the tone of *Paying Guests*, that which is condescending and patronising, and condemns people for being bores however laudable their inner motives might be. One must charitably surmise that Fred's own lameness, obliging him to hobble around with two sticks, made him less good-tempered than usual.

It also further inhibited his social life. The days had long since passed when he felt drawn by magnetic force to a glittering party. 'I had ceased to be diverted by mere gregariousness,' he wrote. 'The elongated dinner-table no longer thrilled me *because* there were so many decorative people sitting round it, nor did I care to squeeze my way up a thronged staircase to emerge in a room packed beyond computation with friends and acquaintances and strangers.'[62] He now despised the 'fashionable folk in Mayfair who would go blindfold to a house if they knew they would get a really good dinner',[63] and did not care to meet new people. He kept a few good friends in 'society' and entertained them in a minor key. Old Lady Radnor was dead, Lady Charles Beresford was dead, but there was still Princess Alice, Countess of Athlone (a grand-daughter of Queen Victoria), whom he knew on such cosy terms that she once bent down and tied his shoe-lace for him;[64] and the Duchess of Sutherland, who wrote to him of that 'absolute and complete friendship which is such perfect satisfaction.'[65] He sometimes stayed with Lord Amherst at Sevenoaks, with Lord Battersea, and with the Duchess of St Albans at Clonmel.

There were, too, occasions on which Fred was summoned by royal command; in 1930, for example, the Prince of Wales bade him dine at St James's Palace and sat him next to M.R. James. (His opinion of the Prince was not improved thereby. 'Pity my father didn't drown him,' he once said.)[66] He could not abide the professional hostesses, such as Lady Colefax the 'lion-hunter', who made it her business to collect people as parrots collect beads, or Lady Cunard with her challenging darts and intimidating manner. On the whole, Fred's social life in his last decade was considerably less frenetic than it had been, as he reverted to a truth he had always known, yet risked forgetting, and which he placed in the mouth of his first heroine Dodo: 'the only pleasure in knowing people is to be intimate. I would sooner have one real friend than fifty acquaintances.'[67]

When the ageing Fred entertained, it was for one to five people, a company small enough for conversation to be unimpeded by the clashing of subjects or voices. Those conversationalists he most admired he celebrated in *As We Were* – Wilde, Henry Higgins, Edmund Gosse – and he appreciated also the whimsy of remarks which appeared irrelevant yet caused a spark, 'using preposterous conversation, as Bismarck used truth, as a valuable instrument to secure definite ends'.[68] His contribution to the table was to tell a story with solemn demeanour, as if amusement was far from his intention, then watch his companions laugh as they caught the point. He was a brilliant mimic, with a repertoire which included virtually every member of the Royal Family, and he relished stories wherein royalty revealed unaccustomed wit. He used to tell, for instance, of the family's annual memorial service on the anniversary of Queen Victoria's death, when Princess Christian had said that the souls of the departed visited the near and dear in the form of a bird, to which Queen Alexandra had responded, 'I am sure Mama's soul would never have made such a mess on my nice new bonnet'. Most of the royal gossip he received from Princess Christian herself, whose imperfect understanding of English led her into some lovely malapropisms. 'Olso,' she once said, 'do you know vot is tact? It is when you do not talk about a cock to St Peter.' It was she, too, who told of her daughter's short and unhappy marriage to a German rascal called Aribert of Anhalt, whose tastes were not predominantly heterosexual. At Fred's table she suddenly ventured an elliptical explanation – 'My poor daughter. Do not ask me. It is all too terrible for her. I cannot tell you anything about it. But she is as she was.'[69]

11   As We Were

Those who revere the name of E.F. Benson primarily for his non-fiction are more than likely to place *As We Were*, which appeared in 1930 (and for which he received a startling advance of £10,000), at the peak of his achievement, and to aver that, even were his humorous novels to slither into the same obscurity which now cloaks his more earnest fiction, his reputation would always stand high in English letters on the evidence of this one book. A magically lucid evocation of Edwardian life, *As We Were* is probably Fred's masterpiece, for it stands the test of being read again and again with renewed pleasure. His artistry was here at its most polished, for the book may be enjoyed not only for its content, being an urbane, witty, acute essay on manners and style lavishly supported by example and anecdote, but also for its elegance of tone. On the grounds of literary merit alone, *As We Were* is a classic example of English prose written by a man of superb education at the height of his powers. And it is one of the best accounts of social and literary London, the High Society of that world which vanished forever in 1914.

Significantly, the manuscript demonstrates that Fred took greater care with this book than with any of his novels. It took him over two months to complete, from 20 September to 30 November 1929, and the pages disclose many alterations and additions, especially those dealing with Oscar Wilde.[1]

In the chapter entitled 'Rebels', Benson devoted some pages to the odd live-in relationship between Swinburne and Theodore Watts-Dunton, in which the former submitted himself willingly to the domestic tyranny of the latter. His unsympathetic treatment of the matter brought from Clara Watts-Dunton a furious accusation of 'contemptible slander' upon her father.[2] That is the only complaint against the book which can be traced; otherwise, it was greeted with a chorus of praise.

In the preceding months Fred had published two more books, a biography of Magellan to join the already popular volume on Sir Francis Drake, and an ambitious novel in which his narrative skill was successfully married to an occult subject. *The Inheritor* combines mystery, terror and a goodly chunk of healthy male beauty to make a tantalising cocktail. Beneath it all lies Fred's serious, reiterated purpose, to demonstrate that inherent evil can only be destroyed, and the victim whose lot it is to carry evil within him be saved, by the intercession of human goodness. Steven Gervase is what we should nowadays term a psychopath, for he is devoid of any understanding of those abstracts which rule our lives – goodness and badness, right and wrong – and has no emotional responses. That he looks so handsome only serves to mask his essential aridity. Steven does not finish, as today he might, in the hands of a psychiatrist or an exorcist, but marries and fathers upon his poor wife a monster, as hideous to the view as Steven himself is to the intellect.

After so much effort, Benson was able to relax with another frivolous adventure, bringing together his two outrageous heroines *Mapp and Lucia*. But that would not be ready until the following year, and in the meantime his life in Rye was assuming the character of permanence. With Madame de Nottbeck he planned, commissioned and saw unveiled in Rye church a memorial window to his brother Arthur. He was a familiar figure in town, respected and liked despite his mockery of Rye inhabitants in *Miss Mapp*. (Possibly the mockery worked to his advantage, for 'Tilling' folk do like to be talked about, whatever the nature of the gossip.) In 1933 he would become a magistrate, to the delight of the town and the amusement of the legal profession. One, however, who was not amused was Julius Bertram of Devon, who wrote rudely to Fred ticking him off for having spoken with disrespect about High Court Judges. (He had suggested their intellects became atrophied in old age.) 'Those like yourself who play at being a judge or a lawyer as an agreeable if rather pompous diversion for an hour or so every fortnight – between games of ball – are indulging themselves in a performance where the trained mind has no part,' he fulminated. Fred was stung into a curt reply, but he should have known that this correspondent was in no sense awestruck by the fame of the Great Author. He returned with a diatribe against 'the complacency, conceit and cocksureness' of Fred's reply. 'I wonder what you know about the rules of evidence, and how many times you have condescended to put pen to paper in taking a note. No sane man would allow *you* to deal with him in any case where he has the right to a jury. But your letter is typical and in its way rather magnificent.'[3]

Fred's standing in the town was further enriched when Queen Mary visited in 1935 and Fred was deputed to show her around the antique shops (a devastating experience for the shop-owners in view of the Consort's raging kleptomania). She afterwards joined him for a chat in private at Lamb House. One does not have to strain one's imagination to picture the Mapps and Plaistows hovering on the street corner, pretending indifference, and chewing over Fred's eminence after the event.

At Lamb House Fred employed a staff of three plus the venerable gardener, seemingly as sturdy as an oak and as timeless, whose care of his plants and vegetables was so consuming that Fred felt like a guest in his presence.[4] Indoors there were Charlie, who ran a cold bath for him in the morning, prepared his clothes for the day and accompanied him everywhere; Ivy the maid; and Rose the cook, later to be Mrs Charlie Tomlin. Fred wrote 2,000 words every day, on the precept that the muse does not come unbidden – it has to be grabbed. A writer, he said, is not some one who *can* write, but some one who *does* write; the work is all. Breakfast was at nine, followed by a read of the newspapers and a word with Rose about the menus for lunch and dinner that day. There were three courses for each meal, and Fred always dressed suitably for dinner, with black tie, even when he was alone. He did not simply ask Rose what she was cooking, but chose the meals carefully, for he had acquired, Heaven knows how, a culinary expertise which was much envied by those who cooked regularly. He invented, for example, a recipe for quail, which one of his admirers thereafter on her menus called *Cailles à la Dodo*.[5] The cellar was well stocked with good wine, and home-made barley-water was very welcome on a hot summer's day.[6]

Having left Rose, Fred worked solidly for two hours, then played the piano before lunch. In the afternoon he rested, took some exercise, had tea, worked for another couple of hours, took a hot bath and changed for dinner. If there were no visitors he might finish the day with more writing or a game of chess with Charlie.[7] Throughout the 1930s the routine barely changed.

When Fred received a proposal from an Austrian professor that he should devote a doctoral thesis to the art of E.F. Benson, one must hope that he smiled. The thesis, *Die Eigenart E.F. Bensons an seinen Hauptwerken aufgezeigt* (EFB's characteristic features as shown by his principal works') by Dr Emil Aldor, was eventually published in Vienna in 1932. Aldor sent a translation to his eminent subject.[8] There were two themes to the study, (a) that modern intellectual women were the kiss of death, and (b) that in the dispute between the generations Benson was on the side of the young.

The Viennese scholar's brief overlooked both Miss Mapp and Mrs Lucas, the two characters who were about to collide in *Mapp and Lucia* and who had now reached the apogee of their absurdity. With this in 1931, and in 1932 a biography of Charlotte Brontë, a sequel to *As We Were*, and another comedy of manners (*Secret Lives*), Benson, too, reached the summit of his powers, expressed in three different moods and developed along three parallel routes. It was a bold stroke to risk the clash of Titans in *Mapp and Lucia*, effected in the simplest manner by having Mrs Lucas rent Miss Mapp's house in Tilling for a period of two months. No sooner is the redoubtable lady ensconced than, by 'showy little dinners and odious flatteries', she manages to supplant Mapp's position in the town, as a result of which the two women are locked in combat. Quaint Irene, with her 'dismal directness', observes the fun and remains the only character not to take these people seriously. It is much to Benson's credit that he contrives a preposterous climax without losing the reader's sympathy: a sudden flood sweeps Mapp and Lucia away on an upturned kitchen table! Fred read the scene aloud to Steven Runciman on the evening of the day he wrote it, to test reaction. He was encouraged.

Charlotte Brontë was a resounding success, and is still regarded with great respect despite the fresh evidence since uncovered by

Winifred Gérin and new insights offered by Margaret Lane. First of all, it is the work of a master story-teller, one who knows how to make his narrative grip and hold the reader captive. It rolls forward with such unerring relish, with such discernment and vivid depiction of its extraordinary cast, that it compels comparison with the very best in the *genre*. Beautifully tempered and measured, with due drama given to the emotional peaks of the story and a sensitive understanding of family tensions, the biography deals most poignantly with the deaths of Branwell, Emily and Charlotte. It also betrays an enviable talent for exposition, with fine literary analysis proceeding from a careful sifting of probability from the debris of invention and romanticism. Moreover, it is concise and arresting.

More than Drake or Alcibiades, *Charlotte Brontë* permitted Fred finally to be admitted among those 'serious' writers whose productions are meant to endure. After years of being tartly dismissed as a lightweight, he was now the subject of earnest scholarly discussion. That doyen of critics, Desmond MacCarthy, devoted a whole programme on the BBC to a review of the book, pointing out that Benson's novels 'seldom made heavy calls' upon his intellect, whereas that intellect 'is in biography under requisition – to our great gain'.

His critics had never bothered to look behind the ease and superficiality of his novels to discover the quality of his mind and acuity of his judgement. These had to be deployed boldly for anyone to notice them, and in *Charlotte Brontë* they were incontestable. As MacCarthy said, 'the first merit of Benson's book is that it sifts legend from truth. There is a minimum of conjecture in it.' In other words, it was a work of academic distinction as well as artistic brilliance. MacCarthy concluded that Fred had done an 'excellent' and 'thorough' job.[9]

E.M. Delafield wrote Fred an ecstatic fan-letter, as did his old friend Ethel Smyth, who loyally never allowed a book of his to pass without sending him a note about it:

> I think it is one of the best biographies I have ever read and far away your best book (so far!). Your style seems to me to have become perfect . . . you seem to have worked up into the region

where your qualities have sweated away all their defects. For
instance your humour. Sometimes I have thought you flippant
– here you are only awfully and discreetly funny now and again.
Another thing – you inspire confidence.[10]

(She had previously told him that his flippancy had been under
control in writing about Alcibiades, to which Fred had mischievously replied that Alcibiades was far more flippant than he.)

As We Are is the kind of book every writer would dearly love
to be invited to do when he has passed sixty (Fred was sixty-five
when it was published), for it tells how appalling everything is
today compared to what it was 'when I was a lad'. Fred looks at
the contemporary world with some bewilderment, despairing at
what passes in the modern day for gentlemanly behaviour or lady-
like quality, and shakes his greying head disapprovingly. Once
more, he writes with supreme elegance, though the subject-matter
be somewhat discursive. Chapters hang together with less cohe-
sion than in *As We Were*. The underlying *leit-motif* is that Fred
knows he is a fossil from a distant era, and does not mind. There
is much about modern literature which he deplores, having no
time at all for James Joyce or Virginia Woolf and being particularly
angry at novels which took the reader too pryingly into the bedroom. Fred's ire is at its fiercest when writing about Arnold
Bennett, whom he clearly detests, and it was this chapter which
'staggered' Hugh Walpole, who wrote to say that its 'sudden
bitterness' was wholly out of tune with the rest of the book.
However, said Walpole, we shall not quarrel as 'I never forget
you were the first person to be kind to me'.[11]

Secret Lives (1932) is one of Fred's most joyous confections.
Set in Brompton Square, where 'surprising passions and secret
lives were seething in unsuspected cauldrons', the plot revolves
around the arrival of a new tenant, Miss Susan Leg, who is so
unimpressive a bore that the neighbours, and in particular Mrs
Mantrip, do not deign to regard her. What they do not know is
that dumpy and tedious Miss Leg is a best-selling novelist under
the pseudonym of Rudolf da Vinci, and Mrs Mantrip, who has
pretensions to intellectual dignity, reads every word of said Rudolf
da Vinci without ever admitting to such a lamentable weakness.

The book ends with a confrontation between the two women in which pomposity explodes like a manic geyser ('It is my privilege to tell you, Miss Leg, that your whole life is a lie, and that from henceforth we are strangers'), and everybody has egg all over his face.

For the last time, Fred has plundered his Marie Corelli scrapbook for the personality of the novelist Susan Leg, whom she resembles in every detail. (Marie Corelli had died in 1924 and was fast being forgotten.) Describing the style of Susan's prose he is describing Corelli with remorseless accuracy:

> It was preposterous to the last degree, but there was a sumptuousness about it, and, though nauseatingly moral in its conclusion, there was also fierceness, a sadism running like a scarlet thread through its portentous pages. Above all, it was written *con amore*; the gusto of Susan Leg blazed in it like some magnificent conflagration . . . in a word, it seemed to him to have all the atrocious qualities of a possible best-seller.

One of Susan Leg's heroines is called Serena Lomond, with the same initials as her creator. Marie Corelli had made Mavis Clare the heroine of her block-buster *The Sorrows of Satan* and endowed her with all the attributes of beauty, talent, musicality, superiority which Miss Corelli thought should be applied to herself. Serena Lomond 'improvised' at the piano, as Marie Corelli had done, and 'said that she heard angels' harps in the air, and just played what they did'. (Marie Corelli had played tediously rehearsed 'improvisations' professionally, under the name 'Rose Trevor'.) The critics did not approve of Serena Lomond, so their wretched scribblings were given to the dog to chew – Miss Corelli trained her dog to do the same. Her second book was called *Amor Vincit*; Marie Corelli had a pierced heart engraved above her fireplace in Stratford-upon-Avon with these words written beneath. Corelli would not allow a photograph of her to be published until 1903, when she was over fifty, and then it was touched up to make her look the age she always pretended to be, twenty-eight. This is mirrored in the theme of the photograph of 'Rudolf da Vinci' which exposes Mrs Mantrip's clandestine delusions. And so on. The whole book is a sequence of revelations about the misguided determination of people to appear as something they are not, and, in its way, though it is written at the expense of Marie Corelli, it is Fred's secret tribute to the woman's glorious obtuseness.

Secret Lives caused some embarrassed consternation among the inhabitants of Brompton Square, and one of them, a Mrs Arkwright, was deputed to write to Fred in Rye and seek elucidation. Fred replied with some cunning, implying more by his words than (he knew) Mrs Arkwright would understand. 'I am delighted to hear that Secret Lives has given amusement to the Square,' he said, 'and I long to know who all the ridiculous people in the book are, for indeed I don't know myself! However, I hope that before long you'll tell me.'[12]

Benson's output in the years of approaching old age was prodigious. He edited and wrote an introduction to the letters of Henry James to his brother Arthur and to Auguste Monod, and followed this with another novel (*Travail of Gold*), another biography (*Edward VII* – which Buckingham Palace had advised him not to write),[13] and another social history – *The Outbreak of War* – which led to an amusing correspondence with the writer/politician Harold Nicolson. Nicolson reviewed *The Outbreak of War* in a manner applauded by journalists who spoil for a fight. It was, he said, 'not only bad, it is deplorable . . . the only interesting thing about this book is the problem of how and why Mr Benson came to write it.' (In fact, that was not a problem at all. Fred was commissioned by the publishers.) Not content with being clever, Nicolson proceeded abjectly to apologise to Fred in private *before* the review appeared, as if to protect himself from any ill-feeling. He sent the following letter:

My dear Benson, I have written a perfectly bloody review of your Great Occasions book which will appear in the Daily Telegraph on Friday. You will probably be amused, as you must feel yourself that the book is not among the more immortal of your works. But I hate being impertinent to the eminent behind their backs, even as I hate being rude to an old friend who has always been very kind to me. So I write to apologise in advance, and to assure you that I should never have reviewed the book at all had I not felt that you are impervious to such abuse. I expect you will forgive me all the same.

As this was a florid example of the kind of hypocrisy he had spent his life mocking, Fred might well have exploded. But he did not. Instead, he sent a note of devastating restraint:

I have now read the gem you refer to in the Daily Telegraph of some day last week, and agree with you: very regrettable. But why apologise if you think it will only amuse me? I don't quite understand, but of course I fully accept your apology, and there is the end of the matter.

This neat and dignified rejoinder stung Nicolson, who obviously felt guilty, into a lengthy further excuse. Fred also mis-spelt Nicolson's name as 'Nicholson', a point upon which the ambitious career man was particularly touchy, as Fred probably knew all too well.

I really mind having hurt your feelings [Nicolson wrote]. It has given me a sore place inside for three days . . . I am *not* a shit and you have made me feel like one. You may be right. In that case it will be of some satisfaction to you to feel that your reproof has gone home like a lance . . . But seriously I think you have hurt my feelings far more than I can possibly have hurt yours.[14]

Fred did not deign to respond to this ludicrous display of squirming. The legacy of Edwardian manners, which were as natural to him as a polite greeting, lent him an august bearing in old age and a silent authority such as to make *arrivistes* like Harold Nicolson tremble. He was not austere, but he was clearly respected.

And he respected others in like measure. A parallel literary squabble occurred with his old friend Hugh Walpole, who he thought might have been mildly offended by some references of his in print. His letter to Walpole, in contrast to Nicolson's to him, is a model of how excuses should be offered. 'I wish to add that I think some of my remarks were very ill-natured, and that I regret them. I fear that arthritis has made me peevish.' Walpole replied, in the same generous spirit, that he knew the remarks 'must have been written before the season of olive branches, and never gave them a second thought in that regard'.[15]

The next four books included a second volume of *Spook Stories*, a fourth Lucia adventure (*Lucia's Progress*), and the last of his big biographies, *Queen Victoria*. With his brother's work on the Queen's letters to draw upon, as well as personal memories to alleviate the toil of archival research, Benson was especially well placed to attempt such a portrait, and it was fortunate that he waited for the sage reflections of his old age before he did so. *Queen Victoria* stands high among the scores of books devoted to the subject and is a solid accomplishment. The book was more widely praised than any of his previous works, even including *As We Were*, as this press notice may demonstrate:

> Long and well-known as a practised novelist and judicious chronicler of the social scene, E.F. Benson has now given us a sprightly and entertaining single-volume biography. There is still room for fresh estimates of the formidable personality of Queen Victoria, and this one will commend itself to many readers who have found Lytton Strachey too satirical and most other writers too fulsome. Mr Benson, as one would expect, has hit upon the right tone, and has sustained it consistently. He is easy, chatty, slightly informal, humorous without being openly satirical, all in the vein of witty and agreeable conversation.
>
> *The Tablet*

Others used such words as 'brilliant' and 'inspiring', 'admirable' and 'alive', and gave the impression that Fred's distinctive combination of talents had at last found fruitful expression. There is another dimension to *Queen Victoria*, and one which the more detailed studies subsequently made by Elizabeth Longford and Cecil Woodham-Smith cannot diminish. The book has something of the nature of a personal gift. The Queen had valued and shown confidence in his father, had been a friend to his mother, and some of her descendants had been among his own friends. His affectionate and human account of her life was in a way a valediction to a crucial personal influence. Fred wanted to celebrate the woman's greatness not as a distant historical figure but as a familiar contemporary placed by Fate on the highest rung. He well knew that future historians would assess her role with greater detachment, and was content that they should, for he was of that rapidly disappearing generation which had lived under her sway.

No one made reference to those scores of forgettable novels which had disfigured his early career; it is doubtful if any of his new admirers were very much aware of them. E.F. Benson was now a man of eminence in the literary world.

Suddenly, the most unexpected honours fell upon his head. In 1933 he was invited by the Town Council to become, of all things, Mayor of Rye, on account of his good work as magistrate and the particular regard in which he was held in the town. The rather aloof mockery to which Miss Mapp had been subjected was either forgiven or, more likely, added to the piquancy of the appointment. At any rate, Fred accepted and was duly invested as the 645th Mayor in 1934, decked in mediaeval costume and welcoming the ceremony and *gravitas* of the occasion with the same relish as he had manifested in Truro, some sixty years before, at the sight of Papa's coat of arms painted on the doors of the Episcopal Carriage. After the procession through town, the Mayor was required to throw pennies from the balcony of the George Hotel to children scrabbling in the street below.

For three successive years Fred kept his Mayoral position (and meagre salary which he had to supplement from personal funds), with Mrs Jacomb-Hood, widow of an old friend, as his Mayoress. His period of office covered the Jubilee celebrations for George V, the succession and abdication of Edward VIII (when a lady-in-waiting to Queen Mary wrote to him from Sandringham about the shame and humiliation they had all passed through),[16] and the Coronation of George VI. A new Lord Warden of the Cinque Ports was appointed in 1935, Fred acting as Speaker of the Cinque Ports in another picturesque ceremony, but he was obliged to forgo his right to attend King George's coronation by reason of his lameness.

Much to his own surprise, Fred took to the minutiae of committee meetings with considerable ease, proving to have the diplomatic skills which were very much needed, as well as the ready knack for summary and concision. He did not care for public speaking,

however, and tried frankly to avoid it. Asked to address the
Whitefriars Club, he declined with the excuse that 'speaking is a
feat of which I am radically incapable. My last attempt was made
two years ago and lasted for three disastrous minutes'.[17] On the
few occasions when, as Mayor, he could not get away with a mere
show of reluctance, his brevity was a notable relief. He once gave
a shelter to the town of Rye, placed at the end of the High Street,
and to celebrate its 'unveiling' he was called upon to say a few
words. After remarking that he had heard the shelter was already
being referred to as 'The Mayor's Hugging Parlour', he continued:

> Never have I contemplated embarking on such intimate and
> sinister (or dexterous) practices there, quite apart from the fact
> that, as long as I have lived in Rye, I have never detected the
> slightest sign in any of its inhabitants that they would consent
> to be my partner in such dark mysteries of the twilight. I repudi-
> ate the notion. I am shocked.[18]

Fred also gave the West Window of Rye Church, executed
according to his own design, as a memorial to his parents. He
contrived to include portraits of his late collie, Taffy, and Charlie
Tomlin in the guise of a shepherd, as well as himself in mayoral
robes.

When his third term of office came to an end, the Town Council
honoured Fred by granting him the Freedom of Rye 'in recog-
nition and high appreciation of the numerous eminent services
rendered by him to the town of his adoption'. Having paid the
statutory fee of twopence, and been given a receipt for it, Fred
made his last public address with suitable, and patently genuine,
modesty:

> I hope you will agree that I have always been eager to listen
> with interest to the eloquence of others, but I think you must
> admit that I have never been very much attached to my own.
> And then I rather dislike superlatives . . . I ask you to credit me
> with preserving what I believe is called a 'rich silence'. It isn't
> quite so rich as it was before your Town Clerk made that
> unexpected raid upon my floating capital.[19]

Noting that he was now immune from arrest on the streets of Rye, he told the famous story of Mark Twain's lament upon the demise of good literature ('Shakespeare is dead, Milton is dead, and I am not feeling too well myself'), then resumed his reserved silence.

In the same year the Fellows of Magdalene College, Cambridge, invited Fred to accept the Honorary Fellowship made vacant by the death of Rudyard Kipling, as a gesture of gratitude towards the munificence of Arthur Benson as much as in tribute to Fred's own eminence, although they rightly insisted upon the latter consideration when they described him as 'the most fitting of all living writers to succeed to Hardy and Kipling'.[20] There was never any hesitation in accepting this very flattering honour, and Fred made the journey to Cambridge, despite painful limbs, to receive his M.A. degree. He then made a generous endowment to pay for a scholarship, and gave the Fellows (at their request) the manuscript of *As We Are*.[21]

Still he wrote books at a furious rate, packing eight in during the last three years of his life. *The Kaiser and English Relations* caused him some bother, as he had originally had 'William II' in the title, and referred throughout the text to 'the Emperor'. His publishers maintained the reader would be confused into thinking that 'William II' referred to a different emperor from the one everybody referred to as the Kaiser. Fred did not think this at all reasonable. 'The mentality of anyone who maintains that the title "The Kaiser" connotes William II, but that the title "William II" connotes somebody else, is, frankly, outside my comprehension.'[22] Nevertheless, he was overruled, and his title amended. Abortive discussions with Metro-Goldwyn-Mayer over film rights for the *Colin* novels ate up time which was becoming ever more precious. Four volumes of social history under the collective title *Old London* were closely followed by *The Daughters of Queen Victoria*, the last of Emmeline Lucas (*Trouble for Lucia*), and that majestic full-stop to an extensive career, which has been much considered in these pages – *Final Edition*. Fred's first title for this farewell tome was *By the Way*, to be replaced by *A Few People* and *Late Edition* before settling into the apt and poignant name by which it is now known. For as the very pages were being delivered to the publisher, Fred fell ill.

He had smoked twenty to thirty cigarettes every day for all his adult life. We find him grabbing the surreptitious smoke after dinner at Lambeth Palace in the 1890s (often joined by Mama in her naughtiest mood); falling asleep in the armchair at Oakley Street with a cigarette next to him; puffing away at Tremans and Brompton Square, and still at Lamb House. At the end of 1939 he began to lose weight, to cough relentlessly, to grow tired for no obvious reason. He did not complain or make a nuisance of himself, but it is not fanciful to suppose he knew his time had come. He was seventy-two. As long ago as 1893 he had written:

> there comes that hour when the whole course of our being is checked, when all the rules and faint ideas that we have ever gathered are subverted, and we go out alone to find what the unknown has to give us. Yet, if the worst gift that death has in store for us is utter forgetfulness and peace, a closing round of the grey limits of annihilation, we face nothing but what we long for.[23]

Death was once given voice by Fred in a short story and a play of the same name. 'To the weary I am rest,' it said, 'to the sad I am consolation. To those that mourn I am comfort, to the happy I am the consummation of their happiness.'[24] It would be difficult to compose a more beneficent view of mortality, nor one so little vexed by regret or uncertainty.

Still, he was uncomfortable. His cousin and heir, Patrick McDowall (whom he knew but scarcely), tried to cheer him up by saying that he should go on 'brightening history', to which Fred plaintively replied, 'I want someone to brighten mine!'[25] Someone who did, with astonishingly neat symmetry, was the woman whose personality had launched him on a literary career – Margot Asquith, the model for his first book *Dodo*. She wrote to him out of the blue from the Tennant family home at Glenconner in North Berwick to tell him how good was his book on the daughters of Queen Victoria. It was, she said, '*brilliantly* written . . . I read it through to 5 a.m.'[26] Lest any doubt lingered, it was good to know that he had been forgiven for the indiscretion of his youth. Margot did not know that Fred was dying.

A specialist at University College Hospital in London suspected cancer and conducted an exploratory operation at the beginning of 1940. The cancerous cells were discovered in Benson's throat, and were so extensive that any hope of recovery was futile. 'When I have to go, I hope to go quickly,' he had said. In hospital he was so obviously weak that friends suspected he had suffered for months without surrendering to complaint. From his hospital bed he told Francis Yeats-Brown, 'It's such a bore, I can't write!' The following week he died, on 29 February, almost certainly happy in the knowledge that he had been active to within a whisper of his term and that *Final Edition* was going to press.

'God could no more have invented cancer than he could have invented sin,' wrote Benson. He was free of anger for his condition at the end, and would have politely refused any attempt to keep him alive. He had prevented doctors from giving his brother Arthur a stimulant which might have stayed his soul from its urgent journey for a few days.[27] But was he prepared to meet his Maker? Did this arch mocker of the human condition believe that the journey had any direction or purpose? The son of the Archbishop of Canterbury was in every important regard a sceptic, an agnostic, a humanist:

The problem of what we are lies at the root of all human anguish. We have creeds, as all mankind have had creeds, since the beginning of the world, all directed against that impregnable rock: 'What are we?' The whole puzzle of life, how we came here, where we are going, what is good, what is evil, all depend directly on that. A creed is a probability to many who do not believe it; to a few who do believe it, a certainty. Yet who has realised for the space of a lightning flash any creed, and has retained it as a creed? For a realised creed is no longer a creed, but an experience.[28]

Benson had seen no lightning flash, had had no such experience. But he was not prepared to dismiss the experience of others any more than he would elevate reason to such a pinnacle as to claim that whatever could not be explained could not be. 'One mystery the more in this illimitable riddle of things, one more confession, "we canot tell", is no startling phenomenon.' The atheist point of view he ridiculed as arrogant. But the stand which excited his scorn more than any other, one which he chastised tentatively while his father was alive and ever more vehemently as he grew older, was the piety of the malicious or self-regarding Christian, as revealed in the odious Edith of *Pharisees and Publicans* and more gently in the humorous ladies of Tilling, Riseholme, or Durham (Brompton) Square who wore one face for God and another for their fellows. 'Milton makes God a bounder, but many pious Christians make him a brute.'[29]

Benson's God was to be found in music, in nature, and in the fine benevolence of human behaviour when it was not directed towards the self. In short, God was revealed in beauty. 'I am a Christian,' says Martin in *The Challoners*, 'and I cannot any longer be of a Church that leaves out beauty from its worship. Why, if you love a thing, if you believe in a thing, you must approach it through beauty, it seems to me.'[30] Or through love. 'All love – the love for children, for parents, for husband, for wife, for lover, for mistress – has something divine about it, or else it is not love.'[31] The supreme exemplar of such love in Benson's life was his mother who possessed what he called 'the divine and human gospel of patience in dealing with people, the patience that teaches us not to pull buds open, however desirable it may be that the flower should unfold.'[32] When E.F. Benson died, it was to the bosom of his mother's God that he was gathered, not to that of his father.

The Bishop of Chichester officiated at Benson's funeral and he was buried in Rye Cemetery. Francis Yeats-Brown contributed a long personal obituary in the *Spectator*. The others concentrated on his literary career, but they could not know that it was as a son and as a friend that this very private man constructed his place in the world, unobserved by his readers and unnoticed by the Society which for so long had formed the overt décor to his life. At the end of 1916, when his mother was recovering from the loss of Maggie and was distressed by the condition of Arthur, she had addressed to him a letter of spontaneous effusion:

You really are the perfectest darling in the whole wide world and have given me such a LEG UP as cannot be described in 'umin langwidge. O Fred, you really ARE. Fred, who has dug his Ma out of a horrid pit and made her think she is the most gifted and delightful and refreshing person in the world.[33]

A few years earlier, his old friend Philip Burne-Jones gave vent to similar devotion and appreciation. 'All good be with you, dear Fred, now and always,' he wrote, 'and I pray the New Year may have nothing but happiness and good luck in store for you and those you love.'[34] It is by such memories that one is blessed.

On the last page of a manuscript he was working on in August 1939, six months before he died but when his increasing discomfort made clear to him that he did not have long to go, he drafted a letter to F.M. Welsford concerning his Will:

I have asked Captain Edwin Dawes of Bank Chambers Rye to act as executor of my Will with you. He is an old friend of mine . . . I am also thinking of buying the Lamb House estate here, in which case I shall have to reduce my pecuniary legacies. If war broke out, I should not do this, but in that case too my legacies would have to be reduced, since there must be a great shrinking of capital.[35]

The writing, smudged and erratic, is that of a very ill man.

In the event, war broke out a week later. He did not buy Lamb House, nor did he change the stipulations of a Will he wrote on 23 August. By the terms of this, Benson left £2,500 to Charlie Tomlin, £100 to Francis Yeats-Brown and £100 to George Plank. Further bequests of £100 each went to London neighbours, the Hon. Eleanor Brougham and the Hon. Mrs Johnstone of Brompton Square, plus £2,000 to Magdalene College for the scholarship he had endowed, and £2,500 to the Cancer Hospital (did he suspect then that he had cancer? The doctors did not diagnose it until later). All his other property, the house in Brompton Square, the silver (both personal and inherited from his father's tenure as Chancellor at Lincoln), his assets, furniture, paintings, and belongings amounting to £10,000, were left without condition to his cousin Patrick McDowall, in order, he said, that the family of his aunt Ada should enjoy more of the fruits of life than they might otherwise have known. McDowall's descendants cherish them to this day. 25 Brompton Square was sold in the 1960s, but almost everything else that Fred knew has been kept, and today adorns at least three scattered houses, breathing into them the life and presence of a man who preferred not to make waves, but constant repeating ripples.

Of the descendants of Christopher Benson of York, no fewer than twelve were published authors, and of these the most enduring fame belongs to E.F. Benson. In his own estimate he had always been 'the family dunce', the one whose future was rendered uncertain by his reluctance to work and his antipathy to 'accuracy'. He fell back upon his ability to write with ease, a talent he owed to genetic legacy and what would nowadays pass for a very superior classical education. He was not vainglorious. He did not nurse an illusory notion of his contribution to English Literature. He did not take himself too seriously. It even seemed to him, in his last decade, that his success had been won without just desert, for he knew that he was intelligent enough to have produced better things. 'I did not feel that I had been selling my soul for lucre and a facile popularity,' he wrote, 'but rather that I had pawned it.'[36] It was then that he turned his mind to the biographies and social histories which are among his finest memorials. But does Benson deserve the feline judgement of one critic who, Miss Mapp-like, asserted that his fiction 'aimed low and hit the target'?[37]

Fred was well aware that the ease with which he could fashion a story was an enemy in disguise. 'My chief danger,' he said, 'the foe by my fireside, was the facility with which I could write readably: that was a handicap rather than an asset.'[38] It was a talent which, for many years, simply could not be reined. Arthur poured out words on to sheets which dropped to the floor and found their way inexorably into print. Hugh wrote 'in furious haste',[39] and Fred himself enjoyed the process so much that he could scarcely bear to interrupt it. 'I've done it all too quickly, I know,' he would say. 'But I couldn't stop, I was so interested.'[40] Clearly he did not suffer the agonies which afflict most writers when faced with blank paper. Most of his manuscripts are dated on page 1, and again on the last page, and they show that Fred's novels usually took three weeks to write. Somewhat ruefully, he noted that the last time he had seen the publisher Heinemann, 'he much deprecated my bringing out books with speed'.[41]

There is a medical view that would attribute this ceaseless activity to brain disease and hold that all three Benson brothers could not stop writing for fear of something worse. 'It seems clear that Arthur's compulsive writing was in part at least caused by his psychosis, and was in some way necessary to him, as an attempt to clear the overloaded circuits of his brain.' All the Sidgwicks as well as the Bensons suffered from this mental disorder, so that when Edward married Minnie, their progeny was doomed to pour words on to pages.[42]

With Fred, however, rapidity of execution by no means implied carelessness of style. He was never slapdash or haphazard in structure, vocabulary or syntax, and his strict adherence to classical rules of balance and harmony ensured that his meaning was always clear. He was a craftsman *avant tout*. Ever since, as a boy, he had discovered 'the infinite flexibility of language, and the joy in the cadences of words',[43] he recognised that clarity resided as much in beauty and simplicity of expression as in content, and his quarrels with other writers usually turned upon their ignorance of or indifference to this cardinal precept. Of Swinburne he had this to say:

The frenzy without which all lyrical utterances are lukewarm causes prose to boil over, for prose, except when delivered with the passion of the spoken voice, does not admit of frenzy, and critical prose, such as Swinburne was composing, loses all force and dignity if fashioned thus. He loaded it with alliteration gone lunatic, he heaped phrase upon phrase, whether for the eulogy of Dickens or the damnation of Dr Furnivall, and instead of using his astounding vocabulary to convey his meaning, let his meaning vanish in order to employ his vocabulary.[44]

By contrast, for Benson the ideal marriage of clarity and beauty was to be found in the Authorised Version of the New Testament (how he would have deplored its subsequent replacement by the vacuous prose of the New English Bible):

I demand – for myself – that prose should have a certain intrinsic beauty of its own quite apart from the meaning it conveys. This beauty is quite consistent with the utmost lucidity and does not depend at all on decoration. The best example I know of it is the Gospels in the Authorised Version of the New Testament: their style reminds one of Holbein's portrait of the Duchess of Milan.[45]

And the real attraction of Charlotte Brontë to him was that she 'wrote fine and apt English, rhythmical and dignified, with that indefinable verbal inevitability which is the hall-mark of the writer.'

The new wave of fiction upon which Fred glowered from his Edwardian eyrie lacked all these qualities, in his view, with its fashion for 'stream of consciousness' and the abandonment of stylistic discipline. In a speech given in Rye, he said he hoped the day would come when we should return 'to the grand imaginative novels of forty years ago' (i.e. in the nineteenth century). He doubted whether people really enjoyed reading modern fiction, but pretended to, just as the man who claims to have spent the morning reading Spenser's *Faery Queene* for the third time 'is lying'. Arnold Bennett earns Fred's most vituperative scorn. He positively loathes Bennett's self-importance and pomposity, and refers to his 'infelicitous gabble . . . He writes so execrably and struts and barks in so provocative a manner.'[46] However else one may adjudge the prose of E.F. Benson, strutting and barking are certainly not among its attributes. Restraint and control (in prose as in life, one might add) are the hallmarks of a style which is dressed with becoming elegance and behaves decorously. Fred also makes a conscious effort to avoid the platitudes which he saw flopping about in the sentences of Desmond MacCarthy, platitudes 'the only remarkable quality of which is that once read they are never remembered'.[47]

The neat balance of this remark, with its unexpected and ironic final word, recalls one of Benson's most frequently employed tools – antithesis, paradox, the revelation of truth through surprise. At the beginning of his career, in *Dodo*, the technique was still essentially Wildean and devoted uniquely to amusement. 'No one means what they say when they pay compliments,' said Dodo. 'They are only a kind of formula to avoid the unpleasantness of saying nothing.' 'Lady Grantham was seized with a momentary desire to run her parasol through his body, provided it could be done languidly and without effort.' 'She devoted her evening to what she called tidying, which consisted in emptying the contents of a quantity of drawers on to the floor of her room, and sitting down beside them.' 'I can't bear conceited men. They always seem to me to be like people on stilts.'[48] Fifty years later, Wilde's influence still lingers: 'It is a mistake deliberately to bore your friends. Most of us do it quite enough while trying to be amusing.'[49] But in the meantime, between *Dodo* and *Final Edition*, Benson has learnt to use the technique in order the better to delineate character. He always claimed that he allowed his creatures to speak for themselves, to reveal themselves through their conversation, but in fact it was Fred's manipulative use of his favourite trick of antithesis which spiked them in the reader's mind. The way in which poor Florence is pictured in *Paying Guests* offers an example. Her father is a hypochondriac and Florence is utterly sacrificed to his service. 'She found herself wondering what would happen if she questioned her father's right to immolate her day and night on the altar of his aches.' 'Her father had seriously taken up the profession of invalidism instead of having no profession at all.' 'She knew well that her interminable ministries to him were not performed out of the bounty of love, but from her own acquiescence in being crushed.'[50]

Sometimes he uses surprise as an insight. 'Deep in the heart of everyone you find what seemed at first their most superficial qualities.'[51] 'The essence of courage is not that your heart should not quake, but that nobody else should know that it does.'[52] Yet again, though he is fundamentally a cerebral writer, not a lyricist; an artist who helps the reader to perceive, not to feel; Benson rises on occasion to paint a bold and simple visual scene, as when Alcibiades stands apart and alone on the deck of his ship. 'From end to end the quay was a blur of massed faces and eager eyes, and all were turned to him, like a bed of flowers to the sun.' In the same book he demonstrates how drama may be injected into a scene by the astute use of syntax and euphony. The final sentence of Chapter 12, when Athens has just lost her entire fleet to Sparta in her moment of abject humiliation, ends with six monosyllabic blows to crush and obliterate the developing crescendo of the preceding words:

> The 'Paralus' carried the news to Athens, and as the tidings spread from Peiraeus to the city, there rose and swelled the sound of lamentation and great mourning, and that night no man slept.[53]

With each of these stylistic devices Benson shows his familiarity with classical literature, and his appreciation that purity of form best conveys accuracy of meaning.

The meaning that it was so important to him to convey is a simple but honourable truth which so often passed unnoticed in his fiction that he began to disguise it in the richest humour. It finds its best expression in the sermon which Mr Banks offers to the assembly of dissimulators and hypocrites at the beginning of Chapter 7 of *Paying Guests*:

> If, dear friends, we all invariably acted on our noble rather than our baser impulses, the world would be a very different place.

Knowing full well that the reader will trot along with this in comfort and not in perturbation, Fred adds, 'there was scarcely anyone in his congregation who grasped the whole of the tremendous truth that lurked in these simple words'. And scarcely anyone of those thousands who laugh out loud at the uproarious capers of Lucia or Miss Mapp grasps the core of E.F. Benson's moral vision – namely that these delectable ladies do themselves a disservice by feeding their vainglory and selfishness when they could be so much richer in spirit were they to direct their energies to the benefit of others. It is not a fresh view of the world, nor a newly-minted philosophy with massive implications, but it is sane, sensible and good, and it is Benson's hope that we may pause in our laughter to ponder a little on what makes Lucia's pretensions so funny or Miss Mapp's mendacity so beguiling. Benson allows us to make fools of ourselves, by being amused at his creatures while taking ourselves so seriously. The purpose of his art, at its best, is precisely to hold a mirror up to nature. The Miss Mapps of his imagination are not grotesque caricatures, they are not invented puppets at whom we can point a finger and consider ourselves apart, they are merely exaggerated versions of ourselves. From his earliest youth Fred was wont to embellish and adorn a story, or prove a point by emphasis; he knew that truth did not necessarily lie in accuracy. The Lucia books are the culmination of this method, and we should be wrong to assume that we may find their characters risible and absurd, yet conclude they have nothing to teach us.

Fred's deepest contempt is aroused by two faults which are too nasty to be counted among the 'follies' of mankind. One is cynicism and the other self-righteousness. About these he is rarely as funny as he might be about mere hypocrisy or pomposity, for cynicism and aggressive piety are positively harmful, even wicked. 'I always a little distrust moral purposes,' says Lady Sunningdale in *The Challoners*. 'If you do a thing with a moral purpose it usually means that you do it, because if you didn't you would be uncomfortable inside. Good people are such cowards, they are afraid of a little pain in their consciences.' Let there be no doubt: E.F. Benson does not consider such a point of view to be amusing – it is detestable. There is the world of difference between such harsh human indifference and the jolly double standards which, as Stephen Pile has written, make the business of a Benson character 'to take the mote out of his brother's eye, while polishing the beam in his own'. There is a vast difference also between the posturings of the pretentious ('all dignity is funny, simply because it is a sham')[54] and the insidious poison of the pious, Benson's second *bête noire*. He saw much of 'Christian hostility' at firsthand in the Church and with Lucy Tait at Tremans, and knew all too well that benevolence before an audience, coupled with a vigorous sense of the guilt of others, could have vicious consequences.

What, positively, Benson applauds is the honesty and integrity of those people who face the Trollopian dilemma of choice between indulgence and duty, and elect the latter. Lord Chesterford in *Dodo* is one such, resembling Plantagenet Palliser in his devotion to what is right and good and his lofty disdain for the shabby or selfish option. Benson says there is something 'divine' in the nobility of his motives. He would use the same word for Violet in *Pharisees and Publicans*, for David in *David Blaize*, and for a dozen other of his characters. Alas, neither Elizabeth Mapp nor Emmeline Lucas would qualify for such an epithet.

Not being a passionate man, Fred could not write passionate stories. Following some robust but clumsy attempts, he recognised where he had failed and why. 'I had often tried to conceal my own lack of emotion in situations that were intended to be moving, by daubing them over with sentimentality.'[55] It was from this realisation and consequent change of direction that issued the glorious nonsense of Lucia, Mapp, Mantrip, Quantock, Plaistow, Leg, Howard and the rest. With this body of comic writing, allied to the pure, limpid structure of his latter non-fiction, E.F. Benson is destined to retain his reputation as one of the great stylists of the Edwardian period. More than anything else, perhaps, it is the recurrence of pleasure which his best books afford that ensures his survival. He always reverted to favourite authors for his most intense enjoyment – to the Greeks, to *Wuthering Heights*, to *Emma* – and if the ghost of this utterly modest man might find some pleasure in his posthumous renown, it would derive from the knowledge that those who read *Mapp and Lucia* or *As We Were* do so again and again.

Bibliography

Manuscript Sources

The principal archive relating to the Benson family is in the Department of Western Manuscripts at the Bodleian Library, Oxford, and is known as the Benson Deposit. It is referred to in the Notes as Dep. Benson, followed by the Box Number.

The Diary of A.C. Benson, in 179 volumes, is at the Pepys Library in Magdalene College, Cambridge. This is identified in the Notes as ACB Diary.

Other papers are to be found at:

The Fales Library, New York University.

The Berg Collection, New York Public Library.

The Library of the University of California, Los Angeles.

The Beinecke Rare Books and Manuscript Library, Yale University, New Haven, Conn.

The Brotherton Library, University of Leeds (Gosse Papers).

The British Library, Manuscripts Room (Gladstone Papers).

The Harry Ranson Humanities Research Center, Austin, Texas.

The National Library of Scotland, Edinburgh.

Longford Castle, Salisbury.

The E.F. Benson Society, EFB's Diary 1887–8.

Lambeth Palace Library (the Ecclesiastical Papers of Archbishop Benson).

Trinity College Library, Cambridge (Archbishop Benson's Diary).

There are three further private collections of letters and papers in West London; in Wiltshire; and abroad. As the owners have requested anonymity, quotations from these papers are referred to in the Notes as 'private collection'.

Books by E.F. Benson

The list hereunder is based upon that compiled by Cynthia Reavell for *E.F. Benson Remembered and the World of Tilling*, by C. and T. Reavell, and published by the Martello Bookshop in Rye. It is supplemented by details gleaned from the bibliography assembled by Bill Taylor for the E.F. Benson Society. To both of these assiduous researchers the author is totally indebted for what follows. Reprints are not included, nor are editions in other languages. Besides which, there are scores of short stories which appeared in disparate journals. An admittedly incomplete list of these is obtainable from the E.F. Benson Society.

1888   *Sketches from Marlborough*

1893   *Dodo*, London, Methuen; New York, Appleton.

         Six Common Things (short stories), London, Osgood McIlvaine; Chicago edition under title *A Double Overture*, 1894, with extra story, C.H. Sergel.

1894   *The Rubicon*, London, Methuen; New York, Appleton.

1895   *The Judgement Books*, London, Osgood & McIlvaine; New York, Harper.

1896   *Limitations*, London, Innes; New York, Harper.

1897   *The Babe, B.A.*, London & New York, Putnam.

1898   *The Money Market*, Bristol, Arrowsmith; Philadelphia, Biddle.

         The Vintage, London, Methuen; New York, Harper.

1899   *The Capsina*, London, Methuen; New York, Harper.

         Mammon & Co, London, Heinemann; New York, Appleton.

1900   *The Princess Sophia*, London, Heinemann; New York, Harper.

1901   *The Luck of the Vails*, London, Heinemann; New York, Appleton.

1902   *Scarlet and Hyssop*, London, Heinemann; New York, Appleton.

         Daily Training (with Eustace Miles), London, Hurst and Blackett; New York, E.P. Dutton.

         'Aunt Jeannie' (unpublished play).

1903   *The Valkyries*, London, Dean & Son; Boston, Page.

         An Act in a Backwater, London, Heinemann; New York, Appleton.

         The Book of Months, London, Heinemann; New York, Harper.

         The Mad Annual (with Eustace Miles), London, Grant Richards.

         A Book of Golf (ed. E. F. Benson and Eustace Miles), London, Hurst & Blackett.

         The Cricket of Abel, Hirst and Shrewsbury (with Eustace Miles), London, Hurst & Blackett; New York, Dutton.

         The Relentless City, London, Heinemann; New York, Harper.

1904   *The Challoners*, London, Heinemann; Philadelphia, Lippincott.

         Two Generations (10-page pamphlet), London, *Daily Mail*.

1905   *The Image in the Sand*, London, Heinemann; Philadelphia, Lippincott.

         Diversions Day by Day (with Eustace Miles), London, Hurst & Blackett.

1906   *Paul*, London, Heinemann; Philadelphia, Lippincott.

         The Angel of Pain, London, Heinemann; Philadelphia, Lippincott.

         'The Friend in the Garden' (unpublished play).

1907   *Sheaves*, London, S. Paul; New York, Doubleday, Page (republished by Heinemann, 1908).

         The House of Defence, London, The Authors and Newspapers Association; Toronto, McLeod & Allen (republished by Heinemann).

1908   *The Climber*, London, Heinemann; New York, Grosset & Dunlap.

The Blotting Book, London, Heinemann; New York, Doubleday, Page.
English Figure Skating, London, G. Bell & Sons.

1909   *A Reaping*, London, Heinemann; New York, Doubleday, Page.

1910   *Daisy's Aunt*, London, T. Nelson & Sons; New York, Doubleday, Page (under title *The Fascinating Mrs Halton*)
The Osbornes, London, Smith, Elder; New York, Doubleday, Page.

1911   *Juggernaut*, London, Heinemann; New York, Doubleday, Page (under title *Margery*, 1910).
Account Rendered, London, Heinemann; New York, Doubleday, Page.

1912   *The Room in the Tower and Other Stories*, London, Mills & Boon.
Mrs Ames, London, Hodder & Stoughton; New York, Doubleday, Page.
Bensoniana, collection of EFB apophthegms, London, A.L. Humphreys.

1913   *Thorley Weir*, London, Smith, Elder; Philadelphia, Lippincott.
The Weaker Vessel, London, Heinemann; New York, Dodd, Mead.
Winter Sports in Switzerland, London, G. Allen; New York, Dodd, Mead.
Introduction by EFB to Waverley edition of Dickens's *Nicholas Nickleby*.
Thoughts from E.F. Benson, compiled by E.E. Norton.

1914   *Arundel*, London, T. Fisher Unwin; New York (1915), G.H. Doran.
Dodo the Second, London, Hodder & Stoughton; New York, Century Company (under title *Dodo's Daughter*, 1913).

1915   *The Oakleyites*, London, Hodder & Stoughton; New York, Doran.
'Dinner for Eight' (unpublished play).

1916   *Mike*, London, Cassell & Co; New York, A.L. Burt, G.H. Doran (under title *Michael*).
David Blaize, London, Hodder & Stoughton; New York, G.H. Doran.
The Freaks of Mayfair, London, T.H. Foulis; New York, Doran.

1917   *Thoughts from E.F. Benson*, compiled by H.B. Elliott, London, Holden & Hardingham.
Mr Teddy, London, T. Fisher Unwin; New York, Doran (under title *The Tortoise*).
An Autumn Sowing, London, Collins; New York, Doran (1918).

1918   *David Blaize and the Blue Door*, London, Hodder & Stoughton; New York, Doran (1918).
Up and Down, London, Hutchinson; New York, Doran.
Poland and Mittel-Europa, London, Hodder & Stoughton; New York, Doran (1919). Reprinted as *The White Eagle of Poland*.
Deutschland Über Alles, republished in *Crescent and Iron Cross*, London, Hodder & Stoughton; New York, Doran.

1919   *Across the Stream*, London, John Murray; New York, Doran.
Robin Linnet, London, Hutchinson; New York, Doran.

The Social Value of Temperance, London, True Temperance Association.

1920   *Queen Lucia*, London, Hutchinson; New York, Doran.
The Countess of Lowndes Square (short stories), London, Cassell.
Our Family Affairs, London, Cassell; New York, Doran (1921).

1921   *Lovers and Friends*, London, T. Fisher Unwin; New York, Doran.
Dodo Wonders, London, Hutchinson; New York, Doran.

1922   *Miss Mapp*, London, Hutchinson; New York, Doran (1923).
Peter, London, Cassell; New York, Doran.

1923   *Colin*, London, Hutchinson; New York, Doran.
Visible and Invisible (short stories), London, Hutchinson; New York, Doran (1924).

1924   *Alan*, London, T. Fisher Unwin; New York, Doran (1925).
David of King's, London, Hodder & Stoughton; New York, Doran (under title *David Blaize of King's*).

1925   *Colin II*, London, Hutchinson; New York, Doran.
Rex, London, Hodder & Stoughton; New York, Doran.
Mother, London, Hodder & Stoughton; New York, Doran.

1926   *Mezzanine*, London, Cassell; New York, Doran.
Pharisees and Publicans, London, Hutchinson; New York, Doran.

1927   *Lucia in London*, London, Hutchinson; New York, Doubleday, Doran (1928).
Sir Francis Drake, London, John Lane the Bodley Head; New York, Harper.

1928   *Spook Stories* (short stories), London, Hutchinson.
The Life of Alcibiades, London, Ernest Benn; New York, Appleton.
From Abraham to Christ (pamphlet based on Warburton Lectures).

1929   *The Male Impersonator*, London, E. Matthews & Marrot.
Paying Guests, London, Hutchinson; New York, Doubleday, Doran.
Ferdinand Magellan, London, John Lane; New York, Harper (1930).

1930   *The Inheritor*, London, Hutchinson; New York, Doubleday, Doran.
As We Were, London, Longmans; New York, Blue Ribbon Books.
Henry James: Letters to A.C. Benson and Auguste Monod (edited by EFB), London.

1931   *Mapp and Lucia*, London, Hodder & Stoughton; New York, Doubleday, Doran.

1932   *Charlotte Brontë*, London, Longmans.
Secret Lives, London, Hodder & Stoughton; New York, Doran.
As We Are, London, Longmans.
The Age of Walnut (introduction by EFB), London, Royal Northern Hospital.

1933   *Travail of Gold*, London, Hodder & Stoughton; New York, Doubleday, Doran.
King Edward VII, London, Longmans.

The Outbreak of War, 1914, London, Peter Davies; New York, Putnam (1934).

1934   *Raven's Brood*, London, Arthur Barker; New York, Doubleday, Doran.

        More Spook Stories (short stories), London, Hutchinson.

1935   *Lucia's Progress*, London, Hodder & Stoughton; (New York under title *Worshipful Lucia*).

        Queen Victoria, London, Longmans, Green.

1936   *The Kaiser and English Relations*, London, Longmans, Green.

        Charlotte, Anne and Emily Brontë (11-page essay), London, Chatto & Windus; New York, Harcourt Brace.

1937   *Old London* (4 vols), New York & London, D. Appleton-Century.

1939   *Trouble for Lucia*, London, Hodder & Stoughton; New York, Doubleday, Doran.

        Queen Victoria's Daughters, New York, D. Appleton-Century; London, Cassell (under title *The Daughters of Queen Victoria*).

1940   *Final Edition*, London, Longmans; New York, D. Appleton-Century.

A selection from other books consulted

Betty Askwith, *Two Victorian Families*, London, 1971.

Michael Baker, *Our Three Selves: The Life of Radclyffe Hall*, London, 1985.

A.C. Benson, *The Life and Letters of Maggie Benson*, London, 1917.

—— *The Trefoil*, London, 1923.

—— *The Life of Edward White Benson*, 2 vols., London, 1899.

—— *Memories and Friends*, London, 1924.

—— (Christopher Carr, pseud.), *The Memoirs of Arthur Hamilton*, London, 1886.

R.H. Benson, *Confessions of a Convert*, London, 1913.

Sir Edward Cadogan, *Before the Deluge*, London, 1961.

Gordon Claridge, Ruth Pryor, Gwen Watkins, *Sounds from the Bell Jar*, Basingstoke, 1990.

Louise Collis, *Impetuous Heart: The Story of Ethel Smyth*, London, 1984.

Michael Cox, *M.R. James*, Oxford, 1983.

Dodo, Newsletter of the E.F. Benson Society.

Richard Ellmann, *Oscar Wilde*, London, 1987.

W.M. Fletcher, *The University Pitt Club, 1835–1935*, Cambridge, 1935.

Phillip Guedalla, *The Queen and Mr Gladstone*, London, 1935.

Robert Hichens, *Yesterday*, London, 1947.

H. Montgomery Hyde, *Henry James At Home*, London, 1969.

Anita Leslie, *Edwardians in Love*, London, 1974.

The Lyttelton/Hart-Davis Letters, London, 1978–84.

Compton Mackenzie, *My Life and Times*, Octave IV, London 1965.

Faith Compton Mackenzie, *Always Afternoon*, London, 1943.

Brian Masters, *Great Hostesses*, London, 1982.

Bibliography

——— *Now Barabbas Was a Rotter: The Life of Marie Corelli*, London, 1978.

David Newsome, *On the Edge of Paradise: A.C. Benson Diarist*, London, 1980.

——— *Godliness and Good Learning*, London, 1961.

——— *A History of Wellington College*, Wellington College, 1959.

Margot Oxford (Asquith), *More Memories*, London, 1933.

Geoffrey Palmer and Noel Lloyd, *E.F. Benson As He Was*, Luton, 1988.

C. and T. Reavell, *E.F. Benson Remembered and the World of Tilling*, Rye, 1984.

Norman Sherry, *Graham Greene*, London, 1989.

Arthur and E.M. Sidgwick, *Henry Sidgwick*, London, 1906.

Ethel Sidgwick, *Mrs Henry Sidgwick: A Memoir*, London, 1938.

Ethel Smyth, *As Time Went On*, London, 1936.

——— *Impressions that Remained*, London, 1919.

Tilling Society *Newsletters*.

Donald Weeks, *Corvo*, London, 1971.

David Williams, *Genesis and Exodus*, London, 1979.

Notes

Chapter One

1 David Williams, *Genesis and Exodus*, p. 141.
2 Dep. Benson, 3/60.
3 ACB Diary, vol. III, p. 10.
4 E.F. Benson, *Dodo*, p. 20.
5 The quotation has generally been attributed to Geoffrey Madan, but it originates in ACB's Diary, vol. CLII, p. 4; ACB probably repeated it to Madan.
6 ACB Diary, vol. LXXX, p. 12.
7 Ibid., vol. CXXXI, p. 76; vol. CXXXVIII, p. 33.
8 Ibid., vol. V, p. 33.
9 Ibid., vol. CLII, p. 4.
10 E.F. Benson, *Dodo*, p. 377.
11 E.F. Benson, *The Challoners*, p. 190
12 A.C. Benson, *The Life and Letters of Maggie Benson*, p. 373.
13 E.F. Benson, *As We Were*, 241.
14 ACB Diary, vol. LXXXV, p. 1.
15 Dep. Benson, 1/72.
16 Dep. Benson, 3/43.
17 A.C. Benson, *The Life and Letters of Maggie Benson*, p. 21; *The Trefoil*, pp. 10, 22; E.F. Benson, *Our Family Affairs*, p. 15; *Mother*, p. 247.
18 E.F. Benson, *As We Were*, pp. 16–17; *Our Family Affairs*, p. 20.
19 ACB Diary, vol. XLV, p. 55.
20 Dep. Benson, 3/59, 3/43.
21 Dep. Benson, 3/48.
22 *The Genealogy of the Benson Family*, prepared by A.C. Benson and privately published in 1895, in a limited edition of 125 copies.
23 Ibid.
24 In private hands.
25 E.F. Benson, *As We Were*, p. 55.
26 Ibid., pp. 57–8.
27 E.W. Benson's Diary is in the library of Trinity College, Cambridge. E.F. Benson's notes taken from it are in the Bodleian Library, Oxford, Dep. Benson, 2/73. These were used for his account in *As We Were*, pp. 60–5.

28 EWB to Minnie Sidgwick, 15 April and 21 June 1853, private collection.
29 EWB to Minnie Sidgwick, March 1853, private collection.
30 University of California, Los Angeles (hereafter UCLA) Library, 177/127.
31 David Williams, op. cit., p. 13.
32 Royal Archives, 'Wellington College Papers', f. 155.
33 13 May 1859, private collection.
34 Dep. Benson, 1/71–1/80.
35 Ibid.
36 Ibid.
37 Royal Archives, 'Queen Victoria's Journal', 4 Nov. 1864 and 12 Dec. 1862.
38 Volume in private collection.
39 A.C. Benson, *The Trefoil*, p. 6.
40 E.F. Benson, *Final Edition*, p. 134.
41 David Williams, op. cit., p. 25.
42 David Newsome, *Godliness and Good Learning*, p. 160.
43 David Williams, op. cit., pp. 32–3.
44 Dep. Benson, 1/83.

Chapter Two

1 A.C. Benson, *The Life of Edward White Benson*, vol. 1, p. 367.
2 Dep. Benson, 1/71–80.
3 Dep. Benson, 3/63.
4 Dep. Benson, 3/66.
5 A.C. Benson, *The Life of Edward White Benson*, vol. 1, p. 353; David Newsome, *A History of Wellington College*, pp. 166–70.
6 A.C. Benson, *The Trefoil*, p. 101.
7 EWB to MB, 21 May, and Dec. 1872, private collection.
8 Dep. Benson, 3/66.
9 A.C. Benson, *The Trefoil*, pp. 62–3; *The Life of Edward White Benson*, vol. 1, p. 363.
10 David Newsome, *On the Edge of Paradise*, p. 25.
11 E.F. Benson, *Our Family Affairs*, p. 28ff.
12 Dep. Benson, 3/46.
13 EFB to Nelly Benson, 21 November 1876, private collection.
14 Dep. Benson, 3/46.
15 E.F. Benson, *Our Family Affairs*, pp. 45–6.
16 E.F. Benson, *David Blaize*, p. 40.
17 Ethel Smyth, *Impressions that Remained*, vol. 2, p. 191.
18 E.F. Benson, *Our Family Affairs*, p. 39.
19 A.C. Benson, *The Life of Edward White Benson*, vol. 1, pp. 227–8.
20 R.H. Benson, *Confessions of a Convert*.
21 A.C. Benson, *The Trefoil*, p. 254.
22 Dep. Benson, 3/59.
23 E.F. Benson, *David Blaize*, p. 73.

24 E.F. Benson, *The Challoners*, p. 19.
25 E.F. Benson, *The Life of Alcibiades*, p. 64.
26 A.C. Benson, *The Trefoil*, p. 59.
27 Dep. Benson, 3/18.
28 Dep. Benson, 1/75.
29 Private collection.
30 A.C. Benson, *The Trefoil*, p. 131.
31 A.C. Benson, *The Life of Edward White Benson*, vol. 1, p. 402.
32 Dep. Benson, 3/19.
33 E.F. Benson, *Our Family Affairs*, p. 61.
34 Dep. Benson, 3/49.
35 E.F. Benson, *Our Family Affairs*, p. 63; A.C. Benson, *The Life of Edward White Benson*, vol. I, p. 485.
36 In *Six Common Things* and *Our Family Affairs*.
37 Dep. Benson, 1/115.
38 David Newsome, *On the Edge of Paradise*, p. 26.
39 E.F. Benson, *Our Family Affairs*, pp. 69–70.
40 Dep. Benson, 3/43.
41 Dep. Benson, 3/49.
42 ACB Diary, vol. III, pp. 10–11.
43 Private collection.
44 Dep. Benson, 3/66.
45 E.F. Benson, *As We Were*, p. 76.
46 A.C. Benson, *The Life of Edward White Benson*, vol. 1, pp. 478–9.
47 E.F. Benson, *As We Were*, p. 78.
48 Diary of E.W. Benson at Trinity College, Cambridge, quoted in David Newsome, *Godliness and Good Learning*, p. 158.
49 EWB to MB, 26 Dec. 1876, private collection.
50 EWB Diary, at Trinity College, Cambridge.
51 Dep. Benson, 3/19.
52 E.F. Benson, *Our Family Affairs*, p. 74; Dep. Benson, 3/19; EWB Diary.
53 EWB Diary, quoted in Newsome, op. cit., pp. 191–2.
54 UCLA Library, 656, Box 1.
55 Rev. C.W. Penny, who had been one of Benson's assistant masters at Wellington College.
56 ACB Diary, vol. VII, pp. 152–3.
57 Dep. Benson, 3/19.
58 Dep. Benson, 1/62.
59 E.F. Benson, *Six Common Things*, p. 29.

Chapter Three

1 A.C. Benson, *Memories and Friends*, p. 41.
2 E.F. Benson, *David Blaize*, p. 9.
3 Fenton J.A. Hort was a well-known scholar and divine, an exact contempor-

ary of Edward White Benson. His son, here mentioned as Fred's companion, grew into Sir Arthur Hort.

4 EWB to MB, 11 May 1878, private collection.
5 E.F. Benson, *Our Family Affairs*, p. 79.
6 EFB to MB, 2 June 1878, private collection.
7 Dep. Benson, 3/65.
8 MB to EFB, Dep. Benson, 3/66.
9 E.F. Benson, *David Blaize*, p. 13.
10 UCLA Library, 177/104.
11 EFB to MB, 24 Nov. 1878, private collection.
12 Dep. Benson, 3/66.
13 EFB to MB, 8 Feb. 1979, private collection.
14 EFB to MB, 8 June 1879, private collection; Dep. Benson, 3/66.
15 EFB to EWB, 6 Dec. 1879, private collection.
16 EFB to MB, 7 Dec. 1879, private collection.
17 E.F. Benson, *Our Family Affairs*, p. 117.
18 Private collection.
19 Dep. Benson, 3/66.
20 MB to EWB, June 1881, and EWB to MB, 21 June 1881, private collections.
21 MB to EWB, 1881, private collection.
22 E.F. Benson, *David Blaize*, p. 107.
23 Dep. Benson, 3/66.
24 David Newsome, *Godliness and Good Learning*, pp. 80–2, 216–17.
25 Royal Archives, 'Queen Victoria's Journal', 22 Dec. 1882; and C 70/24. Also letters in private hands.
26 E.F. Benson, *As We Were*, p. 84.
27 A.C. Benson, *The Trefoil*, pp. 282–3.
28 I am indebted to Dr Robert Runcie, Archbishop of Canterbury until 1991, for showing me Lambeth Palace and pointing out Edward Benson's influence there.
29 E.F. Benson, *Our Family Affairs*, p. 169.
30 Dep. Benson, 3/66.
31 E.F. Benson, *Our Family Affairs*, p. 166.
32 Ibid., p. 165.
33 p. 100.
34 Dep. Benson, 3/65.
35 Dep. Benson, 3/66.
36 Pp. 38, 48, 53, 54. The Diary is in the possession of the E.F. Benson Society.
37 E.F. Benson, *Our Family Affairs*, p. 157.
38 Christopher Carr (A.C. Benson), *The Memoirs of Arthur Hamilton*, quoted in *Sexual Heretics*, pp. 201–2.
39 British Library, Add. MSS 46244, f. 18.
40 2 Nov. 1904. At Humanities Research Center, Austin Texas.

41 Arthur was invited to dine with Henry Irving in London, but his father advised him to wriggle out of it. See E.F. Benson, *Final Edition*, p. 203.

42 For a more detailed account of A.C. Benson's crisis, see David Newsome, *On the Edge of Paradise*, pp. 36–41.

43 ACB Diary, vol. VII, p. 36.

44 Dep. Benson, 3/64.

45 Dep. Benson, 3/62.

46 E.F. Benson, *As We Were*, p. 120.

Chapter Four

1 EWB to MB, 4 Oct. 1887, private collection.

2 Dep. Benson, 3/65.

3 An odd coincidence also makes him distantly related to the mass-murderer Dennis Nilsen, through the latter's great-grandmother, who was a Stephen. See Brian Masters, *Killing for Company*.

4 Walter Morley Fletcher, *The University Pitt Club*, preface.

5 See Ethel Sidgwick, *Mrs Henry Sidgwick: A Memoir*.

6 *As We Were*, p. 50

7 Dep. Benson, 3/65.

8 In possession of the E.F. Benson Society.

9 See *Granta*, vol. 1, no. 9.

10 E.F. Benson, *The Inheritor*, p. 37.

11 Lambeth Palace, Bell Papers, 223.

12 ACB Diary, vol. CXLII, p. 45.

13 Ethel Smyth, *Impressions that Remained*, vol. II, p. 193.

14 Dep. Benson, 3/64.

15 A.C. Benson, *The Life and Letters of Maggie Benson*, p. 91.

16 British Library, Add. MSS 44513, f. 280.

17 E.F. Benson, *Our Family Affairs*, pp. 258–9.

18 Ibid., p. 260; A.C. Benson, *The Life and Letters of Maggie Benson*, pp. 114–19.

19 Ethel Smyth, *Impressions that Remained*, vol. II, p. 246.

20 Lambeth Palace, Benson Papers, 28 Nov. 1890.

21 ACB Diary, vol. XVII, p. 27.

22 E.F.Benson, *Our Family Affairs*, p. 262.

23 Geoffrey Palmer and Noel Lloyd, *E.F. Benson As He Was*, p. 39.

24 Dep. Benson, 3/65.

25 Blackwoods Archive, National Library of Scotland, Edinburgh.

26 E.F. Benson, *Our Family Affairs*, p. 265.

27 13 Aug. 1891, private collection, published in E.F. Benson, *As We Were*, p. 218.

28 E.F.Benson, *The Life of Alcibiades*, p. 19.

29 E.F. Benson, *David Blaize*, p. 251.

30 Richard Ellmann, *Oscar Wilde*, pp. 344–6.

31 Dep. Benson, 3/60, 31 May 1892.
32 Ibid., 3/60, 4 June 1892.
33 E.F. Benson, *Our Family Affairs*, p. 281.
34 Palmer and Lloyd, op. cit., pp. 43–4.
35 E.F. Benson, *Final Edition*, pp. 1–2.
36 E.F. Benson, *Our Family Affairs*, p. 282.
37 Ibid., p. 299.
38 See Brian Masters, *Great Hostesses*, Chapter One.
39 E.F. Benson, *Dodo*, p. 33.
40 Ibid., p. 53.
41 Ibid., p. 58.
42 Dep. Benson, 3/60. 19 May and 23 May 1893.
43 Palmer and Lloyd, op. cit., p. 46.
44 Dep. Benson, 3/60.
45 E.F. Benson, *Dodo*, pp. 366–7.
46 Ibid., p. 79.
47 Ibid., p. 105
48 Dep. Benson, 3/70.
49 Tilling Society *Newsletter*, no. 1, p. 13.
50 Ibid.
51 Margot Oxford (Asquith), *More Memories*, p. 129.
52 12 July 1893, private collection.
53 From private information
54 E.F. Benson, *Dodo*, pp. 76, 90, 99, 102.
55 Ethel Smyth, *As Time Went On . . .*, pp. 205–6.
56 E.F. Benson, *Our Family Affairs*, p. 255.
57 E.F. Benson, *Final Edition*, p. 182.
58 EFB to Edmund Gosse, 7 and 24 October 1893, Brotherton Library, University of Leeds.
59 A.C. Benson, *The Life and Letters of Maggie Benson*, pp. 151, 160, 161.
60 The Hon. Sir Reginald Lister KCMG was Minister Plenipotentiary in Tangier from 1908, and died there, unmarried, in 1912.
61 Palmer and Lloyd, op. cit., p. 50.
62 Robert Hichens, *Yesterday*, pp. 63–5.
63 Palmer and Lloyd, op cit., p. 47.
64 'Poor Miss Huntingford', in E.F. Benson, *Six Common Things*, p. 213.

Chapter Five

1 Dep. Benson, 3/60.
2 Both the books referred to are in a private collection in England.
3 *The Contemporary Review*, July 1895.
4 ACB Diary, vol. LII, p. 44.
5 ACB to MB, 12 Dec. 1895, private collection.
6 MB to EFB, 2 Feb. 1895, private collection.

7 Extracted from various letters MB to Maggie Benson, private collection.
8 Dep. Benson, 3/62.
9 Dep. Benson, 1/77.
10 Lambeth Palace Archives, MS 3406, folio 107.
11 See E.F. Benson, *Mother*, p. 129, and *As We Were*, chapter ten, passim.
12 Letters from Henry James to A.C. Benson, 16 Jan., 5 April, 2 May and 29 June 1896, in private collection. First published in *Henry James: Letters to A.C. Benson and Auguste Monod*, ed. E.F. Benson, 1930.
13 MB to Maggie Benson, private collection.
14 Dep. Benson, 1/77.
15 David Newsome, *On the Edge of Paradise*, p. 61
16 Dr Robert Runcie to the author.
17 Louise Collis, *Impetuous Heart*, p. 40.
18 E.F. Benson, *Our Family Affairs*, p. 322.
19 David Williams, *Genesis and Exodus*, pp. 106–7; E.F. Benson, *As We Were*, p. 114; *Our Family Affairs*, p. 334.
20 Royal Archives, D12/54.
21 Phillip Guedalla, *The Queen and Mr Gladstone*, p. 500.
22 Dep. Benson, 1/77.
23 MB to Duchess of Bedford, 17 Dec. 1896, private collection.
24 Dep. Benson, 1/77.
25 Ibid.
26 Benson himself referred to these criticisms with positive relish in *Our Family Affairs*, pp. 306–7.
27 EFB to Edmund Gosse, 27 April 1894, Brotherton Library, University of Leeds.
28 E.F. Benson, *The Judgement Books*, pp. 119–20.
29 Royal Archives, D12/83.
30 Princess Beatrice to Mrs Benson, 25 Nov. 1897, private collection.
31 Dep. Benson, 3/48.
32 Dep. Benson, 1/77.
33 Dep. Benson, 1/78.
34 Ibid.
35 E.F. Benson, *Mother*, p. 71.
36 E.F. Benson, *Final Edition*, p. 12.
37 E.F. Benson, *The Challoners*, p. 150.
38 Dep. Benson, 1/78.
39 Dep. Benson, 3/62.
40 E.F. Benson, *Final Edition*, p. 12.
41 Louise Collis, op. cit., p. 55.
42 Dep. Benson, 1/78.
43 Dep. Benson, 1/78.
44 Reginald Lister to EFB, 17 Dec. 1897, private collection.
45 Dep. Benson, 3/60.

46 Dep. Benson, 3/62.
47 Ibid.
48 ACB Diary, vol. III, p. 196.
49 ACB Diary, vol. LXXXVI, p. 67.
50 ACB Diary, vol. CXXI, p. 41.
51 ACB Diary, vol. II, pp. 183–4.
52 Dep. Benson, 3/65.
53 Dep. Benson, 3/60.
54 Geoffrey Palmer and Noel Lloyd, *E.F. Benson As He Was*, p. 63.
55 Dep. Benson, 3/65.
56 Dep. Benson, 1/78.
57 ACB Diary, vol. III, pp. 55–6.
58 Dep. Benson, 3/62.
59 ACB Diary, vol. IV, p. 28.
60 Dep. Benson, 1/78.

Chapter Six

1 E.F. Benson, *The Babe, B.A.*, p. 21.
2 Dep. Benson, 3/60.
3 Ibid., 30 Dec. 1900.
4 Dep. Benson, 3/62.
5 Dep. Benson, 3/64, 3/62.
6 ACB Diary, vol. III, p. 196.
7 UCLA Library, William Colles Papers, 2007, fl. 1.
8 MB to EFB, 7 Jan. 1899, private collection.
9 National Library of Scotland, Edinburgh, Rosebery Papers.
10 Dep. Benson, 3/64.
11 ACB Diary, vol. V, p. 63.
12 Dep. Benson, 3/62, 3/64.
13 Mary Benson's Diary, 8 and 12 Nov. 1899, Dep. Benson, 1/78.
14 Dep. Benson, 3/62, 3/63.
15 MB to Adeline, Duchess of Bedford, 12 Oct. 1901, private collection.
16 Dep. Benson, 3/60.
17 *The Saturday Review*, quoted in Palmer and Lloyd, *E.F. Benson As He Was*, p. 169.
18 EFB to William Colles, 21 Dec. 1900, New York University, Fales Library.
19 ACB Diary, vol. XII, p. 63.
20 Ibid., vol. XVI, pp. 151–2.
21 The author is wholly indebted to Michael De-la-Noy for this information.
22 ACB Diary, vol. XI, p. 39.
23 Anita Leslie, *Edwardians in Love*, pp. 159–62.
24 UCLA Library, William Colles Papers, 2007, f. 4.
25 ACB Diary, vol. X, p. 19.
26 *To Whom Did Fred Write After Dinner?*, by Mary Benson, private collection.

27 ACB Diary, vol. CXXV, p. 10.
28 Ibid., vol. XLIV, p. 51.
29 ACB Diary, vol. LI, p. 43; vol. LVI, p. 68.
30 Ibid., vol. LI, p. 51.
31 Ibid., vol. XXXVII, p. 20; vol. XXXIV, p. 39.
32 MB to RHB, private collection.
33 E.F. Benson, *Dodo*, p. 167.
34 ACB Diary, vol. LXXII, p. 61.
35 Ibid., vol. LXXIII, p. 56.
36 E.F. Benson, *The Freaks of Mayfair*, p. 210.
37 ACB Diary, vol. LXXX, p. 8.
38 E.F. Benson, *The Freaks of Mayfair*, pp. 147, 165, 27.
39 E.F. Benson, *As We Were*, p. 283.
40 ACB Diary, vol. LXXVI, p. 13; vol. CXI, p. 4.
41 E.F. Benson, *As We Were*, p. 310.
42 E.F. Benson, *Mike*, pp. 26–7.
43 E.F. Benson, *Secret Lives*, p. 171.
44 ACB Diary, vol. LXXX, p. 13.
45 Ibid., vol. LXXIII, pp. 35, 40.
46 Ibid., vol. LIX, p. 69.
47 Ibid., vol. LXXXIV, p. 64.
48 Faith Compton Mackenzie, *Always Afternoon*, p. 93.
49 ACB Diary, vol. III, p. 100.
50 E.F. Benson, *The Challoners*, pp. 19, 78, 109.
51 UCLA Library, 177/125.
52 ACB Diary, vol. LVII, p. 40.
53 New York University, Fales Library.
54 ACB Diary, vol. LXXIII, p. 53.
55 ACB to MB, 24 Nov. 1905; 19 Oct. 1904, private collection.
56 E.F. Benson, *Final Edition*, p. 40.
57 ACB Diary, vol. XXXIV, p. 39.

Chapter Seven

1 E.F. Benson, *Mother*, p. 222.
2 See G. Claridge, R. Pryor and G. Watkins, *Sounds from the Bell Jar*, p. 171.
3 This account of the onset of Maggie Benson's illness is taken from ACB Diary, vol. XCII, pp. 40–60.
4 David Newsome, *On the Edge of Paradise*, pp. 221–2; ACB Diary, vol. LXXXV, p. 3.
5 ACB Diary, vol. XCIX, pp. 56, 92.
6 Newsome, op. cit., p. 229.
7 ACB Diary, vol. CIII, p. 51.
8 Ibid., vol. CXV, p. 38.
9 Ibid., vol. XCVI, p. 12.

10 MB to RHB, 16 Feb. 1909, private collection.
11 ACB Diary, vol. CXV, p. 43; vol. XCIX, p. 92; vol. LXXXV, pp. 2–3.
12 ibid., vol. CXIII, p. 98; vol. CXI, pp. 6–7.
13 Ibid., vol. CXI, pp. 7, 37.
14 Ibid., vol. C, p. 45; vol. CIII, p. 55.
15 Ibid., vol. CIII, p. 51; vol. CI, p. 64.
16 Ibid., vol. CLX, p. 18.
17 Ibid., vol. CX, p. 22.
18 ACB Diary, vol. CIII, p. 55.
19 Ibid., vol. CXIII, p. 99.
20 Ibid., vol. CXII, p. 6.
21 Dep. Benson, 2/73.
22 ACB Diary, vol. CXI, p. 15.
23 Brian Masters, *Great Hostesses*, pp. 17–18.
24 The album is in private hands.
25 This would be used to good effect in Benson's *Queen Lucia*.
26 *The Book of Fearfuljoy* is in the Bodleian Library, Oxford, Dep. Benson. See also Brian Masters, *Now Barabbas Was A Rotter*, p. 213.
27 EFB to William Colles, 10 April 1905, New York University, Fales Library.
28 New York University, Fales Library.
29 I am indebted to Dennis L. Bird, archivist of the National Skating Association, for this information.
30 ACB Diary, vol. CXVII passim.
31 Arthur and E.M. Sidgwick, *Henry Sidgwick*.
32 ACB Diary, vol. CXX, p. 15.
33 E.F. Benson, *Colin*, pp. 213–15.
34 Archives of the Earl of Radnor, Longford Castle, Salisbury.
35 Faith Compton Mackenzie, *Always Afternoon*, p. 90.
36 Compton Mackenzie, *My Life and Times*, Octave IV.
37 E.F. Benson, *Final Edition*, p. 178.
38 Faith Compton Mackenzie, op. cit.
39 UCLA Library, 177/80, unpublished.
40 See also E.F. Benson, *Up and Down*, pp. 31–6; and James Money, *Capri*, pp. 54, 129–31.
41 Fragment of Yeats-Brown Diary at the Humanities Research Center, Austin, Texas.
42 E.F. Benson, *Mother*, p. 234; see also Geoffrey Palmer and Noel Lloyd, *E.F. Benson As He Was*, pp. 92–3.

Chapter Eight

1 Geoffrey Palmer and Noel Lloyd, *E.F. Benson As He Was*, p. 180.
2 ACB Diary, vol. CXX, p. 48.
3 Ibid., vol. CLXV, p. 1.
4 Ibid., vol. CXLII, p. 37.

5 Dep. Benson, 3/70.
6 UCLA Library, 177/69, unpublished.
7 ACB Diary, vol. CXXXVII, pp. 21, 38.
8 Ibid., vol. LIII, p. 3.
9 Dep. Benson, 3/62.
10 ACB Diary, vol. CXXXVII, p. 49.
11 Ibid., vol. CXLI, p. 14.
12 Ibid., vol. CXXIV, p. 54; vol. CXXXV, p. 1.
13 Ibid., vol. CXXXV, p. 33.
14 Ibid., vol. CXL, pp. 10–13.
15 MB to RHB, private collection.
16 ACB Diary, vol. CXL, p. 44.
17 ACB to MB, 2 Nov. 1912, private collection.
18 ACB Diary, vol. CXXXV, pp. 46–7; vol. CXXXVI, p. 31.
19 Manuscript of *The Hanging of Alfred Wadham* in private collection. Published in *More Spook Stories*.
20 David Newsome, *On the Edge of Paradise*, p. 313.
21 ACB Diary, vol. CLXIII, p. 11.
22 ACB to MB, 20 Jan. 1917; 12 Aug. 1918, private collection.
23 Newsome, op. cit., p. 311.
24 Dep. Benson, 3/69.
25 Foreign Office 395/97, 75033. The author is indebted to Allan Downend for this information.
26 Masterman to EFB, 29 Jan. 1919, private collection.
27 MB to Adeline, Duchess of Bedford, 16 May 1915, private collection.
28 ACB Diary, vol. CL, p. 5; vol. CLII, p. 4.
29 Ibid., vol. CLXIV, p. 32.
30 Ibid., vol. CXLVIII, pp. 46–54; also quoted in Newsome, op. cit., p. 315.
31 Robert Hichens, *Yesterday*, pp. 164–5.
32 E.F. Benson, *Our Family Affairs*, p. 331.
33 E.F. Benson, *Final Edition*, p. 32.
34 E.F. Benson, *Mother*, p. 251.
35 RHB to Canon Ragg, 11 May 1909; New York Public Library, Berg Collection.
36 See Norman Sherry, *Graham Greene*, p. 645; Donald Weeks, *Corvo*.
37 A.C. Benson, *The Life and Letters of Maggie Benson*, p. 329.
38 These are in a private collection.
39 Fragment of RHB Diary kept on a visit to Rome, Nov. 1903, in the Humanities Research Center, Austin, Texas. There is no evidence that St Cecilia ever existed.
40 E.F. Benson, *Final Edition*, p. 120; *Mother*, pp. 277–84.
41 E.F. Benson, *Mother*, p. 256.
42 Fragment of RHB Diary kept on a visit to Rome, Nov. 1903, in the Humanities Research Center, Austin, Texas.

43 Dep. Benson, 3/70.
44 Ibid., 3/68.
45 ACB to MB, 17 Feb. 1911, private collection.
46 ACB to MB, 1915, private collection.
47 ACB Diary, vol. CLXIII, p. 13.
48 Ibid., vol. CLVII, p. 33.
49 ACB to EFB, 12 Jan. 1916, private collection.
50 E.F. Benson, *David Blaize*, p. 259.
51 British Library, Add. MSS 46244, f. 18.
52 Arthur Eckersley to EFB, private collection.
53 Dep. Benson, 3/70.
54 Robert B. Drummey to EFB, 26 Aug. 1917, in Dep. Benson, 3/69.
55 Dep. Benson, 3/70.
56 EFB to Mr Manson, 23 Jan. 1936, UCLA Library, 177/129.

Chapter Nine

1 Now in private collections.
2 ACB Diary, vol. CLIX, p. 10.
3 Dep. Benson, 3/66.
4 ACB Diary, vol. CLIX, p. 33.
5 ACB to EFB, 14 May 1916, private collection.
6 Ethel Smyth, *Impressions That Remained*, vol. II, p. 190.
7 MB to ACB, 9 July 1916, private collection.
8 David Newsome, *On the Edge of Paradise*, p. 342.
9 Humanities Research Center, Austin, Texas.
10 Dep. Benson, 3/48.
11 Ibid., 3/66.
12 Ethel Smyth, *As Time Went On*, p. 242.
13 UCLA Library, 656, Box 1.
14 E.F. Benson, *Mother*, p. 266.
15 Ethel Smyth, *As Time Went On*, p. 146.
16 UCLA Library, 656, Box 1.
17 E.F. Benson, *Mother*, p. 315.
18 ACB Diary, vol. CLXXI, p. 22.
19 In private collection.
20 'By The Way', unpublished manuscript now in a private collection. It was the first draft of what eventually became, in rewritten form, *Final Edition*.
21 ACB to EFB, 24 April 1920, 17 May 1920, in Dep. Benson, 3/69, 3/70.
22 UCLA Library, 177/40.
23 Michael Cox, *M.R. James*, p. 150.
24 UCLA Library, 177/64.
25 Oliver Lodge to EFB, 25 Dec. 1916, private collection.
26 UCLA Library, 177/13.
27 E.F. Benson, *The Freaks of Mayfair*, pp. 52, 61.

28 UCLA Library, 177/54.
29 E.F. Benson, *The Freaks of Mayfair*, p. 197.
30 ACB to EFB, 4 Feb. 1917, private collection.
31 E.F. Benson, *Mrs Ames*, pp. 52, 67, 86.
32 See Brian Masters, *Now Barabbas Was a Rotter*.
33 *Westminster Gazette*, 7 Aug. 1920.

Chapter Ten

1 Manuscript in the Humanities Research Center, Austin, Texas.
2 ACB Diary, vol. CLXVIII, p. 32.
3 Dep. Benson, 3/69.
4 ACB Diary, vol. CLXXII, p. 50.
5 Ibid., vol. CLXXIV, p. 27.
6 Ibid.
7 Ibid., vol. LVII, p. 44.
8 E.F. Benson, *Mike*, pp. 120, 153.
9 E.F. Benson, *The Challoners*, p. 218.
10 E.F. Benson, *As We Were*, p. 235.
11 David Newsome, *On the Edge of Paradise*, p. 368.
12 E.F. Benson, *The Inheritor*, p. 38.
13 *The Lyttelton/Hart-Davis Letters*, vol. III, p. 5.
14 For the Etonian influence see, for example, Sir Edward Cadogan, *Before the Deluge*.
15 Newsome, op. cit., p. 195.
16 Ibid., p. 194.
17 E.F. Benson, *Paying Guests*, p. 224.
18 Ibid., p. 198.
19 ACB Diary, vol. CLXXII, p. 34.
20 A.C. Benson, *The Life and Letters of Maggie Benson*, p. 168.
21 E.F. Benson, *As We Were*, p. 317. See also Timothy d'Arch Smith, *Love in Earnest*, and *Sexual Heretics*, both passim.
22 Private collection.
23 Jack Adrian, Introduction to E.F. Benson, *The Flint Knife*, p. 15.
24 Yale University, Beinecke Rare Books and Manuscript Library.
25 Ibid.
26 EFB to Compton Mackenzie, 8 Sept. 1931, Humanities Research Center, Austin, Texas.
27 Yale University, Beinecke Rare Books and Manuscript Library.
28 See Brian Masters, *Now Barabbas Was A Rotter*.
29 UCLA Library, 177/119.
30 Dep. Benson, 3/69.
31 Brotherton Library, University of Leeds.
32 ACB Diary, vol. CLXXIV, p. 28; vol. CLXXVII, p. 4; vol. CLXXVIII, p. 10.

33 E.F. Benson, 'By The Way', unpublished manuscript in private collection.
34 Ibid.
35 UCLA Library, 177/1.
36 Private collection.
37 Humanities Research Center, Austin, Texas.
38 *The Lyttelton/Hart-Davis Letters*, vol. IV, p 63; vol. I, p. 37.
39 E.F. Benson, *Final Edition*, p. 182.
40 Newsome, op. cit., p. 380.
41 E.F. Benson, *Six Common Things*, pp. 32, 87.
42 Taffy's gravestone, 1928–36, may still be seen in a far corner of the garden at Lamb House.
43 E.F. Benson, *Final Edition*, p. 276.
44 Manuscript in private collection. The play was performed at the Savoy Theatre on 7 March 1906, and appears as a short story in *The Flint Knife*.
45 Dep. Benson, 3/68.
46 UCLA Library, William Colles Papers, 2007, Box 1, f. 7.
47 Humanities Research Center, Austin, Texas.
48 Ibid.
49 New York University, Fales Library.
50 Michael Baker, *Our Three Selves*, p. 279.
51 Private collection.
52 Humanities Research Center, Austin, Texas.
53 UCLA Library, 177/119.
54 UCLA Library, William Colles Papers, 2007.
55 New York University, Fales Library.
56 Lambeth Palace, 19 Nov. 1896; New York University, Fales Library.
57 E.F. Benson, *Colin*, p. 139.
58 UCLA Library, 177/5–7.
59 E.F. Benson, *As We Were*, p. 327.
60 E.F. Benson, *Final Edition*, p. 184.
61 EFB to Edmund Gosse, 3 May 1927, Brotherton Library, Leeds University.
62 E.F. Benson, *Final Edition*, p. 260.
63 E.F. Benson, *Secret Lives*, p. 150.
64 C. and T. Reavell, *E.F. Benson Remembered and the World of Tilling*, p. 58.
65 Dep. Benson, 3/70.
66 Reavell, op. cit., p. 47.
67 E.F. Benson, *Dodo*, p. 384.
68 E.F. Benson, *The Challoners*, p. 268.
69 E.F. Benson, 'Indiscreet Stories', manuscript notebook in a private collection.

Chapter Eleven

1 New York Public Library, Berg Collection.
2 Letter in private collection.
3 Dep. Benson, 3/70.

4 It has been said that Gabriel Gammon, who had worked for Henry James, had been inherited by Fred along with the house. Not so; Fred's gardener was old Mr. Gabriel.

5 Humanities Research Center, Austin, Texas.

6 Tilling Society *Newsletter*, no. 9.

7 Reavell & Reavell, *E. F. Benson Remembered in Rye, & The World of Tilling*.

8 In private collection.

9 Humanities Research Center, Austin, Texas.

10 Dame Ethel Smyth to EFB, 28 June 1932, in private collection.

11 Hugh Walpole to EFB, 29 Sept. 1932, in private collection.

12 EFB to Mrs Arkwright, 27 Sept. 1932, at UCLA Library.

13 Ponsonby to EFB, 10 Nov. 1932, in private collection.

14 All three letters, dated 21 Nov., 30 Nov., and beginning December 1933, are in a private collection.

15 EFB to Hugh Walpole, 28 Sept. 1932; Walpole to EFB, 6 Oct. 1932. Reproduced by kind permission of Sir Rupert Hart-Davis.

16 Dep. Benson, 3/70.

17 Humanities Research Center, Austin, Texas.

18 UCLA Library, 177/106.

19 Manuscript notes, in private collection.

20 21 Dec. 1937, Dep. Benson, 3/69.

21 Palmer and Lloyd, op. cit., p. 159.

22 UCLA Library, 177/121.

23 E.F. Benson, *Six Common Things*, p. 178.

24 Manuscript play, in private collection, subsequently rewritten as a short story and published in *The Flint Knife*.

25 EFB to P. McDowall, 1 Jan. 1940, in private collection.

26 Countess of Oxford and Asquith to EFB, 8 Aug. 1939, Dep. Benson, 3/69.

27 E.F. Benson, *Final Edition*, p. 195.

28 E.F. Benson, *Six Common Things*, p. 163.

29 Manuscript in private collection.

30 E.F. Benson, *The Challoners*, p. 192.

31 E.F. Benson, *Dodo*, p. 269.

32 E.F. Benson, *The Challoners*, p. 246.

33 MB to EFB, 2 Dec. 1916, private collection.

34 Philip Burne-Jones to EFB, 27 Dec. 1909, private collection.

35 UCLA Library, 177/98.

36 E.F. Benson, *Final Edition*, p. 184.

37 David Williams, *Genesis and Exodus*, p. 213.

38 E.F. Benson, *Final Edition*, p. 250.

39 E.F. Benson, *Mother*, p. 250.

40 *Spectator*, 8 March 1940.

41 New York University, Fales Library, William Colles Papers.

42 G. Claridge, R. Pryor, G. Watkins, *Sounds from the Bell Jar*, p. 179.

Notes

43 E.F. Benson, *Our Family Affairs*, p. 202.
44 E.F. Benson, *As We Were*, p. 277.
45 E.F. Benson, *Final Edition*, p. 246.
46 E.F. Benson, *A Criticism on Critics*, UCLA Library, 177/100.
47 Ibid.
48 E.F. Benson, *Dodo*, pp. 236, 309, 372, 421.
49 E.F. Benson, *Final Edition*, p. 209.
50 E.F. Benson, *Paying Guests*, pp. 58–9.
51 E.F. Benson, *Up and Down*, p. 146.
52 E.F. Benson, *David Blaize*, p. 78.
53 E.F. Benson, *The Life of Alcibiades*, pp. 270, 298.
54 E.F. Benson, *Mike*, p. 63.
55 E.F. Benson, *Final Edition*, p. 182.

Index

actual
Index

Index

Index

Index